Lincoln Christian College

S0-FSO-143

WITHDRAWN
University of
Illinois Library
at Urbana-Champaign

THE DEVELOPMENT OF RELIGIOUS
TOLERATION IN ENGLAND

THE DEVELOPMENT

OF

RELIGIOUS TOLERATION IN ENGLAND

FROM THE BEGINNING OF THE ENGLISH REFORMATION
TO THE DEATH OF QUEEN ELIZABETH

by

W. K. JORDAN, Ph.D.

*Instructor in History and Tutor in the Division of History,
Government and Economics in
Harvard University*

LONDON
GEORGE ALLEN & UNWIN LTD
MUSEUM STREET

FIRST PUBLISHED IN 1932

All rights reserved

PRINTED IN GREAT BRITAIN BY
UNWIN BROTHERS LTD., WOKING

283.42
J82
c.2

K. C. Sung

gift

7 June '79

58544

TO

WILLIAM JORDAN

ACKNOWLEDGMENT

This volume owes much to the inspiration provided by the sound scholarship and great learning of Professor C. H. McIlwain, who has been kind enough to criticize the manuscript. Professor R. B. Merriman has followed the study from its inception and has inspired the author by accepting him as a colleague since his first days as a student at Harvard. The author is under a great obligation to Professor W. S. Ferguson and Professor E. A. Whitney for valuable assistance in preparing the manuscript for publication. The author's father and uncle, William Jordan and Elijah Jordan, have been of great service in criticizing the manuscript in points of detail and style which would have escaped one who had not enjoyed the discipline of the classical education of a generation ago.

W. K. J.

CAMBRIDGE, MASS.
October, 1931

CONTENTS

CONTENTS

13

THE DEVELOPMENT OF RELIGIOUS TOLERATION IN ENGLAND

I

THE STATUS OF THE PROBLEM OF RELIGIOUS TOLERATION PRIOR TO THE ELIZABETHAN SETTLEMENT OF RELIGION

A. THE SCOPE OF THE PROBLEMS OF TOLERATION AND PERSECUTION

1. THE CONCEPT OF PHILOSOPHICAL TOLERATION

Abstractions may be interpreted in such a variety of ways that in considering the problem of the development of religious toleration it will be well to define our conception of the content of the term as accurately as possible.

Some of the noblest minds in modern times have suggested that the priceless benefits of toleration rest, not upon a better understanding of the spiritual nature of Christ's teachings, but upon scepticism about the possibility of definitely and dogmatically ascertaining any body of religious truth. It is obvious that few men would seek to persecute another for tenets actually of doubtful validity, or, at best, imperfectly ascertained. Closely allied with this persuasion is the view that modern toleration of religious diversity proceeds from a widespread indifference to the whole range of Christian theology and religious practice. Thus Morley seems to suspect that 'complete tolerance' may mean only complete indifference.

It cannot be denied that scepticism and indifference have been powerful agents in weakening the theory and practice of persecution. But it is an error to say that the indifferent man can be tolerant of a religious belief; he is simply indifferent to it. There can be little doubt that the modern tolerance towards religious diversity has a large content of indifference, but religious toleration was achieved, at least in England,

15

before public indifference to theological questions had attained a place of dominant influence.

Perhaps the finest conception of religious toleration presumes a positive attitude of mind which enables us charitably and sympathetically to hear another man whom we consider to be in error.[1] Philosophical toleration presumes a mind which has definite and pronounced religious opinions, but which is able and willing to concede to other minds the right to retain and practise contrary religious beliefs. This point of view rests its case upon the power of truth to overcome error by the weight of its own virtue. It is distinctly unwilling to force other men's opinions because such an action would hinder the free operation of truth and because it presumes that opinions cannot be changed by any pressure which is not intellectual.

This attitude of mind can be attained only by an Olympian intelligence. History has adequately demonstrated that men who are warmly attached to religious beliefs almost invariably seek to impose them upon others by means which can only be described as one or another kind of pressure. The Church has but rarely claimed that it was able to convert unbelievers by intellectual methods: reliance has rather been placed upon emotional appeal, the powerful influences of the imitative psychology, the miraculous operation of God's grace, and compulsion. The Christian Faith in its very essence teaches

---

[1] This conception has been stated in its classic form by Creighton. (Creighton, M., *Persecution and Tolerance*.) To Creighton, tolerance is a positive virtue in the Aristotelian sense of the term. (*Ibid.*, 122–123.) The virtue of the tolerant man consists in his having opinions, but in not desiring to impose those opinions by external pressure upon another. The truly tolerant man is convinced of the truth of his opinion, but believes that he can win another to his views only by intellectual arguments. That is, he would have no one hold his opinion, however much he may be convinced of its truth, with less reality of perception than his own. (*Ibid.*, 123.) Society has the right to demand that every man should respect the opinions of others, but part of this process may be held to be, that everyone should be permitted to hold positive opinions, which should be submitted to intellectual criticism, and which should not be stifled by social pressure. (*Ibid.*, 124.) Creighton would perhaps define tolerance as "the quick sympathy with another, by which you unconsciously put yourself in his place and appraise not his actual words or deeds, but their origin and their intent." (*Ibid.*, 134.)

that all men who do not embrace a certain body of truth are lost. The Christian must therefore be a missionary. Philosophical tolerance can scarcely be attained by an evangelical intelligence confronted with a soul which may at any moment be consigned to eternal perdition. Philosophical tolerance, when properly analysed, must be regarded as shading into the sceptical attitude of mind.

2. THE MEANING OF RELIGIOUS TOLERATION

We are concerned with the historical content of the term and with the process by which religious toleration was achieved in England. Toleration was attained by the legal guarantee of free belief and the free public exercise of that belief. Legal toleration is limited in its scope, somewhat ignoble in some of its sources, but constitutes, none the less, one of the most significant advances that the human race has ever achieved.

In its legal application the word toleration signifies simply a refraining from persecution.[1] It suggests at least latent disapproval of the belief or practice which is tolerated, and refers to a somewhat limited and conditioned freedom. It involves, as well, a volitional action or state of mind on the part of the dominant party towards a weaker party. It approaches a dispassionate state of mind as a limit, and, as we shall attempt to indicate, is based upon a variety of contributing factors. In its very nature, however, it disapproves, if it does not disallow, the point of view which is to be tolerated.[2] Toleration, therefore, falls considerably short of religious liberty. It presumes an authority which has been and which again may become coercive; an authority which for subjective reasons is not brought to bear upon the dissenting group. It implies, shall we say, voluntary inaction on the part of the dominant group.

The idea of toleration may be said to spring from the theory that the civil power has inalienable and absolute prerogatives. The Government thus elevated may allow certain persons to differ from it in theory and in religious practice. O. W. Holmes

[1] Adeney, C. F., art. 'Toleration,' *Encyc. of Rel. and Ethics*, XII, 360.
[2] See Klein, A. J., *Intolerance in the Reign of Elizabeth*, 5, for the 'positive' view.

must have had this situation in mind when he declared the idea of toleration to be an insult to mankind. Liberty of conscience, on the other hand, springs from the theory that the final object of the State is man, that man is responsible for his own actions, and that the State assumes no responsibility for his thoughts or beliefs. This view would regard the spiritual welfare of the individual as strictly a concern of the individual and his God. It is to be questioned whether we have ever got much beyond the first concept; certainly no progress was made beyond it in England during the sixteenth and seventeenth centuries. Acton has well insisted in a brilliant essay that modern state absolutism has confused the issue of religious freedom, since it condemns as a state within a state every inner group seeking to administer its own affairs. The modern State, he complains, recognizes liberty only in the individual, because it is only in the individual that liberty may be separated from authority.[1] Thus a man is left free to express his personal religious views, but the Church of which he is a member and through which he desires to give reality to his opinions is strictly controlled.[2] Acton urges that religious liberty is a positive right which implies the guarantee that religious communities may attend to the practice of their own duties, the enjoyment of their own constitutions, and the protection of the law, which equally secures to all the possession of their own independence.[3] He protests against the overweening power of the modern State which bends every group consideration to what it conceives to be the duty of preserving order.[4] Such 'statism' may soon result in the tyrannous control of the minorities by the majority for that ephemeral benefit which we describe as the public good.[5]

[1] Acton, J. E. E., *The History of Freedom and Other Essays*, 151.
[2] *Ibid.*   [3] *Ibid.*, 152.   [4] *Ibid.*, 153.
[5] Thus Osborne declares with truth that "Every Calvinist who felt as he took part in the Wars of Religion that he was a sword in God's hand, every Jesuit who faced the rope and the quartering block sooner than acknowledge the Elizabethan Settlement of religion as having spiritual validity, were contending, whether they intended it or not, against the pagan theory of the omnipotent state." (Osborne, C. E., *Christian Ideas in Political History*, 152.) One would, however, question the 'pagan'

We shall, however, be little concerned with the problem of religious liberty; religious toleration had to be achieved before it became even an academic question. Toleration, in the historical and legal sense of the term, represents the withdrawal of external authority from the control over certain ranges of human activity, and is essentially negative.[1] Toleration represents, on the part of the State, a definition of those areas of human conduct over which it professes control. The State reserves the definition of those areas to itself and undertakes the difficult task of fixing the boundary between the free actions of the individual and his religious group and the forbidden sphere of activities, and even opinions, which the State has not relinquished from its control.

3. THE FACTORS UNDERLYING RELIGIOUS TOLERATION

It will perhaps be profitable to attempt to enumerate the elements which have contributed to the development of religious toleration. These forces all operated, though in some instances only to a very limited degree, during the reign of Elizabeth, and had by the conclusion of that reign brought the Government a considerable way towards the point of view which grasps religious toleration as the panacea for the difficult position which diversity and contention impose upon the ruling group. These factors are highly differentiated in character, origin, and operation, and did not readily combine to a common end. For this reason the history of the development of religious toleration is not a simple annal.

Perhaps the most powerful factor in disposing the Government towards toleration was the perception of the dangers inherent to the State in a policy of religious persecution. It was observed that when a religious minority had got itself established it could be rooted out only at the cost of the worst of all types of civil war. When a number of dissenting groups

character of the modern State. It would seem that its advent and its rapid assimilation of the manifold compartments of life and authority were so well supported and so thoroughly condoned by the religious writers of the sixteenth century that it is respectably Christian.

[1] Figgis, J. N., *Studies of Political Thought from Gerson to Grotius*, 4.

had achieved existence, the situation was further complicated. The examples of numerous Continental countries served to convince Elizabethan statesmen that religious minorities could not be exterminated without endangering the very bases of national life.

Closely allied with this influence was the growing secularization of national politics in the sixteenth century. We shall repeatedly urge that the Elizabethan Government was almost completely secular and Erastian in its philosophy and policy. So long as the medieval concept of the spiritual responsibility of the State for the souls of its citizens was truly operative, the Government might reasonably undertake the risk of civil war by assisting the clergy in the extirpation of heresy. But when the aims of the State are secular and when every action is measured by its political reaction, no such heroics will be undertaken. The extermination of heresy involves a crusading psychology, and this mentality was completely absent in the Elizabethan Council. In fact, the Government made most important contributions to the view that the State is concerned only with the external welfare of its citizens and that salvation is a matter which the individual will have to attain by the grace of God and the assistance of the clergy. This view at once dissociated the secular power from any attempt to coerce religious opinion, and placed whatever requirements it chose to frame regarding worship no higher than the grounds of political necessity.

It should be noted, in the next place, that as minority groups develop they tend to acquire increased political strength, aside from the potential threat of civil war. A dissenting group at first tends to attract the poorer and dissatisfied elements of society. Gradually, however, its more radical teachings are softened, it acquires an able and educated leadership, and draws upon the more influential elements of the population. Its communicants will have wealth, influence, perhaps the franchise, and will be able to exert an increasing pressure for religious toleration upon the Government. When the Government is confronted with several such groups, a powerful force for toleration has been achieved. We shall notice that

20

this influence was of great importance in England and that by the close of the century the dissenting groups had considerable support both in the Council and in Parliament.

Closely connected with this influence is the fact that the existence of a number of sects, which the Government does not dare or does not wish to exterminate, weakens and finally destroys the validity of the theory of uniformity. The Government, having disavowed the persecution of heresy for spiritual ends, must rest its case for uniformity upon political arguments or upon the requirements of order and decency in divine service. When, despite restrictive legislation and occasional punishment, several dissenting groups make good their right to existence and disaster does not overtake the nation the theory of uniformity has lost its content. Then, too, the continued existence of a variety of religious groups will sooner or later find reflection in the Government itself. This process occurred with extraordinary rapidity in England. The Elizabethan moderation in religion was to no small degree due to the fact that the inability of the Government to agree on a common policy resulted in a comprehensive compromise. The permanent continuance of repression under such conditions will be at once illogical and impossible.

It cannot be too strongly urged, in the next place, that religious toleration was only achieved in England when the dominant groups no longer had any occasion to fear the consequences of religious dissent. Thus, so long as the Roman Catholics aimed at the overthrow of the Elizabethan Government, so long as those who had profited from the confiscations incident to the Reformation feared for the security of their possessions, and so long as devout Protestants feared for the security of their faith, toleration of Roman Catholics in England was quite impossible. No one who reads the literature of the period can deny that this fear was very real, and fear is the basic cause for all persecution and repression. No Government can be expected to tolerate a group which avowedly seeks its overthrow or which threatens its security. Fear was removed when the minority groups, for various reasons, abandoned their intention of securing control of the agencies of the State in order to impose their beliefs upon the nation; when they placed the emphasis of their teachings upon the spiritual character of religion; when they clearly demonstrated that their religious tenets bore no threat to the social, economic, and political order; and when, for one reason or another, they themselves became tolerant. Most of the minority religious groups in Elizabethan England had not met these requirements and were by admission more intolerant than the Government and the Established Church. It might be held, indeed, that the moderate repression to which they were subjected was not without a salutary effect in compelling them to make a wholly spiritual restatement of their cases.

Further, the development of religious toleration was indebted to the force of economic considerations. The ill effects of persecution and civil war upon trade, the fact that dissent was especially prevalent amongst the commercial groups, and the supposed connection between Dutch prosperity and the religious freedom which obtained there exerted considerable influence in the direction of religious toleration. These influences were not, however, fully operative before the Civil War. The devastating effect of the Religious Wars in France were repeatedly pointed out in Elizabethan literature, and the reviviscent effect of the recent policy of toleration upon commerce was constantly urged as a reason for the acceptance of such a policy in England.

The wide extension of travel during the latter half of the century was likewise a factor contributing to the development of legal toleration. Travellers were impressed with the absurdity of the existence of a half-dozen exclusive "truths" in Europe, all supported by varying degrees of repression. They attained greater sympathy with other faiths and, above all, acquired a comprehensive view of religion which was not without its effect in developing the latitudinarian philosophy. We shall have occasion to indicate the importance of this factor in the writings of at least five Englishmen of our period, and the list could be considerably expanded.

It is probably no exaggeration to say that the fractionization of religion which began with the Reformation never could have been achieved had it not been for the incalculable effect of the invention of the printing press upon the world of ideas. Nor could toleration have been won so quickly by the dissenting groups if they had not had advantage of this powerful instrument of expression. The Middle Ages provide examples of the successful extermination of heretical groups by the concerted action of the civil and ecclesiastical authorities. But governments with far more adequate agencies at their command were to find it quite impossible to eradicate forbidden teachings when those beliefs were disseminated by means of the printing press. A means for spreading ideas widely, cheaply, quickly and accurately had been achieved. The Elizabethan Government endeavoured to check this weapon of minorities by the strictest laws of censorship on printing, but the Martin Marprelate controversy demonstrated that it could not possibly do so, and that its efforts only served to advertise the teachings which it sought to suppress. The cause of toleration could be urged from the comparative safety of pseudonymity and anonymity; prohibited books could be printed abroad and smuggled into England in numbers and distributed with a thoroughness which baffled the Government. The Government, recognizing its inability to suppress this medium of opinion, lent its support to controversial replies which sought to explain its policy and action. The criticism of its repressive policy speedily forced the Government into a defensive position. The literature in favour of toleration during this period was, therefore, not an insignificant factor in the consolidation of a body of opinion, much larger than has been supposed, which was opposed to the persecution of religious beliefs. The Elizabethan Government was highly sensitive to public opinion, and its repeated defences and explanations of its religious policy may be said to be, in no small degree, a recognition of the power of the Press in the moulding of opinion.

Finally, the growth of scepticism and indifference was to make a contribution to the development of religious toleration. These forces were not, however, operative to any marked degree during the sixteenth century.

These influences, when considered in their totality, probably form the major forces which were to result in the achievement of legal toleration in England.

It should be remarked, however, that religious toleration could not possibly have been attained had it not been for the antecedent relaxation of the theory of the persecution of heresy which had been firmly imbedded in the Christian ethic since its rationalization and classical expression by Saint Augustine. The theory of persecution gave way but gradually in the face of the manifest impossibility of securing its enforcement after the Protestant Reformation had shattered the unity of the Christian Church. During the period under consideration most men still adhered to it in theory, and, so far as circumstances would permit, in practice, though clear-sighted men were beginning to disavow it for manifold and complicated reasons.

Persecution of religious heresy rests fundamentally upon the conviction that there is an ascertained body of religious truth which must be believed in its entirety in order to attain salvation. The Church was regarded as the sole custodian of this body of truth, and hence rebellion against the Church was, in part, a rebellion against Truth. Thus, according to universal opinion, all who were external to the Church were doomed to eternal damnation.[1] If men believe beyond the shadow of a doubt that they possess a body of absolute truth necessary to salvation, and that the retention of contrary views places one in the certainty of eternal damnation, they will, sooner or later, persecute those holding heterodox views in order to prevent the spread of infection. Such a view, once its primary premise is accepted, is capable of rationalization, and the medieval Church so rationalized the theory.[2] Expediency may under certain conditions cause those in power to refrain from persecution for a time, but it will in no sense militate against the validity of the theory.[3] The Middle Ages were able to point to the apparent practical possibilities of what was philosophically entertained by the almost complete extermination of several

[1] Lecky, W. E. H., *History of the Rise and Influences of the Spirit of Rationalism in Europe*, I, 360.
[2] Seaton, A. A., *The Theory of Toleration under the later Stuarts*, 5–10.
[3] Lecky, *History of Rationalism in Europe*, II, 12.

plague spots of heresy. Considerable proof may be advanced to demonstrate that a power almost universally supported in an era of imperfect articulation of minority groups and slow communication can actually obliterate opposition opinion. Opinion can under these conditions be controlled.[1]

From this basic theory of persecution it could be demonstrated that heresy was likewise incompatible with a healthy social order. The power of the State was consequently enlisted to enforce the theological dicta of the Church. The Church was able, on the whole, to make persecution effective only by reason of the co-operation of the secular authority. The ruler held his office by virtue of divine commission, and it was therefore necessary for him to assist his subjects in the attainment of salvation by actively co-operating with the Church in the maintenance of an unspotted faith.[2] Heresy was generally regarded as a crime, and since it struck at the roots of salvation, was regarded as the potential source for the corruption of an unlimited number of persons. It was agreed that the heretic's soul could not be saved by punishment, but his removal might check abruptly the further spread of the contamination. Religious persecution was consistently defended for its preventive, not its curative benefits. Thus rationalized, the theory of persecution could be embraced by men whose moral character has cast a beneficent shadow across the pages of history. It became the peculiar evil of persecution, as Lecky has taught us, that it took its seat in the realms of duty and conscience, and was defended by sentiments of the deepest piety.

B. The Renaissance and Reformation in their Relation to the Problem of Toleration

The medieval conception of heresy and the concurrent attitude in regard to the pains which heresy merited were so firmly

[1] Pollock, Sir Frederick, 'The Theory of Persecution' in *Essays in Jurisprudence and Ethics*, 153–154.
[2] We shall observe in later pages that this conception was retained, with certain modifications, in England after the Reformation, and that it was to have an important bearing upon the question of toleration. However, the State, as it became stronger, rapidly diverted the exercise of this duty to its own interest.

imbedded in European thought, and so essential to the preservation of Christian unity, that powerful dissolvents were necessary for the destruction of the validity of the theory and for the weakening of the possibility of the application of that theory. To these two essential elements in the formation of a situation in which toleration could arise in theory and in practice, the Renaissance supplied important contributions, especially in that it presaged the Reformation.

1. THE RENAISSANCE AND THE WEAKENING OF THE AUTHORITY OF THE CHURCH

Lord Acton has taught us in an admirable passage that we owe much of modern liberty to the conflict which raged for four centuries between the claims of the civil and spiritual orders for the loyalty and obedience of man.[1] The rise of modern States and the divorcement of national policy from ecclesiastical ends were to result in the rapid secularization of politics. This tendency was at first vicious in its effect, but was quite conducive to the toleration of opinions which did not threaten the authority or stability of the State. That is to say, the State imposed standards of expression and belief with reference to its own ends, rather than from the point of view of the ultimate spiritual welfare of its citizenry. Perhaps as important, in the long run, was the development of a view of life during the Renaissance which dared to question the absolute character of Christian theology, and which was, on the whole, disposed to philosophical scepticism.[2] The recognition of the fact that 'absolute truth' and 'absolute error' are incapable of logical demonstration greatly weakened the authority of the Church, and created media of thought which are organically linked with the rise of modern rationalism.[3] The authority of the Church over men's minds had also been profoundly disturbed by the Captivity and the Great Schism, while the looseness and the actual tolerance of the Renaissance Papacy

---

[1] Acton, *History of Freedom*, 35.
[2] Matagrin, A., *Histoire de la Tolérance Religieuse*, 131, 140.
[3] Seaton, *The Theory of Toleration*, 19-20.

were not disposed to assist in the restoration of the loyalty of Christendom.

The development of Renaissance philosophical thought did not immediately produce any general rebellion against orthodox belief. The world was gradually assuming an attitude distinctly unfavourable to the teachings of medieval theology; but there was no explosion of hostility.[1] The general tendency of Renaissance scholars was not to contradict or assail the traditional faith, but to keep distinct the spheres of faith and reason, and to practise outward conformity to the creed without any real intellectual submission. What the humanists did was to create an intellectual atmosphere in which the emancipation of reason could begin and in which knowledge could resume its progress.

Matagrin has well emphasized the thought that Abelard's doctrine that faith should be submitted to the judgment of every individual and his disposition to require absolute evidence on any non-apparent question must be regarded as dimly foreshadowing the thought of the Renaissance.[2] In a sense, even the scholastic discussions form an approach to rationalism in their tendency to attempt the demonstration of religion as a metaphysical hypothesis. The scepticism of the Renaissance is likewise exhibited in the latter part of the *Roman de la Rose* when the author unmercifully assails the foolishness and hypocrisy of his age and professes a philosophy, if not sceptical, wholly human.

The Renaissance evolved no system of philosophy, in the strict sense of the term.[3] The thinkers of the period cannot be said to have done more than lead the revolt of reason against scholastic tyranny and obsolete authority. As De Wulf has indicated, the non-scholastic thought of the period is most accurately characterized by its independence of and its indifference to Catholic dogma.[4] The tendency to disregard the teachings of the Church and to pursue philosophy into new realms of

[1] Bury, J. B., *A History of Freedom of Thought*, 73.
[2] Matagrin, *Histoire de la Tolérance*, 132.
[3] Symonds, J. A., *The Renaissance in Italy*, V, 391.
[4] De Wulf, M., *History of Medieval Philosophy*, 464.

consideration by means of new methods of handling ideas may be closely identified with that system of thought which we regard as 'Renaissance.' Pursuing these lines, the thinkers of the period brought scepticism into the world.[1] To be sure, the validity of dogmatic authority was not destroyed, but the logic which undergirded its bases was questioned, and the sphere of its influence narrowed. A fruitful distinction was drawn between the fundamental tenets of religion (all religions) and the non-fundamental appendages of dogma.[2] Men sought to place the important questions of life in the sphere of observation and comprehension, refusing to entrust such concepts longer to the realm of authoritative revelation. Men asked, how can we understand what the manifestations of God's universe are; and the answer came to be that natural intelligence is the surest guide to the solution of these problems. Therewith was developed a principle of religious judgment quite removed from the sphere of religious revelation.[3] When men attempted to place their natural intelligence into direct application to the problems of God and religion, and as they viewed the Church and its theology, their conception and evaluation of orthodoxy changed. Men imbued with such a point of view were inclined towards rationalism, occasionally towards scepticism, and increasingly towards indifference to religion, or at least, to religious fanaticism. In such a culture philosophical toleration could find its roots.

Humanism was to serve as an intermediate stage between scholasticism and rationalism. The Renaissance, in general, may be regarded as the Middle Ages in dissolution. The vast edifice of scholastic theology was being undermined by men who had the energy to divest themselves of orthodox traditions, but who lacked the force and courage to mould the definitive thought of a new system of ideas.[4] Unfortunately, at the moment when the Renaissance philosophers had accomplished the

[1] Freund, M., *Die Idee der Toleranz im England der Grossen Revolution*, 5.
[2] One example, the teachings of Averroes, may suffice. Vide Charbonnel, J. R., *La Pensée Italienne au xvi Siècle et le Courant Libertin*, 161–162, 164–165, 168–169. Renan, *Averhoés et l'averrohoisme* (1861), 205 ff.
[3] Freund, *Die Idee der Toleranz*, 5.
[4] Symonds, *Renaissance in Italy*, V, 392.

groundwork of a rational and liberal system of thought, and, in connection with other forces, had imparted these notions to a fairly large body of men, the deadly influence of the Counter-Reformation extinguished and suppressed Liberal thought in Italy. But the seeds of revolt had been sown and new and fearless hands in the North were to extend and amplify the beginnings which had been wrought in the South.

The Italian Renaissance by a revival of pagan philosophy, which was disburdened of the inexact and coloured interpretation which the Middle Ages had lent to it, and by the establishment of a new and fresh ideal of human conduct, had given birth to the dilettantism of the sceptics and the positivism of the rationalists—tendencies alike favourable to the development of toleration.[1] The intimate and continued contacts of Italy with Byzantine and with Muslim culture had produced a dispassionate tolerance which had gravely weakened the ethnographical conception of a privileged Christendom.[2] Directly classical antiquity became an ideal of life, ancient speculation and scepticism obtained complete mastery over the humanists. As interest in and emphasis on the affairs of this life became stronger the feeling of the need for salvation was progressively diminished. The pleasures and activities of this life tended to exclude concern for the life to come, or to relegate it to a poetic conception which bore but small resemblance to the fixed dicta of orthodoxy.

That religion should again become an affair of the individual, and that it should derive its content from his personal feelings and judgments was, for the scholar, an inevitable consequence of these teachings. The man of pious mien could well be driven to the same position by the evident laxity and corruption within the Church. But the glory of the Italian Renaissance was its individualism and, consequently, it failed to give cohesion and systematization either to tolerant scepticism or to pious discontent.

A tolerant atmosphere had by the various forces which we

[1] Matagrin, *Histoire de la Tolérance*, 147.
[2] Vide Burckhardt, J., *The Civilization of the Period of the Renaissance in Italy*, II, 297–298.

29

have so roughly sketched been created without bursting the unity of the Christian world. It appeared for a brief moment that toleration of religious opinions and freedom of thought might arise within the Church; that the dreams of Erasmus might attain realization. But the very tolerance of the Papacy outdid itself. Christian conscience rightly called for the setting of the ecclesiastical house in order and for the approximation of profession with conduct. It is perhaps the greatest tragedy of modern history that that task could not be accomplished by tolerant, cultivated, and liberal men. The task demanded the efforts of the sterner conscience of the North, little touched by the liberalizing force of Italian humanism. These men took their cue from the humanist's formula of private judgment, but they fashioned their edifice along the lines of absolute right and exclusive salvation. The Catholic Church met the Protestant revolt by setting "right" against "right," dogma against dogma and, while girding herself for the supreme task of her history, found it necessary to extinguish the tolerance which had barely manifested itself. Expression during the Renaissance had developed without conscious antagonism to the Church. Indeed, churchmen had been forward in cultivating the new learning, had encouraged and studied its literature, and had appreciated and promoted its art.[1] But the Reformation, with its attendant incidents, was to make the Church suspicious of movements which might contain seeds of revolt. Italy after 1525 became what Spain had been subsequent to the Moorish wars, sullen in temper and jealous in disposition. When the battle was joined the last vestige of toleration disappeared.[2] Still, the facts of the sixteenth century were to create an impossible 'impasse' in logic and in fact, and from this situation toleration, in its modern meaning, could emerge.[3]

[1] Fairbairn, A. M., in the *Camb. Mod. History*, II, 704.
[2] The disastrous consequences of the struggle induced by the Reformation on the minds of men who had drunk deep of the spring of Renaissance thought, but who were at the same time imbued with the tradition of Catholic unity, may well be demonstrated by a study of More. Cf. *post*, 41–49.
[3] Murray, R. H., *The Political Consequences of the Reformation*, 3; Bury, *History of Freedom of Thought*, 75.

2. THE PROTESTANT REFORMATION AND ITS EFFECT UPON THE DEVELOPMENT OF TOLERATION

The Reformation could scarcely have arisen without the background of humanistic thought. Despite this relationship, however, the Reformation was far from establishing religious liberty and the right of private judgment. What it did was to bring about a set of political and social conditions under which religious liberty might ultimately be secured.[1] The great reformers displayed much more interest in the propagation of spiritual enthusiasm than in the guiding and formulation of Protestant thought. Above all they were deeply religious and their primary aim was the attainment of salvation rather than to secure liberty for the individual. As Tulloch has said, their fundamental aim was the salvation of the human soul rather than the peace of the human mind.[2] The terrific momentum of their enthusiasm was to account for changes which the humanists of the Renaissance could never have accomplished. Nothing was further from the minds of the reformers than the toleration of doctrines other than their own. Each asserted the freedom of his own opinions, while taking little interest that others should be ensured the same measure of liberty. One authority was replaced by another. The authority of the Bible was set up to replace the authority of the Church, but it was the Bible according to Calvin or Luther. The reformers, like the Church from which they had parted, cared nothing for freedom. They cared only for truth.[3] If the medieval ideal was to purge the world of heretics, the object of the Protestants was to exclude all dissentients from the territory under their control.

In considering the influence of the Protestant Reformation

---

[1] Bury, *Freedom of Thought*, 77. The argument (pp. 31–38) rests heavily upon the brilliant analyses of Bury, Figgis, and Acton. At some points, the brilliancy of which could lead to no confusion, footnotes have not been regarded as necessary.

[2] Tulloch, J., *Rational Theology and Christian Philosophy in England in the Seventeenth Century*, I, 3.

[3] Bury, *Freedom of Thought*, 79; Belasco, P. S., *Authority in Church and State*, 20.

upon the development of religious toleration, we must carefully distinguish between its immediate objects and its ultimate effects. The essence of its spirit was the interpretation of creed in the light of reason, and the moral sentiments of human nature.[1] It led men to judge what is true and good by the test of reason rather than by the tenets of tradition. Lecky has rightly suggested that, if little difference appeared in creed, a tremendous shift occurred in the importance of creed. The claims of the right of private judgment could not indefinitely be denied by a system of thought which owed its existence to the triumph of that principle.[2] We may regard the Reformation as representing the unconscious triumph both of the scientific spirit and of human liberty.[3] The Reformers were critically minded theologians who had taken fate into their own hands and deliberately parted with the past and with authority on the basis of rationalism. In the long run, it scarcely mattered that at the same time the Reformers were denouncing the freedom of reason. The Reformation, in so far as it broke the overwhelming power of the Church over the minds of men, made for liberty of dissent.[4] It is better to have three intolerant sects than one intolerant faith. The Church regarded the Protestant sects precisely as it had viewed the earlier heresies. The important fact was the success of the Protestant heresies. A successful heresy may be argued to vindicate the right of heresy by its own continued existence. Thus the Reformation indirectly and involuntarily aided the cause of religious liberty, especially in that the substitution of several truths for one and several authorities for one dealt a fatal blow to the continuance of ecclesiastical authority. Europe was divided by the Reformation into two spiritual camps of fairly even strength. It was the logical aim of the consistently intolerant among the Catholics and Protestants alike to secure the extermination of the opposite religious party. The factual impossibility of this ideal was effectively demonstrated by the

---

[1] Lecky, *History of Rationalism*, I, 365.
[2] Matagrin, *Histoire de la Tolérance*, 153.
[3] Beard, C., *The Reformation of the Sixteenth Century*, 148.
[4] *Ibid.*, 149.

series of religious wars which swept over Europe and the persecuting ideal had consequently to be modified.[1] The continued existence of Protestant and Catholic groups as between nations and within nations, upon the failure of the possibility of exterminating the religious minority within a given area, had to compel the acceptance of some sort of a working system of toleration.

The Reformation likewise assisted the development of toleration by altering the basis of the persecution of dissent. Before its advent Europe was rightly regarded as a unified religious commonwealth, and, as we have attempted to point out, it might be urged that the ruler was bound to assist in the maintenance of the orthodox faith.[2] The disruption of the fabric of Christianity by the Protestant Revolt undermined the logical foundations of the theory of persecution. Then, too, there was less ground for Protestant intolerance. Catholicism was an ancient faith, resting upon long traditions and practices of authority. The Church had been on the defensive since the thirteenth century against ever-rising tides of heresy which washed higher and higher on the rocks of faith. "She might point to the priceless blessings she had bestowed upon humanity, to the slavery she had destroyed, and to the civilization which she had founded. . . . She might show how completely her doctrines were interwoven with the whole social system" and how fearful would be the convulsion if they were destroyed.[3] Upon these bases the Catholic Church had in the Middle Ages exterminated sects which were conceived as threatening the existing social and spiritual order.[4] Further than that, she had condemned individuals whose teachings threatened what was conceived to be purity of dogma. When a large portion of population of a different or schismatical creed was in existence a measured toleration of opinion had prevailed, though political freedom was denied as the source of possible political disorder.[5] Catholic intolerance, we must conclude,

---

[1] Coulton, 'Protestant View of Toleration,' *Contemporary Review*, September 1930, 316.   [2] Creighton, *Persecution and Tolerance*, 112.
[3] Lecky, *History of Rationalism*, II, 57–58.
[4] Acton, *History of Freedom*, 168.   [5] *Ibid.*, 169; cf. n. 2, p. 381.

was handed down from an age when actual unity prevailed and when this unity could be conceived as the sufficient cause for the persecution of those who sought to disrupt it. But it is difficult to condone persecution on the part of a Church which is barely founded, which can show no services, and whose origins are interwoven with the right of private judgment.

The incessant contacts between Protestants and Catholics, and the flow of opposing ideas likewise lent a strong influence towards the rise of toleration. The Reformation was in itself a striking instance of the relativity of all religious truth, a conception which the humanists had gingerly posed as an intellectual thesis. In an absolute sense a body of dogma cannot be true north of the Alps and false to the south of them. It is more probable, the thinking man will come to believe, that both points of view may be largely correct, and that neither may legitimately advance a claim to exclusive truth. A tendency must inevitably display itself, when the first heat of passion has subsided, to stress the points held in common and to regard charitably the points held in dispute. Such a disposition cuts away the claim of absolute truth and with it the claim of exclusive salvation, but it constitutes an escape from the strife and bitterness incident to the clash of opposing systems of 'truth.' 'Relativism' alone afforded an escape from the conflict into which the theologians had launched Europe. Toleration may be approached from any number of angles, but the most important philosophical approach is by the channel of reason.[1] Intelligent men in the sixteenth century, repelled by the harsh dogmatic pretensions of the sects to a complete monopoly of truth, wearied of the eternal insistence on creed, and aghast at the welter of blood and persecution occasioned by these pretensions, turned naturally to test the validity of the assumptions of the theologians, or, at least, suspended judgment until the reformed Churches could advance a clearer justification of their right to persecute.

The Reformation further assisted the growth of toleration in that it was coincident with the rise of national states, and since the rulers of Protestant countries exercised a dominating

---

[1] Matagrin, *Histoire de la Tolérance*, 189

or controlling influence in the determination of religious policy within their frontiers.[1] The growth of national states was, indeed, accelerated by the rapid development of national religious differences.[2] As we shall have occasion to insist later, on whatever grounds persecution was justified in Protestant states, it was practised from political expediency; and of this the State, and not the sects, was the judge. The State regarded certain religious conduct as dangerous and punished it, under the laws of the State, as unpatriotic. England provides the classic example of this line of action. Roman Catholic countries could still persecute from principle; Protestant nations were driven to the arguments of political necessity. The supreme ecclesiastical power in most Protestant states was vested in the sovereign and, since he had other considerations of policy than the religious, he would, sooner or later, modify ecclesiastical fanaticism when it should become an obvious danger to the peace of the realm. The tide of absolutism was running strong when the Reformation came and Luther, at least in his direct influence, appears to have assisted in the final triumph of politics over the moral and spiritual forces which the State for so long had been obliged to heed.[3]

Under these conditions what we may call international tolerance was possible, and it became necessary for the continuation of political life in Europe. This point of view is found clearly imbedded in the formula *cujus regio ejus religio*, which the logic of events forced upon the Empire in the Peace of Augsburg.[4] Theological persecution was discredited through the force of circumstances. The continued existence of Protestant kingdoms was sufficient evidence that international persecution must be formally abandoned. Protestant and Catholic rulers, finding a system of perpetual reprisals intolerable, were practically compelled to permit the existence on some terms of citizens who did not accept the prevailing religion of the

---

[1] We shall be especially interested in tracing the influence of this factor in our consideration of England. No Protestant country presented so Erastian a situation.   [2] Creighton, *Persecution and Tolerance*, 112.
[3] Acton, *History of Freedom*, 42.
[4] Haynes, E. S. P., *Religious Persecution*, 72–73.

State.[1] The Peace of Augsburg likewise witnessed the definite abandonment of the theory that no heretic might rule a Christian State.[2] The possibility or the validity of occasional persecution was not abandoned, but the ideal of medieval intolerance was definitely discarded. The establishment of the right of migration, though it was held that unity of religion was essential to the welfare of the State, was tantamount to the admission that no real ground could be found for the execution of an heretic for the sake of his soul.[3] We have come a long way from the Middle Ages. Persecution for the sake of political reasons was upheld since the age-old union of Church and State was retained, and it was very clearly regarded as unsafe to the body politic to permit the existence of more than one religion within a given State. But no claim was advanced to the right to disarm thought or to exterminate heresy.[4] The theory that one religion is needful to the State, but that it might vary as between States, was a distinct step towards the modern theory that the State exists indifferently to confessional distinctions.[5]

In this stage of development uniformity of religion was held to be essential to the well-being of the State. Religious dissent may entail banishment; but an imperial Church and a common religious law are definitely abandoned. Each State is left free to go its own way. With the attainment of this attitude the last vestige of the theory of universality has been destroyed.[6] Political entities are to be regarded as religious entities. The right of the State to embrace Protestantism is not conceded, but once a State makes good its revolt, its position is given the sanction of law. A State may, as in the case of England from the Reformation until the defeat of the Armada, be threatened for having withdrawn from the ancient faith, but such international righteousness displays itself as limited strictly by considerations of political ends. The moment England had achieved a secure settlement of her religious problem she

[1] Pollock, *Theory of Persecution*, 158.
[2] Figgis, J. N., in the *Camb. Mod. Hist.*, III, 754.
[3] *Ibid.*   [4] *Ibid.*, III, 755.   [5] *Ibid.*
[6] The attainment of this point of view must have been in close connection with the development of International Law. It is perhaps significant that Bodin was a Politique, and that Gentilis and Grotius were dissenters.

had little to fear from united Catholic action against her for spiritual reasons. This fact was scarcely appreciated in England before the death of the Queen, but it became increasingly operative as a factor for toleration. International toleration results from the increased power of the national states. The acceptance of the theory of sovereignty by the nations of Europe permitted no distinction in law between a Catholic state and a Protestant country.[1]

With the factual attainment of international tolerance the responsibility for the handling of the problem of dissent may be said to have been shifted to the national State. No State during the period under discussion was prepared to permit full liberty of conscience and worship. In England, however, an interesting and momentous advance was made towards toleration under the enlightened leadership of Burleigh and the Queen. The State endeavoured to frame the religious settlement along lines of comprehension and maintained a reasonably moderate interpretation of the laws against nonconformity. The Government, in addition, sought to differentiate between persecution of conscience and restriction of liberty of worship. The former it consistently declared to be beyond the province of governmental concern; the latter it held was a function of Government since public safety and order were vitally concerned. Until the plots coincident with the Counter-Reformation obliged a strict programme of repression, the Government permitted a large degree of freedom of conscience and even freedom of worship. Religious programmes involving sedition were punished, but were dealt with as political crimes. The Government made no real effort to attain religious uniformity beyond the prohibition of outward services in sectarian churches. This attitude may be characterized as an attempt to secure the political advantages of uniformity while, as Figgis says, "putting dissent in the category of an unrecognized but permitted vice."

The next stage in the development of toleration for political ends did not occur everywhere in Europe in the sixteenth

[1] This principle is of fundamental importance with Grotius, and, to a lesser degree, with Bodin.

century. The logical conclusion of the Wars of Religion would have been the extermination of the dissenting minorities in any given country. But as time went on and when it became apparent to wise and patriotic observers that the terrible waste of blood and funds was accomplishing the ruin of the State rather than the destruction of the sects, a new position had to be assumed. By 1600 it had become quite apparent, after a rather complete trial in France and the Netherlands, that heresy could not be exterminated by the sword. Heresy had come to stay, and it remained for the State to accept the fact, to arrange the legal and political structure to accommodate a necessary nuisance, and to secure the dissenting bodies to the State by ties of patriotism and loyalty. When once avowed heretics are permitted to live, and the principle of toleration is so far established that the terms and conditions of it can be discussed, persecution may be said to have been driven from its high theological seat.[1] The State admits by its actions that there are limits within which religious belief is an affair not of certainty but of opinion; and the repression of religious opinion, so far as it continues, proceeds not from the requirements of spiritual welfare, but from reasons of social and political necessity or expediency.[2] More important, when the theological grounds of persecution are abandoned, it will be held, sooner or later, that strict theological uniformity cannot be enforced and that each soul will have to attend to its own salvation.[3] These related developments may best be traced in France during the sixteenth century, and they found their culmination in the Edict of Nantes. A little later the same trends found their conclusion in Holland, while in England the full recognition of these principles did not come before the closing years of the seventeenth century. In other European states, legal toleration was postponed until much later, and in some cases did not occur until the late years of the past century.

To these forces which were steadily making for at least partial toleration of dissent, the reformers opposed a dogmatic system little less severe and quite as rigid as that of the Church

[1] Pollock, *Theory of Persecution*, 158.
[2] *Ibid.*   [3] *Ibid.*, 160.

from which they had sprung.[1] The reformers by their discussions and controversies loosed zeal and enthusiasm so acrimonious and passionate that the cause of moderation and toleration was seriously impaired. The entire weight of the reforming energy was confined to dogmatic channels. The germs of rationalism, so implicit in the revolt, were soon suppressed and denied. Conscience was the last tribunal to which men were referred for the supreme authority of their creed. "There was much doubt as to what historical authorities were most valuable, but there was no doubt that the ultimate basis of theology must be historical."[2] The subsidence of the rational side of Protestantism arose not only from the character of the reformers, but also from the nature of their position. The tremendous surge of enthusiasm which the reformers had loosed did its work too well. It not only snapped the bonds of ecclesiastical authority, but threatened to dissolve the bonds of civil authority. Protestantism had barely arisen when its authors sought to anchor it with bonds of discipline and dogma. They found it necessary to fix restraints upon the spirit of enquiry, to limit the right of private judgment, and to mould the great spiritual enthusiasm of the movement into the cold forms of creed.[3]

These facts account, at least partially, for the extremely dogmatic character which Protestantism soon displayed. If the rich spiritual character which Protestantism had assumed was to be controlled to constructive ends, it must be consolidated, clarified, and defined by dogmatic formulae. It has been well argued that this process alone enabled Protestantism to withstand with even partial success the counter-surge of Rome.[4] In the second half of the sixteenth century Protestantism was almost stationary in character. Professor Smith has well pointed out that after 1560 Protestantism lost more territory in Europe than it gained.[5] It had been crystallized into churches, and had consolidated its theology. The men who had been largely responsible for the accomplishment of this task had

[1] Lecky, *History of Rationalism*, I, 365.　　　　[2] *Ibid.*, I, 369.
[3] Tulloch, *Rational Theology and Christian Philosophy*, I, 5.
[4] *Ibid.*, I, 5-6.　　　[5] Smith, P., *The Age of the Reformation*, 388 ff.

set up what they regarded as a definite system of truth against a definite system of error. In consequence, the questioning side of Protestantism was to go into a protracted eclipse. But the very fixity of Protestant dogma and its inability to permit of flexibility was directly to be the cause of further revolt along lines of religious liberty within the Protestant communion. The clergy of the sixteenth century was almost unanimous in its opposition to toleration. Indeed, at the close of the next century Bossuet was able to maintain that the right of the civil power to persecute heresy was one of the points on which Catholics and Protestants alike were in agreement. The dominant cause of Protestant, as well as Catholic, intolerance was the firm belief in the possibility of attaining absolute truth and the intimate connection of this notion with the doctrine of exclusive salvation.[1] The dawn of toleration witnesses in all countries the rise of a point of view which tends to regard doctrines merely as the vehicles of moral sentiment, and which, while it greatly diminishes their value, simplifies their character and lessens their number.[2]

C. THE ENGLISH BACKGROUND

It is not within the proper scope of this study to trace carefully the progress of the English Reformation or the development of English theory with respect to the power of the magistrate in the Church, save as they seem to hinge upon the question of toleration. There is, as well, during the period prior to the accession of Elizabeth little to arrest us with regard to the accretion of opinion against the persecution of religious divergence. English opinion remained essentially medieval with respect to this question, and the dissolution of the ancient faith had not proceeded far enough and had not been under weigh long enough to make the question of toleration one of vital importance.[3] There are surprising utterances, but they appear to be isolated, exceptional, and, generally speaking, unconnected with trends of major importance.

[1] Lecky, *History of Rationalism*, II, 61.   [2] *Ibid.*, II, 62.
[3] Acton, *History of Freedom*, 51.

1. THE REFORMATION DESTRUCTIVE TO HUMANISTIC TOLERANCE

We have mentioned above the effect which the Protestant Reformation had upon the tolerant position of the humanists, and upon the drift within the Church to arrive at a more lenient construction of dogmatic thought. These important humanistic developments had scarcely struck root in England with the Oxford group than the chilling blasts of theological controversy brought them, so far as possibilities of major influence were concerned, to a fairly abrupt conclusion.

The attitude of the humanists when confronted by the dissolution inherent in the Protestant Revolt constitutes a highly important index to the reaction which the movement generally inspired in sensitive men whose cultural roots struck deeply into the past. It was again proved that radicalism is fatal to liberalism. These men believed that the Church could and was cleansing herself, and that within her communion freedom and tolerance of thought and worship could best be secured. Profoundly influenced by an historical sense, they beheld all that they considered fine and good in European civilization going down in red ruin and anarchy. Protestantism, in its initial stages, was perhaps attractive to an Erasmus because of its insistence upon the rights of conscience and the validity of private judgment; but dogmatic Protestantism was quite as repellent as dogmatic Romanism, and with less *raison d'être*.[1] Instinctively the humanist who had so far advanced thought and learning crept back to the shelter of an institution which symbolized peace, order, and unity. Deformed as the Church was it appeared infinitely better than a fractionalized religious society whose chief characteristics seemed to be intolerance, dogmatic insistence upon the exclusive character of its truth, and the disruption of the bonds of the social order. More and Erasmus especially evidence this tendency.

More, in the *Utopia*, written in 1516, advanced a well-defined system of religious toleration. The Utopian theory of toleration, as has been well said, may be characterized as a

[1] Allen, P. S., *Opus Epistolarum Des. Erasmi Roterodami*, III, 587 ff., 527 ff., 540 ff.; *Ibid.*, I, 29; Epist. MLX, 1210c.

conception of religious liberty arising in a great mind as a possibility; and it may have been conceived as desirable at the time he wrote.[1] It is the humanist who speaks. Some of the Utopians adore the sun, others a star, others a deified man, while the philosophers worship a Great Unknown.[2] But all men acknowledge a Supreme Being called Mithra. All men are permitted as a principle of State to hold any religious opinion they may prefer. It is perhaps significant that the Utopians are not represented as Christians. The limit of their creed was to forbid disbelief in either divine providence or in a future life in which the just would be rewarded by God's presence. However, even those who retained these heresies, if they refrained from any attempt to disseminate their errors, were not amenable to punishment.[3] Heretics in these particulars were not permitted to hold office, since such views were regarded as ignoble, and government requires a noble mind. Utopus, the first king, had ordained toleration on the very interesting grounds that God Himself might have inspired men with a variety of religious beliefs.[4] The people were persuaded that "it is not in a man's power to believe what he list, no, nor they constrain him not with threatenings to dissemble his mind and show countenance contrary to his thought. For deceit and all manners of lies they do marvellously abhor." The 'Established Church' of Utopia had little power, and its creed was exceedingly simple. The priests were few and were selected by popular vote.

More's noble representation of an ideal spiritual commonwealth was not out of harmony with the advanced thought of the intellectual community of which he was so distinguished a member. As Professor Coulton has well remarked, it seems improbable that on so serious a subject he would have portrayed a system which he would not gladly have seen accepted in the England of his own day.[5] The toleration of the *Utopia* may be regarded as the finest expression of the humanistic

[1] St. John, W., *The Contest for Liberty of Conscience in England*, 15.
[2] More, Thomas, *Utopia*, 209–210.
[3] *Ibid.*, 215–216.   [4] *Ibid.*, 214.
[5] Coulton, G. G., *Protestant View of Toleration*, Cont. Rev., 777, 316.

culture of the period. Lord Acton has admirably sketched the wide extent of religious freedom that existed in the period 1510–1530. At the time of the publication of the *Utopia*, the storm of religious controversy had not yet broken over Europe. Erasmus warmly praised the 'light and liberty' which he found in Rome in 1515. In France the Inquisition found its powers severely curtailed and the French bishops declined to bring accused heretics before it.[1] Lutheran teachings were spread in the French Court with the connivance of the king. In Savoy the Waldensians were permitted to worship without interference. The Hapsburgs had attempted persecution at the beginning of the Reformation, but Ferdinand, as early as 1526, acknowledged the factual operation of the principle *cujus regio ejus religio* in his dominions. The Catholics and the Utraquists had arrived at a fruitful and tolerant settlement of the religious affairs of Bohemia a decade earlier. In Venice, the Greek Catholics worshipped in separate churches with little or no interference. The Diet of Denmark, in 1527, assigned equal rights to Catholic and Protestant subjects. The Thomas More of 1516 drew heavily upon the ideas of toleration which were fairly generally received by men of his intellectual status at that time.[2] The test of the strength and permanence of his ideas had yet to come.

When More wrote the *Utopia* he had no personal knowledge of heretics, and no conception of the assaults which they might make upon the institutions which he revered. The Lutheran Revolt, the horrors of the Peasants' Rebellion, and the dangerous views of the Anabaptists and of the other strange sects which he saw springing up mushroom-like over all Europe profoundly altered his views. To More civilization and order were very nearly synonymous.[3] His views upon many matters were advanced far beyond his age, but his faith was firm in a civilization based upon Catholicism. His sensitive spirit realized almost more than anyone of his generation, save Erasmus, the terrific shock which the bases of society had

[1] Kitchin, G. W., *A History of France*, II, 310.
[2] Murray, *Political Consequences of the Reformation*, 246.
[3] Murray, 'Utopian Toleration,' *Edin. Rev.*, No. 447, 101.

suffered.[1] While realizing the urgency of material corrections in the Church, his sentiments and instincts were violated by the radical programme which Protestantism proposed for the attainment of these corrections. He was by nature repelled by the idea of radical change. It would almost appear that he and his group had set under weigh forces whose outcome was to be far different from what they anticipated, and whose consequence was to fill them with horror.[2]

Thus we may expect to find in More's later writings expressions wholly contradictory to the words of the *Utopia*. The sentiments of the *Utopia* are free, frank, and warm, and appear to come from the heart of the man.[3] The words of the *Confutation*, on the other hand, are those of an official who is justifying a political action by stilted, well-worn figures of speech, which impress one as being unworthy of the man.

In 1526 the *Index Librorum Prohibitorum* was established in England, and More was commissioned by Tunstall to read various heretical works in order to refute them. An examination of his controversial works displays the tragic effect which the Reformation had upon him.

Heresy, More wrote in the *Apology* (1533), is not only a grave spiritual sin meriting severe punishment, but is "the wurste cryme that canne be."[4] It is, in fact, a more serious crime than treason.[5] Heresy, "wherby a Christen man becommeth a false traytour to God is in al lawes spiritual and temporall both, accompted as greate a crime as is the treason committed against anye worldlye man."[6] An heretic under trial should be deprived of knowledge of his accusers, he urged in *The Debellacyon* (1533).[7] His fear of heresy and of its consequences is strikingly shown when he advises Christians: "Wee should haue none other communicatiō with heretikes, but onely of reprouyng their heresy and giuyng them warning to leaue. And yet not euery man be bold to talke to long with them not

---

[1] Stratford, E. Wingfield, *History of British Civilization*, I, 394.
[2] Murray, R. H., 'Utopian Toleration,' *Edin. Rev.*, No. 447, 102.
[3] Creighton, *Persecution and Tolerance*, 108.
[4] More, Thomas, *The Apology of Syr Thomas More, Works*, 866.
[5] *Ibid.*, 910.
[6] More, Thomas, *The Debellacyon, Works*, 995.　　　　[7] *Ibid.*, 987.

euen therof neither, . . . lest as the pestilēce catcheth some tyme the leche that fasting commeth very nere, and long sytteth by the sicke mā busye aboute to cure hym; so some folke fainte and feable in the faythe matched with a felowe stobourne and stronge in heresy, may sooner hymself take hurte, than do the tother good."[1]

More would show little mercy to heresy and he doubts the possibility of its cure in most cases, "So harde is that carbuncle, catching ones a core, to bee by any meane well and surely cured. Howebeit God so worketh, and sometime it is. Towarde the helpe wherof, or if it happely be incurable, then to the clene cutting oute that parte for infeccion of the remenāt, I am by mine offyce in vertue of mine othe, and euerye officer of iustice through the realme for his rate, right especially bounden, not in reason onely and good congreuence, but also by plaine ordinaunce and statute."[2] Thus the humanist was driven to the refuge of an outworn medieval figure and to a plea of duty to the State in justification of his personal position. Later, when confronted by another 'duty of office,' he found that personal judgment and conscience constituted a higher basis of decision. The humanist also descended to the language of controversy in his antipathy for Luther and Tyndale, whom he regarded as principally responsible for the disasters that had befallen Christendom. He savagely attacked the heresy of Luther, not as an error, but as a crime against religion and society. He branded Luther as "an apostate, an open incestuous lechour, a playne limme of the deuill, and a manifest messenger of hell."[3]

More's most coherent exposition of the duty of persecution is to be found in the *Dialogue*, which has been somewhat neglected for the *Confutation*. He urged that fear of the dissolution of religion and the rending of the civil structure have been the causes "that Princes and people have bene constrayned to punishe heresyes by terrible death. . . ."[4] He endeavoured to

[1] More, Thomas, *The Answer to the First Part of the poysoned booke*, *Works*, 1036.
[2] More, Thomas, *The Confutacion of Tyndales Answere*, *Works*, 351–352.
[3] More, Thomas, *The Dialogue of Syr Thomas More*, *Works*, 247.
[4] *Ibid.*, 274.

explain why consistent persecution should be adopted as a policy in his own day, while admitting that Christ and the primitive Church did not advocate or practise such repression.[1] Persecution, he argued, proceeds not only from concern for the spiritual welfare of mankind, but "also of the peace amõg ... the princes people." The heretics in the early Church were gently dealt with because they refrained from violence. But "as for heretykes risyng among our selfe, and springing [out] of ourselfe, be in no wyse to be suffered, but to be oppressed and ouerwhelmed in the beginning."[2] Heresy, if treated mildly, will only spread the faster and will eventually be the harder to eradicate. Then, leaning heavily on the logic of Augustine, he pointed out how comparable the situation in Germany was with the disorder and chaos that appertained in the Christian fold during the lifetime of the great Father. If it were just and necessary to suppress heresy then, it is just and necessary at the present time. The English law plainly indicates that heretics should be burned and that law should be enforced.[3]

Using language reminiscent of the Middle Ages, he argued that it is the highest duty of the Christian ruler to maintain and nourish the true religion.[4] He laid great stress on the political consequences of dissension: there is great danger that the State will be broken up, property destroyed, and that the subjects will be "destroyed by common sedicion, insurecion, and open warre, within the bowelles of their owne lande." These dire dangers may be avoided "by punishmēte" in the beginning, "of those fewe who be the first, which few wel repressed, or yf nede so require utterly pulled up, ther shall farre the fewer have lust to folow."[5]

[1] More, Thomas, *Dialogue, Works*, 110, 274, 275.
[2] *Ibid.*, 276.   [3] *Ibid.*, 276 ff.
[4] Christ's teachings of mercy in no sense "bind a man that he shall of necessitie against the comen nature suffer another manne causelesse to kyll hym, nor letteth not any manne frõ the defēce of another, whom he seeth innocente and invaded and oppresed by malice (i.e. by heresy). In whiche case bothe nature, reason, and Goddes beheste byndeth, fyrst the prynce to the safe garde of hys people." (*Dialogue, Works*, 278–279.) The prince is surely bound not to "suffer thys people to bee seduced and corrupted by heretikes [since] the peryll shall in thorte [short] whyle growe to as greate peril" as if infidelity were abroad in the land.
[5] More, Thomas, *Dialogue, Works*, 279, 285–286.

This discussion, though it clearly indicates the change that the Protestant Revolt had worked in the mind of More, adds little to the doctrine of persecution. His theory is not placed upon the lofty plane of Saint Thomas. The whole of More's later writings are pessimistic and fearful. Persuasion he considered of little avail, for "a man maye with as much fruite preache to a post" as to an heretic. In the closing words of the *Dialogue* More demonstrated perfectly the fundamental psychological factor underlying intolerance; the instinctive conviction that the persistent retention of an opinion which we regard as patently erroneous is a certain indication of the stupidity, stubbornness, and perversity of the holder.[1] More's pessimism and fear are strikingly demonstrated in a conversation with Roper.[2] Roper had just commended his father-in-law on the happy state of the realm where "no heretic durst show his face" and where "so loving obedient subjects all in one faith agreeing together." But More, conscious of the restless currents of thought that underlay the Henrican calm, replied, "Troth it is indeed, son Roper, . . . and yet, I pray God that some of us, as high as we seem to sit upon the mountains treading heretics under our feet like ants, live not to see the day that we gladly would wish to be at league and composition with them to let them have their churches quietly to themselves, so that they would be contented to let us have ours quietly to ourselves."[3] One is tempted to express an historical regret that this pithy exposition of legal toleration could not have been More's own conviction. But an age cannot transcend itself. The fact that Europe appeared to the great humanist to be "on the brink of red ruin and the breaking up of laws" moved him to support a desperate attempt to check the onrush of the apparently destructive forces of the new order at whatever cost.[4]

[1] More, Thomas, *Dialogue*, *Works*, 286 ff. It remained for Acontius first to analyse and expose this basis of persecution. His treatment has never been equalled. Vide *post*, 318–323.
[2] Roper, William, *The Life of Sir Thomas More*, 35–36.　　　　[3] *Ibid.*
[4] These words recall in striking manner the effect which the French Revolution and, more recently, the Russian Revolution had upon liberal thought in Europe. The effect of the Protestant Reformation with its attendant social and political disturbances upon the tolerant humanist recalls the effect of the French Revolution upon, shall we say, Burke.

Chambers' able paper has done much to remove the stigma of actual persecution from More's reputation.[1] During the period of his administration of office there appears to have been no capital punishment of heresy in the diocese of London.[2] The wave of persecution began in 1531, and, though More was still in office, power had slipped from his hands. Stokesley was responsible for the executions which occurred in the closing months of More's tenure of office,[3] though it must be noted that More defended both the conduct of the trial and the judgment of the clergy on the heretics.[4] But this fact, agreeable as it is to the admirers of More, can scarcely remove the weight of the reasoned arguments of his later writings on the subject of heresy and its treatment. He may not have burned heretics, his sensitive spirit may actually have been repelled by the thought of human suffering, but he had placed himself intellectually upon the side of that very action. More exercised an intellectual influence that completely dwarfs any political power he may have wielded. He should therefore be judged in this particular by his intellectual attitude on the subject. It might well be argued that considerably more moral responsibility must be attached to the intellectual dicta of the humanist on the subject than to the brutal application of those dicta by a Stokesley.

Chambers has well pointed out that More was deeply imbued with the current conception of political obedience. He never actively protested against the order by law established. He entertained convictions of conscience which he held in violation of the law, but these he held upon principles of right and reason. But he did not believe that he could advance those views against the State at the cost of sedition.[5] Chambers' proof rests upon the convincing account of Harpsfield which described the trial and death of More. "For I assure you," More said, "that I have not, hitherto to this hour, disclosed and opened my conscience and mind to any person living in all the world."[6]

[1] Chambers, R. W., *The Saga and the Myth of Sir Thomas More*.
[2] *Ibid.*, 19.   [3] *Ibid.*, 19–20.   [4] Hall, *Chronicle*, 828.
[5] Chambers, *Saga and Myth of More*, 48–51.
[6] "Pourveu que telle conscience, comme est la mienne, n'engendre scandale ou sedition à son Seigneur: vous asseurant que ma conscience ne s'est descouverte à personne vivant." (Emmanuel MSS., fol. 50b.)

This attitude in the face of danger recalls the doubts that Cranmer suffered during his trial. More maintained with fine conviction that conscience and belief are free, but held that the public expression and dissemination of illegal opinions constituted an act of sedition which even the considerations of a sincere conscience could not condone. To this extent he did not recede from the teachings of the *Utopia*. It is pleasant to recall that More would never have suffered death under Elizabeth, for this view had much in common with her public policy in the matter of belief contrary to the established religion.

2. THE DEFINITION OF THE FUNCTIONS OF THE MAGISTRATE IN THE CHURCH

The attitude which is generally held as to the nature of the Church and the power of the ruler in the Church is naturally of importance for the development of religious toleration. Any religious order which is conceived as embracing the entire realm, which will permit of no dissent, and which is subject to the civil power, with a more or less nominal allowance for freedom of doctrine, can scarcely be conducive to the toleration of dissenting minorities. The English Reformation sloughed off the English Church from the Church Universal, though every effort was made by Henry VIII and his divines to retain and maintain the catholic character of the Church. However, whatever catholicity the English Church managed to retain was national rather than international in character.

Stephen Gardiner, writing in 1535, gave typical definition to the English national Church. The Church, he said, "sygni-fieth that onli multitude of people, which being vnited in the profession of Christe, is growen into one bodie."[1] The Church was declared to be coterminous with the realm, and over the Church in each realm the king had been set as its head.[2] Gardiner sought to set at rest very natural questions which might follow upon the momentous changes in the organization of

[1] Gardiner, Stephen, *De Vera Obedencia*, xix.
[2] He is "also the head of the same men, when they are named the Church of England. . . ." (Gardiner, *De Vera Obedencia*, xix.)

the English Church. It is all very clear, at least to Gardiner. There is no cause for confusion—"Shal the terming of words, in as much as they have no other vse but to signifie thynges, be of such force in thys cause, as to turne the nature of things thēselves vp side down?" Englishmen are at once subject to the king as citizens of the realm and "in that he is a Christian dwelling in Englande, he is demed to bee of the Churche of Englande."[1]

A Necessary doctrine and Erudition for any Christen Man (1543) was a semi-official attempt to answer the question.[2] The Catholic Church is represented as a group of local churches, each with its proper head, more or less different in form, but united in true Christian profession and by the fact that all its members are called of God.[3] Geographically the members are separate and have particular heads, but spiritually they form one Catholic Church.[4] As Allen remarks, the *King's Book* clings with one hand to a broken ideal, while it smashes it with the other.

The power of the King in the Church of England was, in fact, stronger than even a Gardiner would have cared to admit. Audley's interpretation of the royal supremacy, as reported by Gardiner, shows at once a significant resentment among the laity at clerical privilege and power and the fact that the Crown in Parliament was master of the ecclesiastical household. In 1547 Gardiner wrote to Somerset that when the Bishop of Exeter and his Chancellor had been cited for praemunire, he had reasoned with Audley that "it seemed to me strange that a man, authorised by the king (as, since the king's majesty hath taken upon himself the supremacy, every bishop is such a one), could fall in a praemunire."[5] Audley had answered him in Parliament and had invited him to "look at the Act of Supremacy, and there the king's doings be restrained to spiritual jurisdiction; and in another act it is provided that no spiritual law shall have place contrary to a common

---

[1] Gardiner, *De Vera Obedencia*, xx.
[2] The work passed through no less then ten editions in the year of its publication.   [3] *A Necessary Doctrine*, art. ix, Dv. ff.
[4] *Ibid*.   [5] *The Acts and Monuments of John Foxe*, VI, 43.

law or act of parliament. And if this were not . . . you bishops would enter in with the king, and, by means of his supremacy, order the laity as ye listed. But we will provide . . . that the praemunire shall ever hang over your heads; and so we laymen shall be sure to enjoy our inheritance by the common laws, and acts of parliament."[1] This appeal to the common law and to the power of Parliament was a somewhat premature expression of a possible avenue by which religious liberty might be secured. Audley appeared to fear the power of the Crown under the Act of Supremacy and he insisted that the King should be restrained to a purely spiritual jurisdiction within the Church, and that no spiritual law should be contrary to the common law or parliamentary enactment. Appreciating more fully than most of his countrymen that the control of the Church in spiritual matters had been largely absorbed by the Crown, he proposed to restrict that jurisdiction by constitutional formulae. For the time being the Crown was to a large degree master of Parliament because its interests happened to coincide with the interests of that body, and the King was, at the same time, master of the ecclesiastical structure which Parliament had erected under his direction. But in later days Parliament was not to forget that that body which alters a structure so profoundly in one particular may likewise alter it in another.

The English reformers, with their Continental contemporaries, were likewise in agreement as to the power of the magistrate in the Church.[2] Cranmer, on the day of Edward's coronation,

---

[1] *The Acts and Monuments of John Foxe*, VI, 43.

[2] Bullinger regarded it as the "office and duty of the magistrate to advance religion." He is the guard of faith and must be learned in God's Word. He must put down heresy; and the Bible expressly commands the ruler not to spare heretics. (Bullinger, *Decades*, II, 308–309, 319–322.) There was, however, little agreement in regard to the proper means of exercising this function. Beza held the essentially Romanist view that the State should simply carry out the orders of the Church. Jewel would regard the king as something more than the mere instrument of ecclesiastical policy. (Jewel, *Works*, IV, 991.) Becon likewise held that the ruler was more than the mere hangman of the Church. (Becon, *A New Catechism Set forth Dialoguewise*.) Naturally, the issue is of considerable importance in its connection with toleration. A profound difference will ensue when the State persecutes for its own purposes rather than at the behest of the Church.

51

reminded him that "being God's vice-regent, and Christ's vicar in his own dominions, he was obliged to follow the precedent of Josias; to take care the worship of God was under due regulations, to suppress idolatry, remove images, and discharge the tyranny of the Bishop of Rome. . . ."[1]

Hooper held that the magistrate was set by God in his Church "for the defence of the good and godly, and to chasten and punish the wicked. . . ."[2] He is likewise commissioned by God "to take away and to overthrow all idolatry and false serving of God, to destroy the Kingdom of Anti-Christ and all false doctrine, to promote the glory of God, and to advance the Kingdom of Christ, to cause the word of the gospel everywhere to be preached, and the same to maintain unto death; to chasten also and to punish the false prophets, which lead the poor people after idols and strange gods, and instead of the gospel preach and teach the fables and traditions of men, to the dishonour of God and Christ His Son, and to the great decay of the whole Church. . . ."[3] Hooper left no doubt of his conception of the magistrate's power in the Church, and his views on the treatment of heretics in his confession of faith.[4] It is the high duty of the magistrate, not only to punish infractions of the civil law, "but also such as blaspheme the living God,[5] as godly kings and rulers have done. . . ."[6] The writer was frank in admitting that the punishment of heresy cannot result in the construction of correct opinions, but, for that matter, neither can the punishment of civil

---

[1] Collier, J., *An Ecclesiastical History of Great Britain*, V, 177.
[2] Hooper, J., *Brief and Clear Confession*, art. 78 (*Works*).
[3] *Ibid.*, art. 79 (*Works*). Vide also *Early Writings*, 435.   [4] *Ibid.*
[5] It is interesting to reflect that Luther, after his earlier tolerance, came to advocate the punishment of the Anabaptists on the grounds of their blasphemy. As Beard has well said (Beard, C., *The Reformation of the Sixteenth Century*, 178), blasphemy is a word by which the religious opinions of a minority, if sufficiently unpopular, have always been designated. Misbelief when it reaches a certain hazily defined point becomes an insult to the majesty of God, Luther held. The unbeliever, or the misbeliever, deserves punishment of a severe nature for this offence.
[6] "For although a civil law and punishment cannot change the heresies of the mind, neither the desire that men have to do evil. . . ." (Hooper,*Confession of Faith, Works*, 87.)

offences change the desire of men to do evil.[1] But, none the less, "when they break forth against the honour of God, and trouble the commonwealth, they should be punished. For the magistrate is as one that hath the two testaments tied at his neck, and should defend them as his own life; and therefore Saint Paul calleth him not only the revenger of evil, but the maintainer of good. . . ."[2]

Perhaps Becon's observations upon the power of the magistrate in the Church and the proper treatment of heretics will suffice for a typical instance of the orthodox position on these questions during the period prior to the accession of Elizabeth.[3] In the dialogues between father and son found in his *Catechism* we learn that heretics deserve the same treatment as idolaters and false prophets. The magistrate may punish them "and also take them out of this life, if they will not repent, amend, and come to the truth."[4] Again, "The magistrate beareth not the sword in vain. If he that beareth false witness against man is worthy of death . . . is he worthy of less punishment that beareth false witness against God. . . ."[5] However, it is to be desired that ". . . the magistrate would first of all gently and lovingly deal with heretics, and see unto what conformity he could bring them with his wisdom and counsel, and also suffer

[1] Hooper, J., *Works*, 87.
[2] *Ibid.*, 87. In preaching before Edward VI, Lent, 1550, Hooper said, "Beware of this ungodly pity, wherewith all men for the most part be very much nowadays cumbered withal. . . . Foolish and preposterous pity hath brought both king and laws, not only of this realm, but also of God, into contempt; and daily will more and more, if it be not foreseen." (*The Third Sermon on Jonah, Early Writings*, 481.)
[3] In the interesting *Necessary and Fruitful Dialogue*, ascribed somewhat uncertainly to Bullinger and Veron, it is held to be the duty of the Christian king to destroy such blasphemers as the Anabaptists and Papists. The ruler should seek out "suche runnegates, and withoute any favoure or mercye, to punyssh them that all other may take example by them." (*Prologue*, no pagin.) With Hooper, he would decry foolish sympathy with such persons; "better it is yf two or three be thus extremely punished, thē thousands, should through their wicked counsails and entisements, most miserably and to the great losse of the countrey, perish." (*Prologue*.) It seems possible that Bullinger was the author of the Latin version of the *A most necessary and frutefull Dialogue*, and that John Veron was the English translator. The B.M. copy (1551) was published at Worcester and not, as usually catalogued, at London.   [4] Becon, T., *A New Catechisme sette for the Dialoguewise*, 312.
[5] Becon, T., *Catechisme*, 313.

them to have access unto such as be godly learned, which may yet once again have conference with them."[1]

The Marian attempt to restore Catholicism with its coincident severity induced highly radical views on the subject of the powers of the magistrate in the Church from a number of the leading Protestants who had taken refuge on the Continent. Their views, as then expressed, may be said to have had relatively little influence on the development of English thought on the subject, especially since many of them were quick to reverse their position upon the erection of a 'true Church' under Elizabeth. The radical tenor of their views did, however, demonstrate the suspiciously intimate connection between political fact and theological theory. We may perhaps regard Poynet's *Treatise of Politike Povver* (1556) as typical of this section of thought.

Poynet teaches us that some groups, especially the Anabaptists, would lend too little obedience to the magistrate. On the other hand, the 'Papists' "Racke and stretche out obedience to muche, and wil nedes haue ciuile power obeid in all things. . . ."[2] The truly Christian man finds his position between these extreme views. He will seek out the will of God and refuse obedience to the mandates of wicked men. He will take especial care that in obeying the commandment of the inferior he does not violate the commandment of the highest power. Poynet urged that God has appointed the civil power to jurisdiction over certain aspects of life, but He "hathe not geuen it pouer ouer the one and the beste parte of man, that is, the soule and conscience of man. . . ."[3] We must measure our obedience to the civil ruler by our duty to God. "If the ministers of the Ciuile power commaunde thee to honour and glorifie God, as God wil be honoured, to defende . . . thy countreye against the enemies, to doo suche thinges as be for the wealthe and benefite of they countreye, . . ." we must as part of our duty to God lend our full obedience. "But if the ministers of the ciuile power commaunde thee to dishonour God, to com-

---

[1] Vide Becon, *Catechisme*, 312–315, for this interesting discussion.
[2] Poynet, John, *A Shorte Treatise of Politike Povver* (no pagin.).
[3] *Ibid.* (no pagin.).

mitte idolatrie," and the like it would dishonour God to lend obedience to the ruler. The prince "can but take from men their goodes and liues: but God can take from vs bothe goodes and bodie, and cast bothe body and soule in to hell."[1]

The argument of Poynet was, of course, presented in order to justify opposition and rebellion to Mary and her Roman Catholic policy. The argument of this section of the book hinges squarely onto the famous chapter, *Whether it be lawfull to depose an euil gouernour, and kill a tyranne.*[2] We are chiefly interested in the implications of the writer's theory of obedience. Poynet placed the responsibility of determining what was and what was not the true command of God upon the individual Christian. This view might lead to spiritual anarchy in actual fact, but it would necessarily lead to toleration as well. Perhaps, however, toleration in itself is a species of spiritual anarchy. The spiritual determinations of the individual derive a sacrosanct character from the view that the voice of God speaks directly to the individual Christian. No logic and no force may invade the sanctity of that relation. Thus, though it were better that a tyrant should be killed properly and decently, if a "priuate man haue som special inwarde comaundment or surely proued mocion of God," such an act may rightfully be carried out by the individual Christian.[3] The Reformation had truly released tremendous forces by its emphasis upon the essential individuality of Christianity.

These radical teachings were likewise advanced by Christopher Goodman in his *How Superior Powers oght to be obeyd of their Subiects.*[4] The Commandments of God, he urged, must take precedence over the requirements of the civil magistrate.

[1] Poynet, *Shorte Treatise* (no pagin.).
[2] The argument for tyrannicide is based chiefly upon the examples of the Old Testament, the instances in history, and the testimony of the Law of Nature. The doctrine, with Poynet, was unquestionably presented chiefly to vindicate the deposition or assassination of a prince who, like Mary, set up a false religion which was enforced upon the nation. It is therefore curious to find in the book no specific statement that the introduction of a false religion or the persecution of the faithful warrant such extreme action. The implications, however, are strong and the high validity of the private commission from God (*see below*) probably suffice for his purpose.
[3] Poynet, *Shorte Treatise* (no pagin.). [4] Published in 1558 in Geneva.

In fact, "to obeye man in anie thinge contrary to God, or his precepts thoghe he be in hiest auctoritie, or neuer so orderly called . . . is no obedience at all, but disobedience."[1] Any obedience which violates the will of God is disobedience,[2] for all the powers of the earth are not to be compared with God.[3] The test of obedience resides not in the character or the legitimacy of the title of the ruler, but in the comparison of his commands with the word and will of God.[4] Hence if they transgress God's laws and command others to follow them in their iniquity, "then haue they lost that honor and obedience which otherwise their subiectes did owe vnto them: and oght no more to be taken for Magistrates; but punished as priuate trāgressors. . . ."[5]

As in the case of Poynet, the responsibility for the determination of the legitimacy of the ruler's commands would appear to rest in the conscience of the individual Christian's judgment. Not only the magistrates, but the common people as well were declared to be responsible for subjecting the prince to obedience to the laws of God.[6] An idiot is dispossessed of power, and much more reasonably should "vngodly rulers, maynteyners of idolatrie ād tyrannie" be stripped of their power in order to prevent injury to God's purpose.[7] The true subject will refuse to obey a wicked commandment of the ruler. But he has a positive duty as well in the event of such a command, "in dooing the contrarie; euerie man accordinge to his vocation and office."[8]

Goodman's arguments were, of course, principally directed against the 'idolatrous' policy of Mary. He urged that it was the duty of the English people to rise and eradicate the worship which was blasphemous and idolatrous.[9] "And thoghe it appeare at the firste sight a great disordre, that the people shulde take vnto them the punishment of transgression, yet, when the Magistrates and other officers cease to do their duetie, they are as it were, without officers, yea, worse then if they had none at all, and then God geueth the sworde in to

---

[1] Goodman, *How Superior Powers oght to be obeyd*, 42–43.
[2] *Ibid.*, 43.   [3] *Ibid.*, 47; 59, 60–61, 116.   [4] *Ibid.*, 118.
[5] *Ibid.*, 118–119.   [6] *Ibid.*, 142 ff.   [7] *Ibid.*, 143, 73–74, 196.
[8] *Ibid.*, 63. See also 43, 59, and 72.   [9] *Ibid.*, 181–184.

the peoples hande, and he himself is become immediately their head. . . ."[1]

These radical Protestant doctrines were promptly repudiated upon the accession of Elizabeth and the restoration of the Reformation in England. Goodman and Poynet were opportunists and, like the Jesuits, suited their arguments to the exigencies of the moment. But their strong insistence upon the right of private judgment, their implied doctrine that the ruler has only a limited power in spiritual affairs, and their championship of resistance to a civil power that was considered by the elect as tyrannous and idolatrous were not to be without consequences in the development of the concept of religious toleration. For a brief moment, as it were, the powerful potentialities of Protestantism as a political dissolvent were disclosed.

3. EARLY EVIDENCES OF TOLERANT THOUGHT: 1530–1558

English thought with respect to the problem of heresy was, if possible, more uniformly intolerant than was Continental opinion prior, at least, to 1558. Unorthodoxy was as yet completely disorganized; religious changes came too frequently to permit of literary expressions in favour of toleration by any important group which happened for the moment to be oppressed; and as yet no party of consequence had arisen, in the absence of a strictly enforced and obviously permanent settlement of religion, which could seriously undertake a deliberate programme of repression.

There were, however, unquestioned symptoms of tolerant opinion during this period of stress and strain; points of view which are with difficulty attached to any considerable body of opinion and which should be regarded as isolated statements whose value is exaggerated by the almost unbroken darkness of the canvas upon which they appear.

Shortly prior to 1530 a little book called *The Sum of the Scriptures* filtered into England.[2] It was among the first of the

---

[1] Goodman, *How Superior Powers oght to be obeyd*, 185.
[2] I know of no copy of the book. Wilkins, *Concilia*, III, 730–733, gives excerpts of the heretical opinions which were found in the work. We gather, from his citations, that the book was about 121 (double pages) in length.

works which prepared the way for the reception of Baptist teachings in England. It must have attained some prominence since it was formally condemned upon royal command by Warham in 1530.[1] The book advanced the Anabaptist doctrine that among the people of this world who belong to the Kingdom of God there is no place for the temporal sword, which appertains to the unrighteous.[2] Christ has not ordained any temporal sword in his spiritual kingdom, although temporal justice is admitted to belong to the secular kingdom which lies outside the Church.[3] "Christen men amonge themself have nought to doo with the sworde nor with the lawe, for that is to them nether nedefull nor profitable; the secular sworde belongeth not to Crists kingdome, for in it is noon but good and justice."[4]

Destructive as Anabaptist tenets may have been to the authority of the State, their views would indirectly have favoured the development of religious toleration.[5]

The literary and parliamentary debates on the *Ex Officio*

[1] Wilkins, *Concilia*, III, 727.
[2] "There be two soorts of people in the worlde, oon is the kingdome of God, to which belongyth all true cristen people, and in this kingdome Criste is king and lorde, and it is impossible that in this kingdome, that is to say, amonge very true cristen men, that the swerde of justice temporall shuld have ought to doo." (*Ibid.*, 732.)   [3] *Ibid.*   [4] *Ibid.*
[5] The Church, they would say, is composed only of those who seek and attain baptism after the spiritual experience of conversion (Regeneration). The Church, then, consists of those true believers who have found God through personal conversion and who have, in token of their experience, sought baptism. They held that baptism can only be effective when taken as an act of personal faith and as a symbol of a new spiritual life. (Jones, R. M., *The Church's Debt to Heretics*, 233.) It follows that the Church can only be a voluntary organization in the strictest sense of the term. According to their view, it would be absurd to hold that the Church could be created by state edict, or that a Christian could be made by coercion. Force can only lead men to the profession of an experience they have never undergone. The State Church would be branded by the Anabaptist as an essentially artificial creation of a wicked civil power. As Allen has well pointed out, this theory gained rapidly during the sixteenth century, and came to be an important factor making for toleration. (Allen, J. W., *Political Thought in the Sixteenth Century*.) He takes the view that the persecution of the sect was so vigorously prosecuted principally because of their anarchistic tenets. (*Ibid.*, 42.) Modern theory would agree that the State was justified in punishing their overt actions of sedition and violence. Indeed, a modern Government would probably be even quicker to recognize and punish such actions. But the Anabaptists present a unique problem in that their political views are a secondary

58

Oath at the very dawn of the English Reformation displayed at once a spirited resentment at clerical privilege and corruption and a genuine fear that the clerical courts might so construe and prosecute heresy that the liberties of the laity would be endangered. Gardiner has suggested that the inception of the controversy between Sir Thomas More and St. Germain over the *Ex Officio Oath* was inspired by Henry VIII at the moment when the monarch was marshalling every possible force to meet the crisis of the break with Rome.

In 1532 St. Germain's *A Treatise Concernynge the Division betweene the Spiritualtie and Temporaltie* appeared.[1] The work assailed the greed and rapacity of the clergy. Following More's reply in the *Apology*, St. Germain published in 1533 his *Salem and Bizance* in which the claims of the common law were elevated beyond those of the ecclesiastical law. He accused the clergy of inordinate ambition and greed, of self-seeking, and of a wholesale neglect of their legitimate functions of spiritual guidance and leadership.[2] In a later work, *Dialogue Betwixt a Doctor of Diuinity and a Student of the Laws of England*, St. Germain likewise insisted that a common law when brought into collision with a decision of the canon law takes precedence.

The anti-clerical sentiments of Parliament and the attitude of its members towards trials for heresy were demonstrated in

---

and derived expression of their basic religious doctrines. A perplexing problem arises. Can the State punish political views which are an indirect consequence of religious opinions if it professes to tolerate all religions? Acton has said that in reality little religious liberty actually exists even in modern States. The Government tolerates opinions to a point, fixed in law, where such opinions become, or threaten to become, civil disorder. Acton further extends his argument to the view that while a large liberty of opinion and a legal and social guarantee to the right of free opinion exists there is, none the less, a very limited guarantee of the right to express that opinion, especially by an organized body. Governments, in other words, are tolerant of opinions, but are quick to repress such expressions of opinion as may be dangerous to the *status quo*. No satisfactory answer to this problem exists. Perhaps we are all partially, if not wholly, intolerant when our security, our property, and our sentiments are endangered.

[1] The book was published anonymously.
[2] Hume, M. B., *History of the Oath Ex Officio in England*, p. 34, for an excellent discussion of this controversy.

the dramatic petition of the House of Commons to the King against the harsh dealings of the ecclesiastical courts.[1] It was alleged that in heresy cases the questions were so cleverly framed as to trap a simple or a "well wytted layman" into confusion. It was petitioned that the laity should not be subjected to the pleasure of the ecclesiastical courts, and that they should not be made subject to the oath *ex officio* which left to them only the alternative of abjuration or the penalty of being burnt for heresy.[2] The King, upon receiving the petition, answered that the judges should not be too light of credence and pass sentence without a hearing for the accused.[3] The ordinaries in their reply admitted the possibility of isolated instances of injustice, but took the position that they were responsible for the spiritual well-being of the realm and hence for the prosecution of heresy.[4] To their knowledge no person had sustained punishment save upon clear evidence of guilt.[5]

At about the same time Thomas Starkey in his important *Dialogue Between Cardinal Pole and Thomas Lupset* denied the theory that virtue could be enforced by law.[6] He would seek to limit the authority of law in human affairs. In objecting to Pole's programme for an ideal state to be achieved by legislation, Lupset suggested that men cannot be made virtuous by legislative enactment.[7] Virtue consists in the knowing and seeking of virtue from inward desire rather than from fear. In the

[1] *Lett. and Pap., Henry VIII*, V, 1016.
[2] Hume, M. B., *Ex Officio Oath*, 40.
[3] Hall, E., *Chronicle*, 784–785.   [4] Wilkins, *Concil.*, III, 750.
[5] The ordinaries protested that they have never "enterprised anything" against the people of the realm without due cause. They "only have, as we dare surely affirm, with all charity exercised the spiritual jurisdiction of the church, as we are bound of duty, upon certain evil disposed persons, infected and utterly corrupt with the pestilent poison of heresy. . . ." (*Ibid.*) They traced the complaints against their authority to sedition and error, and they urged that "varriance and debate" will result in the division and desolation of the land. (*Ibid.*) The act of 25 Henry VIII, c. 14, repealing the act of Henry IV and authorizing the oath *ex officio*, and the power of the bishops to burn heretics, was the unfortunate result of this agitation.
[6] The book was written between 1536–1538. The Dialogue probably presents the economic and religious views of Starkey rather than those of Pole.
[7] Starkey, T., *A Dialogue Between Cardinal Pole and Thomas Lupset*, 206.

absence of this indwelling virtue compulsion is without effect.[1] Such a position would, it may be inferred, exclude the magistrate from power in the Church in so far as that authority was argued to rest upon the theory that the magistrate's chief care was that of enforcing the true worship of God.

A highly important attack upon clerical power, for our purposes, and an early and neglected utterance in favour of religious toleration, is to be found in Brinklow's *Complaynt of Roderyck More* (c. 1542).[2]

Brinklow vigorously denied the right of the ecclesiastics to imprison men. It is especially wrongful for the bishops to imprison those who contend against them.[3] If two men fall into a religious dispute, it would be better to put both in prison and assure each an impartial trial. "Bysshops ought no more to be lordys of presons, than was Chryst and his Apostyls, which were often imprysoned, but thei neuer presonyed man. . . ."[4] He complains bitterly that ". . . there were neuer so cruel lawys made under the sonne, as the most part of the lawys that haue bene made within these fewe yearys past. Death, Death, euyn for tryfls, so that thei folow the High prystys in crucyfyeng Christ. . . ."[5] If those responsible for these laws truly love God and desire to follow the example "of them which ground all their iustice vpon gods word," they should follow the example of several cities in Germany that have adopted the following course in cases of heresy:—"Thei lay no snarys nor grynnys

---

[1] Starkey, T., *A Dialogue Between Cardinal Pole and Thomas Lupset*, 206.
[2] Brinklow appears to have been a Grey Friar in London at one time. He must have left the order, however, for he later appears as a mercer and citizen of London. He was married, and died in 1546. Cowper, his editor, believes he was the eldest son of a well-to-do leaseholder of Berkshire. (*Complaynt of Roderyck More*, ed. by J. M. Cowper, v.) The treatise is a rather violent arraignment of economic, legal, moral, political, and religious conditions in his time. The language occasionally overrides the bounds of restraint. The writer was a Protestant, and evidently knew something of German conditions. The treatise has been reprinted several times. There are four copies of the first edition in the British Museum. There was a printing in Savoy, n.d.; Geneva, 1545; Geneva, 1550.
[3] "Wherfore I say, it is not lauful that any parson that preacheth, teacheth, or wryteth the lawe of the gospel, shuld be put in to the handys of the bysshops with whom thei contend." (Brinklow, *Complaynt*, 28.)
[4] *Ibid.*, 30.   [5] *Ibid.*, 31.

to catch mennys lyues from them, as doo our forked beare
woluys; but in case any heretycke do hold an vngodly opynyon
contrary to the Scripture, and so be a teacher or a seducer of
the pepyl in their wicked sectys" he is called before a justice.[1]
Learned men are then called to expound the Scriptures to
him and persuade him to abandon his heresy. If he will not do
so, he is not killed, but is banished from the country.[2] In case
the heretic should return to the city, or country, despite his
legal banishment, he will be put to death for breaking a temporal
law[3] and not "for his faythes sake." "Neither put thei any man
to death for their faythes sake; for fayth is the gift of God only
. . . so that no man can give another fayth. Now let all men
judge, whether these men or our blody bysshpos goo nerest
the Scripture."[4]

In these few lines a rough conception of toleration is sketched.
Those who persecute do not follow the example of Christ.
Persecution is often the mark and symbol of the faithful.[5]
"The pore sort," he says, "seke the blode of no man, but are
content to spend their own blode, to call all men vnto Christ
by his word, with the losse of their lyues."[6] True Christians
do not persecute heresy. He apparently considered heresy to
be dangerous to religion and as sufficiently serious to warrant
banishment. An heretic should not be put to death as an heretic,
but only if he proves himself incorrigible both to the State and
Church. This view is considerably in advance of the era in
which Brinklow lived and is perhaps in part explained by his
eagerness to divest the spiritual courts of their coercive power
rather than by any well thought out idea of religious toleration.

About two years later George Joye, a violent Protestant, in

---

[1] Brinklow, *Complaynt*, 31.
[2] ". . . if he contynue in his wickydnesse, or at the first will obstynately
contynue and resyst the manyfest truth, than thei banyssh him their contry
or cyty ypon payne of his head." (*Ibid.*, 32.)
[3] *Ibid.*   [4] *Ibid.*
[5] In another connection Brinklow makes this even clearer, "I wold fayne
axe a questyon; whether those that persecute, or those which are persecuted,
be more lyke wolues? Thow seist that those which be persecuted, are very
pore men in the sight of the world (although thei be riche in God) and
neyther they nor none of their doctryne neuer persecuted man vnto death."
(*Ibid.*, 72.)   [6] *Ibid.*, 73.

his *A Present Consolation for the Sufferers of Persecucion for Ryghtwysenes*, denounced the practice of persecution, at least of his own radical group.[1] He contended that persecution and bloodshed had been tried with no success both in Germany and France.[2] The long attempt to eradicate heresy has borne no fruits. "The gospell standeth and shall stande neuerthelesse."[3] No contrary action of man can permanently or seriously obstruct the dissemination of the spiritual message of the Word of God.[4] The writer urged, quite logically, that if the opponents of Protestantism were in the right, they would not need to employ "against us swerde and sper."[5] He pointed out that the persecutions of heresy in the era of the early Church only contrived to increase the vigour and determination of Christ's followers and to fire their zeal.[6]

Joye did not pause to consider what procedure was to be taken with one who is an heretic according to his view of the

---

[1] The date of Joye's birth is uncertain. He was a native of Bedfordshire, and was graduated A.B. from Cambridge in 1513. In 1527 he was cited to appear before Wolsey for holding Protestant opinions, but he fled to Strassburg. While there he began a series of translations of various books of the Old Testament. He was living in Antwerp in 1534 (*D.N.B.*, xxx, 219), where he continued his translations. He met Frith and Tyndale while there, and may have assisted Tyndale in his translation of the New Testament. (Strype, *Cranmer*, 115.) It is certain that he came to the assistance of the great translator in his bitter controversy with More. (*D.N.B.*, xxx, 220.) The two men quarrelled when Joye issued a new edition of Tyndale's New Testament without the knowledge of the translator. Joye answered Tyndale's reproaches somewhat unsatisfactorily in his *Apologie Made by George Joye to satisfye if it may be, W. Tyndale*. In the following year Edward Foxe wrote to Cromwell in his behalf (*L. & P., Henry VIII*, 823), and he was permitted to return to England. He was residing in London in 1541, and was in business as a printer (Cooper, *Ath. Cantab.*, I, 115). He was obliged to flee again, because of his religious views, in the following year. He was deeply moved by the execution of Barnes, and attacked Gardiner violently. (Strype, *Mem.*, II, 1, 52.) The work under consideration appeared in this period (1544), and Joye removed to Geneva shortly after its publication. His works were listed among those to be burned in 1546. He returned to England upon the accession of Edward VI, but died in 1553. (Cooper, *Ath. Cantab.*, I, 115.)
[2] This idea, repeated in much the same terminology, suggests a literary acquaintance with Brinklow.   [3] Joye, G., *A Present Consolation*, F. 4.
[4] *Ibid.*, F. 5.   [5] *Ibid.*, no pagin.
[6] ". . . the cruellier thei persecuted the faith in Chrust, the wyder it spred, the deper it roted, and the higher it grewe and encreased, ād the more and mightier was the noumbre of the crystianes." (*Ibid.*, no pagin.)

Bible and revealed religion. He was solely concerned with the spiritual consolation which might be afforded to those who suffer for the sake of 'truth.' He would seem, at times, to be on the verge of making a general denunciation of religious persecution but his eyes did not survey a wider field than his own conception of the content of the Christian faith.

Somewhat more interesting is the sentence which stands nobly but in complete isolation in Lord Stafford's free translation of Fox's *De vera differentia regiae potestates et ecclesiasticae*.[1] ". . . In the churche," he asserted, "it is necessarye to conuerte them that be wyllyng and not by coacion or compulsiō for we haue no power geuē to vs by the lawe that by aucthoryte of sentence we may constrayne any mā to refraine from his offences and vices. . . ."[2]

Robert Barnes, who was himself a martyr to the persecuting programme of the Henrican Church, boldly enunciated a theory of a spiritual Church which does not persecute, and whose members are free, in so far as their spiritual lives are concerned, from the interference of the State. In his *What the Church is: and who be thereof, and whereby men may know her*,[3] he compared the administration of the bishops with that of the true Church of Christ. "The church suffereth persecutions and you withstand all thinges and suffer nothing. You oppresse euery mā, and you will bee oppressed of no mā. You persecute euery man, and no man may speake a worde agaynst you, no though it bee neuer so true. You cast euery mā in prison, no mā may touch you, but he shal bee cursed. You compell euery mā to say as you say, and you will not once say as Christe saythe. . . ."[4]

Barnes drew a clear and important distinction between the civil and spiritual powers.[5] He lent full obedience to the civil

---

[1] The *De vera differentia regiae potestates et ecclesiasticae* appeared in 1534, and Stafford's translation under the title, *The True Dyfferēs betwen ye regall power and the ecclesiasticall power*, with a dedication to Somerset, followed in 1548. The book is extremely rare.
[2] Stafford, Lord, *The True Dyfferēs*, 33.
[3] The treatise was written between 1539 and 1544, and was first published in the great collection of the works of Tyndale, Frith, and Barnes in 1572-3.
[4] Barnes, Robert, *What the Church Is*, *Works*, 250-251.
[5] Barnes, *Mens Constitutions*, *Works*, 292-300.

power, for we "must bee obedient in all thynges that pertaine to the ministration of this present life and of the commō wealth. . . ."[1] The prince, even if a tyrant, cannot be resisted by force of arms. But the writer went far beyond most of the reformers in excluding the prince from interference in the affairs of the true Church. Most of the divines of the period contented themselves, in considering this delicate problem, with the rather empty statement that a command of the king which is against the ordinances or revealed will of God is not to be obeyed. They likewise excluded the king from the ministration of the sacraments and the formulation of doctrine. But the subsidiary questions, which are of the utmost importance, of who is to interpret and define a collision of regal and divine command; what Christian action is to be in such instances; and the precise frontiers of temporal and divine jurisdiction remain in shadowy and unprecise definition. The doctrine of loyalty to the will of God in the face of governmental authority may, if properly and logically extended, virtually exclude secular interference from the spiritual life of mankind. The importance of such a doctrine for the development of toleration and civil liberty is apparent.

Barnes, it would seem, provided the best analysis of these problems that had appeared to the middle of the century. He held that if the king should forbid or command anything in God's Word, or anything which was necessary to the Church, "or any other thynge that is agaynst Christ vnder a temporall payne, or els vnder a payne of death"; Christians are not to obey.[2] If the king will not yield to intercession in such instances, "they shall keepe their Testament, with all other ordinaunce of Christ, and let the kyng exercise his tyranny if they cannot flee."[3] The king, under no circumstances, is either to be resisted or obeyed.

There can be little doubt that the interpretation of what is essential to the faith, of what constitutes the "Testament of Christ," by this reasoning, resides in the conscience of the Christian man and not in the definition of king or prelate.

[1] Barnes, Robert, *Mens Constitutions, Works*, 292.
[2] *Ibid.*, 294.   [3] *Ibid.*

Toleration hovers on the edges of such a doctrine. We are told that to deny the testament of Christ is to deny Christ. Christians will therefore "boldely confesse, that they haue the veritie, and will thereby abyde. . . ."[1] God will protect His people and revenge them. "The truth of god and his childrē bee alwayes in persecutiō, but the ende is alwayes glory vnto them."[2] Such quiet but determined courage, such a magnified view of the possibility of the individual's capability of attaining religious certainty, if properly understood, would have deeply disturbed the Erastian mind of Barnes's sovereign. Powerful currents of thought had been loosed which acquired dignity and stubborn consistency in the conviction of the Protestant that God's hand rested upon him.

Barnes abruptly stated that the temporal power "commaundeth nothing as conscerning the conscience, but all onely as conscerning the ordering of worldly thinges, and therefore; it mynistreth a temporall payne ouer the body onely and therwith is cōtent."[3] ". . . Therefore must we of that part that beelongeth to this lyfe bee subiect vnto powers, that is vnto men that doe minister worldly things with some honour, but as conscerning that part, whereby we beleeue in God and bee cauled vnto hys Kingdome, we ought not to bee subiect vnto any mā that will peruert that same thing in vs that hath pleased God to geue vs to eternall lyfe."[4] Thus, even if we are commanded to do an indifferent thing, we should not obey, "not because it is euill to doe, but that it is damnable to bee done as a thyng of necessitie."[5]

An obscure and very rare book published in 1547 and of uncertain authorship, emphasized the spiritual nature of Christ's kingdom and the obligation of all Christians to employ only weapons of the spirit in seeking the attainment of that Kingdom on this earth.[6] The author insisted that the Kingdom of God "standeth not in a carnall dominion or powre; But

---

[1] Barnes, *Mens Constitutions, Works*, 295.   [2] *Ibid.*, 296.
[3] *Ibid.*, 297.   [4] *Ibid.*, 300.   [5] *Ibid.*
[6] The *A bryefe and plaine declaracion of certayne sentēces in this litle boke folowing* . . . was published, probably in London, in 1547. It is signed B. J., and the authorship may probably be ascribed to J. Bale or J. Bradford.

lykewise as the Lorde is a spirite . . . euen so is hys Kyngdome spirituall inwardly within vs . . . and not of this worlde."[1]

The whole purport of the Gospel is that Christ's followers must suffer and in no wise attempt to avenge evil. By God's help true Christians will not stray from His teachings and precepts. They will, in addition, hold it for a dreadful abomination that men should "cast away the weapons wheruthe the apostles haue fought . . ." and "put vpon them the harneys of Dauid."[2] The doctrine of Jesus was one of peace. Christians, therefore, may fight only with the Word and the Spirit of the almighty God.

Henry VIII regarded it as a divinely appointed duty to maintain peace in religion. "He sent to the scaffold those who maintained the authority of the Pope, and who, by so doing, assailed the national independence. He sent to the stake those who preached new doctrines, and by so doing, assailed the national unity."[3] Henry was able to deal in summary fashion with all forms of dissent from the Establishment because he so thoroughly typified the needs of the nation. The persecution of heresy was held to be an essential attribute of the royal power. There were strong grounds for believing that if the flood of new opinions were allowed to take root and to acquire strength, those who held them would at once begin to persecute the vanquished followers of the old creed.[4]

However, the assumption by the State of an overweening power in the doctrinal and administrative structure of the Church indirectly weakened the validity of the theory of persecution. So long as the Church monopolized the persecution of heresy its policy in this respect would likely be spiritual. Heresy will be a spiritual crime subject to spiritual judgment. But when the State assumes the task of directing the Church, heresy will inevitably become a political crime, or at least an offence which will be judged by political concerns. The theological formulae will still be employed but the application will become increasingly devoid of spiritual content. The spiritual society, in its effort to prevent the corruption and disruption

[1] *A bryefe and plaine declaracion* (no pagin.).　　　　　　[2] *Ibid.*
[3] Gardiner, S. R., *History of England*, I, 10.　　　[4] *Ibid.*, I, 11.

of the body of truth necessary for salvation, could command almost universal respect and support. It could adduce a sincere and water-tight logic in support of its policy. But the transfer of this power to the State placed a different complexion on the issue. Intelligent men will soon suspect that the coercion of opinion and the persecution of Nonconformity, though clothed in the same outward garments, proceed from different motives. Men will soon question the competence of the civil power to determine religious truths; for the judgment of what is and what is not heresy involves that capability. Men will soon suspect that the State has simply absorbed another of the rapidly dwindling compartments of authority, that it is administering it to its own ends, and finally that, however serious political treason may be, religious treason has lost all content.

Under Edward VI, as well, fairly definite limits were set to religious belief and the right of private judgment. The faith of the Church must at once be Catholic and national. The aliens who sought refuge in England from Spanish bigotry and the artisans who were attracted from abroad by economic inducements offered a difficult problem in connection with this theory. They refused to conform to the Second Act of Uniformity and were permitted to conduct their own services for a time.[1]

The policy of the Government under Edward VI was, in general, firm but not harsh when measured by the accepted canons of the times. Foxe tells us that "During the whole time of the six years of this King, much tranquillity, and, as it were, a breathing time was granted to the whole Church of England; so that, the rage of persecution ceasing, and the sword taken out of the adversaries hand, there was now no danger to the godly, unless it were only by wealth and prosperity,

---

[1] *Acts of P.C.*, IV, 160–161. Thus when John à Lasco came to England to set up an exile church in which foreign Protestants might worship according to their consciences, he soon ran afoul the English laws. (Krasinski, V., *History of the Reform. in Poland*, I, 259–264.) This group claimed immunity from episcopal control and the liberty to employ certain rites contrary to the practice of the English Church. Cranmer was largely instrumental in allowing a considerable measure of toleration to foreign Protestants, and yielded. A second church was soon set up at Glastonbury. (Strype, *Cranmer*, I, 335–353.)

which many times bringeth more damage in corrupting men's minds, than any time of persecution or affliction. Briefly, during all this time, neither in Smithfield nor any other quarter of this realm, were any heard to suffer for any matter of religion, either papist or protestant . . . except only two, one an English woman, called Joan of Kent; and the other a Dutchman named George. . . ."[1]

Somerset was a man of tolerant temper and of considerable breadth of mind. In the early days of his administration the Six Articles Act was repealed, permission was given to print and expound the Bible in English, and the royal supremacy, while it could not be assailed in writing, might be denied in speech without penalty.[2] Somerset, in fact, appears to have been more interested in abolishing what he regarded as unjust and brutal restrictions on conscience than in constructive ecclesiastical statesmanship. He seems to have been persuaded that the theological clamour of the period might best be controlled by giving it opportunity to dissipate itself through fairly free discussion.[3] The ensuing wave of religious controversy, however,

---

[1] Foxe, John, *Acts and Monuments*, V, 704. The two heretics who were burned in the time of Edward VI held very radical opinions. Joan Bocher denied the humanity of Christ, and George van Parris the divinity of Jesus. (Pollard, A. F., *Cranmer*, 261–263; Wriothesley, C., *Chron.*, II, 47; Dixon, R. W., *History of the Church of England*, III, 237, 272–273.) According to the apparently apochryphal account of Burnet, Cranmer was employed by the commissioner to persuade the King to sign the warrant for Joan's execution. Edward was averse to bloodshed, and for some time refused. Cranmer argued his case from the law of Moses which consigned blasphemers to stoning. Impiety should be punished by the prince, just as the King's deputies were obliged to punish crimes against the King's person. Burnet tells us that Edward signed the warrant, telling Cranmer that if he did wrong, he did so in submission to the Archbishop's authority who would answer to God for it. (Burnet, G., *History of the Reform.*, II, 204.) Every effort seems to have been made to secure a recantation, Cranmer and Ridley taking her into custody in their own houses in an effort to dissuade her from her beliefs. (Neal, D., *History of the Puritans*, III, 335.) The examination of Philpot in November 1555, preparatory to his own execution, shows the normal view taken in this period of the treatment of heresy. He told his judges, "as for Joan of Kent, she was a vain woman (I knew her well), and a heretic indeed, well worth to be burned, because she stood against one of the manifest articles of our faith, contrary to the Scripture." (Foxe, VII, 631.)

[2] Froude, J. A., *History of England*, (1870), V, 63–64.

[3] Clark, H. W., *History of English Nonconformity*, I, 125.

alarmed Cranmer and persuaded him that the time had come to constitute a definite basis for the Church of England and to remove that basis from the province of controversy.

Cranmer was persuaded that "no state could be in safety when there was toleration of two religions." His goal was uniformity, but he was not a man to crush, without discrimination, all obstacles that deterred the attainment of that end. In his efforts a constant restraint is evidenced. His moderation is displayed in the two Acts of Uniformity of which he was the principal author.[1] The Church was committed to a theory which embraced the entire nation and enforced worship within that Church, but it was enforced with notable moderation. Cranmer attempted to use pressure rather than persecution.[2] He envisaged a reformed Church which should retain as much as possible of the dignity of the old Church. The mark of this Church was to be unity and purity of belief and practice.[3] This reformed Church was regarded, ideally at least, as embracing all the Protestant Churches and Cranmer made a genuine effort to bring about that ideal.

The Archbishop's view of religion was broad and extended beyond the frontier of the nation. Thus in March 1552 he wrote to Calvin, "as nothing tends more injuriously to the separation of the Churches than heresies and disputes respecting the doctrines of religion; so nothing tends more effectually to unite the Churches of God, and more powerfully to defend the fold of Christ, than purer teaching of the gospel, and harmony of doctrine. Wherefore I have often wished, and still continue to do so, that learned and godly men, who are eminent for erudition and judgment, might meet together in some place of safety . . . and comparing their respective opinions, they might handle all

---

[1] The first applied only to the clergy; the second was more stringent, and insisted on attendance at public worship, but attached only ecclesiastical penalties to neglect. Imprisonment was the severest penalty imposed upon attendance at unauthorized worship.

[2] Thus when Hooper declined to take the see of Gloucester on account of vestarian scruples, Cranmer subjected him to the persuasion of all the bishops and to a few weeks of honourable imprisonment before which Hooper gave way.

[3] Clark, H. W., *History of English Nonconformity*, I, 137–138.

70

the heads of ecclesiastical doctrine, and hand down to posterity, under the weight of their authority, some work not only upon the subjects themselves, but upon the forms of expressing them."[1] The Protestant Church must follow the example of the Roman Catholics in the Council of Trent and come to some definite agreement on the essential doctrines. This unity was desirable to Cranmer both as an ideal of infinite spiritual value and as a defensive measure against the mounting power of the Catholic reaction.[2] "It cannot escape your prudence, how exceedingly the church of God has been injured by dissension and varieties," especially with respect to the doctrine of the Eucharist, which he seems to regard as of fundamental importance in the constitution of doctrine.[3] In a letter to Melanchton of the same month he suggested England as a "safe and friendly meeting place" and insisted that "although all controversies cannot be removed in this world . . . it is never the less to be desired that the members of the true Church should agree among themselves upon the chief heads of ecclesiastical doctrine."[4]

This proposal of Cranmer is important for our consideration. The Archbishop expressed a desire to simplify dogma by the assumption that the doctrine of the Eucharist is the essential corner-stone of the faith. For ideal and practical considerations he appears ready to waive minor differences in order to attain Christian unity. We would perhaps err in ascribing the knowledge to Cranmer, but the Protestant sects had already sufficient

[1] Cranmer, T., *Remains and Letters, Works*, II, 432.
[2] *Ibid.*, II, 432–433.   [3] *Ibid.*, II, 433.
[4] It is interesting to note that there was considerable fear among Catholics that union might result from the conversations of this period. In a memorandum preserved among Cecil's papers, and apparently from the hand of Sidney, it is observed that "Edward (VI) . . . by his crafty and politick counsell hath absolutely brought in heresy, wch if not by art or other endeauours speedily ouerthrown or made infamous, all other foreign Hereticks will unite with yr new Heresy now among yr selues lately planted, and so haue bishops as you haue, And it is the opinion of our learned now at Trent, that the Schisms in England by Edward Counsel established will reclaime all the foreign Sects vnto their discipline, and thereby be one Body vnited, for Caluin, Bullinger, and others haue wrote vnto Eduard to offer their services to affect and unitie, also to make Eduards and his heirs their Chief Defenders." (Delph, May 5, 1549. *Stow MSS.*, 155, 9.)

national and internal differences to make such a programme impossible beyond a loose agreement upon incontrovertible principles of faith. One of the most fruitful sources for toleration was the gradual disposition to discredit dogma, to simplify doctrine, and to insist upon the spiritual nature of Christianity as opposed to the unyielding shell of doctrinal accretion. But in an age when theological controversy was bitter, when it was actually enjoyed for its own sake, and when doctrinal correctness was the badge of spiritual health, such a programme was quite impossible. The logical genius of Calvin realized this fact and the reply to Cranmer was cool.

A unique view for this period was urged by William Thomas in his *Third political Discourse for the Kings Study*.[1] He pointed out that "the Turk" compels no man to alter his religion within his dominions and suggested that because of this policy "he is the more able to enjoy so large an empire." "But if he thought he might bring all men to Mahomet's law, as he seeth the contrary, he would use that rigour in religion that he doth in other things."[2] This argument will recur frequently during the reign of Elizabeth.

In concluding our survey of Pre-Elizabethan thought on the question of religious toleration, it will be well to notice in some detail the work of two important but neglected writers. The first is William Turner, an extraordinarily versatile and irritable man who, as a Marian exile, had drunk deep at the spring of Continental Protestantism.[3] His *Neue Dialogue* appeared about

---

[1] In Strype, John, *Ecclesiastical Memorials*, II, 2, 377–381. Thomas appears to have been a Welshman who graduated from Oxford in 1529. (Wood, *Athenæ Oxon.*, I, 218.) During the late years of Henry VIII's reign he travelled abroad, and in 1548 was in Venice. (*Acts of Privy Council*, I, 176.) He returned to England in 1549, and was a year later appointed a clerk of the Privy Council. (*Acts of P.C.*, II, 433; III, 3–4.) He undertook the self-appointed task of acting as a political mentor to the King, and wrote six short political discourses which are printed *in extenso* by Strype. (Strype, *Ecc. Mem.*, II, 2, 365 ff.) He was an ultra-Protestant, and was executed shortly after the accession of Mary. (*D.N.B.*, lvi, 196.)

[2] Strype, J., *Ecclesiastical Memorials*, II, 2, 381.

[3] Turner was a Cambridge graduate (1536), and became in 1538 the Senior Treasurer of Pembroke Hall. From 1534 to the time of the accession of Edward VI he appears to have resided abroad, and while there adopted rather advanced Protestant views. He returned to England in 1548, and was

1548,[1] and in 1551 his more important *A Preseruatiue, or triacle, agaynst the poyson of Pelagius* was published in reply to a manuscript work of one Robert Cooche.[2]

Turner, in the *Preseruatiue*, compared the Anabaptists with the water-snake of fable with its seven heads. "For as out of one bodye rose seuen heades: so out of Pelagius rose vp these seuen sectes: Anabaptistes, Adamites, Loykenistes, Libertines, Swengfeldianes, Dauidianes, and the Spoylers."[3]

The author, deliberately digressing from his consideration of original sin, says that some would urge the employment of those weapons against "thys many folde monstre" that the Papists are accustomed to use against the Protestants.[4] Thus Knowledge, in the *Neue Dialogue*, reflects that recently in England, and at the present moment on the Continent, men are commanded on pain of death to believe in the doctrines of the Roman Catholic Church. He denied that Christians are obliged to lend obedience to any religious command unless "that they commaunde, be conteyned in ye expressed worde of God."[5] If the ruler "woulde commaunde men to beleue,

---

constituted physician and chaplain to Somerset. It has been tentatively suggested that he held a seat in the House of Commons at one time. (*D.N.B.*, lvii, 363.) Somewhat later he became Dean of Wells, and in the following year the *Preseruatiue* appeared. He was deposed with the accession of Mary, fled abroad, and did not return before 1559. (*Machyn*, 210.) At that time he was reinstated in his deanery, but almost immediately entered into a long and acrimonious controversy with the Anglican party. His advanced views led to his suspension from the preferment in 1564. Turner died in 1570. His views on religion were tolerant and considerably in advance of his age. (Vide also, Wood, *Athen.*, I, 362–364; Strype, *Mem.*, II, 1, 111.)

[1] The work was probably published shortly after his first return to England. A second edition may have appeared in 1549. The book is rare.

[2] This work is likewise rare. The full title is, *A Preseruatiue, or triacle, agaynst the poyson of Pelagius, lately renued, and styrred vp agayn, by the furious secte of Anabaptistes.*

[3] Turner, *A Preseruatiue*, Intro. (no pagin.).

[4] *Ibid.* (no pagin.). It is interesting to note, however, that Turner was unable to retain his tolerant notions during the Marian persecutions. In his *A nevv booke of spirituall Physik*, published in 1555, he held that the nobility of England were responsible to God for the rooting out of false worship. It "belongeth . . . vnto them, to destroye all false and conterfet religion, and to destroye all false teachers and preachers, and to mayntayne the true learnynge of almyghtye God, . . ." (no pagin.); vide also, 12 ff.

[5] Turner, *Neue Dialogue* (no pagin.).

that thynge to be a worshyppynge of God, which is eyther
vnspoke of in the written worde of God, or contrary vnto the
same worde, or if he shoulde forbid this word or anye part
of it, we are not boūd to obey him in this case."[1]

The writer had no sympathy with the use of force in overcoming heresy. For the grievous sin and crime of blasphemy
he would, apparently, prescribe banishment with the penalty
of death for return.[2] He regarded heresy as "no materiall
thynge, that we must fyght withal, but gostly...."[3] It is therefore
"moste mete, that we should fyght with the sworde of goddes
word, and with a spirituall fyre against [them?] Elles we are
lyke to profit but a little in our besynes."[4] He urged that Christ
and the Apostles employed and authorized only the weapons
of the spirit, and concluded that earthly weapons have no
power against a spiritual force.[5] Thus we are reminded that
"when as the enemie is a spirite, that is, the goste of Pelagius,
that olde heretike: ones welle laid, but now of late to the great
treperdie of many raysed vp agayn: the wepones, and the
warriers that must kyll thys enemie, must be spirituall."[6] We
have not been left defenceless in the struggle of the Church
with the evil of heresy, for the spiritual weapons at our command
are many and powerful. "We may haue enough out of the
store house, or armoury of the Scripture to cōfound and
ouertrow all the gostly enemies, be they neuer so many."[7]
These weapons constitute the sole defence of the Church.

The second work, by an anonymous Anabaptist, may be
found, at least in substance, in the reply which the formidable
John Knox saw fit to give to it under the imposing title, *An
answer to a great nomber of blasphemous cauillations written by
an Anabaptist, and aduersarie of God's eternal predestination,*

---

[1] Turner, *Neue Dialogue* (no pagin.). The Dialogue represents Mistress
Mass as on trial before Palemon, the judge, for heresy. The argument is, of
course, that since the mass cannot be supported from the Scriptures we are
not obliged to lend obedience to a command to observe it.
[2] *Ibid.*   [3] Turner, *A Preseruatiue*, Intro. (no pagin.).
[4] *Ibid.*   [5] *Ibid.*   [6] *Ibid.*
[7] *Ibid.* Turner also suggests that education will be an efficacious means for
the combating of heresy, but he does not develop this interesting and fruitful
notion.

confuted by John Knox.[1] The identity of Knox's adversary is not well established. It appears that Knox used a manuscript copy of the work,[2] and it is quite certain that he was acquainted with the author.[3] Laing, the able editor of Knox's works, advances the suggestion that the Anabaptist author was Robert Cooke, a man of some learning and at one time a keeper of the wine cellar at the English court.[4] The work was probably published in 1559.[5]

The "adversary" sketched in a brief compass a noble and reasoned condemnation of the persecution of heresy. God does not persecute: this may be taken as the primary thesis of the work.[6] On the other hand, "your chief Apollos be persecutors,

[1] Knox's *Answer* appeared in 1560, about a year after the work of the Anabaptist.
[2] "The copie which came to my hands was in that place imperfecte, for, after the former wordes, it had onely written, etc." (Knox, *Works*, V, 122.)
[3] Vide, Knox, *Works*, V, 183, 127, and especially 223.
[4] *Ibid.*, Intro., 16.
[5] Knox's attack on the Anabaptist was first printed in Geneva in 1559. An edition was published in London in the following year, of which the McAlpin Library is fortunate enough to possess a copy. A third edition appeared in 1591.
[6] Knox, in his refutation of the work under consideration, adds little to the systematized logic of Calvin and Beza in support of a Protestant theory of persecution. Fundamentally, he seems to hold that persecution rests upon the duty of Christians to 'hate,' "and in his heart and mouth condemne, that which God Himself hath condemned." (Knox, *Works*, V, 223.) The Old Testament is once more brought forward to prove that "The Law of God . . . will witness that no less oght the murtherer, the blasphemer, and suche other, to suffer death, then that the meeke and the fearer of God should be defended." (*Ibid.*, V, 223.) The disposition of the upholders of persecution to levy blasts from the Old Testament, and of those rare persons who supported a more tolerant conception of Christ's religion to answer from the Gospels leads to an impasse. So long as both sides agree that both Testaments are equally binding, equally inspired, and equally adducible little intellectual progress can be made in the solution of the question. We will be interested in observing the gradual development, on the one hand, of rationalism, and, on the other, of a simplification of dogma as curatives for the rancour and aimlessness of theological disputation. Knox provides an interesting and close-knit definition of the term blasphemy, which was employed to excuse a variety of persecuting actions by the Reformers. Blasphemy consists not only in the denial of the existence of a God, but likewise in esteeming too lightly the power of an admitted God. In addition, "To have, or to sparse abrode, of his Majestie such opinions as may make his Godhead to be doubted of; to depart from the true honouring and religion of God to the imagination of man's inventions; obstinately to maintain and

75

on whom the bloode of Servetus crieth a vengeance, so doeth
the blood of others mō, whom I coulde name. But forasmuch as
God hath partly alreadie reuenged their bloode . . . with the
same measure wherewith they measured to others, I will make
no mention of them at this time."[1] Indeed, there is little
necessity for attacking them for these men have "for a perpetuall
memoirie of their crueltie, sett furth bookes, affirming it to be
lawfull to persecute and put to death such as dissent from them
in controversies of Religion, whome they cal blasphemers of
God."[2] The Anabaptist then laid bare the essential psychology
of intolerance: that dissenting minorities, during the period of
their own persecution, cry for tolerance, but when they have
gained the ascendancy they, as majorities, persecute dissent in
their own turn. These men, who now write books upholding
persecution, "afore they came to autoritie, they were of an
other judgment, and did bothe say and write, that no man
ought to be persecuted for his conscience saik; but now they
are not onely become persecutors, but also they have given, as far
as lieth in them, the sword into the hands of bloodie tyrantes."[3]

Christians, he urged, are as sheep sent among wolves, and
the sheep cannot destroy the wolves. "Mark how ye be fallen
into most abhominable tyranny, and yet ye see it not." The
disposition towards persecution, like most of the Calvinist's
errors, he blames on the doctrine of predestination; . . ."ye
walk even after the lustes of your heartes, thirsting after bloode
and persecuting poore men for their conscience saik, ye be
blinded, and see not yourselves, but say, Tush, we be pre-
distinat; what so ever we do, we are certen we can not fall
out of God's favour."[4]

In a noble passage the Anabaptist demonstrated that those
who persecute and those who tolerate dissent and disagreement

defend doctrine and diabolicall opinions plainely repugning to Gods trueth;
to judge those things which God judgeth necessary for our salvation, not
necessarie; and finally; to persecute the trueth of God, and the members of
Christes Bodie." (Knox, *Works*, V, 224–225.) The definition certainly covers
every conceivable form of unbelief and misbelief. It is to be regretted that
Cooke, or whoever the Anabaptist may have been, did not have occasion to
reply to Knox.   [1] Knox, *Works*, V, 207.
[2] *Ibid.*, V, 207–208.   [3] *Ibid.*, V, 208.   [4] *Ibid.*

in religious questions are in reality motivated by two widely different conceptions of God. It might be suggested that one is essentially an Old Testament conception, while the other finds its source in the New Testament. "As these goddes be of contrarie nature, so do they begette children of a contrarie nature; the fals god begetteth unmercifull, proud, ambitiouse, and envifull children; bloody persecutors of others for their conscience saik; evill speakers, impacient, contenciouse, and seditious children. And they be like unto their father in that they speake one thing with their mouth, and think another with their heart. They can never be without filthy thoghtes and wicked motions, for such poyson do they receave of their father. The trew god begetteth mercifull, humble, lowlye, and loving children; abhorring from blood, persecuting no man ..."[1]

The argument of the Anabaptist against persecution was essentially religious in character. Persecution was declared to be foreign to the nature and meaning of Christianity. He drew a clear distinction between civil and spiritual offences, "externall crimes hath no affinity with matters of religion." The State cannot legitimately interfere in a province wherein it has no jurisdiction. Difference of opinion in matters of religion were held to be inevitable and wholly legitimate. The Word of God is a sufficient rule of conduct and when it does not clearly specify a rule of conduct or faith each man may choose for himself.

4. CONCLUSION

We have endeavoured to enumerate and to estimate those forces which contributed most largely to the development of religious toleration in England. It has been suggested that religious toleration, in so far as it has historical significance, has been granted by Governments, apparently as a free action but in reality to relieve the weight of the combined forces demanding some legal sanction for at least limited religious freedom. The State renounced its control over certain areas of human interests in order to prevent the disruption of the body politic. The freedom granted to religious communities

[1] Knox, *Works*, V, 419.

was limited in quality and in degree, but sufficient for the exercise of normal religious activities. This freedom was withheld until such a time as the dissenting religious groups abandoned, or relegated to theory, their intention of mastering the agencies of the State in order to impose a variant intolerance upon the nation.

The attainment of religious toleration could only be accomplished by the complete dissipation of the Christian theory of persecution of heresy. This theory had been rationally stated and historically solidified during the Middle Ages, and so long as the concept of the universal State and the universal Church remained and had appreciable content it could not easily be uprooted.

Religious orthodoxy was first seriously questioned and considerably weakened by the tendency of Renaissance thought critically to examine the bases of its omnicompetent pretensions. Renaissance thought was, in this particular, unsystematic, individualistic, and, to a certain degree, unconstructive, but it gravely weakened the logical cement which had for so long retained intact the structure of religious persecution. This thought tended to approach the problem of toleration from the point of view of scepticism and, since it was spreading with such a powerful contagion, it appeared possible that toleration might be accomplished through the liberalizing of orthodox thought.

The Reformation finally destroyed the logical basis for the theory of religious persecution. At the same time, it overwhelmed the humanism and liberalism of Renaissance thought by dividing Europe into several armed theological camps. Each theological group bent every effort to the tasks of defence and offence and would permit no weakening internal division.

The Reformation in its ultimate effect gave powerful stimulus to and, indeed, made necessary the development of religious toleration. The doctrine of private judgment; the fact that heresy had vindicated its physical ability to exist in Europe; and the immediate necessity for arriving at a formula of international toleration soon obliged a softening of the doctrine of persecution. Further, the new creeds could not claim those cultural and historical services which had softened and rendered logical the Catholic theory of persecution. The greatest cataclysm in the cultural history of the western world had occurred and the Protestant faiths could not indefinitely adduce reasons for their intolerance which ignored that cataclysm to which they owed their very existence.

The Reformation, likewise, assisted the development of religious toleration since it was achieved in most countries by the bestowal of much of the power and wealth hitherto wielded by the Church upon the national ruler. The sovereign was motivated by essentially political considerations and could not for long claim the spiritual concern which the medieval ruler might rightfully adduce when he brought pressure to bear upon dissenting groups. In England, at least, the Government very soon admitted that its punishment of dissent was inspired solely by secular considerations and the intellectual basis for persecution was at that moment abandoned. The State had by this admission practically abandoned its claim to rule on correct dogma and withdrew itself a considerable way from that intimate concern for the spiritual welfare of the citizen which so characterized medieval politics. The State had thereby placed the responsibility for the salvation of its subjects upon their own spiritual shoulders.

Meanwhile, for various reasons, the early Protestant creeds had crystallized into dogmatic systems quite as exclusive and intolerant as the one from which they had revolted. For some time, therefore, evidences of sentiment in favour of religious toleration must be sought outside the established Protestant Churches. However, the principle of toleration was implicit in the theory and in the fact of the Protestant Revolt and the individualism and the spiritual freedom inherent in the system of thought could not long be curbed. There resulted, especially in England and Holland, in the closing years of the sixteenth century, a Second Reformation, almost as profound in its consequences as the earlier movement. This revolt against Protestant orthodoxy and dogmatic rigidity finally swept away the pretensions of Protestant intolerance and laid bare the solid foundations of a system of religious toleration which had been slowly and obscurely under construction by many hands through several decades.

In England, the effect of the Protestant Reformation upon the mind of Sir Thomas More may be taken as typical of the consequences of that movement upon humanism.

The English theologians attempted with ill success to retain the fiction of catholicity, while stressing the independence of the geographically separated portions of the true Church. Anglican theory in this respect was cast in such a wise as to accentuate the power of the monarchy in the national Church. The magistrate was regarded as the earthly head of the Church, was declared to have a heavy responsibility for the spiritual well-being of his subjects, and was held to be charged with the duty of punishing heresy. In fact, the totality of the medieval conception was retained to be applied, however, in a medium which bore but scant resemblance to the medieval spiritual structure.

During the Marian Reaction important denials were made of the power of the civil ruler in the Church and of the power of the magistrate to coerce religious opinion. These advanced Protestant thinkers sought to limit the civil power to a strict attendance upon its secular responsibilities. They stretched the principle of private judgment to its logical point and the acceptance of their position, while involving spiritual anarchy, would have resulted in religious toleration.

The pre-Elizabethan period was not without tolerant literature, and some of the sentiments expressed in that era must be regarded as historically of the first importance. Opinion in favour of toleration was not, however, well focused or powerful and lacked the influence which may be achieved only by the adhesion of an articulate group to those principles. Because of the isolated and highly individualistic character of these utterances any general summary of their content would be inaccurate. Suffice it to say that, considered *in toto*, these pleas covered the entire range of the intellectual and spiritual arguments for religious toleration and that we will find them repeated and expanded during the reign of Elizabeth.

The greatest importance, from the point of view of religious toleration, must be attached to the fact that religious policy was by the circumstances of the English Reformation placed definitely in the hands of the monarch. Henry VIII dealt in a summary fashion with dissent and his actions provoked few protests because his policy was so carefully attuned to the requirements of national life. But the assumption by the State of the responsibility for religious repression inevitably meant that heresy would be interpreted, not as a spiritual crime, but as a political offence. The old theological formulae will still be employed but they will speedily lose all content. Men soon doubted and eventually denied the competence of the State to deal with opinions and sentiments which reside so completely in the realm of the human conscience. Under these circumstances, a wise Government would not long employ the brutal coercion which had been the Henrican reply to dissent. In the next reign intelligent pressure was substituted for bald force, and Cranmer sought to lay down a comprehensive ecclesiastical structure into which the vast majority of Englishmen could be coaxed with a minimum of compulsion. The first victory of toleration had been won and, excepting for the irrational return to the older policy by Mary, the substance of that victory was to be retained and gradually to be expanded until freedom of worship had been won.

II

THE DOMINANT GROUPS DURING THE REIGN OF ELIZABETH: DEVELOPMENT OF GOVERNMENTAL AND ANGLICAN THOUGHT WITH RESPECT TO RELIGIOUS DISSENT TO 1576

1. THE ELIZABETHAN SETTLEMENT OF RELIGION

The character of the Elizabethan Settlement of religion was to play an important rôle in the development of religious toleration. Because of its moderate and comprehensive scheme of doctrinal organization it represented in itself a noteworthy advance over the fixity of most Protestant dogmatic systems. The Settlement was imposed by a State harassed by many vexatious problems, of which religion loomed as highly important, with the frank object of obtaining religious peace. When the trappings of ecclesiastical terminology and the theories of continuity are pushed aside we find the State enthroned as the arbiter of religious opinions. So long as the State regarded uniformity of worship as essential to its well-being, persecution will be expected. But persecution will result from political motives rather than from purely spiritual ideals of a perfect society. Once the State is convinced that uniformity cannot be attained by persecutions; or, more important still, that uniformity is not necessary to a well-ordered or closely knit State; or, that the continued aggravation of minority groups may result in catastrophe, the bonds of repression will be somewhat relaxed.

We will find these forces to be powerfully operative during the reign of Elizabeth. The Government steadfastly maintained that it did not propose to persecute conscience, and that it dictated modes of worship essentially for political ends. If these tenets were advanced for political purposes at the beginning of the reign, they had, by the conclusion of the reign, achieved substantial reality. Half the case for religious persecution had been abandoned. For in the first stage of persecution the mere

82

retention of certain religious opinions was regarded as a punishable offence. This view of persecution implied that the State was vitally interested in the maintenance of pure faith for the sake of the faith, and presumed that the State was competent to pronounce upon the validity of theological questions.[1] England, by the time of Elizabeth, however, had advanced to the position wherein dissenters are persecuted, not so much because of the essentially evil character of their beliefs, though this may formally be argued,[2] but because adherence to those beliefs is deemed to be dangerous to the established order. The State has relinquished the claim to punish opinion, though it may continue to order outward conformity, and it will confine its attention to the effects of religious conduct upon the interests of the State, and will profess to punish instances of dissent upon the basis of a civil action.[3]

It is particularly interesting to study the opinions of the dominant political and religious group on the question of religious toleration because the ultimate solution of the problem may be said to reside within the disposition of that group. We shall therefore investigate, not only the expressed and implied sentiments of the official groups, but the views of the leaders in the Establishment. As is normal, lay opinion ran considerably in advance of clerical theory. We will find little in the opinion of the typical Elizabethan bishop to distinguish him, in respect to the question of toleration, from Calvin or Beza, but we will find much to distinguish the policy of Elizabeth and her ministers on this important question from that of her father and sister.

The English Reformation was the least heroic of them all, the least swayed by religious passion, or moulded and governed by spiritual and theological necessity.[4] The settlement was dictated by national policy and by considerations of safety. The conception of religion as a thing private and individual did not emerge until after a century in which religious freedom normally meant the freedom of the State to persecute religion,

[1] Seaton, *Toleration under the Later Stuarts*, 5.
[2] Thus the Government in sentencing Protestant heretics continued to employ the medieval formulae in support of its actions. Cf. *post*, 297 ff.
[3] Seaton, *Toleration under the Later Stuarts*, 6.
[4] Tulloch, *Rational Theology and Christian Philosophy in England*, I, 37.

not the freedom of the individual to worship God as he pleased.[1] It is important to remember that there dwelt deep in the Queen's nature a love of order, a meticulous exactness which could not endure loose ends.[2] Disorder in the Church betokened at once a threat to the State and an indication of the insufficiency of the loose ecclesiastical structure. To attain peace and order considerable compromises were allowed, much was officially winked at when it was regarded as desirable. Elizabeth was no zealot. She desired to frame a structure which would not permit the exercise of fanatical zeal. She desired a system— regular, stable, moderate and respectable. Perhaps Tennyson only slightly overstated it when he characterized the settlement as "faultily faultless, icily regular, splendidly null."

It will be necessary to view the legal framework of the Establishment only so far as it touches upon the question of toleration. The settlement of the English Church was based upon the Acts of Supremacy and Uniformity[3] and no substantial change was made in the structure until 1689.

The Act of Supremacy did not restore the Henrican title of Supreme Head, but it gave the Queen all the spiritual and ecclesiastical power that heretofore had been legally exercised by the Crown.[4] The Crown was specifically vested with the power of "the visitation of the ecclesiastical state and persons, and for reformation, order and correction of the same and of all manner of errors, heresies, schisms, abuses, offences, contempts and enormities. . . ."[5] The Act further imposed an oath upon all ecclesiastics and Crown officials known as the Oath of Supremacy in recognition of the authority conferred by the Act,[6] and imposed a series of penalties culminating in forfeiture and death upon those who persisted in supporting "the authority of any foreign prince or prelate."[7] It was insisted as a principle of politics crystallized in creed that there should be no recognition of papal supremacy in England. Catholic belief was not forbidden or outlawed. From the beginning,

[1] Tawney, R. H., *Religion and the Rise of Capitalism*, 175.
[2] Clark, *History of English Nonconformity*, I, 155.   [3] 1 Eliz., cs. 1 and 2.
[4] 1 Eliz., c. 1, section 8.   [5] *Ibid.*   [6] 1 Eliz., c. 1, section 9.
[7] 1 Eliz., c. 1, section 14; Prothero, G. W., *Select Statutes and . . . documents*, xxxi.

the State announced that it would punish only those actions on the part of Catholics which by its own interpretation it considered harmful to the safety of the realm. "It was only after the pope had absolved her subjects of their allegiance; it was only after groups of English Catholics conspiring with foreign potentates had plotted against her life; it was only after Jesuits and seminaries . . . abroad had undertaken a systematic invasion of her kingdom to preach disobedience to her laws, that she exchanged her mild policy for one of much greater severity."[1]

Toleration was deliberately excluded by the Act of Uniformity which authorized and imposed the ecclesiastical system erected by the Settlement of Religion upon the Realm to the exclusion of all others. The Second Prayer Book of Edward VI was adopted with certain modifications and its use was made obligatory by severe penalties upon the recalcitrant ministers.[2] Heavy penalties were levied upon any person depraving the Prayer Book or hindering its use.[3] Conformity was sought by inflicting a fine upon all those absenting themselves from church services.

The Settlement of Religion was essentially political and national in character. In the Protestant-Catholic disputations at the beginning of the reign,[4] the Protestant supporters especially stressed the distinction between the universal, truly Catholic Church and the Roman Church. They claimed at once a more comprehensive communion than that enjoyed by Rome, and, at the same time, sought to establish a narrow, national body which should have the right to erect an independent government and ritual.[5] Both of these tendencies when logically extended lead towards toleration.

The doctrine set forth by the Elizabethan Settlement was, in essence, that conscience was free, although the public exercise of any but the established religion was not to be tolerated. Unsatisfactory as this was it represents an immense

[1] Read, C., *Mr. Secretary Walsingham and the Policy of Queen Elizabeth*, II, 272.　　　[2] 1 Eliz., c. 2, section 2.　　　[3] *Ibid.*, c. 2, section 3.
[4] Frere, W. H., *The English Church in the Reigns of Elizabeth and James I*, 23–24.
[5] Ranke, L. v., *A History of England . . . in the Seventeenth Century*, I, 231.

advance over the opinions which had prevailed in England a generation before.[1] This advance may be held to proceed from the nature of the religious situation at the Queen's accession and from her own religious inclinations. Elizabeth found two nicely balanced parties at the time of her accession, and she was able, with remarkable skill, to exclude the predominance of either. The Anglican party in 1558 was practically non-existent. Buckle has well called this the first instance in Europe of a Government existing in good order without the participation of the spiritual authority.[2] The State was able to secure an immediate and a firm control of religion which could not be shaken from its grasp during the reign of Elizabeth. Upon the clashing groups the State was able to impose a moderate and comprehensive settlement.

The moderate nature of the Elizabethan Establishment likewise proceeded from the personal character of the Queen. She knew too well the blighting results of persecution and the dangers which occurred to the State when a minority group was repressed to the point of explosion. These dangers she proposed to avoid. Her policy may be an example of 'trimming,' but she made ground. She perhaps had little religious enthusiasm herself.[3] She did not share the uncompromising zeal of either Catholic or Protestant. Whether or no the opinion, "all differences between Christians *n'était bagatelle*" because "there is only one Jesus Christ and one faith . . . all the rest is a dispute over trifles," was really voiced by her, it is highly typical of her religious point of view. Excessive doctrinal enthusiasm wearied and annoyed her. She found herself completely lacking in sympathy with the logical bent of the Calvinist and with the passionate zeal of the Romanist. She desired to avoid undue zeal, and middle courses do not inspire particularly warm enthusiasm. Neither zealous Catholic nor ardent Protestant would be satisfied with such a settlement,[4] but

[1] Gardiner, S. R., *History of England*, I, 13.
[2] Buckle, H. T., *History of Civilization in England*, I, 338.
[3] Read, *Mr. Secretary Walsingham*, II, 271.
[4] Thus Jewel wrote to Martyr in 1559 that there appeared to be "a seeking after a golden, or, as it rather seems to me, a leaden mediocrity; and are crying out, that the half is better than the whole." Jewel, *Works*, IV, 1210.

Elizabeth and her most trusted councillors were not extremists and they believed that the nation, harassed by a series of violent changes in faith, would support the obvious sanity of her policy. The Queen, always an accurate judge of her people, correctly presumed that the "sweet reasonableness" of her policy would win the support of the mass of Englishmen. Thus fortified dissent could be handled.[1] The Settlement was so skilfully and quickly executed that even the Catholics had little time or cause actively to exert an opposition. Generally speaking, the more advanced and impatient Protestants were not summoned to leadership either in Church or State.

Every religious action was viewed and tested in the light of its relation to the security and well-being of the State. We shall have occasion to stress the repeated contention of the Government that it had no desire to force conscience or to compel faith. There was no indication throughout the long reign that the Queen was motivated in any degree by those spiritual ideals which so largely dominated the public conduct of her sister. Thus she accepted the uniform Catholicity of Ireland, and, save for a very brief attempt in 1559, left unenforced the nominal fine of 1s. for recusancy. Political order must not be disturbed by adherence to the medieval view of the State which conceived it as responsible in no small degree for the eternal salvation of its subjects. The Government's aim was not to 'decatholicize England,' unless its insistence that Catholic policy must confine its operation to the limits of the law may be so regarded.[2] Elizabeth and Cecil repeatedly stated that the

[1] Klein (13–14) has advanced the view that one of the chief factors in the policy of moderation was that Elizabeth was assisted by national indifference to religion. The view would appear to be an overstatement. In fact, few periods in history, and perhaps no period in English history, display greater popular interest in religious matters; few periods have produced so great a body of religious literature, both systematic and controversial. The feelings of the mass of Englishmen may have been more moderate than before, but even this is to be doubted on the basis of the evident interest and enthusiasm. England was caught in a great revival of religious enthusiasm, which, as some one has well said, made the Englishman "theologically disputationous" for the first time in his history. The moderate character of the religious settlement rested rather upon the appreciation of the danger of precipitating religious strife if either of the extreme positions should be adopted.

[2] Hollis, C., *The Monstrous Regiment*, 37, for the opposite view.

Catholics could be won only by education and preaching. These efforts were relegated to the proper specialists; the Government's mission lay in preventing and in curbing the appearance of faction. She was an exact observer of two State maxims, "never to force men's consciences" and "never to suffer factious practises to go unpunished."[1] Her primary aim was to secure peace abroad and quiet at home and to attain these ends she was willing to juggle with creeds and dogmas.[2] She was a staunch believer in the formula, *cujus regio ejus religio*, but, since she had no decided religious zeal, she was willing, in some degree, to mould the settlement in accordance with the desires of her people.

Elizabeth's great minister, Cecil, offered the support of a powerful and patient ability in the attainment of the desired end. He appears as something of an opportunist in religious matters. He had conformed under Mary and, though a Protestant by choice, his State policy was not often affected by his religious sympathies. For reasons of State he favoured a *via media*; he accepted the principle of an established Church as a political necessity; and regarded dissent as a dangerous species of rebellion, whether Catholic or Protestant. Conformity he regarded as necessary, for he could not conceive of a State without a religion.[3] In his opinion, civil obedience presumed compliance to the religious order of the State, but he did not require that such obedience should be more than outward.[4] He was too wise and observant to believe that faith could be changed by punishment. Therefore, though he could not concede liberty of worship, he did concede liberty of conscience. Privately he seems to have sympathized with Protestant dissenters, but this attitude was reflected but slightly in his public

[1] Echard, L., *The History of England*, 415.
[2] Read, *Mr. Secretary Walsingham*, II, 271.
[3] Peck, F., *Desiderata Curiosa*, I, 44. "He held also, that there cold be no government where there was division, and [consequently, that] that State cold never be in Safety, where there was [a] Tolleration of two religions. For there is no Enmytie so greate as that for Religion and therefore they that differ in the Service of [their] God, can never agree in the Service of theire Contrie."
[4] Green, J. R., *History of the English People*, III, 244.

policy.[1] In fact, he discounted the importance of religion in public affairs, and to whatever persecution he lent his support he was singularly free of religious animus.[2] He was essentially a *Politique*.

The Government, on the basis of the initial legislation, proposed not to interfere with men's consciences. If they lent formal obedience to the religion by law established, they were welcome to think as they pleased.[3] Under Mary, and before, no distinction had been drawn between inner belief and outward conformity. Every Englishman had been called upon to adjust his conscience as well as his conduct to the policy of the State. The Elizabethan Settlement betokened that the persecution which had sought to vindicate this policy had only served to defeat it. The Government, especially in its handling of Catholic dissent, refused to accept the moral responsibility involved in religious persecution for its own sake.[4] To Cecil persecution was a necessary evil, which found its sole justification in political grounds. Persecution with him and with the Queen had no moral content. It is most significant that the Government felt it necessary to make repeated appeals to public opinion on the subject; that it felt obliged to justify what a generation before would have been the obviously correct policy.[5] In the noble words of Green, "Instead of strengthening religious unity, it gave a new force to religious separation; it enlisted the conscience of the zealot in the cause of resistance, it secured the sympathy of the great mass of waverers to those who withstood the civil power."[6] Though the repeated declaration that men's consciences were not to be meddled with implied

[1] Frere, *English Church*, 51–52; Arber, E., *Martin Marprelate Controversy*, 41–48.   [2] Read, C., *Eng. Hist. Rev.*, January 1913, 37.
[3] Thus Grevil comments that in the face of a growing faction within the nation "she was content to let devout conscience live quietly in her Realmes: . . ." Grevil, Sir Fulke, *Of the Life of the Renouned Sr. Philip Sidney*, 194. Professor Meyer's comment in this connection is very apt; "Elizabeth and her ministers were never guilty of allowing religious passion to endanger the well being of the nation." Meyer, A. O., *England and the Catholic Church Under Elizabeth*, 188.
[4] Figgis, J. N., *Political Thought in the Sixteenth Century*, C.M.H., III, 755.   [5] *Ibid.*, III, 755.
[6] Green, *History of the English People*, III, 244.

a step forward in securing liberty of conscience, it implied no advance in the securing of liberty of public worship. On the incompatibility of freedom of worship with public order, Cecil and Beza would have found themselves as one. This notable attempt at Erastian secularization of religion might conceivably have won the day under the able guidance of the Queen's ministers but for the recrudescence of the theocratic spirit of Calvinism and the militant efforts of the Society of Jesus.[1]

Bacon, in opening the first session of the Parliament that was to frame the legislation undergirding the ecclesiastical settlement, presaged in his address the moderate policy that was to be assumed. In respect to religion, he said that "the Queen desired they would consider of it without heat or partial affection, or using any reproachful term of papist or heretic, and that they would avoid the extremes of idolatry and superstition on the one hand, and contempt and irreligion on the other. . . ."[2] They were to avoid sophistical and "too subtle speculations," and were instructed to "endeavour to settle things so as might bring the people to an uniformity and cordial agreement in them."[3]

The Act of Supremacy was not passed without provoking, in both houses, notable protests against its intolerant character.[4] In the Commons a member attacked the bill on the grounds that no ecclesiastical penalty could rightfully be enforced beyond excommunication. "Though in the old law idolatry was punished with death; yet, since the coming of Christ, who came to win the world by peace, the greatest punishment taught by the Apostle was that of excommunication."[5] Religion, he urged, cannot be advanced by violence. This Member was evidently not a Catholic, for he regarded the Marian bishops as "bloodsuckers and murderers, worse than Caiaphus and Judas."[6] He pointed out the essentially illogical character of persecution when he enquired how the advocates of the

---

[1] Haynes, *Religious Persecution*, 89.
[2] Burnet, G., *History of the Reformation*, II, 605.
[3] *Ibid.*   [4] Frere, *English Church*, 20–21.
[5] Strype, *Parker*, I, 246.   [6] *Ibid.*

Supremacy Bill could possibly desire to set up a law which they had branded as tyrannous and illegal under Mary.

Archbishop Heath (York) attacked the Bill on the more limited grounds that spiritual supremacy does not properly appertain to the secular ruler.[1] He covered familiar ground when he pointed out that if spiritual supremacy belongs to the King, Herod was supreme head of the Church at Jerusalem and Nero of the Church at Rome.[2] If Christ left the headship of his Church in temporal hands, then it was either without a head for three centuries, or under the spiritual supremacy of pagan emperors.[3]

The legal power which the legislation of the religious settlement gave to the Crown is an important matter for our study. If the civil ruler is in reality the supreme judge of doctrine and ceremony and the source of ecclesiastical discipline, several factors of importance for the development of religious toleration may ensue. The policy which the dominant religion assumes towards heresy will inevitably be, or become, political in nature. Such an Establishment will, sooner or later, alienate and antagonize men of deeply spiritual nature who have become cognizant of the secular character of the State Church. We may expect, as well, the development of a body of believers who deny that the State has any connection at all with the exercise and promotion of religion. In especial, persecuted minorities will seek to establish their right to exist by a partial or a complete denial of the age-old union of the ecclesiastical and the secular governments, which, in the case of England, meant the practical absorption of the former by the latter, the State alone having given the theory of persecution actual significance.

The Act of Supremacy placed no definite limits on the legal power of the Queen in the Church and appears, in fact, consciously to avoid an exact definition. The Queen repeatedly disclaimed the power of regulating doctrine and of exercising purely spiritual functions.[4] The Queen sought in the Admonition

---

[1] Strype, *Annals*, I, 2, 399–407.
[2] *Ibid.*, I, 2, 401. [3] *Ibid.*, I, 2, 402.
[4] *S.P. Dom. Eliz.*, xv, 27; xxvii, 40; Neal, I, 91.

at the conclusion of the *Injunctions of 1559* to explain her position. Many of the Catholic clergy had taken the stand that the oath admitted the authority of the Queen both in respect to doctrine and the administration of the service of the Church. The power of the Queen in the Church was declared to be precisely that of her father and brother.[1] It was denied that the Queen "may challenge authority, and power of ministry of divine service, in the Church" beyond that exercised by Henry VIII and Edward VI.[2] This authority and power, so far as it is here defined at all, seems to be that the Queen "under God" has "the sovereignty and rule over all manner of persons . . . either ecclesiastical or temporal, soever they

---

[1] Text of the *Admonition* follows:—

Elizabeth's Admonition, in explanation of her supremacy. 1559

The Queen's majesty, being informed that, in certain places of the realm, sundry of her native subjects, being called to ecclesiastical ministry of the Church, be, by sinister persuasion and perverse construction, induced to find some scruple in the form of an oath, which, by an act of the last parliament, is prescribed to be required of divers persons, for their recognition of their allegiance to her majesty, which certainly never was ever meant, nor, by any equity of words, or good sense, can be thereof gathered, would that all her loving subjects should understand that nothing was, is, or shall be meant or intended by the same oath to have any other duty, allegiance, or bond required by the same oath, than was acknowledged to be due to the most noble kings of famous memory, king Henry the eighth, her majesty's father, or king Edward the sixth, her majesty's brother.

And further, her majesty forbiddeth all manner her subjects to give ear or credit to such perverse and malicious persons, which most sinisterly and maliciously labour to notify to her loving subjects, how, by words of the said oath, it may be collected that the kings or queens of this realm, possessors of the crown, may challenge authority, and power of ministry of divine service, in the church; wherein her said subjects be much abused by such evil disposed persons. For, certainly, her majesty neither doth, nor ever will, challenge any [other] authority, than that was challenged and lately used by the said noble kings, . . . which is and was of ancient time due to the imperial crown of this realm, that is, under God to have the sovereignty and rule over all manner of persons born within these her realms, dominions, and countries, of what estate, either ecclesiastical or temporal, soever they be; so as no other foreign power shall or ought to have any superiority over them. And if any person, that hath conceived any other sense of the form of the said oath, shall accept the same oath with this interpretation, sense, or meaning, her majesty is well pleased to accept every such in that behalf, as her good and obedient subjects, and shall acquit them of all manner of penalties, contained in the said act, against such as shall peremptorily or obstinately [refuse to] take the same oath. (In Dodd, Charles, *Church History of England*, (Tierney edit.), II, ccl-ccli.)   [2] *Ibid.*

be: so as no other foreign power shall or ought to have any superiority over them."[1] The commentators of the period were

[1] Text of the *Admonition*.

It is interesting to compare the various Protestant Confessions of Faith on this important issue. Thus the Augsburg Confession of 1530 avers that "Christians, therefore, must necessarily obey their magistrates and laws, save only when they command in sin; for then they must rather obey God than man" (Itaque necessario debent Christiani obedire magistratibus suis et legibus; nisi cum jubent peccare, tunc etiam magis debent obedire Deo quam hominibus) (Art. XVI, *Corpus. Reform.*, XXVI, 263 ff.). Article VII, which treats of the ecclesiastical power, is somewhat more explicit: "Seeing then that the ecclesiastical power concerneth things eternal, and is exercised only by the ministry of the Word, it hindereth not the political government any more than the art of singing hinders political government. For the political government is occupied about other matters than is the Gospel. The magistracy defends not the minds, but the bodies, and bodily things, against manifest injuries: and coerces men by the sword and corporal punishments, that it may uphold civil justice and peace. Wherefore the ecclesiastical and the civil powers are not to be confounded. The ecclesiastical power hath its own commandment to preach the Gospel and administer the Sacraments. Let it not by force enter into the office of another. . . ."

("Itaque cum potestas ecclesiastica concedat res aeternas, et tantum exerceatur per ministerium verbi: non impedit politicam administrationem; sicut ars canendi nihil impedit politicam administrationem. Nam politica administratio versatur circa alias res, quam Evangelium: magistratus defendit non mentes, sed corpora et res corporales adversus manifestas injurias, et coercet homines gladio et corporalibus poenis, ut justitiam civilem retineat.

"Non igitur commiscendae sunt potestates ecclesiasticae civilis: ecclesiastica suum mandatum habet Evangelii docendi et administrandi Sacramenta. Non irrumpat in alienum officium . . . .")

The great Belgic Confession of 1561 goes far in denying the right of the civil magistrate to bind the conscience of the Christian. Article XXXII, *'On the order and discipline of the Church,'* states, "In the meantime we believe, though it be useful and beneficial, that those who are rulers of the church institute and establish certain ordinances among themselves for maintaining the body of the Church; yet they ought studiously to take care that they do not depart from those things which Christ, our only Master, hath instituted. And, therefore, we reject all human inventions, and all laws which man would introduce into the worship of God, thereby to bind and compel the conscience in manner whatever. Therefore we admit only of that which tends to nourish and preserve concord and unity, to keep all men in obedience to God."

However, Article XXXVI of the Belgic Confession, which is more specifically concerned with the power of the civil magistrate, would appear to lend the prince almost as much power within the Church as the English settlement. Thus, ". . . He [God] hath invested the magistracy with the sword, (for the punishment of evil doers, and for the praise of them that do well— pour punir les méchants, et maintenir les gens de bien, Insertion of 1619),

somewhat clearer in their definition of this point. Cecil was of
the opinion that the Queen enjoyed privileges in the Church
equal to those formerly exercised by the Pope, and at least
equal to those of the Archbishop in the English Church.[1]
The Crown, in fact, claimed and exercised all the functions
which had been absorbed from the papacy. Jewel held that
the laws gave to the ruler "that prerogative and chiefty that
evermore hath been due unto him by the ordinance and Word
of God; that is to say, to be the nurse of God's religion; to
make laws for the Church; to hear and take up cases and
questions of the faith, if he be able; or otherwise to commit
them over by his authority unto the learned; to command the
bishops and priests to do their duties, and to punish such as
be offenders."[2] Parker enquired, "Who will doubt anything
that passes from that authority?"[3] At a later date Hooker held
that ". . . when the whole ecclesiastical state, . . . do need
visitation and reformation; when, in any part of the Church,

and this office is, not only to have regard unto and watch for the welfare of
the civil state, but also that they protect the sacred ministry, and thus may
remove and prevent all idolatry and false worship; that the Kingdom of anti-
christ may be thus destroyed, and the Kingdom of God promoted. They
must, therefore, countenance the preaching of the Word of the Gospel
everywhere, that God may be honoured and worshipped by every one, as
He commands in His Word."

(Original text may be seen in *La Confession de foi des églises réformées
Walonnes et Flamandes*, published at Brussels in 1854 by the Société
évangélique Belge. The English text is that authorized by the Reformed
Dutch Church of America.)

The Calvinist hatred of error and blasphemy disposed them to grant to
the magistrate large powers in the eradication of false beliefs,—powers which
were quite inimical to their conception of Church independence. Calvinism
always presumed, however, that sooner or later the civil power would carry
out its spiritual duties at the command of the Church.

The thirty-seventh article of the English Confession of Faith (1563) fails
satisfactorily to define the problem. (Vide Hardwick, C., *History of the
Articles of Religion*, 277 ff.) The framers of the Settlement must have realized
that they were on delicate ground, and they preferred, as in the case of
doctrine, to leave much undefined. The unofficial views of the theologians
and the officials of the period constitute a far better index to thought on the
subject than the cold definition of the creed.

[1] Parker, Matthew, *Correspondence*, cclxx (Parker to Cecil, July 1, 1569).
[2] Jewel, John, *Works*, III, 167; I, 396–397; III, 98; IV, 975–980, 959–960.
[3] Parker, *Correspondence*, cclxx (Parker to Cecil, July 1, 1569).

errors, heresies, schisms . . . are grown, which men in their several jurisdictions either do not or cannot help; whatsoever any spiritual authority or power (such as the legates from the see of Rome did sometimes exercise) hath done or might heretofore have done for the remedy of those evils in lawful sort" has been granted to the Crown by the law of England.[1]

The necessity for a strong Government in England and the ability and adroitness of the Tudors had absorbed most spiritual jurisdiction to the Crown and had almost extinguished the long distinction between the spiritual and the temporal powers. To all intents the government of the English Church has become Erastian.[2] Law compelled recognition of the royal supremacy and attendance at authorized churches. The Government employed the episcopal system and the ecclesiastical courts to enforce these measures. The Crown proclaimed from time to time that it did not and could not regulate religious truth, but from the point of view of dissenting groups this view was a patent legal fiction. "Law recognized that the determinations of civil authority concerning religious belief and observance, must be consistent with the word of God; and the law . . . assumed that they were always so."[3] The Bible was conceded to be the infallible standard of religious truth, but the Crown in Parliament had undertaken to lay down a legally binding interpretation of that truth. This position was inherently contradictory to the underlying principles of the Protestant Reformation and an increasing body of evidence demonstrated that the Government pursued civil ends in its religious policy rather than lending its efforts to the salvation of souls. Many men, perhaps most men, yet believed that discussion and Bible reading might result in an ideal religious commonwealth, but few men could long hold that religious truth was determinable by legislative enactment, The governmental view conceived religion as a function of the social order; and such a conception could satisfy no truly religious man.

[1] Hooker, Richard, *Of the Laws of Ecclesiastical Polity*, VIII, viii, 5.
[2] Klein, *Intolerance in the Reign of Elizabeth*, 70.
[3] Allen, J. W. *Political Thought in the Sixteenth Century*, 172. This interpretation of the character of the Settlement owes much to the inspiration of Tulloch and the masterful analysis of Allen.

The Establishment which Elizabeth and her ministers sought to enforce by law was vague in definition, comprehensive in content. Perhaps the Government envisaged a loosely organized ecclesiastical structure in which men of every religious conviction could find themselves a measurably comfortable dwelling place. The conception failed to take into account, however, the almost universal conviction that exact religious truth might be ascertained by Bible reading and discussion, and the as yet latent revolt of many men at any attempt of the State to impose fixed religious formulae upon a nation. Elizabeth succeeded in maintaining the Establishment intact because she was content with the tremendous influence which a capable Government can attain by abstaining from demanding precise definition of its power, by yielding here and crushing there. The Settlement, because of its character, was a long step towards toleration. So little was clearly stated in doctrine that only zealous dogmatism would be driven into revolt. Men of all shades of religious opinion remained within the Church during Elizabeth's reign. The question of toleration during her reign never assumed outstanding significance because of the essentially tolerant character of the governmental position.

Measured by contemporary standards, the attitude assumed by the Elizabethan Government towards dissent was fairly moderate. Whatever programme of repression the churchmen undertook required the sanction and co-operation of a ministry which was objective in outlook and unclerical in character. In repeated instances clerical policy was tempered by the Government to which it was referred. The law was never delivered into the hands of the ecclesiastical authorities to enforce without the deterrent of state review and control.[1]

The somewhat implicit resolution of the Government to leave unmolested those persons who undertook the vows of loyalty, and who lent formal conformity by their attendance at public worship marks a distinct advance towards the attainment of legal toleration. We are interested not so much in the fact that Elizabeth persecuted less rigorously than most con-

[1] Klein, *Intolerance*, 90.

temporary Governments but that she persecuted from motives which were quite different from those which had actuated her father and sister. The Government proposed to tolerate dissenting opinion on the grounds that opinion could be changed only by education and by the slow process of example, while prohibiting the public exercise of dissenting beliefs which were interpreted as inimical to the public weal. The State, in fine, undertook the hazardous and difficult task of defining what constituted dangerous expressions of opinion. Under the great Queen the definition was broad enough to permit of the formation of powerful and articulate minorities which threatened serious opposition unless the State undertook to enlarge the frontiers of permitted belief and worship to the point of toleration. Each group, with one or two important exceptions, asked for toleration for itself alone, but the totality of demands may be said to pose the question of legal toleration for all sects which do not outrage law and order.

The body which was the final centre of decision in religious matters, although small, reflected almost every shade of religious conviction. The men who composed the royal Council must have realized, from their own example, the futility of attempting to encase the religious life of a people within the rigid moulds of a doctrinal system imposed and enforced by the agencies of the State.

Cecil, the chief of this great group of statesmen, some years later emphasized these tendencies while considering the problem of the Roman Catholics, the most powerful of all the dissenting groups at that time, in their relation to the State. "To suffer them to be strong with hope, that with reason, they will be contented, carrieth with it, in my opinion, but a fair enamelling of a terrible danger."[1] Men naturally resent not only a "present smart," but seek to revenge what they regard as past injury. When occasion affords opportunity "they will remember, not the after slacking, but the former binding; and so much the more, when they shall imagine this relenting to proceed from fear: For it is the poison of all government, when the subject

---

[1] Burleigh's Advice to Queen Elizabeth in Matters of Religion and State, *Harl. Misc.*, VII, 57.

thinks the prince doth anything more out of fear than favour."[1]

The nation, in other words, has committed itself to the Protestant cause, and there can be no retreat from this position. But the assumption of this policy does not imply that the Catholics should be goaded to desperation.[2] He almost summarized the Government's policy towards dissent when he reflected, "and therefore, though they must be discontented, yet I would not have them desperate; for, amongst many desperate men, it is like someone will bring forth some desperate attempt." Dissenters are to be made as uncomfortable as possible and every effort is to be made to secure uniformity in religion, but not at the cost of civil war. Cecil displayed himself as a true *Politique*. Uniformity is not abandoned as the ideal, but it is not worth the risks of civil war.[3] Hence especial care should be taken in submitting the Oath of Supremacy so that those who refuse it must be considered as guilty of civil treason. Only those persons who will not bear arms against any foreign prince or power seeking to invade the realm are to be considered as traitors. There is to be no extension of the law of treason, though, we may infer, there may be a considerable tightening of its application. He seems disposed to regard the Oath of Supremacy as the equivalent of an Oath of Allegiance in order to preclude any charge of persecution of conscience in dealing with those who refused to take the oath.

Cecil's programme for the Catholic problem likewise involved the systematic education of the Roman Catholics. A definite programme of preaching and teaching should be undertaken. The "preciser sort," who are the worst enemies of Rome,

---

[1] Burleigh's Advice to Queen Elizabeth in Matters of Religion and State, *Harl. Misc.*, VII, 57.
[2] ". . . there is no way but to kill desperates, which, in such a number as they are, were as hard and difficult, as impious and ungodly." (*Ibid.*, VII, 57.)
[3] The view is strikingly similar to those expressed a few years later by the *Politiques* in France. A comparison with the position of La Noue (*Discours Politiques et Militaires*, 1587); Bodin, *Rep.*, IV, 754–758; L'Hôpital in his speech at Orleans in 1560, *Œuvres complètes*, I, 395 ff., and especially in his *Traité de le Reformation de la Justice*. Vide also his *Coll. de Poissy*, I, 469–479.

should be utilized for the achievement of the plan.[1] In addition, the Catholics must be deprived of all civil power; "for to compel them you would not; kill them you would not; so, to trust them you should not. . . ."[2] Upon the assumption of such a policy, he urged, none would be executed "but very traitours, in all men's opinions and constructions. . . ."[3]

2. INITIAL PROCEDURE AGAINST NONCOMFORMITY

The Government, in its initial contacts with the Catholic problem, displayed its intention of proceeding along the lines which were sketched by Cecil. Thus, when several members of the Council urged the Queen to punish the deprived bishops she replied, if we may trust Strype, "Let us not follow our sister's example, but rather shew that our reformation tendeth to peace, and not to cruelty."[4]

In accordance with this policy, Thirlby and Boxal[5] were ordered by the Council to be removed from London in 1563, when the plague was prevalent there. They were removed to Parker's house at Bekesborn where Thirlby lived until his death seven years later.[6] In 1560 the Council permitted the imprisoned bishops to dine together and upon the outbreak of the plague they were sent to the various bishops for greater safety.[7] Nowell in his *Reproof* remarked somewhat caustically that the Oath of Supremacy was never required of them and "they pined not, but fared well, and of other men's cost too. . . . They were neither whipped nor scourged, as some of them used others. And that in sickness time, they had their progresses both for health and pleasure too." Rome itself commented favourably upon the kindly treatment of the deposed Catholic leaders. In 1559 it was said there that "the Queen, notwithstanding her perversity in religion, has not as yet shewn any

[1] Burleigh, Advice, *Harl. Misc.*, VII, 58.   [2] *Ibid.*, VII, 59
[3] *Ibid.*, VII, 59.   [4] Strype, *Annals*, I, 1, 219.
[5] The Bishop of Ely and the Dean of Windsor.
[6] Strype, *Parker*, I, 278.
[7] The Anglican bishops were instructed to "give them convenient lodging, each of them one man allowed them, and to use them as was requisite for men of their sort; and that they should satisfy his Lordship for the charges of their commons." (Strype, *Parker*, I, 279.)

disposition to deal rigorously with the persons of those lay lords and church-men who have refused to take the oath of obedience or deny the Catholic religion, but has merely deprived them of their offices and benefices, still suffering them to abide in the realm, and in some cases to live abroad in the enjoyment of their revenues. . . ."[1] Indeed, the writer was so impressed with the moderation and lenity of the Queen that he believed that she might in time "restore the obedience of the realm to the Apostolic See, and to return to the Catholic religion."[2]

The Royal Commission of Visitation, in its attempt to weed out the Catholic clergy, was not unmindful of the sentiments of the district in question. In large areas no changes were undertaken in the ranks of the lower clergy. The Reformation was so carefully and adroitly accomplished that we may believe that the mass of the laity was quite unaware of the gravity of the change which was occurring.[3] The Government had no desire fundamentally or radically to alter the religious attachments of the average Englishman.

Archbishop Parker had shown considerable moderation in the execution of the Oath of Supremacy. He had privately dispatched letters to the various bishops, warning them that caution should be taken in the administration of the law. The bishops were instructed not to tender the oath for the second time before laying the facts of the case before him in writing.[4] He likewise wrote to Cecil that he was pleased with most of the bishops and with their willingness to co-operate with him in his programme. Parker regarded himself as cleaving to a middle course between the somewhat rigorous policy of the Queen and the advanced opinions of many of his colleagues.[5] In so far as possible, he proposed to refrain from employing

---

[1] *Roman Calendar*, I, 27.   [2] *Ibid.*, 27.
[3] As Lever expressed it to Bullinger, ". . . The prebendaries in the cathedrals, and the parish priests in the other churches, retaining the outward habits and inward feeling of popery, so fascinate the ears and eyes of the multitude, that they are unable to believe, but that either the popish doctrine is still retained, or at least that it will be shortly restored" (July 1560). (*Zurich Letters*, First Series, XXXV.)   [4] Strype, *Parker*, I, 248.
[5] "And where the Queen's highness doth note me to be soft and easy, I think divers of my brethren will rather note me, if they were asked, too sharp and too earnest in moderation." (Strype, *Parker*, I, 249.)

58544

the power of the State in the execution of the laws respecting religion.[1]

The power delegated to the prince by the Settlement received, in 1562, literary defence in the *Apologia Ecclesiae Anglicanae* by Jewel.[2] Five years later his *A Defense of the Apologie of the Churche of Englande* followed in reply to the attack of Harding on the earlier work. The English Church, Jewel held, grants "no further liberty to our magistrates than that we know hath both been given them by the Word of God, and also been confirmed by the examples of the very best governed commonwealths."[3] The prince may not lawfully claim the title or exercise the functions of Supreme Head, but he is the highest judge of all his subjects, whether lay or ecclesiastical. The Christian prince "hath the charge of both tables committed to him by God, to the end he may understand that not temporal matters only, but also religious and ecclesiastical causes, pertain to his office; . . . ."[4] The king may claim no ministerial function; doctrinal ascertainment, the sacraments, and preaching belong to what we may describe as a specialized body of Christians. But the prince has a very real duty in fostering true religion and in insisting upon the proper functioning of the ecclesiastical machinery.[5]

The king's duty extends to the restraint and persecution of unbelief and error for "God by his prophets often and earnestly commandeth the King to cut down the groves, to break down the images and altars of idols, and to write out the Book of the law for himself. . . ."[6] Good kings have always considered it a sacred duty and trust to reform religion and to keep the clergy at their duties. Harding, he said, would make the king the servant of the priest, "to draw his sword, and strike when

---

[1] Strype, *Parker*, I, 250.

[2] The first edition appeared anonymously; later editions appeared in 1581, 1584, 1591, 1606, 1614, etc. An English translation was brought out in the year of the first edition as, *An Apologie, or answer, in defence of the Church of England, concerninge the state of religion used in the same*, etc. At least eight editions of the translation were subsequently to appear.

[3] Jewel, John, *Defence, Works*, IV, 973. [4] *Ibid.*, IV, 975.

[5] That is, "We say not the prince is bound to do the bishop's duty. . . . But thus we say, the prince is bound to see the bishops to do their duties." (*Ibid.*, IV, 976.) [6] *Ibid.*, IV, 977.

Lincoln Christian College

and whomsoever the priest biddeth." Jewel, with most of his contemporaries, found in the Old Testament ample proof that the king was set above the priest.[1] "By histories and by examples of the best times," I say, "good princes ever took the administration of ecclesiastical matters to pertain to their duty."[2]

Substantially the same view was expressed in the *Articles of Religion* agreed upon in the Convocation held in the early months of 1563. Thus the chief government of the Church is entrusted to the Queen. Still, "wee giue not to our princes the ministering, either of God's Word, or of the sacraments, the which thing the Iniunctions also lately set foorth by Elizabeth our Queene, doe most plainely testifie. . . ."[3] The power of the ruler in the Church was defined as that which God in his Word has always bestowed upon godly princes. This power was stated, with more caution than by Jewel, as the "rule over" all "estates and degrees committed to their charge by God, whether they be Ecclesiasticall or Temporall," and the restraint by the civil sword of the stubborn and the evil doers.[4]

The Parliament, which was in session at the time when Convocation approved the Thirty-Nine Articles of Religion and showed considerable Protestant sympathy by failing by one vote to eradicate several liturgical and disciplinary survivals from the old worship,[5] was dominated by fear of France and Spain. We may observe in this Parliament the psychology which was later to dictate the policy of the Government towards the Roman Catholics of the realm. The penalties for recusancy were drawn tighter in order to guard against political emergency.[6]

In the first session of the Parliament an Act was passed "for the assurance of the Queen's majesty's royal power over all estates and subjects within her Highness' dominions."[7] Any person maintaining the "jurisdiction, authority, or preeminence" of the pope should, upon conviction, "incur into the . . . penalties of praemunire," and, in the event of a conviction for a second offence, should incur the penalties of treason. The

---

[1] Jewel, *Defence*, IV, 980.   [2] *Ibid.*, IV, 981.
[3] *Articles agreed upon by . . . convocation*, art. 37.
[4] *Ibid.*   [5] Strype, *Annals*, I, 1, 502–503.
[6] Frere, *History of the English Church*, 99.   [7] 5 Eliz., c. 1.

same penalties were likewise prescribed for refusal to take the oath of allegiance.[1]

The bill met with sharp opposition in both Houses. Montagu in the Lords and Atkinson in the Commons expressed sentiments in their criticism of the oath which are of importance in tracing the development of religious toleration.

The Catholic Lord Montagu raised the objection of conscience in speaking against the bill.[2] The measure, he urged, was quite unnecessary, since the Catholics of the realm "disturb not, nor hinder the public affairs of the realm, neither spiritual nor temporal: they dispute not, they preach not, they disobey not the queen, they cause no trouble nor tumults among the people: so that no man can say, that thereby the realm doth receive any hurt or damage by them."[3] In other words, Montagu sought to prove that the argument of political necessity which was being advanced in support of the measure was wholly

---

[1] 5 Eliz., c. 1, sects. vii, ix.

[2] Lord Montagu (Anthony Browne) was born in 1526, the son of Sir Anthony Browne, who was an executor of Henry VIII and the guardian of Edward VI. He was related, through his mother, to the powerful Nevil family. He was throughout his life a staunch Roman Catholic. Browne was imprisoned for a short time in 1551 for hearing mass, but a year later Edward VI visited him at his seat. He was created Viscount Montagu upon the accession of Mary (*Cal. S.P. Dom.*, iv, 21), and was made master of the horse in the same year. Montagu was a member of the commission which treated with the papacy for the return of England to the Roman obedience, and appears to have been a personal friend of the Queen (Froude, VII, 17–18). He was made a member of the Privy Council in 1555. (*D.N.B.*, vii, 40.)

He, with the other pronounced Catholics in the Privy Council, was deprived of his seat upon the accession of Elizabeth (Froude, VII, 17–18). In 1560–1561, however, he was employed by the Queen on a special embassy to Madrid. He appears to have undertaken the mission against his will, and was sent because his brave stand against the Settlement would make him acceptable to Philip (Froude, VII, 191–192). From this time forward, however, he seems to have enjoyed the confidence of the Queen. Elizabeth repeatedly displayed her willingness to overlook differences in religion so long as she was certain of political loyalty on the part of her subjects. Montagu was one of the commissioners for supervising the levying of the subsidy in Surrey in 1559 (*Cal. S.P. Dom.*, Eliz., iv, 23), and in 1574 returned the muster rolls for Sussex (*Ibid.*, xcviii, 12). He sat in the trial of Mary Queen of Scots and led a body of troops in the famous review at Tilbury. (Hallam, *Constitutional History of England*, I, 162.) In 1591 he entertained the Queen at his seat in one of the magnificent festivals which she loved so well. He died in the following year.　　　　　　　[3] Strype, *Annal*, I, 1, 442.

unjustified on the basis of Catholic action since the Queen's accession.

In addition, the speaker condemned the proposal as unjust in spirit and in essence. He disclaimed any intention of examining the verity of any religion. Truth in religion is measured and revealed by the action of time alone. But he did plead that Englishmen should not be compelled to believe in the Protestant faith under pain of death.[1] Force, in this particular, he branded as contrary to the law of nature and the civil law. He urged nobly that "No man can or ought to be constrained to take for certain that that he holdeth to be uncertain: for this repugneth to the natural liberty of man's understanding: for understanding may be persuaded, but not forced."[2] A finer plea for the sanctity of honest scruple and for the freedom of human conscience could scarcely be enunciated. The religious fervour and dissension which the Reformation had engendered had convinced Montagu, if we may regard him as speaking his true thoughts, that absolute truth in religion may not easily be defined and that honest doubt was justified by the facts of the situation which he saw about him on the floor of Parliament. Belief should not be compelled "till all opinions come to one: and that there be one faith, one God, and one Trinity." This is especially true because of the uncertain status of Protestant authority. "It is sufficient, and enough for protestants," he urged, "to keep the possession of the churches, and the authority to preach and excommunicate, not to seek to force and strain men to do or believe by compulsion that they believe not; and not to swear, and to make God witness of their lies."[3]

[1] Both Elizabeth and Cecil would have agreed with this, and would have denied that the Government intended any such attempt. The Government was concerned in this instance only with the erection of provisions for the punishment of certain actions which it held to be treasonable, and which, unfortunately, were imbedded deep in the faith of most zealous Catholics. It might be held with reason that the Government's conception of treason was far more open to attack than its view of the rights of conscience. Montagu here raised an important question, which is not yet settled, as to what the State's attitude should be in the case of religious belief which happens to lie foul of what the State regards as requisite to public order and national safety.   [2] Strype, *Annals*, I, 1, 443.
[3] Strype, *Annals*, I, 1, 443; Hallam, H., *Constitutional History of England*, I, 116–117.

The bill, since it violates the rights of conscience, cannot be enforced. It compels men to a choice of lying, dying, or rebelling. The good prince will seek to avoid laws that tend to the provocation of civil discord.[1]

In the House of Commons, Atkinson spoke against the bill, in the first place, because the penalties prescribed were too rigorous. The common law, in his estimation, had never accounted the maintenance of the jurisdiction of the Pope a treasonable offence;[2] but rather praemunire. He confessed his ignorance of the Scriptures, but held it to be a commonplace that Christ preached a doctrine of peace. The most grievous punishment reserved to His Church is excommunication. "Religion," he held, "must sink in by persuasion, it cannot be pressed in by violence."[3] Atkinson observed acutely that the very persons who protested most vehemently against the Marian persecutions were now endeavouring to erect precisely the same repressive system. He regarded the existing legislation as quite sufficient to secure the safety of the State, as had been demonstrated by the peace and order that had appertained since the accession of Elizabeth.

The member expressed no doubt, if the Act were passed, that most Catholics would not accept it.[4] But it would be foolish to presume that the mere acceptance of the oath would suffice to change the heart of the subscriber. Nor would the passage of the bill serve as a preventive of sedition, for "If men were seditious before, now will they become ten times more seditious."[5] In his closing remarks Atkinson made an eloquent plea for greater tolerance and charity. "Let us, therefore, for the honour of God, leave all malice, and not withstanding religion, let us love together. For it is no point of religion, one to hate another. Let us make an end of division, for fear lest our enemies, who are mighty, and now in the field, might peradventure, finding us at dissension among ourselves, the easilier vanquish us. . . . Let us, for the love of

[1] Strype, *Annals*, I, 1, 445; Hallam, I, 116–117.
[2] *Ibid.*, I, 1, 447–448.   [3] *Ibid.*, I, 1, 450.
[4] Quite aptly, he remarked, "many a false shrew there is, that will lay his hand to the Book, when his heart shall be far off." (Strype, *Annals*, I, 1, 453.)
[5] *Ibid.*, I, 1, 454.

God, forget and forgive all griefs for the Commonwealth's sake, and let us love one another; for so shall no division work for the desolation of our kingdom."[1]

Atkinson here uttered a doctrine which resembles the spirit of the *Politiques* in France. Persecution is wrong from the point of view of religion because it finds no warrant in the teachings of Christ. But as important, he urged that the State may exist without uniformity of belief. Persecution and repression serve only to weaken the front which the State presents to its enemies. He almost urges that the State rests upon bases apart from religion. The fibre of the State is found in loyalty and patriotism, and these vital forces may be secured without the brutal cohesion of oppression. Germany, he remarked, has learned after terrible experiences "that the papist and protestant can now quietly talk together, and never fall out about the matter" of religion. Men that offend by their dissent "offend not as murderers and thieves do, that is, of malice and wicked intent, but through conscience and zeal . . ." and "such offenses cannot easily be punished without injury to the soul and body. . . ." "Though some peradventure have offended you; yet do not for their sakes punish the rest, who never offended you; but rather, for the other's sakes, who are the greater number, forgive all."[2]

These utterances on the floor of Parliament represent the highest and completest expressions of a tolerant point of view that we find in the early years of the Queen's reign. We are perhaps warranted, as well, in taking them to reflect a considerable body of opinion which had come to realize the futility, if not the injustice, of persecution. The Government had itself tacitly recognized similar ideas. No lay person had been compelled to subscribe. The Government had, as Fuller puts it, charitably presumed "that where parishes were provided of pastors orthodox in their judgments, they would, by God's blessing on their preaching, work their people to conformity to the same opinions."[3]

Already, however, the child-like faith of the reformers in

[1] Strype, *Annals*, I, 1, 454.   [2] *Ibid.*, I, 1, 455.
[3] Fuller, T., *Church History of Britain*, IV, 319.

the power of truth to overcome error was weakening before the obstinate refusal of the Roman Catholics readily to accept that truth. As we have seen, even Cecil believed strongly in the possibility of eradicating error by preaching and teaching. By degrees, however, the Government and the Parliament receded, though never wholly, from this admirable position. The Act of 1563 empowered the bishops to tender the Oath of Supremacy, not only to persons holding Church preferments or official positions in the State, but to large bodies of men; and it was enacted that all who refused the oath should be visited with severe penalties.[1]

The Queen, at about the same time, sketched the attitude of the Government towards dissent in a letter to the Emperor who had petitioned Elizabeth to cherish her Catholic subjects rather than to persecute them.[2] He further requested that English Catholics might be permitted freely to exercise their religion in at least one church in each city.[3]

Elizabeth, in her reply, emphasized the moderate policy of the Government in suspending sentences which were legally binding. She found it impossible to permit the Catholics to have free churches since such an action would constitute a violation of the laws of the realm and would result in danger to the State. "It would be to sow various religions in the nation, to distract the minds of honest men, and to disturb religion, and the present quiet state wherein it is."[4]

We are only indirectly interested, at this point, in the struggle which began to shape itself with Puritanism about 1564. The Puritans claimed that a scriptural warrant must be demonstrated for every detail of public worship and thereby challenged the authority of the Church in ordaining the form of the service. They answered the argument of the Establishment, that matters of indifference lay within the province of human arrangement, by an assault upon these points as idola-

[1] Gardiner, *History of England*, I, 13.
[2] Strype, *Annals*, I, 2, App., 572–573, (September 1563).   [3] *Ibid.*
[4] "Vero templum diversis ritibus, praeterquam quod aperte pugnat cum nostri parliamenti legibus nihil aliud esset, quam serere religionem ex religione, distrahere mentes bonorum, alere studia factiosorum, religionem et rempub. perturbare in hoc jam quieto statu nostro...." (Strype, I, 2, 574.)

trous and popish. There was, as yet, no divergence in doctrine, but there was a vigorous attack upon the bases of ecclesiastical authority as defined by the laws of the realm. We shall consider the relation of the Puritans to the question of toleration in later pages, but at this point it may be well to estimate the implications of the position of the dominant groups towards the Puritan demands.

The Queen, in early 1565, complained to Parker that the bishops were making no concerted effort to secure uniformity of service and charged that their negligence had resulted in variety and disorder. She demanded that legal proceedings should be undertaken in order to check these evils, and that scrupulous care should be exercised in the bestowal of benefices. About a month later the Archbishop published a summary of the varieties existing in the service. Although personally averse to compulsion, Parker, in consultation with a small group of bishops, prepared in March 1565, a book of articles which was designed to remedy the situation. The Queen, however, was loath, perhaps because of the decided antagonism of the Puritan wing of the Council, actively to support the policy which she had demanded. Parker wrote to Cecil that "If the Queen's majesty would not authorize it, the most part (of the orders) were like to lie in the dust, for execution on their parties, laws were so much against their own private doings."[1] Parker appears to have believed that many of the influential clergy were so far in opposition that they would ignore or oppose any attempt to enforce the established order, unless the Government were willing to commit itself to a definite policy of enforcement.[2]

Spite the efforts of the Archbishop and his entreaties to the Government, he could not at this time overcome the opposition of a considerable element in the Council which was avowedly hostile to a strict enforcement of the existing ecclesiastical laws, much less willing to sanction the formulation of additional measures.[3] Parker was well aware of the seat of the opposition

[1] Strype, *Parker*, I, 316.
[2] *Cal. St. Pap., Dom.*, xli, 43 (December 14, 1566).
[3] Strype, *Parker*, I, 317.

to his efforts and pleaded that "It was better not to have begun except more were done: and that all the realm was in expectation." He insisted that if the Council did not lend a helping hand "all that was done was but to be laughed at."[1]

Somewhat later Parker wrote to Cecil that he had desisted from urging conformity upon the clergy for a time because of "the political considerations which they who were the secret friends to non-conformity urged."[2] More recently he had attempted to carry out the express injunction of the Queen, somewhat against his own judgment and conviction, only to see his programme defeated by opposition within her Majesty's Government. He and his commission had power to deprive and imprison Nonconformists, "But there are some of these men who offer themselves to lose all; yea, and their bodies to prison, rather than they would condescend."[3] He probably expressed his own convictions when he pleaded that he was not prepared to adopt a rigorous policy, "having no more warrant and help; lest after much stirring, he might do little in the end but hurt."[4] In spite of the tightening of the bonds by the ecclesiastical authorities, yet did the Queen and "Her commissioners dispense or wink at many divines who could not comply, and yet had and retained still dignities in the church."[5]

Elizabeth continued to withhold her confirmation from the Book of Articles, hoping that vigorous action in London might secure the desired end,[6] or, perhaps, desiring to make a test of some particular district. The lack of consistency on the part of the Government at this juncture admirably displays the moderate and political character of its ecclesiastical policy. It proposed to provoke no general opposition even to secure what it considered an ideal religious community. Much was winked at, much countenanced; and any efforts of repression were to be conducted gradually and carefully. In so far as possible, it desired the ecclesiastical courts to undertake the disagreeable

[1] Strype, *Parker*, I, 317.   [2] *Ibid.*, I, 423.
[3] *Ibid.*, I, 424.   [4] *Ibid.*, I, 424–425.   [5] *Ibid.*, I, 375.
[6] Parker had, somewhat earlier, attempted with no success to make a test case of Paul's Cross.

task without the public approval of the Government. The ecclesiastical courts, on the other hand, insisted that the Government should share in the odium attached to any effort to attain uniformity. It would appear that those in authority had come to a realization of the dangers attached to any programme of repression and that they were measuring their actions before a powerful body of public opinion which was opposed to any policy which savoured of religious persecution. Ideal spiritual considerations, as Parker indicated, were sacrificed to the more immediate demands of policy. The divisions within the Council, as within the nation, were already becoming an effective check upon bigotry and severity. The Government from its very constitution was impelled towards a policy of moderation and politic compromises. The Queen would do no more than promise the unhappy Archbishop the support of part of the Privy Council to whatever actions he might undertake on his own account.

Parker, failing to secure legal sanction for his *Book of Articles*, issued it in more moderate guise as the *Advertisements*. The *Advertisements* were issued only for his own province and bore only an implied legality. The preface indicated that they had been formulated by the "strait" command of the Queen so that "some orders might be taken whereby all diversities and varieties among them of the clergy and the people . . . might be reformed."[1] It is interesting to notice that Parker and his colleagues considered it necessary to disclaim any divine sanction for their orders and that any intention of binding conscience was disavowed; "These orders and rules ensuing have been thoughte meete and convenient to be used and folowed; nor yet prescribinge these rules as laws equivalent with the eternall worde of God, or of necessity to bynde the consciences of her subjectes in the nature of them considered in themselves, or as they should adde any efficacye or more holynes to the vertue of publique prayer, and to the sacraments. . . ."[2] They should be considered only as "temporall orders meere ecclesiasticall, without any vayne superstition,

---

[1] Prothero, *Select Statutes*, 192.
[2] Cardwell, E., *Documentary Annals of the . . . Church of England*, I, 323–324.

and as rules in some parte of discipline concerning decency, distinction, and order for the time."[1]

The mundane and cautious policy of the Queen was well displayed by her attitude towards Parker in consequence of the friction which preceded the publication of the *Advertisements*. Parker had spoken his mind on several occasions on the subject of Elizabeth's desertion of the cause which she had inaugurated. The Queen found it necessary, in her public capacity as it were, to rebuke Parker publicly for his indiscretion.[2] On the following day, so Parker wrote to Lady Bacon, she took occasion privately to express a very different sentiment towards him and his policy.[3] A better illustration could scarcely be found to illuminate the character of the Queen and to demonstrate that she was employing her power in the Church primarily for political ends. Elizabeth was wholly willing to tack the sails of ecclesiastical policy in order to gain momentum for her political designs.[4]

---

[1] Cardwell, E., *Documentary Annals of the . . . Church of England*, I, 323–324.

[2] Strype, *Parker*, I, 514.

[3] Parker wrote to Lady Bacon: "I will not be abashed to say to my prince that I think in conscience, in answering to my charging. As this other day I was well chidden at my Prince's hand; but with one ear I heard her hard words, and with the other, and in my conscience and heart, I heard God. And yet her Highness being never so much incensed to be offended with me, the next day coming to Lambeth bridge into the fields, and I according to my duty meeting her on the bridge, she gave me her very good looks, and spake secretly in mine ear, that she must needs continue my authority before the people, to the credit of my service." (Strype, *Parker*, I, 514.)

[4] This fact, and the generally tolerant intentions of the Queen, are displayed by a conversation which the Spanish ambassador, De Silva, reported to his master as having had with Elizabeth. De Silva accompanied the Queen on her progress through Norfolk in 1568, and was impressed by the joy with which she was acclaimed by an aged and popular priest. The ambassador remarked that he was very glad that the priest "should show so openly the goodwill and affection with which the Catholics had always served their sovereigns, and that she might be sure their fidelity was advantageous to her, in order to check the disobedient people in the country." De Silva continued that he had on several occasions advised the Queen "not to allow them to be molested or maltreated." The Queen in reply declared that she had followed his advice and would continue to do so. One of the things she had "prayed to God for when she came to the throne was that He would give her grace to govern with clemency, and without bloodshed, keeping her hands stainless." (De Silva to the King, July 10, 1568. *Span. pap., Eliz.*, II, 37.)

3. THE FIRST TEST OF THE POLICY OF MODERATION: THE ROMAN CATHOLIC PROBLEM, 1569–1576

The Government was obliged by 1570 to meet the first serious test of the strength of its religious policy because of the refusal of many Catholics to accept the settlement of religion, and in consequence of the decision of the Papacy actively to assist the Jesuit programme for the conversion of England. We shall be concerned later with the connection of the Catholic problem and the development of toleration,[1] but it will be necessary at this point briefly to trace the attitude of the Government towards what had become by 1570 a problem of major importance.

The arrival of Mary in England in 1568 and the immediate focusing of Catholic intrigue about her, the serious blunder of the papal Bull of excommunication, and the Rebellion in the North forcibly impressed the Government with the necessity of tightening the bonds of conformity.

During the first decade of the reign the great majority of English Catholics had satisfied the Government of their political loyalty and had found themselves able to conform occasionally without damage to their conscience.[2] Many of them had been able to hear mass in country houses, or in the chapels of ambassadors from Catholic Powers, and, on the whole, the authorities had carefully refrained from any general inquisition into the consciences of the Catholic subjects.[3] During this period the average Catholic appears to have attended divine service at the established churches often enough to satisfy the local authorities, while grasping such opportunities as presented themselves for the celebrating of mass privately.[4]

[1] Chapter VI.
[2] Simpson, R., *Edmund Campion*, 18–19; Poynter, J. W., *Reformation, Catholicism and Freedom*, 102–103.   [3] *Hatfield MSS.*, II, 222.
[4] Thus 13 Eliz., c. 2 (Act against the bringing in of Bulls), asserted that one effect of the papal Bull of excommunication had been to induce Papists to secure absolution from Roman Catholic priests and to withdraw and absent themselves from divine services. The Church, as late as 1571, was not seriously averse to the practice of occasional conformity. In that year the Bishop of Quadra excused the English Catholics from attending the required services on the grounds that the Book of Common Prayer contained no false doctrines, and that it was consistent with the Bible.

Coke, at the trial of Garnet in 1605, perhaps overstated the religious peace of the first twelve years of the reign, but his comments were largely true. He declared that "before the Bull of the Impius Pius Quintus, in the eleventh year of the Queen, wherein her majesty was excommunicated and deposed, and all they accursed who should yield any obedience to her . . . there were no recusants in England, all came to the church (however popishly inclined, or persuaded in most points) to the same divine service as we now use; but thereupon presently they refused to assemble in our churches, or join with us for publick service, not for conscience or any thing there done, against which they might justly except out of the Word of God, but because the Pope had excommunicated and deposed her majesty, and cursed those who should obey her."[1]

Two years later, while instructing the grand jury at the Norwich assizes, Coke argued that, though the Elizabethan settlement had completely altered the basis of religion, "the estate of Romaine Catholiques in England" was for a decade "tollerable, though some were committed in the beginning of her coming to the crowne. . . ."[2] Even those men were imprisoned, he held, solely because their precedent actions had cast justifiable doubt upon the sincerity of their allegiance. "But as well those so restrayned, as generally all the papists in this kingdome, not any of them did refuse to come to our church, and yield their formall obedience to the Lawes Established."[3] It was not until 1569, he said, that the fact or the term of recusancy made its appearance in England. The Queen was compelled by the endless plots and efforts of the Jesuits to pass legislation which was calculated effectively to control her rebellious subjects and to prevent the successful issue of the papal designs on her kingdom.[4]

Though the evidence of Coke must be discounted, there can be no doubt that a large measure of toleration of Roman Catholicism obtained during the early years of the reign. The

---

[1] Garnet, during the trial, admitted that, "I know divers myself who before that Bull refused to go to church all the time of Queen Elizabeth, though perhaps most Catholics did indeed go to church before." (*State Trials*, II, 222.)   [2] *The Lord Coke, his speech and Charge*, 12.
[3] *Ibid.*, 13.   [4] *Ibid.*, 15.

Church of England did not pursue the policy of a persecuting church and the English Catholics long believed that the Queen was open to conviction.[1] The moderate and secular policy which the Queen had adopted towards religion had borne rich fruit.[2] None but the most bigoted Roman Catholic could allege that a systematic programme of repression preceded the offensive policy of the Counter-Reformation. Thus the Catholic author of *Leycesters Commonwealth* introduced a "certaine lady of the Court" to say, "I doe well remember the first douzen yeares of her highnesse raigne, how happy, pleasant, and quiet they were, with all manner of comfort and consolation. There was no mention then of factions in religion, neither was any man much noted or rejected for that cause; so otherwise his conversation were civill and courteous. No suspition of treason, no talke of bloudshed, no complaint of troubles, miseries or vexations. All was peace, all was love, all was joy, all was delight."[3]

Had the English Catholics been left to themselves it is possible that the practice of occasional conformity would have continued to satisfy the requirements of the State and that Catholic repression might have been avoided.[4] We may say with certainty that every action and pronouncement of the Government was a pledge to that policy. When contemporary thought on the subject of religious uniformity is borne in mind, it is amazing to see how little real persecution of religion occurred during

[1] Thus as late as 1565–1566 we find Richard Shacklock inviting her "to come out of the cockering boat of schismatical noisomeness into the steadfast ark of Noah."

[2] "Untill the tenth of her reign her times were calm and serene, though sometimes a little overcast, as the most glorious Sun-risings are subject to shadowings and droppings-in; for the clouds of Spain and the vapours of the Holy League, began then to disperse and threaten her serenity; . . ." (Naunton, R., *Fragmenta Regalia*, 29–30.)

[3] *Leycesters Commonwealth* (Burgoyne, F. J., ed.), 218–219.

[4] In the diocese of Carlisle there was no evidence of recusancy until the Jesuits began their offensive programme. None of the old priests in the diocese had anything to do with the new religio-political policy. "It was a new and alien institution, half religious and half political, glowing with enthusiasm and tainted with treason, bringing diastrous consequences to those who came under its spell." (Wilson, J., in *V.C.H.*, Cumberland, II, 82.) In Dorset no conviction had been pressed against a recusant before the year 1582. (*V.C.H.*, Dorset, II, 30.)

the first ten years of the reign. The legal fine of twelve pence a Sunday for absence from authorized services was not systematically collected.[1] The anti-Catholic laws, it is true, were severe, but they were administered with almost non-enforceable laxity.[2] No Catholic was executed during a period of eleven years and even when the policy of the State became more rigorous punishment was held to be purely for political ends.[3] The laws of the realm were regarded as a potential weapon against the

[1] Cecil wrote in 1581, while urging the execution of the statutes of that year against recusants: "The causes that moved the renewing of this law was for that it was seen that the pain being no greater than xii pence, no officer did seek to charge an offender therewith, so that numbers of evil disposed persons increased herein to offend with impunity." (Quoted in Read, *Walsingham*, II, 273.)

[2] During this period the chief disabilities of the Catholics were: No Catholic could hold any office or employment under the Crown, or any ecclesiastical preferment in England, or take a university degree; because of the oath renouncing the authority of the Pope, and acknowledging the supremacy of the Queen, which was exacted in such cases. (1 Eliz., cs. 1, 2.) In addition, no Catholic could be present at mass, since the Prayer Book was ordered at all divine services. (1 Eliz., c. 2, sect. 14.) Further, no Catholic could absent himself from the appointed services of the Established Church under 1 Eliz., c. 2, sect. 14. It was, finally, illegal for a Catholic to speak, write, or circulate any arguments in favour of the ecclesiastical contentions of his Church, or to derogate the royal supremacy or the Prayer Book. The penalties legally operative upon the infraction of these laws ranged from one shilling for absence from church on Sunday or on a holy day to death under conviction of treason upon repeated convictions for maintaining the claims of the Pope. These laws remained in force throughout the period of this essay, and constituted the basis for the Government's eventual repression of Roman Catholics. The statutes were not formally abolished until 1829. The Act 5 Eliz., c. 1, extended the operation of the Oath of Supremacy to a greater number of officials than had been affected by cs. 1, 2, of 1 Eliz., including schoolmasters, lawyers, and members of the House of Commons. The refusal of the oath for the first time entailed the punishment of outlawry and confiscation, as did the advancement of the claims of the Pope by writing or speech. The penalty of high treason ensued in the event of a second conviction. The troubles of the period 1568–1570 resulted in the passing of four new treason laws (13 Eliz., cs. 1, 2; 14 Eliz., cs. 1, 2) against the supporters of Mary and persons bringing in papal bulls. The remaining anti-Catholic acts of the reign will be considered in later pages.

[3] As King James said, "The trewth is, according to mine owne knowledge, the late Queen of famous memory neuer punished any papist for religion." Eldon in a speech in the Lords (1810) commented, "The enactments against the Catholics were meant to guard, not against the abstract opinions of their religion, but against the political dangers of a faith which acknowledged a foreign supremacy." (Twiss, H., *Life of Eldon*, II, 124.)

Catholics in case their religious activity should in the future come into conflict with what was considered to be the best interests of the State. The Marian clergy had, for the most part, conformed and those who could not in conscience accept the oath were treated with fine moderation.[1] Elizabeth and her ministry had established and maintained with tolerable uniformity a policy of leniency towards English Catholics.[2] The expressed policy of the Government should have made it clear to Roman Catholics that this moderation would continue to prevail until religious nonconformity showed indications of passing into political disobedience.

Only when the Government became convinced that the Roman Church had adopted a militant programme against the Crown as inimical to the reconversion of the realm; only when this programme was seen to include the active support of all English Catholics who could be persuaded to support seditious designs which were clothed in religious terms; and only when England found herself alone and in apparent danger of losing her very identity, were the bonds of repression drawn tight. The purpose of this stringency, if we may trust the unanimous evidence of those who wrote and spoke for the Government, was to choke the rising head of treason.[3] But it unfortunately happened that in the effort to destroy treason the finest sentiments of conscience and faith were sometimes crushed under the weight of an inclusive law. A nation which, correctly or incorrectly, conceives itself to be in danger will be neither meticulous in the choice

[1] Gee holds that not more than 2½ per cent. of the clergy were deprived as a result of the transition in religion. (Gee, H., *The Elizabethan Clergy*, 237 ff.) Pollen, who represents the other extreme, places the number of deprivations at six hundred, or about 8 per cent. of the eight thousand clergymen. (Pollen, J. H., *English Catholics in the Reign of Elizabeth*, 40.) The laity were scarcely disturbed during the first decade of the reign. (The *Cal. Dom. Add.* (1547–1565) lists only sixteen recusants as in prison in 1561, xi. 45.) [2] Klein, *Intolerance in the Reign of Elizabeth*, 35. [3] Without doubt the Elizabethan Government was materially assisted in meeting the Catholic problem by a deep-seated fear of internal disorder which had been present in the English consciousness since the Wars of the Roses. This fact assists, as well, in explaining why the nation cheerfully and enthusiastically subordinated religious as well as constitutional considerations in order to enable the Government the more capably to meet its external and internal foes.

of its weapons nor prudent in their exercise. This psychology was admirably illustrated in the speech of the Lord Keeper in the Star Chamber in 1567 when he professed his aversion to "extreme and bloody laws." It may be argued, he said, that a rigorous execution of the penal laws will make them bloody, "and for extreeme and bloody laws I have neuer liked them, but when the execution thereof . . . by touching half a dosen offendors may sufficiently warn half a hundred, I thinke these laws nor the execution thereof may justly be call'd extreme or bloody."[1] The situation with regard to the proper enforcement of the law was likened to the difference between whipping and hanging; "Indeed though whipping may be thought extreme, yett by whipping a man may escape hanging . . . and better it were for a man to be twice whipped then ones hanged."[2]

The Catholic Church began to exert militant efforts for the reconversion of England shortly after the accession of the stubborn and drastic Pius V to the papal throne in 1566. The new Pope appears to have been persuaded by the Consistory that an offensive policy against the Queen would compel her to follow the example of King John.[3] Pius granted authority to Sanders and Harding to reconcile those English Catholics who had placed themselves in a position of schism by the practice of occasional conformity. By this step Rome brought to an issue a matter which the English Government and the majority of its Catholic subjects would have preferred undefined. In 1567 a formal Bull of absolution further defined the papal policy. Cecil was gravely alarmed as early as January 1568 when he notified the ecclesiastical commissioners that an effort was being made to "withdraw men away from allegiance and conformity," and ordered a strict watch to be maintained on the actions of all ministers.[4] In May of the same year the situation was rendered acute by the arrival of Mary who at once became the pivot around which the Catholic activity revolved.

In the Catholic and conservative northern counties resistance to the ecclesiastical laws spread rapidly and was further stimulated by the arrival in early 1569 of Dr. Morton with a papal

---

[1] *S.P. Dom., Eliz.*, xliv, 52 (November 28, 1567).   [2] *Ibid.*, xliv, 52.
[3] Pollard, *Political History of England*, 369.   [4] Frere, *English Church*, 141.

commission and 12,000 crowns to be employed in fostering resistance, if not rebellion. The ensuing Rebellion in the North and the stupendous papal blunder of the Bull *Regnans in Excelsis* brought to an end the praiseworthy efforts of the Government to secure by a broad and inclusive religious policy the formal adherence of the Catholics to the religious settlement. The rash action of Pius V, in effect, compelled Catholic Englishmen to choose between loyalty to the Government and loyalty to their spiritual head.[1] No people have ever faced a more difficult intellectual choice. The papacy had opened a question which the superior policy of the Queen and her ministers had carefully avoided. The Catholic policy of the Government during the first decade of the reign had perhaps not been very honest, as it had consisted essentially in restraint from the enforcement of the laws against Catholics in return for a perfunctory recognition by them of the Settlement without any impingement upon their spiritual beliefs, but it had been adequate for the securance of a large measure of toleration.

The papacy, on the other hand, by bringing the question of spiritual and civil obedience to a precise definition had made it virtually impossible for an English Catholic to be at once a loyal subject and a devout son of the Church.[2] The view

[1] The Bull of Excommunication declared the Queen's subjects "absolved from the oath of allegiance, and every other thing due unto her whatsoever; and those which from henceforth obey her are innodated with the anathema . . ." (Wilkins, *Concilia*, IV, 260.) Elizabeth was declared to have overthrown the true faith and to have set up an heretical establishment, and was therefore declared excommunicated and "deprived of her pretended title to the kingdome . . . and of all dominions, dignity, and privilege whatsoever, . . ." Her subjects were commanded and interdicted "all and every the noblemen, subjects, people and others aforesaid, that they presume not to obey her, or her monitions, mandates, and laws; and those which do the contrary we do innodate with the like sentence of anathema." (Wilkins, *Concilia*, IV, 260–261.)

The Bull was a political and diplomatic blunder of the most serious sort, as the King of Spain realized (Innes, A. D., *England Under the Tudors*, 415.)

[2] This view is well illustrated by an incident which is reputed to have occurred at the execution of Campion. "Do you renounce the pope?" asked Knollys of Campion. "I am a Catholic," he replied. Whereupon a bystander cried out, "In your catholicism all treason is contained." (Froude, J. A., *History of England*, XI, 357.) Vide also Stratford-Wingfield's remarks in this connection, *British Civilization*, I, 429, and Moreton, H. A., *La Réforme Anglicane*, 256.

118

became a political commonplace that Roman Catholicism and treason had become synonymous terms.[1] The papacy had demanded the complete subordination of political loyalty to religious zeal. Such a view ignored the fact that Englishmen of this period were almost hysterically loyal to the Crown and that the papal policy must inevitably come into conflict with the profoundest ties of national life. The papal programme further failed to consider that the Queen was well armed for just such an emergency and that there was in existence in England the machinery and the power adequate for the extinction of a dangerous minority. It is to the eternal credit of the Elizabethan Government that this machinery was never set into more than partial operation and that no campaign of annihilation was undertaken. The dramatic incidents of the period were so coloured by subtle propaganda that the Counter-Reformation programme of Rome was made to appear as a direct assault upon the identity and very life of the English State. The Government was afforded unexcelled opportunities for calling forth national enthusiasm against foreign usurpation and Elizabeth and her ministers forged every possible weapon in the flames of sedition.

The crisis served to augment the prestige and power of the Crown. Cecil was resolved firmly to punish all evidences of civil disloyalty and to dissociate, in so far as possible, the disloyalty of every individual from his religious convictions. The Government had taken the position that it intended to punish civil crimes on a purely civil basis, and a long step had been taken toward the assumption that the religious convictions of the subject are of no particular concern to the Government.[2]

[1] Innumerable examples could be drawn from the literature of the time. An especially interesting statement of the English case against Catholicism is to be found in Hastings, Sir F., *A Watchword to all Religious, and true-hearted Englishmen*, especially p. 79 ff. Hastings held that the papal excommunication was the root of Catholic sedition, ". . . from this Bull bellowing out these monstrous sounds all the troubles, rebellions, and treasons plotted against her Maiestie haue proceeded." (*Ibid.*, 27.)
[2] A paper of 1565 presents an extraordinarily cool and Erastian view of the Catholic problem. It was no zealot who suggested that recusants should be fined, since this punishment would "procure to the queen's majesty suche present proffit, without anye her charge, and restore her to suche perfait

There is much truth in the pungent analysis which Fuller made of the situation; "Indeed, hitherto the English papists slept in a whole skin, and so might have continued, had they not wilfully torn it themselves; for the late rebellion in the North, and the pope thundering out his excommunication against the Queen, with many scandalous and pernicious pamphlets daily dispersed, made her majesty about this time first to frown on papists, then to chide, then to strike them with penalties, and last to draw life blood from them by the severity of her laws...."[1]

Cecil was careful to explain in connection with the policy which the Government had found itself obliged to adopt, that "there shall be no colour or occasion gyven to shed the blood of any of her majestys subjects that shall only profess devotion in their religion without bending their labours maliciously to disturb the (common) quiet of the realm, and therewith to cause sedition and rebellion to occupy the place of peace against it...."[2] Hard upon this pronouncement came the Ridolfi plot, an attempt by a Catholic faction to depose Elizabeth in favour of their co-religionist, Mary Stuart.[3] Elizabeth met these overt actions with a more rigid execution of the laws which she had in hand. In general, there was no substantial change in the character of the penal laws before 1581.

The rebellion of 1570 and the policy of repression which the Government had undertaken against the political aspects of Catholicism called forth an extended statement from the Government of its position with regard to the general question

knowledge, howe, when, and where, to punishe all that from tyme to tyme, will wilfullye offende, as that it will redounde to suche her continuall greate gayne, as none of her ancestors of this three hundred years had ever more, or the like." (*S.P. Dom. Eliz.*, xxxviii, 41.) The man who wrote this must have had *The Prince* upon the shelves of his library.

Aylmer expressed a similar view in 1577 when he suggested to Walsingham that stiff fines "will weaken the enemy, and touch him much nearer, than any paine heretofore inflicted hath done." (*S.P. Dom.*, *Eliz.*, cxiv, 22 (June 21, 1577).)

As the Puritan pamphleteers pointed out with great detail, however, Aylmer had an uncommon appreciation of the value of money. See especially, *Oh Read Ouer D. Iohn Bridges*, 8, 9, 36, 21.

[1] Fuller, T., *Church History of Britain*, IV, 371–372.
[2] *S.P. Dom.*, *Eliz.*, lxxiii, 49 (August (?) 1570).
[3] *Ibid.*, lix, 10, 11–12, 19.

of freedom of conscience and the requirements of the State with regard to the loyalty of its subjects.

In the *Declaration of the Queen's Proceedings* in Church and State Elizabeth endeavoured to set forth the principles which had dominated her policy in civil and religious matters.[1] She invited comparison between her Government and that of her predecessors and denied that any breach had been made with the past. The keynote of the document is the elaborate attempt to prove that there had been no persecution of conscience.[2] She appealed to all men to choose between the Government which she had given to England during the twelve years of her reign and the platform of the men who were sowing rebellion and dissolution of laws in the North.[3]

She attributed the rebellion to a variety of causes; ". . . In some part there wanted not external incitements and provocations to animate and stir our people to withdraw their natural duties from us and our laws. . . ."[4] But these factors could not have led to rebellion had there been not deliberate provocation by "malicious persons" who "first inveigled some few of our nobility . . . with a false fear of our indignation towards them . . . and next . . . abused another sort and greater number with false persuasions of some general severity, intended by us and our ministers against them, only in respect of opinions in religion, when no[5] such thing did appear, or was in any wise by us meant or thought of. . . ."[6]

The Queen proposed to outline the past policy of the

---

[1] The original draft of the treatise is among the Hatfield manuscripts (1450). E. W. Collins has ably edited the document, and the page references are to his edition. A draft with certain revisions and alterations is to be found in the Records Office (*S.P. Dom., Eliz.*, lxvi, 54), and the more important of those changes will be indicated in the discussion of the document. (February (?) 1570.)

[2] The document is to be compared with Burleigh's order in council of June 1570. (*S.P. Dom., Eliz.*, lxxi, 16 (17).) Cf. *post*, 127–128.

[3] The paper was evidently written sometime after the first rebellion had been suppressed and before the uprising of Leonard Dacre; i.e. *c.* January 1570. The latter rebellion probably caused the suspension of the publication of the paper, and there is no indication that it was ever published. Certainly, however, the Government spent considerable time upon the document, and it may be regarded as official.   [4] *Queen's Proceedings*, 36.

[5] *Ibid.* Elizabeth adds, "Token of any."   [6] *Ibid.*, 36–37.

Government in order to expose the falsehoods that the rebels had spread abroad and to indicate "what course we intend, by God's grace to hold towards all persons, except by contrary behaviour and contempt of any of our subjects, we shall be induced to make alteration therein."[1]

With reference to civil policy, she stressed the clemency of her rule and the absence of compulsion in her Government. None the less she had repressed crime and had given England peace and quietness. She had endeavoured to avoid the pains and costs of wars abroad, and had refrained from unusual taxes and impositions.[2] She pointed with justifiable pride to the contrast with the England of her predecessors and to the turbulent state of affairs on the Continent.

She asserted that it had been her intention, in religious affairs, "to cause" her people "to live in the fear and service of God, and in the profession of the Christian[3] religion." She recognized that this portion of her policy had been subject to the greatest criticism and "because in some things the ecclesiastical external policy of our realm by laws differeth from some other countries" certain foreign powers have attempted to withdraw her subjects from their natural obedience.[4] The Queen pointed out that the power appertaining to the Crown in matters of religion was established by law and represented an ancient prerogative. Her definition of that power did not differ materially from that of the formal statement found in the Injunctions[5]: for it is not to be understood "that thereby we do either challenge or take to us . . . any superiority to ourselves[6] to define decide or determine any article or point of the Christian faith and religion, or to change any ancient[7] ceremony of the church . . . or[8] the use of any function[9] belonging to any ecclesiastical person[10] being a minister of the Word and[11] sacraments in the Church. But that authority

---

[1] *Queen's Proceedings*, 38.   [2] *Ibid.*, 39.
[3] *Ibid.* Elizabeth adds, "faith and."
[4] *Queen's Proceedings*, 41.   [5] Cf. *ante*, 91–93.
[6] Elizabeth's additions in this important portion of the documents are, of course, of especial interest. For 'ourselves' read 'ourself.'
[7] Add, 'rite or.'   [8] Substitute, 'that we do challenge or use.'
[9] Add, 'or office.'   [10] Add, 'of what degree soever.'   [11] 'Or.'

which is (yielded to us and)[1] our crown (consisteth in this)[2]; that . . . we are . . . bound (to direct)[3] all estates, being subject to us, to live in the faith and the obedience[4] of Christian religion, and to see the laws of God and man which are ordained to that end be duly observed, and the offenders against the same (duly)[5] punished, and consequently to provide, that the church may be governed and taught by archbishops, bishops,[6] and[7] ministers (according to)[8] the ecclesiastical ancient policy of the realm, whom we do assist with our sovereign power . . ."[9] This power in the Church she regarded as essentially one of "care of souls" and only by the exercise of this prerogative is the Christian ruler to be distinguished from the pagan prince.

She assured her Catholic subjects that the Government had no intention that any of its subjects should be molested either by "examination or inquisition in any matter, either of[10] faith, as long as they shall profess the Christian faith,[11] not gainsaying the authority of the holy Scriptures (and of)[12] the articles of our faith contained in the creeds (Apostolic and Catholic). . . ."[13] The Government demanded of its subjects only their adherence to the general framework of dogma which both Protestants and Catholics regarded as infallibly true. This attempt of Burleigh and his mistress to define the body of doctrine which must be believed as a minimum in order to assure immunity from prosecution for heresy is a noteworthy advance towards tolera-

[1] Substitute, 'annexed to.'   [2] Substitute, 'we take to be.'
[3] Substitute, 'in duty to God to provide that.'
[4] Add, 'and observation.'   [5] Substitute, 'justly.'   [6] Add, 'pastors.'
[7] Add, 'such other ecclesiastical.'   [8] Substitute, 'and curates as by.'
[5] *Queen's Proceedings*, 42–43.   [10] Add, 'their.'
[11] Add, 'in.'   [12] Substitute, 'nor denying.'
[13] Substitute 'received and used in the Church.' In writing to Walsingham with regard to the religious obstacles to the marriage negotiations of 1571, Elizabeth expressed the same view: ". . . Yet mean we not to prescribe to him, or any person, that they should at our motion, or in respect of us, change their religion in matters of faith; neither doth the usage of the divine service of England properly compel any man to alter his opinion in the great matters now in controversy in the Church; . . ." (Digges, D., *The Compleat Ambassador*, 100.) The Government repeatedly insisted that it had no desire or intention to compel faith. As we have had occasion to point out, the attainment of this policy was an achievement of great importance in the development of religious toleration: it was, in fact, a necessary stage in that development.

tion. It would appear that only atheists and Unitarians would be excluded from this broad view of Christianity. The attempt to lay aside the crystallized mass of dogma and reduce Christianity to its simplest elements, in this case no doubt unconsciously undertaken, was to prove one of the most fruitful sources of toleration.[1]

[1] We will note in detail the development of this tendency, especially in the case of Acontius, in England in later pages. Considerable efforts were made in this direction on the Continent during the course of the century. In general it is to be noted in connection either with mysticism or Unitarianism: strange bedfellows at first glance. Hans Denck, the early Anabaptist, in whom we find a noble strain of spiritual mysticism, appealed to all Christians to cease bickering over the non-essentials of religion and to unite as brothers on the common principles of their religion. All externals are for the sake of love, and not love for their sake. (Denck, *Vom Gesitz Gottes*, 33, in Jones, R. M., *Spiritual Reformers*, 28.) Denck weakened the claims both of ecclesiastical and of Scriptural power (*Ibid.*, 21) to the point of extinction. Somewhat later Sebastian Franck held that "Nobody is master of my faith, and I desire to be the master of the faith of no one. I love any man whom I can help and I call him brother whether he be Jew or Samaritan. . . . I cannot belong to any separate sect" . . . "but I hold as my brother, my neighbour, my flesh and blood, all men who belong to Christ among all sects, faiths, and peoples scattered over the whole world . . ." (Franck *Apologia to Das Verbütschierte Buch*, 5–8, in Jones, R. M., *Sp. Reformers*, 52). The mystics were, however, highly individualized Christians outside the main currents of Protestant thought.

More important was the work of Socinus and the early Unitarians, which seems to have influenced both Castellion and Acontius. Faustus Socinus made his great contribution to the theory of toleration in his reduction of the matters of faith essential to salvation to a few broad and easily comprehensible principles of the New Testament upon which all men could agree. (Harnack, *History of Dogma*, VII, 166. See also the *Catechism of Rakau* (1609) and the *First Unitarian Confession of* 1574.) Castellion came near to saying that the belief in one God and in Christ His Son was sufficient to salvation. (*Traité des Hérétiques*, 29, 66.) Coornhert, who was profoundly influenced by Castellion, held that true religion was a matter of the spirit and is attained quite independently of creed and dogma. Religion of the heart can never be attained "through force, tradition, or hearsay." (Coornhert, *Wercken*, III, 413–427; I, i ff.). All creeds and sacramental systems, he held, are but partially true, and are only imperfect expressions of eternal verities. They have no direct connection with the attainment of salvation, and should be regarded merely as means of direction. The Church has been torn with doctrinal strife all too long. When men come to ascribe to them only a symbolic value, as Christ taught, they will be able to abandon their intolerant strife and unite in the Gospel of love which Christ taught. (*Ibid.*, III, 413 ff.) He would say that dogmatic speculation is precisely what the term implies, and that it transcends our knowledge and should therefore be ignored. It is especially reprehensible to attempt to enforce a system of speculation

The Government likewise pledged that no subject should be persecuted for "matter of ceremonies," or any other external matters appertaining to the Christian religion, "as long as they shall in their outward conversation show themselves quiet and conformable, and not manifestly repugnant and obstinate to the laws (of the realm),[1] which are established (for frequentation of divine service in the)[2] ordinary churches, (in like manner as all other laws are whereunto subjects are of duty and by allegiance bound)."[3]

If this outline of church policy should be challenged by any "potentate in Christendom," the Queen expressed her willingness to defend it in any general council of the Christian nations and to correct it if it does not "satisfy the university of the good and faithful." The Queen argued that her merciful and mild Government in religious affairs had been taken as an opportunity by some men to undermine the obedience of her people, "to commit treasons or rebellions, and to adhere to external and strange power, having no interest in their persons by laws divine or human."[4] In order that the "craftiness of these seditious and pernicious persons" might not again induce rebellion, and in order to suppress the disobedience that has manifested itself as a result of a mistaken conception of her leniency, the Queen proposed to punish those who had

---

upon other people. Upon these grounds Coornhert refused to establish an additional sect and another doctrinal system. He did consent to the establishment of the Interim-Church (Compare Schwenkfeld's conception of the "Still-stand." Arnold, *Kirchen und Ketzer historien*, Th. II, Bk. xvi, cxx, A 5 ff.), but its only creed was to be the Confession of God and of Christ as sent of God. (*Wercken*, I, 554 ff.) Somewhat later (1582), in his masterful *Critique* of the Belgic confession, he bitterly assailed the rigid doctrinal orthodoxy of Calvinism. Doctrinal disputation is vain. "Those who would seek to penetrate the mysteries of God are confounded. . . . Leave to one side those useless things which are closed to all, but which fill the eyes of those who pretend to know, but who do not exhibit themselves as better." We are only required to believe that "which will lead to perfection, and that, God, the source of all excellent grace, has dispensed to all through Jesus Christ our Lord" (Coornhert, *Preface of Abridged Critique, Wercken*, Vol. III). The development by the Remonstrants of this position belongs to the history of the seventeenth century.   [1] Omit.

[2] Substitute, 'by the whole realm for resorting to their.'

[3] Substitute, 'or places of common prayers, and using there of divine services.'   [4] *Queen's Proceedings*, 45.

been "manifestly disobedient against us and our laws."[1] However, she desired to assure all other of her subjects that if they were obedient to her laws "that they shall [2] certainly and quietly have and enjoy the fruits of our former accustomed favour[3] lenity and grace in all causes requisite, without any molestation to them by any person by way of examination or inquisition of their secret[4] opinions (in)[5] their consciences, (for)[6] matters of[7] faith."[8] In conclusion, the Government admonished "all such obedient subjects to beware[9] that they be not brought in[10] doubt of this our (grant by any)[11] imagination of[12] lewd and seditious reports and tales[13] at any time hereafter, when they shall behold or hear report of the execution of justice against traitours or seditious persons or[14] manifest contemners and offenders (against)[15] our laws. . . ."[16]

This interesting document sought to dissociate the punishment of sedition and treason from the persecution of religious opinion, and it was a successful attempt to draw the very thin line that occasionally exists between the two. Spite the dangers which beset the land at the moment, the paper does not impress one as the utterance of a frightened Government seeking to justify its actions and to rally support to itself. The tone of the paper, on the contrary, is calm and objective. The most striking feature of the document, and this applies as well to the numerous utterances of similar nature, is that the Government recognized the existence of a body of opinion which required an explanation of its procedure. We may believe that no such opinion had existed to an important degree under Henry VIII, or even during the reign of Mary. The paper provides concrete evidence that a considerable number of Englishmen had become convinced that religious persecution

---

[1] *Queen's Proceedings*, 46.   [2] Add, 'freely.'   [3] Add, 'mildness.'
[4] Omit, 'secret.'   [5] Substitute, 'for.'
[6] Substitute, 'in.'   [7] Add, 'their.'
[8] Add, 'remitting that to the supreme and singular authority of almighty God, who is the only searcher of hearts.'
[9] Substitute, 'all our good and obedient subjects.'
[10] Substitute, 'into any.'
[11] Substitute, 'gracious determination and grant by the.'
[12] Add, 'any.'   [13] Add, 'to be stirred up.'   [14] Add, 'against.'
[15] Substitute, 'of.'   [16] *Queen's Proceedings*, 46.

per se was either wrong or impolitic. The Government, always sensitive to opinion, found it necessary to say that it held precisely those convictions, and that its policy towards its Roman Catholic subjects was dictated by considerations which involved the primary function of Government; the maintenance of order. Certain passages indicate that Burleigh and Elizabeth had the foreign audience in mind, but the manifesto was primarily intended for domestic consumption. The Government promised freedom of conscience under a very comprehensive formula and it implied that it would not concern itself too meticulously with illegal aberrations from the Established service so long as the exercise of religious belief found no association with political disloyalty. Under the prevailing political situation the Government could go no further.

Four months after the drafting of the document just reviewed an order in the Court of Star Chamber further exemplified the attitude of the Government towards its Catholic subjects. The statement appears to have been inspired by the petition of certain Protestants of Cirencester against the Catholics of that place.[1] The petitioners recommended to the Council "That it would please their lordships to remove and weed out the above named persons from having any authority; and through examining them, to bolt out a number of their affinity."[2]

The Government, in reply, branded as "utterly untrue" the reports which were said to be abroad that it intended a systematic inquisition and examination of men's consciences in matters of religion.[3] The Government pledged that so long as its subjects obeyed the laws of the realm, "hir matys meaning is not to haue any of them molested by any inquisition or examination of their consciences in causes of relligion. . . ."[4] The purpose

[1] Strype, *Annals*, I, 2, 371–372.
[2] The Catholics in question were apparently magistrates in Cirencester. (*Ibid.*, I, 2, 371.)
[3] "Where certen rumors are caried and spredd amongst sondry hir maties subiects, that hir maty hath caused or will hereafter cause inquisition and examination to be had of mens consciences in matters of religion. Hir maty wold haue it knowen that such reports are vtterly vntrue and grounded ether of mallice or of some feare more then there is cause." (*S.P. Dom. Eliz.*, lxxi, 16. See also the Proclamation of July 1, 1570; *Ibid.*, lxxi, 34.)
[4] *Ibid.*, lxxi, 16.

was rather to regard all men as good and faithful subjects without regard to their religious opinions so long as they did not "by their open dedes and facts declare themselues wilfully disobedient to breke hir lawes. . . ."[1]

The Queen sought to place the basis of loyalty to the State upon political grounds and denied the necessity of uniform religious opinion for the existence of a well-ordered Government. The basis of punishment was declared to be wholly civil and the State expressed its disinterest in the private religious opinions of its subjects. This is not an unimportant step on the road to religious toleration, even though the document reiterates in the strongest terms the determination of the State to enforce public conformity to the civil and the religious laws for political reasons. The right of free belief was granted; the right of the free expression of that belief was denied. For if the laws of the realm should be broken, the Government will be compelled to punish the offenders "according to their deserts; and will not forbeare to inquire of their demeanors, and of what mind and disposition they are, as by hir lawes hir maty shal find it necessary."[2] In conclusion, the proclamation strongly asserted that the Queen "meaneth not to enter into the Inquisition of any mens consciences, as long as they shall obserue hir lawes by their open dedes. Being also very loth to be provoked by the overmuch boldness and wilfulness of hir subiectes to alter hir naturall clemency into a princely severity."[3]

At about the same time a curious and enlightened proposal was sent to Burleigh by the Catholic Sir John Nevill "for the surety of the queen and state," and to bring about some toleration for Catholics.[4] Nevill suggested that a sort of international pact should be arranged, including the Pope and foreign princes, whereby the revolting northerners should be restored to their estates "with a toleration through the realm to live with safety of conscience, and have churches appointed."[5] All persons who were then in prison on religious charges should be released. One-half of the confiscated estates should be restored and the Queen of Scots should be sent home in safety. Nevill argued

---

[1] *S.P. Dom. Eliz.*, lxxi, 16.   [2] *Ibid.*   [3] *Ibid.*
[4] *Ibid. (Add.)*, xviii, 28 (1) (April 3, 1570).   [5] *Ibid.*

that the acceptance of his suggestion would serve to "save much bloodshed, and obtain peace," while the Queen would "be assured to have the said Lords and all the rest obedient subiects."[1] Though the writer had an obvious personal and political interest at stake the proposal is highly interesting as one of the first suggestions by a layman that only by a policy of toleration and freedom of worship could peace and order be maintained in England. The proposal that such a settlement might be arranged by an international pact was quite extraordinary and would suggest a keen perception of the dangers which England might incur if she were to attempt such a policy without international sanctions.

The legislation of 1571 against the recusants was the reply of the harassed Government to the disturbances which the militancy of Catholicism had inspired. After extended discussion the 'Act whereby certain offences be made treason,'[2] the 'Act against the bringing in and putting in execution of bulls and other instruments from the see of Rome,'[3] and an act confiscating the goods of fugitives abroad who bore no licence, were passed.

This body of legislation greatly increased the scope of Catholic repression.[4] The definition of treason was so enlarged as to

---

[1] S.P. Dom. Eliz. (Add.), xviii, 28 (1).   [2] 13 Eliz., c. 1.   [3] Ibid., 2.
[4] The repression from this time forward was, of course, highly rigorous when viewed by modern standards. The extent and severity of persecution was, however, quite relative to the danger in which the State conceived itself to be from the efforts of the militant Catholics at home and abroad. Even when the laws were strictly enforced a great many instances of individual relaxations of the laws may be cited. Such cases may be adduced from the Acts of the Privy Council almost at random. Thus in 1573 may be noted a "Letter to the Lord President of the North and Lord Archebisshop of York, that whereas sute had ben made unto them by the Deane of Powles for the libertie of his brother John Townley, esq., who was content to cume to churche and only refused to receve the communion, and yet nevertheles was committed prisoner there; for that pryson was sumwhat noysum and that by sum more curteous usage he wold be soner brought to conformitie, they thought good to recommend the matter unto them to be used as they shuld see cause, either to banishe him out of Lancashire, to remaine at his howse in Lincolne and there repaire to his parishe churche, or otherwise as they shuld see cause." (Acts of the P.C., viii, 170–171; December 1573.) In the following year the Privy Council protested to the Ecclesiastical Commission in the case of the detention of Standen and Bonham that though they would be "glad to assiste them in any lawfull cause against

include reconciliation with Rome, the introduction of papal bulls, and of material objects like crosses, pictures, and Agnus Dei, from Rome. Any attempt to carry a papal bull into execution was regarded as treasonable. As Prothero has well suggested, the effect of these measures was to render the quarrel irreconcilable—it was henceforth impossible for anyone to be at the same time a good Catholic and a good subject.[1] The avowed policy of their Church had rendered the very exercise of their faith a matter of grave suspicion and many Englishmen could agree with a show of reason that a choice must be made between Catholicism and the continuance of a stable Government.[2]

We are far more interested, however, in a bill which was introduced in the same Parliament, probably on April 4, 1571, 'for coming to church and receiving the communion.' The measure would have provided the Government with an instrument for readily distinguishing between its conforming and its nonconforming subjects.

The proposed measure was twice assailed by Aglionby as subversive to the rights of conscience and as extending in its application beyond the proper jurisdiction of human law.[3] The speaker argued that conscience is not discernible to the world and hence no positive human law can possibly force it. The conscience of man he declared to be "eternal, invisible, and not in the power of the greatest monarchy in the world, in any limits to be straitened, in any bounds to be contained, nor with any policy of man, if once decayed, to be again raised."[4]

such as refuse to conforme themselfes to the Uniformitie of Religion, yet can not their Lordships like that men shold be so long deteyned without having the cause examined, and therefore desire them to proceade in suche cases more spedelye hereafter, and to examine the said complainantes cause: and in case any be so sick that they cannot well there continew, to suffer them to be bailed till their cause be endid." (*Acts of P.C.*, viii, 235–236; May 1574.)

In cases of illness or threatened illness the Council showed itself willing to relax the imprisonment of recusants by releasing them on bond, or by some similar arrangement. (*Ibid.*, xi, 15, 21, 51, 162, 174; 1578–1580.) Urgent business was likewise a valid reason for granting bail. (*Ibid.*, xii, 51, 254, 264, 298; 1580–1581.)   [1] Prothero, *Select Statutes*, Intro., xlviii.
[2] This argument is well presented in *Lansdowne MSS.*, xcvii, 10.
[3] Brook, Benjamin, *The History of Religious Liberty*, I, 359.
[4] Cobbett, William, *Parliamentary History*, I, 763.

Even the Turks and the Jews, he argued, require no more than an outward observance of the law. Thus he would admit compulsory attendance at church services, but he held enforced participation in the communion to be wrongful and sinful. There is a vast difference between forcing attendance at church and compelling men to receive the sacrament.[1]

The speaker cited Cicero and Saint Paul to prove that it was wrong to take property from men in order to force them to do what they cannot do in good conscience.[2] The early Church provides no example of this kind of compulsion. The Bible exhorts men to come to the communion, but it does not command them to do so. "For us to will and command men to come, because they are wicked men, is too strong an inforcement, and without president."[3] This brave and enlightened speech from the floor of the House of Commons must be regarded as of great importance in the early literature of religious toleration and it indicates that such a position could be assumed in Parliament without especial danger of punishment. The Puritan Strickland, in reply, sought to prove by the Bible that the prophets had constrained the consciences of men, and Norton argued that the communion was the only possible device by which the Papists could be detected.[4]

[1] Cobbett, William, *Parliamentary History*, I, 763.   [2] *Ibid.*, I, 764.
[3] D'Ewes, Sir Simonds, *Journals of all the Parliaments During the Reign of . . . Elizabeth*, 177.
[4] After considerable negotiation the Bill passed the Commons, and on May 17th it was passed on its third reading in the Lords with four dissenting votes. The Queen apparently refused her assent to the measure, for no more is heard of the Bill. There appears to be no record of Elizabeth's or the Council's attitude towards the measure, and no definite explanation for her rejection of it. Such information, needless to say, would throw further and valuable light on the moderate policy of the Government. Is it not possible that Burleigh and the Queen regarded it as a serious infringement upon that sanctity of conscience which they had just enunciated as a governmental policy?
It cannot be too often reiterated that Elizabeth's chief concern was not that men worshipped truly, but that they worshipped in such a way as not to conflict with the aims of the State. A few days after the passage of the Bill by the Lords, John Baptista Castagna (the Archbishop of Rossano) characterized the religious policy of the Queen quite accurately when he wrote: "The Queen feels no great interest in any faith or any sect, but that she has no other thought than to keep herself on the throne in whatever

4. The definition of the anglican position on the question
   of dissent

a. Carleton

The Government, during the parliamentary session which we have just been considering, for the first time felt the weight of the growing Puritan opposition to the settlement of religion. The appreciation of this resistance was reflected in a long paper written by one Mr. Carleton, which was sent to Burleigh by Thomas Cecil.[1] The document is long and concerns a variety of subjects, but of particular interest was his proposal to suffer "the precise sort to inhabit Ireland." The writer realized the permanent character of the religious differences which divided England and he foresaw grave dangers to the State unless the mounting pressure of religious repression were somehow relieved.

England, he said, must carefully weigh its state, for she can scarcely defend herself since she is united in no one faith. He divided the subjects of the Crown into the Papists, atheists, and Protestants. The first two groups he declared to be dangerous to the realm, and they should be removed. But they are favoured and condoned because England is peaceful and "wee . . . dare not displease them."[2] The writer expressed the hope that disaster would not come during the lifetime of the Queen, but he looked forward to the day of sorrow that must come. In order to guard the realm against the dangers incident to a divided State, he proposed an association for the

way she can, and by means of that religion which may best serve her purpose. . . . She is coming to disrelish having so many malcontents within and without her realm solely for religion's sake; perchance also the persecutors of the Church are now satiated." (John Baptista Castagna to the Cardinal of Como, June 1571; *Roman Calendar*, II, 406.)

The same point of view was displayed by the Queen in her reply to the Puritan clamour of 1570, when she said quite bluntly: "That she did not inquire into the Sentiments of People's minds, but only required an external conformity to the Laws, and that all that came to church and observed her instructions should be deemed good subjects." (Oldmixon, J., *History of England*, 410.) Then the Queen sought to define the rather metaphysical distinction between a man's duty to God and his duty to the State.

[1] *S.P. Dom. Eliz.* (*Add.*), xxi, 121 (1572?).   [2] *Ibid.*

defence of the Gospel, Queen, and State. Essential to such a plan, however, was the utilization of the increasing numbers of the "precise sort" of Protestants who "cannot be perswaded to beare lykinge of the queene's proseedings in relygion, . . ."[1] In spite of the Queen they insist upon having their own churches, upon meeting together, and upon worshipping as they choose. He regarded their actions as a serious offence, yet they may not "be punished for the same, because they are the quene's owne bowells, her dearest subjects, the servants of God, and such as doe tread the straighte pathe of the Lord to Salvation. So that eyther the (churche?) of Englande must be framed to theire appetyte, or els they must be suffred, wth out blame, to proscede as they beginne."[2]

Carleton, in his analytical manner, pointed out three possible means "to satisfy these grieffs, and relive this people." The Puritans might be suffered to leave the realm, but this he regarded as too heavy a loss to the State. Again, they might be permitted to "dwell here as they doe, suffered to congregate in companyes together, and to have their owne churches."[3] The writer was not wholly convinced of the efficacy of religious toleration, for he dismissed this solution with the observation that "as one countrye is best governed by one kinge or quene so the same and they bothe oughte to be directed by one course of law."[4]

The writer therefore proposed that several English gentlemen should be placed in charge of an enterprise to "deliuer this realme of all the presyse ministers and greatest parte of the people that folowe them, to the nombre of 3,000 men, enter Irelond, inhabite the same, and there live under the quene's subjectyon, accordinge to the faithe of good subjects and lawes of this realme, the churche's constitution only excepted."[5]

Carleton realized that continued divergence in religious matters, when accompanied by the persistent restraint of law, must inevitably lead to serious dangers to the State. He hoped

[1] S.P. Dom. Eliz. (Add.), xxi, 121.   [2] Ibid.   [3] Ibid.   [4] Ibid.
[5] Ibid. Carleton would have had the colony planted in Ulster, which he regarded as the greatest source of danger to England, since "it borderethe uppon the Skott. . . ."

that, if the Puritan opposition could in some manner be appeased, the Catholic danger might be removed by the concerted action of an overpowering majority of opinion. The document testified to his conviction that belief and conscience could not be forced, and to the fact that thinking Englishmen of his day were prepared to concede that the settlement had settled nothing. Toleration was still too radical a departure from current politico-religious thought to be accepted as a solution for the dilemma in which the State found itself, but in the same breath Carleton admitted that toleration was the only ultimate solution. If the Puritans cannot be tolerated in England they will have to be tolerated in Ireland, repaying the motherland by providing a buffer against external dangers. The writer, like many men of his generation, still embraced the age-old theory which regarded uniformity as essential to a solidly based state. He therefore shrank from the idea of religious toleration, though he was driven to admit that the fact of diversity had made it necessary for the continuance of a peaceable order of society. One is, in this connection, reminded of the acute observation of Figgis that religious liberty arose, not because the sects believed in it, but out of their passionate determination not to be extinguished, by either political or religious persecution.[1]

A fragmentary argument is to be found among Burleigh's papers which advanced an even more tolerant view.[2] The writer sought to justify the toleration of the Roman Catholic mass on highly interesting grounds. "If the meat which was of the infidels dedicated to idols might be used and suffered of the Christian Corinthians with a safe conscience; then the mass which the papists use may be now used and suffered of the right Christians with a safe conscience."[3] The author pointed out that though Christ completely abrogated the Old Testament, Paul permitted the exercise of Jewish rites as without harm either to the Jews or to the Christians. Thus he commanded "that none should condemn the Jews, which for conscience and religion durst not eat that was forbidden by

[1] Figgis, J. N., *Political Thought in the Sixteenth Century*, in the *Camb. Mod. Hist.*, III, 768.
[2] Written about 1573. Strype, *Annals*, II, 2, 474-475.   [3] *Ibid.*, II, 2, 474.

the abolished laws of Moses."[1] With this example before us; "How then can we rightly condemn them, which for ignorance use the mass with such holiness, . . . as the papists? For as they judge it necessary for salvation, and for worshipping of God, so did the Jews judge the abolished law of Moses to be."[2] We should tolerate the superstitious use of the mass just as Paul bore with the adherence to the abrogated law of Moses.

This argument would appear to indicate that important and telling criticisms might be levelled at the theory and practice of enforced conformity from the great source of all Christian doctrines. The Protestant Reformation had enshrined the Bible with an aura of absolute and determinable truth; had created what Troeltsch aptly terms a Bibliocracy. The Protestant theory of persecution rested essentially upon the generally entertained conviction that absolute truth could be ascertained by reference to the inspired and revealed Word of God. Arguments against persecution, therefore, when based upon the Bible had in their turn a powerful effect. The absolute character of Christian dogma began to be dissipated almost as soon as the Reformation movement had reached its zenith. The ever-increasing multitude of sects, the acrimonious disputes and controversies within particular sects, and the evident impossibility of arriving at agreement by Bible-reading, preaching, and prayer served at once to engender that doubt which leads to rationalism, and that latitudinarianism which leads to an attempt to simplify creed in order to attain comprehension.

b. The Privy Council

The Privy Council, in a letter to the Dutch Church in London, which was permitted to conduct its services in a manner not in accord with the prescribed religion, virtually admitted the operation of these forces. The Council professed to find beneath the differences in externals a core of religious unity. Since the inception of Christianity men have worshipped

[1] Strype, *Annals*, II, 2, 475. [2] *Ibid.*

God in a variety of manners.[1] "And yet," they said, "one and the self-same religion" is practised, "if the prayers are don in truth to the true God, and no impiety and superstition mixt with it. In divers places and countries the same God, whose is the whole world, is believed and adored of divers nations, and in divers tongues and languages, and in divers manners, and with varieties of cloathing and ceremonies; yet is it the self-same faith, the same religion, the same Christ, and God the Father of all."[2]

Admitting the relativity of externals, the Council confessed that it regarded the customs of the Dutch Church as good and "fittest for you," nor did it propose to compel it to accept the worship of the English Church. In return the Council expressed the hope that "you in anothers commonwealth, will not be so ungratefully curious, that you will condemn those customs which wee have bin moved to establish out of the principles of true pietie and religion . . . as most proper for our people."[3]

The fact of extensive and firmly rooted differences of opinion with respect to every phase of religion had become by 1573 an inescapable actuality. In October of that year the Queen issued a proclamation "against the despisers or breakers of the orders prescribed in the book of common prayer."[4] The proclamation admitted the failure of the governmental programme to effect a comprehensive uniformity in religion. The religious settlement "is now of late of some men despised and spoken against, both by open preachings and writings, and of some bold and vain curious men, new and other rites found out and frequented," which has led to the development of sects, diversity, disputation, and schism within the realm.[5]

c. Hutton

A fortnight earlier the Dean of York had written to Burleigh with even more than his normal pessimism, in regard to the

---

[1] For "in divers churches, ever since the Christian religion had a beginning, divers waies and ceremonies have been used, som standing, som falling on their knees, others flat downe, have addressed and prayed to God." (Strype, *Annals*, II, 2, 517.)   [2] *Ibid.*, II, 2, 517–518.   [3] *Ibid.*, II, 2, 518.
[4] Cardwell, Edward, *Documentary Annals of the . . . Church of England*, I, 383.   [5] *Ibid.*, I, 384.

mounting dissension in the Church.[1] He regretted that when the unrest had begun some more definite policy had not been pursued. The discontent should either have been appeased or the programme of uniformity should never have been undertaken. For "the envious seedsman of tares, while we slept in security, hath so prevailed that now it is almost too late to seek for a remedy. At the beginning it was but a cap, a surplice, and a tippet; now, it is grown to bishops, archbishops, and cathedral churches, to the overthrow of the established order, and to the Queen's authority in causes ecclesiastical. These reformers would take the supreme authority in ecclessiatical matters from the prince, and give it unto themselves, with the grave seignory in every parish."[2]

d. The Whitgift-Cartwright Controversy

It may be argued that religious toleration in England developed principally because of the fact that these differences in belief were able to get themselves established and from the realization of intelligent men that any attempt to eradicate these distinctions would seriously endanger the stability and peace of the nation. The great controversy between Whitgift and Cartwright afforded clear proof of the existence of these differences. Their discussions likewise illuminated the attitude of the spokesman for Anglicanism and the Puritan champion on the manifold considerations which bear upon religious toleration. We shall confine ourselves as strictly as possible to those aspects of the writings of the two men which relate organically to the question of toleration, and we shall be especially interested in noting the attitude of Whitgift, as the spokesman for Anglicanism, towards this question.[3]

[1] Matthew Hutton to Burleigh, October 6, 1573. (*Hatfield MSS., H.M.C.*, II, 60.) [2] *Ibid.*
[3] A fuller discussion of the connection of Puritan thought with the question of toleration will be found in Chapter IV, Pt. A.
We are greatly indebted in the analysis of this controversy to the important study of Mr. A. F. S. Pearson, *Thomas Cartwright and Elizabethan Puritanism.* In numerous instances page references have not been regarded as necessary,—the writer's debt to Mr. Pearson is of a more general nature.

The First and Second Admonitions to Parliament had appeared by 1573 and Whitgift's *Answer* was published in 1572 as the official apology for the Established Church. Thomas Cartwright's *Replie to an Answere* joined the controversy in the following year, and Whitgift's great *Defense of the Aunswere* was published in 1574. Cartwright's *The Second Replie* (1575) and *The Rest of the Second Replie* (1577) completes the literature of the discussion.

In a sense, Whitgift was a more typical and accurate spokesman for Anglicanism than was Hooker. He dealt with the problems of his Church as a practical, hard-working ecclesiastic rather than with the objective gaze of the philosopher. He wrote to defend the Church, of which he was as early as 1573 an important member, from specific attacks by the Puritans, and not to lay down an imposing and majestic interpretation of its relation to the State and to Christendom. We may well read Hooker to appreciate the best of the Elizabethan age, while we read Whitgift to appreciate more accurately that which was typical of that age.

Whitgift saw in the Puritan protest an attempt to dissolve the fabric of the English Church by a process of indirection. He compared them both with the Anabaptists and the Catholics. Cartwright, in reply, held that the Puritans sought not the destruction of the Church of England but its reformation. He acknowledged, as freely as would Whitgift, that Church and State stood in the same relation as the twins of Hippocrates, which prospered or languished together. The improvement of the one will result in the improvement of the other.

Cartwright held that the Church of England should be reformed strictly to conform with the model of the Apostolic Church; that it should base its organization as well as its doctrine squarely upon the Bible. Its form and government were fixed by its founder who in his wisdom "desired not the slightest deviation." Whitgift was disposed, on the contrary, to regard the Church as an evolving, living body which had been designed by its founder to adapt itself to the requirements of the changing ages. Cartwright, he held, envisaged a Church set upon two rotten pillars; that the Church should have no government but that prescribed in the Apostolic age, and that nothing which had been abused by Rome should be retained in its structure.[1] The Bible, Whitgift argued, leaves much to the discretion of the Church. We are bound by no hard and fast rule. It is wise to consult the Scriptures, but we are not bound to abide by them in matters of government and form. The end of an institution, and not its origin, should govern the formulation of its policy. The Church of England will find its best and truest course in a judicious adaptation of the Apostolic government which we find described in the Bible to its own requirements and purposes.

The Anglican view of the nature of the Church, as developed by Whitgift, was considerably more tolerant, at least in its possibilities, than was the rigid literalism of Cartwright. He denied that the policy of the Church was fixed beyond the possibility of advantageous change. His vindication of rationalism in ordering the services of the Church is almost as far-reaching as that of the more famous Hooker. Following Whitgift's argument, the Church could, in the event such a change appeared to be essential to its peace and continuance, recognize the right of groups that had become factually divergent to worship as they pleased. Cartwright's view, on the other hand, postulated an absolute truth, a rigidly defined dogma, and an inflexible Church government, deviation from which would place the dissentients and those who condoned their dissent under the wrath of God.

In considering the relationship existing between Church and State, a problem of prime importance in connection with religious toleration, Cartwright declared that we owe obedience to the civil ruler, but that we should always remember that the prince is to govern by the Word of God, and that he must relinquish any part of his government which infringes upon the legitimate province of the Church.[2] He assailed the Erastian character of the Church of England when he repudiated the doctrine that the Church should be framed to meet the necessities of the State, "as if a man should fashion his house accord-

---

[1] Whitgift, *Def. of the Answer, Works*, I, 6.
[2] Cartwright, *Reply* in Whitgift's *Works*, III, 189.

ing to his hangings." "The commonwealth," in fact, "must agree with the church, and the government thereof with her government."[1] Whitgift in an acute reply pointed out that this view virtually deprived the civil ruler of all ecclesiastical power,[2] and would logically presume the subjection of the ruler and of the State to the whims of the ecclesiastical power.[3] The civil ruler, he observed, under such an arrangement would of necessity "be of some peculiar church and congregation. . . ."[4]

Cartwright declared that, though the civil magistrate is the head of the State, Christ alone is the head of the Church. The civil magistrate as a Christian is only a lay member of the Church and possesses no peculiar powers in it. The Church of Christ was formed without the assistance of any magistrate. "It is absurd to say that the ministers now, with the help of the magistrate, can lay surer foundations of the Church . . . than the Apostles could. . . ."[5] As the head of the State the ruler is a great ornament in the Church, "yet he is but a member of the same."[6] This theory of the relation of the ruler to the Church would appear to be disposed towards toleration, since it would eliminate persecution from State policy, but in reality the ruler would become little more than the agent for the execution of the will of the spiritual order.[7] The degree to which toleration would be admitted would depend upon the attitude of the Church rather than upon the policy of the State, and Cartwright later revealed that the attitude of his particular Church was highly intolerant in character.

Whitgift, on the other hand, held that though the civil ruler might not assume such properly ecclesiastical functions as

---

[1] Cartwright, *Reply*, Whitgift's *Works*, III, 189.
[2] Whitgift, *Def. of the Ans.*, *Works*, III, 189–190.   [3] *Ibid.*, III, 191.
[4] *Ibid.*; Whitgift, *Table of Dangerous Doctrines*, *Works*, III 554.
[5] Cartwright, *Reply*, Whitgift's *Works*, I, 389.   [6] *Ibid.*, I, 390; III, 198.
[7] Cartwright insisted that it was the duty of the ruler to reverence the Church and to seek to carry out the laws of God respecting religion. The ruler, like any other member of the congregation, he regarded as amenable to its discipline to the extent of excommunication. (Cartwright, *Rest of the Second Replie*, 65.) The Church must be completely independent of the State in purely religious affairs. Cartwright expressed the utmost loyalty to the Queen (cf., Whitgift, *Works*, III, 314), but regarded the further reformation of the Church as necessary (*Ibid.*, III, 324).

preaching, administering the sacraments, and the like, the view "that he hath no authority in the Church to make and execute laws for the church, and in things pertaining to the church, as discipline, ceremonies, etc.," is false by the Word of God and the testimony of learned men.[1] The ruler has a corrective and a disciplinary function to perform which is quite independent of the order or command of the Church officials. Thus the prince should impose a quiet order, preserve the peace of the Church, and plant the religion that "he in conscience is persuaded to be sincere."[2] For the magistrate is the chief governor of the Church under Christ, and he is especially charged with its welfare.[3] He therefore concluded that "it is not meet that anything touching the government of the Churches, or any public function pertaining thereunto, should be otherwise done, than he shall think convenient and profitable for the present state of it."[4] The Anglican charged Cartwright with allowing no more authority to the prince in the Church than did the Roman Catholics.[5] He pointed out that the early emperors had great authority in "making ecclesiastical orders and laws, yea, and . . . in deciding of matters of religion, even in the chief and principal points."[6] He declared the Puritan views to be conducive to schism and dissension.[7]

Whitgift thus frankly faced the fact that the Elizabethan Government controlled the Church, and endeavoured to construct a theoretical apology for this situation. The prince derived his power in the Church as an heritage from the spiritual power with which the Middle Ages had clothed his office. Whitgift regarded this power as positive in its effect, and would scarcely have admitted that the prince could employ the Church for an evil or a secular purpose. The importance of the Anglican admission, for our purpose, lies in the fact that the State was very definitely shaping ecclesiastical policy, along lines believed to be most consonant with its secular ends. The burden of enforcing a uniform worship and belief rested upon the State.

[1] Whitgift, *Answer to the Epistle*, *Works*, I, 22.   [2] *Ibid.*, I, 22–23.
[3] Whitgift, *Defence of the Answer*, *Works*, I, 393.   [4] *Ibid.*
[5] *Ibid.*, III, 297–300.   [6] *Ibid.*, III, 306.
[7] *Ibid.*, III, 318; Sermon Preached at St. Paul's (1583), *Works*, III, 592.

The State had definitely renounced any attempt to compel the latter, and contented itself with intermittent efforts to enforce the former. The State declined to do the bidding of religious bigots; persecution had descended from the high seat of a spiritual idealism which envisaged a truly universal Church to the seat of a Council table which measured action by reaction, policy by counter-policy, and ideal considerations by the requirements of necessity.

An examination of the views of the protagonists in regard to their interpretation of the Bible and their view of the Judicial Laws of the Old Testament reveals more clearly their respective positions on the question of toleration. Cartwright regarded men as bound by the general rules of the Scriptures which he proceeded with normal Calvinist certainty to expound.[1] Whitgift assailed the implicit presumption of the Cambridge divine and remarked with one of the few attempts at humour in the work that if his opponent would "hold you here" for a minute they would soon be agreed.[2] Both men, in theory, were agreed that the Bible must be given a supreme authority in the affairs of the Church. They clashed rather in their interpretations of the Word.

Cartwright discovered a fast and complete Church and discipline clearly laid down for the construction of the earthly 'ecclesia.' This Church and discipline happened to be Presbyterian in character, and he desired to impose it by logic and perhaps by force upon the realm. Whitgift was unable to find so definite a pronouncement of these matters in the Bible. The Bible, he said, contains everything essential to salvation, but it in no sense ordains a Presbyterian Church and discipline as part of the essential scheme of salvation.[3] Cartwright demanded a Church in which the leadership and will of Christ should permeate its every agency and activity. Whitgift declared that the Church was free in all matters excepting dogma.[4]

The views of the two men with regard to the interpretation of the Bible and the ideal function of the Church was displayed

[1] Cartwright, *Reply*, Whitgift's *Works*, I, 190–191; 194–195.
[2] Whitgift, *Def. of the Ans.*, *Works*, I, 195.
[3] *Ibid.*, I, 191–192; 194–195.   [4] *Ibid.*, I, 175, 222; II, 425 ff.

by their discussion of the Judicial Laws of the Old Testament. This discussion was important in displaying the extent to which the two men were disposed towards the toleration of misbelief. Cartwright held that the Scriptures were equally binding in all parts and therefore the death penalties pronounced by the Old Testament for blasphemy, heresy, adultery, and murder should still be enforced.[1] He regarded the opinion that the Judicial Law of Moses no longer bound the Christian world as tantamount to the view that the Old Testament no longer bound us at all; "for surely, if these two places agree not unto us in time of the gospel, I know none in all the Old Testament which do agree."[2] It is not given to us to add or to detract from the Word of God. The Judicial Laws are universally equitable and have never been annulled.[3] The enforcement of the command of capital punishment for infractions of these laws is part of the duty of the ruler, and the assistance of the prince in that high duty constitutes the sole excuse for the presence of the bishops in Parliament.[4] Though the Lord does not so severely revenge by bodily punishments as he did in the days of the old dispensation, no liberty has been granted to the civil power to relax its efforts in the enforcement of these laws.[5] On the contrary, the civil ruler should be even more vigilant in his activities since the Lord has so far withdrawn His hand.[6] The same severity of punishment that was employed

---

[1] Cartwright, *Reply*, Whitgift's *Works*, I, 264; *Sec. Reply*, 101.   [2] *Ibid.*

[3] Cartwright, *Second Reply*, 94. The argument was considerably amplified in the *Helpes for the Discovery of the Truth in Point of Toleration*, first printed in 1648, and attributed somewhat doubtfully to Cartwright. The writer held that Christ came not to save men from the corporal death of the judicial law, but from the death of the spirit. (*Helps for Discovery*, 4.) If Christ had released men from the Judicial Law, he would have preached the intelligence of that release. (*Ibid.*, 5.)

On the contrary, the apostle has put a sword in the hand of the magistrate, "and in the use of it maketh him a Minister and servant of the vengeance and justice of the Lord against sinne: He striketh through this opinion, which imagineth that our Saviour Christ came to hang the sword of the Lords Justice upon the pleasure and will of man." (*Ibid.*, 6.) The magistrate can no more ignore the command of the Lord, than can a sheriff ignore the command of the magistrate. (*Ibid.*, 6.)

[4] Cartwright, *Second Reply*, 102-104.

[5] Cartwright, *Helps for Discovery*, 11.   [6] *Ibid.*

against false prophets then, ought likewise to be exercised to-day.[1] "If this be extreme," Cartwright grimly declared, "I am content to be counted with the Holy Ghost."[2]

This fearless literalism definitely committed the Church and the State, which was conceived as its agent and assistant, to a policy of persecution of heresy and blasphemy for spiritual ends.[3] Whitgift was repelled by the thought and argued acutely that if we are still bound by the Mosaic Law we are likewise bound by the ceremonial and judicial precepts of the law. "I am not so Jewish," he wrote, as to think that "we are bound either to the ceremonial or the judicial law." The precepts in Deuteronomy in their relation to us, "doth not extend any further than to such things as God hath commanded or forbidden us that be Christians to do in his word."[4]

Cartwright condemned the denial of the binding character of the judicial laws against heresy and blasphemy as constituting an heresy. For such a view is tantamount to the belief "that there is a gentler and a severer God, one under the Law, and another under the Gospel." To say that God was in the time of the Old Testament, a severer punisher of sin, and that now he is not, "at so great hatred with it, but that he will have it gentlier and softlier dealt with, is even all one in effect with that which supposeth two Gods."[5] In fact, infractions of the law in the present-day should be more severely punished since our knowledge is greater.[6] In the true kingdom of Christ the false prophet will be put to death even by his own father and mother. Cartwright conceded that some of the Judicial Laws, apparently the ceremonial precepts, were given with reference to particular regions and peoples, and in such instances the prince, retaining the marrow of the laws, might alter the circumstances of their application with reference to time and place.[7] But this relativism was unimportant in his theory, for to say that "any magistrate can save the life of blasphemers, contemptuous and stubborn idolaters, murderers, adulterers,

[1] Cartwright, *Helps for Discovery*, 12.   [2] *Ibid.*, 13.
[3] Osborne, C. E., *Christian Ideas in Political History*, 141.
[4] Whitgift, *Def. of the Ans., Works*, I, 265.
[5] Cartwright, *Reply*, Whitgift's *Works*, I, 329.
[6] *Ibid.*; *Helps for Discovery*, 11–12.   [7] *Ibid.*, 1–2.

incestuous persons, and such like, which God by his judicial law hath commanded to death, I do utterly deny. . . ."[1] These laws have a constant and eternal efficacy.[2] If a man who has taken the physical life of another man is worthy of death, it is far more equitable that a man who has destroyed the spiritual life of another should suffer death.[3] In fact, the efforts of the State should be more inclined toward the punishment of spiritual crimes than civil offences.[4]

Whitgift rose to his finest height in attacking the intolerance of Cartwright. He pointed out that to apply the Puritan's system of thought would be to upset the entire legal and constitutional scheme of England.[5] He said bluntly that the Judicial Law must be left to the discretion of the magistrate who may add to or detract from it, and who may alter it as conditions may demand.[6] In a noble passage he asserted that ". . . neither was the law then cruel, neither yet the gospel is now dissolute for the greatness of forgiveness; but in both, though diversely, the loving kindness of God remaineth."[7] The Law of God is full of mercy, "because hereby the people should rather be purged of their sins than condemned." Repentance alone can cure sin, and repentance, he would seem to say, can be attained only by the operation of subjective forces within the individual soul. Following the early words of Luther, he explained that under the Gospel the prophecy of Zachary referred not to the physical destruction of the heretics: "That is to say, they shall destroy him, not with iron or brazen armour and weapons, but with the Word of God. . . ."[8] He denounced Cartwright's view as bloody.[9]

The notions of the two men on the general problems of liberty

---

[1] Cartwright, *Reply*, Whitgift's *Works*, I, 270.
[2] Cartwright, *Helps for Discovery*, 3.   [3] *Ibid.*, 13.
[4] *Ibid.*, 13–14.   [5] Whitgift, *Def. of the Ans.*, *Works*, I, 273.
[6] *Ibid.*, I, 278; *Table of Dangerous Doctrines*, *Works*, III, 552; *A Godly Sermon preached at Greenwich*, *Works*, III, 576.
[7] Whitgift, *Def. of the Ans.*, *Works*, I, 330.   [8] *Ibid.*, I, 332.
[9] Whitgift was almost prepared to say that stubborn, blasphemous persons might be considered as under the operation of the law. But he refused to make this intolerant step; "neither have you any example of such extremity committed by a true Christian towards a repentent idolator, from the nativity of Christ unto this hour. . . ." (*Works*, I, 332.)

of conscience were not so clearly developed. In reply to Cart-wright's argument that the fixing of holy days was an abridg-ment of Christian liberty, Whitgift made an important generali-zation. The magistrate, he argued, has power over all external and bodily matters. Thus he may compel a man to labour or to rest. The liberty that God has given to man, "which no man ought to take away from him, nor can if he would, is liberty of conscience, and not of worldly affairs."[1]

In indifferent matters, on the other hand, the will of a private man is subject to those who exercise a legally constituted power over him.[2] Whitgift held that the so-called indifferent matters, upon which the Church of England was so insistent, were not 'trifles,' but were "convenient and necessary for order and decency." Whoever refuses to obey the laws appointing and regulating them must be regarded as a contemner and a dis-obedient person.[3] ". . . If any man shall say that this is to bring us again in bondage of the law, and to deprive us of our liberty, I answer, no; for it is not a matter of justification but of order; and to be under a law is no taking away of Christian liberty. For the Christian liberty is not a licence to do what thou list, but to serve God in newness of mind, and that for love, not for servile fear. Of themselves therefore they be but trifles, but, being commanded by the magistrate to be used, or not to be used, they are no trifles. . . ."[4] Those men who refuse the appointed services of the Church, when so understood, encourage dissension, the breaking down of laws, and obstruct the spread of truth.[5]

Cartwright would appear to include the English Catholics as blasphemers and idolaters worthy to be punished under the meaning of Zachary.[6] He argued that any man who has fallen away from God and who seeks to draw others to his heresy is amenable to the Judicial Law. "If this be bloudie, and extreme. . . . I am contente to be so counted with the holie goste . . . and althoughe in other cases of Idolatrie, uppon repentance liffe is giuen . . . yet in this case of willing

---

[1] Whitgift, *Def. of the Ans., Works,* II, 570.   [2] *Ibid.,* II, 571.
[3] *Ibid.,* III, 488.   [4] *Ibid.*
[5] *Ibid.,* III, 489.   [6] Cartwright, *Reply,* Whitgift's *Works,* I, 333.

sliding backe, and moving others to the same, and other some cases, whiche are expressed in the lawe, as off open, and horrible blasphemie off the name of God: I denie that uppon repentance, ther oughte to followe anie pardon off death, whiche the Iudiciall law dothe require."[1] The magistrate should compel them to hear the Word preached, and if examination displays that they have not profited from the opportunity to abandon their idolatry, they should be punished by the magistrate.[2] As their "Contempt groweth, so increase the punishment, until such time as they declare manifest tokens of unrepentantness; and then, as rotten members that do not only no good nor service in the body, but also corrupt and infect others, cut them off. . . ."[3]

Whitgift appears deliberately to avoid an important issue which his opponent had so clearly set out.[4] In order to defend the concept of the national Church, he declared that even blasphemers and Papists must be counted of the Church until they are excommunicated from it. Thus Papists at heart who are willing to conform have a ready and unassailable defence.[5] He appears here in an awkward fashion to pronounce a liberal theory of comprehension. Earlier, however, he had argued that Catholics might be compelled to communicate.[6] He specifically branded Cartwright's severity in dealing with persons who are outside the Church as not of the Word of God.[7] But he failed to utilize this excellent opportunity to denounce the general implications of Cartwright's system of repression. If the future archbishop had desired to construct a genuine theory of comprehension and toleration, he would have done so at this point.

In concluding our examination of the controversy, it may be well to note Whitgift's defence of the governmental policy towards the Puritans. In reply to the charge of the *Admonition* that the Puritans were being genuinely persecuted because of

[1] Cartwright, *Second Reply*, 115–116.
[2] Hunt, J., *Religious Thought in England*, I, 55.
[3] Cartwright, *Reply*, Whitgift's *Works*, I, 386.
[4] Whitgift, *Def. of the Ans.* I, 387 ff.　　　　　　[5] *Ibid.*, I, 386–387.
[6] Hunt, *Religious Thought in England*, I, 55.
[7] Whitgift, *Def. of the Ans.*, *Works*, I, 388.

"unbrotherly and uncharitable" removal from office, he compared the Puritans to a "shrewd and ungracious wife, which, beating her husband, by her clamorous complaints maketh her neighbours believe that her husband beateth her. . . ."[1] Cartwright was classed with the men of whom Saint Paul spoke, who knew nothing as they ought to know—the contentious and vainglorious, who provoked and envied one another. He denied that the Puritans were persecuted, and held that they were not severely dealt with.[2] The Puritans have a custom, he held, of crying persecution when they are unable to secure what they desire. In fact, lack of severity was suggested as the chief cause of their 'licentious liberty.' "You are as gently entreated as may be, no kind of brotherly persuasion omitted towards you, most of you as yet keep your livings, though some one or two be displaced. You are offered all kinds of friendliness, if you could be content to conform yourselves; yea, but to be quiet and hold your peace."[3]

The Establishment, in other words, demanded at most conformity for the sake of decency and law. Whitgift came close to saying that if the Puritans would only hold their peace they would be permitted to worship about as they pleased. He, and the Government for whom he spoke, resented not so much the demands of the extremist party within the Church for freedom of belief and worship as the insistence of that group that the religious and disciplinary notions which they regarded as absolutely true should be enforced upon England. Intolerance, it was felt, could be met only with intolerance.

Whitgift charged the Puritans with unwillingness to refrain from their extreme missionary impulses. "You . . . most unchristianly and most unbrotherly, both publicly and privately, rail on those that shew this humanity towards you, slander them by all means you can, and most untruly report of them, seeking by all means their discredit."[4] The Established Church, he said, sought only to execute the laws, being bound by oath so to do. He acutely suggested that if the extremists could not in good conscience carry out the functions to which

[1] Whitgift, *Def. of the Ans., Works*, III, 320.   [2] *Ibid.*
[3] *Ibid.*   [4] *Ibid.*

they were pledged by oath and law to attend, they should resign their livings and pulpits.[1] He accused them of intellectual dishonesty in swearing by laws and in accepting benefits which they could not in conscience maintain as required. The Anglican logic was almost convincing when Whitgift declared, ". . . I think it much better, by removing you from your livings, to offend you, than, by suffering you to enjoy them, to offend the prince, the law, conscience, and God."[2] A Church, in order to exist, must have a determined practice and discipline.[3] The Church strives 'modestly and soberly' to defend the truth, and cannot justly be accused of persecution.[4] "We therefore exhort you, if there be any fear of God before your eyes, any reverence towards the prince, any desire of promoting the Gospel, any loving affection towards the Church of Christ, to submit yourselves according to your duties to godly orders, to leave off contentiousness, to join with us in preaching of the Word of God, and beating down the kingdom of Anti-Christ, that this your division procure not God's wrath to be poured upon us."[5]

A survey of the writings of Whitgift and Cartwright, from the point of view of religious toleration, leads to the conclusion that at this time Anglicanism, even when under attack, could portray itself in a far more moderate guise than Puritan extremism. Whitgift viewed the Church and the Bible with considerable rationalism. He regarded religion as a cloak which might be shaped to the form of the wearer so long as its stuff was of the genuine material. The Anglican vigorously rejected the harsh mandates of the Old Testament with respect to the punishment of heresy and blasphemy, and upon that basis alone could a logical system of religious persecution for spiritual ends be framed.[6]

---

[1] Whitgift, *Def. of the Ans.*, *Works*, III, 321.   [2] *Ibid.*, III, 321, 324.
[3] "Is it meet," he enquired, "that every man should have his own fancy, or live as him list?" (*Ibid.*, III, 321.)
[4] *Ibid.*, III, 462.   [5] *Ibid.*, III, 463.
[6] The Protestant apologists for religious persecution rested their case almost entirely upon the Old Testament, since the fact of separation prevented the incorporation of the logical teachings of the Roman Catholic Church in this particular *in toto*. Cf. Melanchton, *Bretschneider, Corpus Reform.*, II, 17–18, to Frid. Myconio, February 1530; II, 549, to Myconio,

Cartwright, on the other hand, was caught in the strictness of his own interpretation of the Bible, and his philosophy rejected the nascent germs of rationalism which were making their appearance in sixteenth-century thought. His system was one of rigid literalism. His conscience obliged him to lend full obedience to the judicial ordinances of the Old Testament; and had his party been in power, in theory at least, he would have put to death all practising Roman Catholic priests, and other "blasphemers and idolaters."[1] The intolerance of the man proceeded rather from a bigoted and literal reading of the Bible than from intolerance of heart. Pitiless logic may lead, on occasion, to pitiless conclusions. He aimed at the ascendancy of his own system, and not at liberty of conscience for all men.[2]

The system which Cartwright envisaged was to be practically the supreme power in the land, at least in all matters which could, under a broad definition, be considered as religious or moral. The secular power was to serve the Church, to enforce its decisions, and to secure for it the spiritual monopoly which it claimed.[3] He hoped to substitute one intolerant system for another; if anything, an intolerance that was in spirit more severe and in scope more inclusive.

Whitgift's defence of the Establishment rested upon the lower grounds of the requirements of the times as determined by reason, but therein lay a better avenue for the advent of religious toleration. The Church, for the sake of order and decency, must require a precise order and discipline, but that discipline, he was prepared to say, would not be so extended as to crush out the possibility of growth and change. Whitgift probably would have agreed with Parker when he wrote to

October 1531; XII, 697–698, De haereticis puniendis per magistratum; II, 711–712, to M. Bucer, March 1534; IX, 133 (1557); IX, 77, to N. Palladio, February 1557; VIII, 362, to J. Calvin, October 1554; and esp. VIII, 520–523, concerning the execution of Servetus. See also Calvin, Opera, I, 229–230, LIII, 140–141; the Defensio; and Beza, De haereticas, esp. 139–151.

[1] Cartwright, Second Reply, 117.   [2] Pearson, Thomas Cartwright, 406.
[3] "Heretics and schismatics" were to be "beaten down into dust." "False teachers," even if repentant, should not be permitted to live. (Cartwright, Helps for Discovery, 12–13.)

Burleigh in 1575, "Doth your Lordship think; . . . that I care either for cap, tippet, surplice, or wafer bread, or any such? But for the law so established esteem them."[1] Parker expressed his desire to enforce uniformity because "contempt of law and authority would follow . . . unless discipline were used."[2]

Such a position is far more flexible and adaptive than a system fixed immobile in divine precept. Yet it must not be assumed that either Whitgift or Parker would have admitted that the English Church was motivated in its actions by mere policy. Nor would either have admitted the truth or the desirability of the fact that the State to which so much of ecclesiastical jurisdiction had been surrendered, was dominated in its policy increasingly by considerations of political interest, and that therein lay the way for the future development of religious toleration. The development of such a trend was slow and often obscured by the religious terminology in which secular policy often chose to clothe itself. In addition, actions frequently occurred which were wholly contradictory to the development of this trend. Thus in 1575 a special commission was handed down to Sir Nicholas Bacon for the burning of two Anabaptists which was couched in a language and in a spirit wholly reminiscent of the worst periods of religious persecution.[3]

e. Pilkington and Sandys

The Anglican theory of the proper course in dealing with dissent and Nonconformity was further developed in this period in the sermons of Edwin Sandys, who was consecrated Archbishop of York in 1576, and in the writings of James Pilkington, Bishop of Durham, who died in that year. Discontent and dissent had reached such an acute stage by this time that the question of repression required an extended treatment. Both Sandys and Pilkington expressed views considerably more intolerant than those of Whitgift and they dealt somewhat more specifically with the problem of what course the ruler should take when confronted with instances of stubborn Nonconformity.

[1] Strype, *Parker*, II, 424. [2] *Ibid.*, II, 424.
[3] Wilkins, *Concilia*, IV, 281.

Pilkington, in discussing the prince's duty in the Church, held that "Their duty is not to suffer God's enemies to invade or hurt, slander or blaspheme, those that they have charge over, but to draw the sword, if need be, to drive away such wolves, and punish such wicked tongues. . . ."[1] The magistrate is charged with the care of religion and he must not suffer the Church, its doctrine, or ministers to be "ill spoken of, reviled, defaced, nor overrun."[2] He must strive to defend the Church both with the Word and with the Sword.[3] For princes are divinely charged to maintain true religion and to suppress superstition and idolatry.[4]

Sandys, in various sermons preached between 1568 and 1580, developed this view somewhat further. In preaching before the Queen, he urged that English Protestants were in full agreement upon the substance of religion; "We all build upon one foundation, Christ Jesus, slain and offered up for our full redemption, according to the doctrine of the Scriptures."[5] This, however, was not to Sandys, or to his Church, a sufficient basis for unity of belief. It was rather the greater pity that there should be so much dissent in matters of minor importance. Contention in these matters serves only to hinder the progress of the Gospel.[6] "The ministry cannot well be executed without her rites: which rites are left indifferent to every policy. So that they be not disagreeing to the Word; so that they tend to edification; so that they be seemly, and according to decent order."[7] There is no cause, for the sake of a few indifferent and doubtful rites, to tear down the entire ecclesiastical structure in the name of Reformation.

The king, Sandys held, serves God as a man in one way, and in another manner by virtue of his office. The chief point of his duty to God consists in purging and cleansing the Church[8] "from all false doctrines: from all idolatry and superstition." The ruler was enjoined to fear the Lord, to serve Him in zeal

---

[1] Pilkington, James, *Exposition on Nehemiah* (Parker Soc. Ed.), 360.
[2] *Ibid.*   [3] *Ibid.*, 361, 429.   [4] *Ibid.*, *Works*, 640–642.
[5] Sandys, Edwin, *Sermon Before the Queen*, Strype, *Annals*, III, 2, 67.
[6] *Ibid.*, III. 2, 67.   [7] *Ibid.*, III, 2, 67.
[8] Sandys, *Sermon Preached at York* (ii), *Sermons*, 43.

and in truth, and to cast out from the Church all blasphemy, idolatry, and simony.[1] The prince is charged with a burden of souls.[2]

After the king has assisted in achieving a proper ecclesiastical structure, he must assist the Church by the exercise of a distinctly moralistic function. The prince must attempt to bring all his people to conform themselves to the preaching of the Word.[3] "Although conscience cannot be forced; yet unto external obedience, in lawful things, men may lawfully be compelled."[4] Erring men should be obliged to place themselves in a receptive position,[5] "For though religion cannot be driven into men by force, yet men by force may be driven to those ordinary means whereby they are wont to be brought to the knowledge of the truth."[6] With curious logic Sandys argued that it was profitable to force men to do that which was good for them. The Church may justly compel her lost children to return to the way of salvation, since these lost sheep compel others to destruction.[7] He argued that no man could reasonably deny the justice of forcing men to hear the Word. It therefore "appertaineth . . . unto princes that fear God, . . . to compel every subject to come and hear this Word, lest the church by this evil example should be greatly offended. . . ." "To see

[1] Sandys, *Sermon Preached at York*, (ii), *Sermons*, 43.   [2] *Ibid.*, 44–45.
[3] "As the ministers are to be provided for, that the Word may be preached; so the people must be brought to conform themselves to the thankful receiving thereof. . . . And this care also pertaineth to the godly prince and good magistrate. . . ." (*Ibid.*, 46.)   [4] *Ibid.*, 46.
[5] "Such stray sheep . . . as will not of their own accord assemble themselves to serve the Lord in the midst of His holy congregation, may lawfully and in reason ought to be constrained thereunto." *Ibid.*, 192.   [6] *Ibid.*, 192.
[7] Sandys, *Sermons*, 46. Despite his admission that conscience could not be forced, Sandys here laid down a programme of action which presumed that very notion. Sandy's theory of compulsion was far more intolerant than that of Whitgift. Whitgift, at least in theory, based his conception of uniformity upon the requirements of decency and proper order, ecclesiastical and civil. There is not the slightest indication that he believed anyone's views could be changed by enforced attendance at the established services. Sandys, on the other hand, believed that if men could be forced into church they could be won by the play of the power of truth upon their minds. He belonged to the older group of Anglican thinkers which had not yet abandoned the obviously invalid theory that truth must prevail over all men if only the proper means for its reception could be provided.

the gospel everywhere preached, the ministers provided for, and the people compelled to hear the word . . . this is the fear of God which Samuel requireth."[1]

A more succinct statement of the advanced Anglican position with respect to the question of toleration could scarcely be found. The king's prime duty was represented as the maintenance and advancement of the true faith. The notion that men may openly profess diversity of religion was held to be dangerous, not only to the Church, but to the commonwealth. "What stirs diversity of religion hath raised in nations and kingdoms, the histories are so many and so plain, and our times in such sort have told you, and with further proof I need not trouble your ears."[2] He laid down as his platform for the perfect society the beautiful but rapidly vanishing ideal which for ages had intrigued the minds of the noblest men: "One God, one king, one faith, one profession, is fit for one monarchy and commonwealth. Division weakeneth; concord strengtheneth . . . but conformity and unity in religion be provided for; and it shall be a wall of defence for this realm."[3] If Sandys really believed that this ideal was attainable in his age, he misread every sign of the time.

The Archbishop, in a sermon whose diction and simple power mark it as a literary masterpiece, compared the Church of England to a carefully nurtured vineyard supervised by a skilful overseer.[4] The vineyard has, by the care of the overseer, been well cleansed of thorns and thistles and has been fenced by the laws of discipline.[5] The plantation will be fruitful only under conditions of civil and spiritual peace, while plague and spiritual famine will follow upon disorders and dissensions.[6]

The chief enemies of the prosperity of the vineyard are the heretics, schismatics, and atheists who, like foxes, seek the ruin and overthrow of the vineyard of the Lord. The chief task of the overseer is to snare these enemies. Ideally, the foxes should be taken into the Church and converted into

---

[1] Sandys, *Sermons*, 46.   [2] *Ibid.*, 49.
[3] *Ibid.*, 49; also Sermon xix, *Sermons*, 380–381.   [4] *Ibid.*, 57.
[5] *Ibid.*, 60.   [6] *Ibid.*, 62.

sheep. For meeting the inroads of these enemies "The minister hath his nets . . . withal, the magistrate hath his traps."[1] The net of the minister is the Word of God and the example of a righteous life.[2] But if this ideal means should fail, the misbelievers must be cut off or tied up, and, in this case, the responsibility passes from the Church to the State.[3] The magistrate must set the traps of the law and by death, exile, confiscation, or imprisonment seek to punish and restrain their ravages.[4] Reminiscent of Cartwright was his argument that the Laws of Moses authorized the prince to destroy the rebellious foxes.[5] However, Sandys tended to regard confiscation as the best means for restraining misbelief since "There can be no sharper punishment, to a worldly-minded man, than to be taken in this trap."[6]

f. Minor Theorists

The growing dissatisfaction within the communion of the Church of England, the accumulating weight of Catholic dissent, and the evidence that the dominant Protestant group was in danger of fractionization had led to a fuller consideration of the Anglican theory of conformity. Alexander Nowell in his *Reproof of M. Dorman*, and Geoffrey Fenton in his *A Form of Christian Policy*, were moved by these considerations to place their support on the side of enforced conformity.[7]

Sandys, *Sermons*, 70.   [2] *Ibid.*, 71–72.
[3] *Ibid.*, 72.   [4] *Ibid.*, 439–440.   [5] *Ibid.*, 72–73.
[6] *Ibid.*, 73. "Touch them by the purse: it is the most easy . . . way, whereby to take and tame these foxes." *Ibid.*, 74.
[7] *The Reproufe of M. Dorman his proufe of certaine Articles in Religion*, etc., was published in 1566. Fenton's *A forme of Christian pollicie*, etc., was published eight years later.

     Alexander Nowell (*c.* 1507–1602) was a native of Lancashire and was educated at Oxford, where he is said to have shared quarters with John Foxe. He was appointed master of Westminster school in 1543, and was installed as prebendary of Westminster eight years later. (Le Neve, *Festi*, III, 351.) He was elected to Mary's first parliament, but was debarred from his seat because of his place in the Convocation. He soon lost his preferment, and retired to Germany in 1554. While there he adopted views shading towards Presbyterianism (*D.N.B.*, xli, 244), but conformed and was in 1560 made Dean of St. Paul's. He held that position for forty-two years.

The examples of Moses and Joshua were again monotonously urged to prove that the king had been set over the priest in order to direct and correct him.[1] Both tables have been committed to the Christian king by God. The king's highest duty lies in the ordering of the Church and in the preservation of true faith. The prince, not being an expert, should not attempt to judge all ecclesiastical causes, but the principal and ultimate authority resides in him.[2] The Christian ruler should "set foorth the godly doctrine" and should forbid the exercise of the Roman faith as repugnant to God.[3]

Fenton strongly urged the duty of the ruler to assist the Church by restraining misbelief and by compelling conformity. He held that since "many men eyther by a vice in nature, or corruption of maners, carrye this frowardnes that without compulsion they wil not bee drawen to doo or bee good; it belongs to the Magistrate . . . to drawe them to the hearing of the Worde by perswasions and al easy meanes, and where they find no willing conformitye in any, let there bee constraynt by fine, and afterward according to the nature and continuance of their resistance to gods woorde . . . to proceede by seuerity and rigour of justice."[4] The spiritual sickness of man is so grave a condition that the magistrate will be guilty of a grave neglect of duty if he does not employ "compulsion by paines and punishment for the hearing of Gods woorde."[5]

The ponderous work of John Bridges on *The Supremacy of Christian Princes*[6] shed a somewhat softer light on the attitude

Nowell was "a polished scholar, a weighty and successful disputant, and a learned theologian." (*D.N.B.*, xli, 247.)

Fenton's work was published as 'gathered out of the French,' but appears to represent his own views.   [1] Nowell, *Reproof*, 146 ff.
[2] *Ibid.*, 161.   [3] *Ibid.*, 161, 162; 171–172; 194.
[4] Fenton, G., *A Forme of Christian Pollicie*, 21–22.   [5] *Ibid.*, 22.
[6] The work was published in 1573 under the title, *The Supremacie of Christian Princes, ouer all Persons throughout their Dominions, in all causes so wel ecclesiastical as temporall, &c.* This huge work of more than 1100 pages failed to shed new light on its central argument: that the prince enjoys supremacy in all ecclesiastical matters.

John Bridges was educated at Pembroke Hall, Cambridge, receiving the B.A. degree in 1556 and the M.A. degree four years later. He entered the lists as a controversial writer in 1573 with the work under consideration, which was in form an answer to the recent books of Stapleton and Sanders.

of the churchmen towards dissent and heresy. Bridges retained much of the older trust in the efficacy of Biblical instruction and evangelical preaching to overcome error, and he clearly avoided a direct consideration of the problem which dissent created for a Government which acknowledged a moralistic function. His central position appears to have been that the Bible was quite competent for the overthrow of any heresy.[1] The Word, he said, is likewise the sole guide for the defence of the faith, for the definition of heresy, and for the conversion of misbelievers.[2]

The writer was obviously puzzled by the problems which he had raised for consideration. "Nowe what muste the prince heere do: must he not examine and searche out" and, his logic impelled him, "punish . . . whome he findeth to be the heretike. And thus, if ye wil needes haue death the punishment, in Gods name euen death be it."[3] But his acceptance of this position was guarded. The Catholics have demonstrated the evils inherent in religious persecution too clearly for the Church of England to embrace it as a policy.[4] They have been guilty of proceeding upon the basis of the Old Law and of forgetting that the Law of the Gospel is "of grace and full of mercie."[5] We must remember that "the gospell . . . killeth not, but laboureth to saue. . . ."[6] Only indirectly can we find any justification for the capital punishment of heretics in the Bible.[7]

We have perhaps examined enough of Anglican literature in the middle portion of Elizabeth's reign to determine the attitude of the leaders in the Church during that period towards the manifold issues which relate themselves to the question

He was made Dean of Salisbury in 1577. He was a prolix writer, and his *A Defence of the Government Established in the Church of Englande for Ecclesiasticall Matters* (1587) ran to 1412 pages. The latter work was an attack upon Calvinism, and was chiefly distinguished as the immediate cause for the outbreak of the Martinist controversy. Bridges was elevated to the see of Oxford in 1605. Surprisingly little is known of his long and distinguished career. (*D.N.B.*, VI, 320–321; Strype, *Annals* and *Whitgift, passim.*)
[1] ". . . there is no heresie defended neuer so frowardly, of any obstinate heretike, but the worde is able to conuince it to be an heresie." (Bridges, J., *The Supremacie of . . . Princes*, 323.)
[2] *Ibid.*, 323. [3] *Ibid.*, 606. [4] *Ibid.*, 610–611.
[5] *Ibid.*, 613. [6] *Ibid.* [7] *Ibid.*

of religious toleration. The writings of Whitgift, in particular, would seem to indicate that the Anglican communion was attempting to maintain a policy of comprehension and toleration in the face of great difficulties not of its own creation. But the views of Pilkington and Sandys and, on the whole, of the minor writers of the period evidenced a growing disposition to justify the employment of vigorous repression in cases of dissent and misbelief.[1] However, Anglicanism did not venture to place the *raison d'être* for this policy higher than the requirements of ecclesiastical and political order.

The Anglican apology for persecution rested principally upon the large powers which obtained to the ruler in the Church. As we have observed, this position, by indirection, leads to toleration once the State is convinced of the impossibility or of the inherent danger involved in the suppression of religious opinions. We shall, therefore, be obliged to focus rather more attention upon the development of governmental opinion and policy than upon the more finely spun elaborations of ecclesiastical theory. The Puritan theory, which made the State the executive agent of the Church for the forcible moulding of a Christian commonwealth, as we shall indicate in greater detail in later pages, had none but intolerant connotations. Alongside these main currents of thought, however, was the emerging sectarian theory which denied, usually for obvious reasons, that any connection existed between Church and State.

Occasionally this view was combined with a genuine theory of religious toleration, and, if not, the teeth were drawn from persecution by the complete exclusion from spiritual affairs of that power which was alone capable of executing a programme of repression. Sectarian opinion was therefore highly important

[1] Grindal's famous Defence of Prophesying in 1576 constitutes an important, but isolated, exception to this tendency. He displayed essentially Puritan resentment against the overweening power of the secular authority in the Church, and admonished the Queen to distinguish between the civil and the spiritual spheres. (Fuller, *Church History*, IV, 451–452.) The language which Grindal used in rebuking the Queen is reminiscent of Knox's fatherly lectures to Mary Queen of Scots. Elizabeth, however, was not moved to tears, but to a demonstration of the amplitude of that power which the Archbishop had so nobly protested.

in so far as the development of a 'pure theory' of toleration was concerned, but of distinctly minor importance in the achievement of that theory because of the disadvantageous position in which minority groups must labour.

5. CONCLUSION

In summary, the thought of the dominant groups in England had by 1576 produced no general analysis of the problem of toleration. Occasional and important individual suggestions had been made, but these conceptions had not yet attached themselves to a considerable or a powerful body of opinion. Nor is there evidence that the writings of the Continental exponents of religious toleration had as yet begun to influence these groups to an appreciable degree.[1] The Elizabethan Government had, none the less, kept the way open for the development of toleration.[2] The governmental policy of cleaving to the *via media* found warm support in a large and influential body of opinion. There were many in England who were more anxious to preserve the unity of the Church than the form which was rapidly making that unity impossible. Men were beginning to enquire whether it was well "that fruitful and pious men who preached the same doctrine as that which was held by their conforming bretheren, and whose lives gave at least as good an example as that of any bishop in England, should be cut short in their career of usefulness merely in order that the clergyman who officiated in one parish might not scandalize the sticklers for uniformity by wearing a surplice, whilst the clergyman who officiated in the next parish wore a gown."[3]

[1] The first notice of Castellion's writings is found in a letter from Knollys to Burleigh and Leicester on September 29, 1581, warning them that steps must be taken to seize the printers of Castellion's books so that the "pestilent doctrynes thr of may be . . . found and suppressed." He regarded Castellion as especially dangerous because he advanced Anabaptist and Free-Will doctrines. (*Lansdowne MSS.*, xxxiii, 84.) Generally speaking, Castellion's *Traité des Hérétiques* had little influence in England before the appearance of the Dutch edition in 1610. Bodin's influence began to exert itself in England about 1580. The views of the *Politique* school became current in England during that decade. The Continental apologists for toleration had already profoundly influenced certain of the dissenters and laymen.

[2] Allen, *Political Thought*, 234.
[3] Gardiner, S. R., *History of England*, I, 41.

Toleration had during the period under discussion made important advances. The comprehensive and moderate character of the Settlement of Religion at the beginning of the reign had made it possible for a wise and cautious Government consciously to abstain from any general persecution of religious dissent. Repression was applied with a severity which stood in direct relation to the amount of civil danger which the Government believed to be present in a particular religious practice at a particular time. As the Government defined its policy more fully in secular terms, it became increasingly wary of entangling itself in any effort to enforce religious uniformity for spiritual ends. A clear and important distinction was repeatedly drawn between the persecution of religious beliefs and the punishment of religious actions which the Government happened to believe were inimical to the best interests of the body politic, and the weight of this distinction was on the side of religious liberty.[1]

The Government was obliged to modify this policy towards

[1] Professor G. G. Coulton presents an interesting criticism of Elizabeth's religious policy in his valuable article 'A Protestant View of Toleration.' (*Cont. Rev.*, No. 777, September 1930, 310–319.) In commenting on Saint Bernard's sermons on the Canticles (the 64th, 65th, and 66th), in which Bernard outlined his theory of persecution, he suggests that the view of the saint and the policy of the Elizabethan Government are highly similar. Bernard held that in the absence of the restraint of heretics from subverting others, "it is better, beyond all question, that they should be coerced with the sword than that they should be permitted to bring many over to their own error." This notion Professor Coulton would regard as "exactly the policy of Elizabeth four and a half centuries later." (314.)

It would seem, however, that the Church, at least in the Middle Ages, was almost solely concerned with the spiritual and doctrinal implications of heresy. The political and social views of its victims were occasionally utilized to secure the more eager participation of the secular authority in the execution of its persecuting policy, but this emphasis was quite subsidiary to the real purpose of its punishment.

Elizabeth and her Government, on the contrary, on no occasion proceeded against a Nonconformist purely or principally because of the spiritual dangers involved in misbelief. The medieval jargon was still employed, but it did not conceal the essentially political motives underlying her persecution of Nonconformity. In fact, every pronouncement of the Government on the subject sought to indicate the highly important transition in point of view which distinguished not only St. Bernard from Elizabeth, but Mary from Elizabeth. The complete Erastianism of the great Queen can scarcely be too vigorously maintained.

the close of the period under consideration on the side of severity in order to cope with militant Catholicism which, from the perspective of the period, threatened the security of the State. In addition, the Government was harassed by the growing vigour of Puritan opposition to the policy and character of the Establishment, an opposition which it was disposed to curb to a more limited degree. The Government was in fairly complete control of the agencies of repression and it employed those instruments throughout our period judiciously and with a remarkable absence of religious bigotry.

We have estimated the strictly ecclesiastical thought of the period as considerably less tolerant than the thought and practice of the Government. However, the views of the greatest of the apologists for the Church of England during this era were, in comparison with those of his Puritan opponent, surprisingly moderate. The Anglican Church was permeated with the spirit of rationalism in its interpretation of discipline, ecclesiastical structure and policy. In especial, the willingness with which the ordering of the Church and the responsibility for the punishment of heresy and Nonconformity had been surrendered to the magistrate reduced Anglican intolerance to the complexion of the policy of the State, and that policy was dictated by rationalism and by mundane considerations.

Notable pleas for toleration of religious opinions and modes of worship had been raised during the period, and it may be suggested that there was a far larger body of opinion which was favourably disposed towards religious toleration than has ordinarily been supposed. There was, however, during these years no extended or analytical defence of the concept of religious toleration which may be associated with the dominant groups, whether in Parliament, the Council chamber, or the Church of England.

As Mr. J. W. Allen has well pointed out, there were in 1576 many real difficulties which prevented the assumption of a consciously tolerant policy by those who were in authority in Church and State. In the first place, religious toleration presumes the view that the magistrate is not invested with the duty of maintaining the true religion.[1] As we have seen, no person who spoke for those in authority was prepared to admit this revolutionary doctrine. The English view had not yet completely turned from the contemplation of the magnificent vista which the Middle Ages had raised, a conception so noble in design that it must eternally haunt the minds of the finest men.

In addition, it was still generally believed that religious truth could be exactly ascertained, and it followed that the prince had a high duty to assist to a greater or lesser degree in the advancement of that truth. We shall suggest in later pages that the rapid dissolution of this notion during the second half of the Queen's reign was a factor of immense importance for the development of religious toleration.

It was likewise generally believed, and especially by the Government, that if men were permitted to worship as they pleased, though the right of free belief had been conceded, the dissolution of the fabric of society must ensue. Religious unity was regarded as a national necessity in the face of an hostile Europe. The constant menace from abroad made men feel that it was necessary to enforce some degree of uniformity, if not truth. Men conformed because unknowingly the highest allegiance had come to be granted to the State and not to religion.[2] Men often supported the theory of persecution with the outworn formulae of the Middle Ages when actually they were motivated by the powerful currents of the new nationalism. Perhaps, however, the principal reason that no full-blown theory of toleration appeared from the dominant groups is to be found in the fact that a large degree of actual toleration appertained through the whole of the period just considered.

[1] Allen, J. W., *Political Thought*, 235.   [2] *Ibid.*, 236.

III

THE DOMINANT GROUPS DURING THE REIGN OF
ELIZABETH: DEVELOPMENT OF GOVERNMENTAL
AND ANGLICAN THOUGHT WITH RESPECT TO
RELIGIOUS DISSENT FROM 1576 TO 1603

1. THE GOVERNMENT AND ROMAN CATHOLIC NONCONFORMITY,
1576–1583

The principal testing ground for the Government's theory
of uniformity lay in the handling of the Catholic problem
which was by 1576 assuming critical proportions. It will not
be necessary for our purpose to trace in detail the progress
of the Catholic problem: we shall be more concerned with the
shadow which the problem cast upon the question of toleration.
The general effect of the penal laws had been materially to
reduce the number of confessing Romanists while heightening
the enthusiasm and activity of those persons who continued
to cling to the old faith. The party diminished in numbers,
but individually its members were tested and refined by
persecution.[1] The effect of the seminaries and colleges abroad
and the missionary activities of the Jesuits was to lend to English
Catholicism a Roman and a foreign complexion and inspiration
which soon cast upon it a distinctly disloyal appearance.

The Privy Council was the principal organ for the handling
of the Catholic problem and Sir Francis Walsingham was by
position and temperament fitted to be its chief executive officer.
Walsingham's attitude towards the repression of Catholicism
may be taken as typical of the governmental position. Without
doubt his personal religious convictions inclined towards
Puritanism.[2] But, as Read has demonstrated, he was primarily

[1] Pollard, *Pol. History of England*, 371.
[2] Thus Camden speaks of him as a sharp maintainer of the purer religion.
(Camden, Wm., *Annals*, 394.) His home and university training and his
experience while abroad during the reign of Mary had determined his
religious convictions before his entry on public life. (Read II, 258–259.)
Elizabeth often complained that he was more interested in the advancement

a statesman and carefully discriminated between his private religious convictions and his public duty.[1] He rarely, if ever, aided the Puritan cause by an official action. He desired to secure reformation within the Church by public authority and realized that under the existing constitutional system toleration for advanced Puritanism could never be secured by brooking the Queen's will. Realizing the situation, he feared that the extreme Puritan demands would alienate her even further. His attitude was well shown when the English merchants residing in Antwerp proposed to alter their service in accord with the suggestion of Travers, their Puritan Minister. Such an action, he wrote, would assure the antagonism of the Queen.[2] "I do not write this as one that misliketh of such a form of exercise of prayer; but I would have all reformation done by public authority."[3] He held that it would be dangerous to the state if every man possessed authority to order religion. "If you knew with what difficulty we retain what we have, and that the seeking of more might hazard that, you would, Mr. Davison, deal warily in this time, when policy carrieth more sway than zeal."[4]

Like most of his contemporaries, Walsingham was impressed with the tightening circle of Catholic danger. Protestantism in England was gravely threatened, and for the time being the bonds of cohesion must be tightly drawn in order to present a united front to the arch-enemy. When that danger had passed, we may believe, the bonds could be relaxed and reformation proceed. This attitude characterized many patriotic Englishmen, who personally desired reformation and further latitude, to the time of the Glorious Revolution, and it somewhat obscures the extent of tolerant sentiments. As a statesman Walsingham keenly felt the great danger incident to internal dissension, and he regarded unity as the immediate end to be attained.[5]

of his own religious views than in the welfare of his country. He was regarded as the Protestant chief by the Churches abroad, was the benefactor of Cartwright, and dissenting clergymen often appealed to him for aid.

[1] Read, *Walsingham*, II, 262 ff. The discussion of Walsingham's thought is considerably indebted to Dr. Read's able work.

[2] *S.P. Holland and Flanders*, VI, 54 (May 8, 1578). [3] *Ibid.*

[4] *Ibid.* [5] Read, *Walsingham*, II, 266.

"... Civil and domestical broils come very evil to pass in this common combustion abroad. The time requireth an unity and perfect agreement rather in them that make profession of that truth, which is elsewhere so impugned and hath so mighty enemies and so cruel wars kindling against it in these days amongst our fellow members abroad."[1] Unity in England, he says, will be a bulwark at home and an assistance to the distressed cause of Protestantism abroad. "But if we shall like to fall to division amongst ourselves, we must needs lie open to the common enemy and by our fault hasten or rather call upon ourselves our own ruin."[2]

Walsingham was intensely hostile to the Catholics, whom he held to be the chief enemies of Protestantism and the greatest menace to the security of the State. His share in the persecution of Catholics who fell under the scope of the penal laws finds rationalization in this view rather than in any personal conviction that men should be persecuted for religious opinions alone.[3] He dealt with the Catholics not so much as enemies of the Established Church as enemies to the State and public order. He watched them, tracked them down, and occasionally tortured them because he regarded them as traitors to all that was dear to him.

Burleigh's sober analysis bore a somewhat different view. While he urged sharp repression of the seminary priests and of the political connotations of the counter-Reformation, he, like Elizabeth, distinguished carefully between the leaders and the laity. We should never proceed to capital punishment for such men. The Catholics should never be driven to despair.[4] We should rather mitigate the oath imposed upon them and should never drive them to an absolute choice between their religious inclinations and their political duties.[5] At the same time the Government must never relax its energy so as to awaken in the hearts of Catholics any hope that their demands will be granted. To do so would only render them the more

---

[1] (1578) In regard to Protestant dissensions in Scotland. Read, *Walsingham*, II, 266, from *Hall MSS*. 6992, 50.   [2] *Ibid.*
[3] *Ibid.*, II, 269-270.   [4] Ranke, L. von, *History of England*, I, 300.
[5] Cf. *ante*, 97-99.

obstinate and determined. In other words, "we do not wish to kill them, we cannot coerce them, but we dare not trust them." Burleigh, in the consultation at Greenwich in 1579, especially urged their complete exclusion from political power.[1] It is likewise important that the Queen should bind the House of Commons to her by every tie of gratitude. To accomplish this end he would grant political toleration to the dissenting Protestants, permitting them to worship and catechize as they chose, since they are the best preachers, the most ardent Protestants, and the arch-enemies of Rome.

In the same year Walsingham advised his agents to deal somewhat more gently with recusants in order to avoid the danger of desperation. "I thought good not as a councillor . . . but as one that wisheth well the common cause of religion, to signify unto you, by these letters, that though, in due and necessary policy, it were fitt that Papists who will not conform themselves to resort to public prayer, should receive punishment due to their contempt, according to the laws provided in that behalf: yet the time serveth not now to deal therein, and therefore I cannot but advise you and such others of the best affected gentlemen in that shire to forbear to persecute by means of indictment such as lately were presented whose names you certified up: . . ."[2]

Thus the policy of repression which the Government was on the verge of assuming in 1579 displayed in its inception a large recognition of the requirements of policy, and a disavowal of persecution of religious belief *per se*. The Government assumed, with justice, that the most nominal obedience to the ecclesiastical laws was a sufficient badge of loyalty, and it displayed no interest in probing beyond this required degree of conformity.[3] Every inducement and effort were employed to secure this nominal adhesion to the establishment. Thus in 1576 the Privy Council wrote to the keeper of Gatehouse with regard to Hugh Erdswicke, a recusant, who had petitioned for release on the score of ill-health, instructing

[1] Murdin, W., Ed., *Collection of State Papers*, II, 340.
[2] *S.P. Dom.*, XLV, 27. Unsigned. Read ascribes to Walsingham (1579?).
[3] Cf. *Acts of Privy Council*, IX, 15 (August 16, 1575.)

the jailer to present the recusant to the Dean or some of the prebends at Westminster in order to "prove by persuacion whether he may be induced to conform himself *onely* in going to the churche without any furder constrainte of his conscience, . . ."[1] Again, because one Evans Fludd "is so far forthe reclaimed that he is willing to come unto the churche to hear Diuine Service and Sermons," his release was ordered by the Council.[2] In 1580 we find a circular letter from the same body to the Sheriff of Lancaster stating that "wheras it pleased her Majestie to graunt him [the sheriff] under the Great Seale of Englande the penalties imposed by lawe uppon certaine persons in Lancestire, transgressours of the statutes for matters of religion, whereby her Majesties intention being to terrifie the offendours, and that the penaltie might rather be moderated by some gentle composicion . . . then the extremitie were sought by th' entier execucion of the statute," persons refusing to conform are to be required to make compositions, rather than to be imprisoned.[3]

The Church had surrendered to the State the task of attempting to secure the conformity and uniformity which it regarded as ideal, and the State proceeded squarely along sectarian lines.[4] It is interesting to speculate what might have occurred had bigoted ecclesiasticism been in control.

Prior to 1580, Elizabeth and her Council had evidently entertained the typical Reformation notion that the recusants might be won by a policy of preaching and conciliation to support the settlement of religion. After 1580 she and her Council as evidently proceeded against them on the supposition that they were potential, if not actual, enemies of the State.[5] The Parlia-

[1] *Acts of the Privy Council*, IX, 295 (February 20, 1576).
[2] *Ibid.*, X, 359–360 (October 29, 1578).   [3] *Ibid.*, XI, 446 (April 14, 1580).
[4] Thus in 1578 the Queen pressed Mendoza, the Spanish Ambassador, for peace in the Netherlands on the basis of Ghent. The essentially political view which the Queen took of religion is shown when she urged that no peace could be attained there without the granting of some measure of toleration. She declared herself unable to see why the King of Spain cared "if they go to the devil in their own way." (*Sp. Papers*, 1578, June 17th, II, 515. Mendoza to the King.) In England, she said, Catholics were punished only for refusing to acknowledge her as Queen. (*Ibid.*)
[5] Read, *Walsingham*, II, 286.

ment of 1581 showed its perceptions of the dangers feared by
the Council by increasing the penalties of recusancy in a new
"Act to retain the Queen's Majesty's subjects in their due
obedience."[1] Mildmay summarized the Government's view
when he urged that there were two parties contending for both
the civil and ecclesiastical supremacy of England. The Queen
on the one side, and the Bishop of Rome and his followers on
the other, were represented as the two antagonists, and Englishmen had to choose between them. To be loyal to the Roman
See is treason to the Queen. The law adjudged all persons who
should withdraw subjects of the Queen from their allegiance
to her, or from the established religion, or who should "move
them to promise any obedience to any pretended authority
of the See of Rome" to be guilty of high treason.[2] In addition,
all persons who were willingly "absolved or withdrawn" from
obedience to the Queen and the Establishment, were, upon
conviction, to incur the penalties of high treason.[3] Besides
dealing with the Jesuits, the Act made the participation in mass
punishable by fines and imprisonments;[4] punished recusancy
by a penalty of £20 a month;[5] and ordered sharp penalties
imposed upon the dissemination of slanderous news and libels.[6]

[1] 23 Eliz., c. 1.   [2] 23 Eliz., c. 1, Sect. 1.   [3] *Ibid.*
[4] 23 Eliz., c. 1, Sect. 3.   [5] 23 Eliz., c. 1, Sect. 4.
[6] 23 Eliz., c. 2. This Act was to be employed, however, principally against
the sectarians. The disposition of the Government to provide itself with
machinery for the handling of any Catholic emergency which might arise,
but to temper the enforcement of such legislation, is shown directly after
the passing of these acts. Many recusants were soon imprisoned or placed
in the charge of persons who were competent to give them instruction in the
true faith. But in the summer of 1581 the Council decided that all recusants
who were in prison for "not conformitie in the matter of religion" should
be released under bail under the following conditions: The released person
was not to pass out of the realm without license; he was to remain within
three miles of his house; was not to entertain or to resort with Papists or
Jesuits, etc. (*Acts of Privy Council*, XIII, 41). (For a copy of the *Conditions
of the Bonds of the Recusants* (August 1581) see *Egerton Papers*, 85). There
are scores of orders for release during late 1581–early 1582 with bails ranging
from £20 to £1,000 (*Acts of the P.C.*, XIII, 41). Those refusing to accept
these conditions were often released for terms under bail (XIII, 304, 325).
The Government displayed marked toleration, for many who were thus
favoured appear immediately to have begun to spread propaganda or otherwise to violate the conditions of their bail (*Acts of the P.C.*, XIII, 189,
238, 287, etc.).

The feeling of the majority of Englishmen that a policy of toleration for Catholics was quite impossible, was perhaps shown by Fulke's *A Briefe Confutation of a Popish Discourse* (1581). The work was a somewhat unimportant reply to Parsons' *Certain Reasons why Papists refuse to come to Church*. Parsons argued "Surely as I am nowe mynded, I woulde not for tenne thousande worldes, compell a Iewe to swear that there were a blessed Trinitie. For albeeyt the thinge never so true, yet should hee bee damned for swearing agaynst his conscience, and I for compelling him too committe so heynous and grievous a sinne."[1] Fulke seized upon his words "as I am nowe mynded" as indicative of the danger involved in any possible leniency towards Catholics. "You doe well to adde the condition of your present perswasion, that you maye leaue a place, to chaunge your mynde, when you shal bee better aduised. And sure I am, that either you are a Schismatike from all your fellow Papistes, or if the law were in youre hande, you would shewe a practise contrary to this protestation . . ."[2] In other words, Englishmen were afraid that if the Papists were permitted to go unchecked, they would succeed in overthrowing the Government and in establishing their own religion by force. England was afraid and when the dominant group is in fear, toleration is impossible. For toleration must be regarded as the result of social development and it rests essentially on the basis of empiricism. Essentially we are tolerant because no harm results from our being so.[3] The bases of national life were discerned to lie far deeper than religious uniformity, and only when it became apparent that national and institutional life could continue in spite of dissenting views of religion was toleration at hand.

The repressive measures which the Government had deemed it necessary to undertake against its Catholic subjects were excused and explained in the *Execution of Justice in England*, a semi-official governmental apology which appeared in 1583, probably from the hand of Burleigh.[4] Perhaps the most sig-

[1] Fulke, *Brief Confutation*, 10.   [2] *Ibid.*
[3] Creighton, *Persecution and Tolerance*, 114.
[4] First Ed. *The Execution of Justice in England for Maintenance of Publique and Christian Peace.* (Anon.) C. Barker, L, 1583; 2nd Ed. with small

nificant thing about the treatise is the fact that it was felt to be necessary. The publication of the treatise was a tacit admission that the Government recognized the existence of a considerable body of opinion opposed to religious repression. The work sought, therefore, to prove that England was persecuting, not religious opinion, but treason and disloyalty.

Burleigh pointed out that after some years of quiet, Englishmen who had heretofore supported the religious laws had been incited to take up arms against their Queen.[1] The expressed resolution of this group was to depose the Queen and to set up an adherent of its own faith as ruler. The Catholics have held that the cause of their disturbances "was for the religion of Rome, and for maintenaunce of the . . . Pope's authoritie."[2] As a matter of fact, Burleigh gravely urged, several of the ringleaders have never shown a shred of religious conviction in their private lives. The entire responsibility for the situation was ascribed to the papal Bull of excommunication, to the deposition of the Queen, and to the absolution of English subjects from their rightful loyalty to their ruler. To accomplish their purposes foreign princes have been incited to wage war on England, seminaries have been erected "to nourish and bring up persons disposed naturally to sedition," and priests and disguised Jesuits have crept into England further to spread their designs.[3] The general policy of this group has been, in short, conducive "ot horrible vprores in the realmes, and a manifest blooddy destruction of great multitude of christians."[4] This party lacks only a favourable opportunity to demonstrate itself as openly traitorous to the realm. Those who have been apprehended have " not being delt withall vpon questions of religion, but iustly, by order of Lawes, openly condemned as traitours."[5] Offers of mercy were extended, and if accepted

changes, C. Barker, L. 1583; *Justitia Britannica*, 2 pts., Vautroullerius, 1584; *D'Executie van iustitie*, Middleburgh (Schilders), 1584; *l'execution de iustice faicte en Angleterre*, T. Vautroullier, 1584; *Alto della guistitia d'Inghilterra*, G. Wolfio, 1589. Copies of all in B.M. The book was barely published when it attained wide circulation by numerous reprints and translations. (Destombes, 332.)

[1] Burleigh, *Exec. of Justice.*, *Harl. Misc.*, II, 123.   [2] *Ibid.*
[3] *Ibid.*, II, 124–125.   [4] *Ibid.*, II, 125.   [5] *Ibid.*

they were spared, but otherwise these leaders were convicted and executed as manifest traitors by the ancient laws of the realm.

The writer charges that the priests who were coming into England pretend that they come "to informe or reforme mens consciences from errors in some poynts of religion," when in reality they propose to execute the self-expressed design of the Pope. It is the highest duty of the Queen and her Government to prevent, if need be by the sword, the success of these designs which would result only in civil war with all of its terrible incidents. He pointed out that many Englishmen differed from the Established Church in matters of religion, "yet, in that they doe also professe loyaltie and obedience to her majestie, and offer readily, in her majesties defense, to impugne and resist any forreine Force, though it should come, or be procured, from the pope himself; none of these sort are, for their contrary opinions in religion, prosecuted, or charged with any crymes or paines of Treason, nor yet willinglie searched in their consciences for their contrarie opinions, that favour not of treason."[1] Thus many dignitaries of the Marian Church "were neuer, to this day, burdened with capitall Peanes, nor yet deprived of any of their goods, or proper livelihoods, but only remoued from their ecclesiasticall offices, which they would not exercise according to the Lawes."[2] Such of them "as yet remayne, may, if they will not be authors or instruments of rebellion or sedition, inioye the Time that God and nature shall yeelde them, without danger of Life or member."[3]

Burleigh made the most advanced concession that the Government had ever unofficially seen fit to admit when he said that the State had chosen to disregard the fact that many prominent Catholics, to the Government's knowledge, held the opinion "that the pope ought, by the authoritie of Gods worde, to be supreame and onely Head of the catholique church, through the whole world, and onely to rule in al causes ecclesiasticall; and that the queenes maiestie ought not to be the gouernour

---

[1] Burleigh, *Execution of Justice, Harl. Misc.*, II, 126.
[2] *Ibid.*, II, 127.   [3] *Ibid.*

over any of her subiectes in her Realme, being persons ecclesiasticall; . . ."[1] even though these opinions are tinged with illegality. In other words, the Government judged that no one should be prosecuted for upholding the purely spiritual power of the Papacy or for denying the purely spiritual power of the Queen.[2] No one had been placed in danger of life who had not actually supported the contents of the papal Bull.[3]

He called attention to the fact that Elizabeth, by Catholic admission, put to death not more than sixty persons in twenty-five years for causes in which religion was involved; while Mary in five years executed five times as many, under circumstances of the greatest cruelty.[4] The tolerance of the Elizabethan Government is especially manifest, when it is recalled that those who perished under Mary "Never . . . denied their lawfull Queen, nor maintained any of her open or forreine enemies, nor procured any rebellion, or civill Warre, . . . nor with drewe any Subjectes from their obedience, as these sworne seruantes of the pope have continually done."[5]

In appealing to the sovereigns of Europe against the papal claim to the power of deposition, Burleigh pointed out that this presumptive right struck at the root of the sovereignty of every State. The claim is wholly unscriptural, and the early

---

[1] Burleigh, *Exec. of Justice, Harl. Misc.*, II, 128.   [2] *Ibid.*, II, 128.
[3] Thus Sanders, Parsons, Hart, and other Catholic writers are guilty of treason.
[4] Burleigh, *Exec. of Justice, Harl. Misc.*, II, 131. Assuming all the Roman Catholics were executed for faith, rather than for treason, Elizabeth put to death for catholicism an average of four persons for each year of her reign; while Mary put to death for Protestantism fifty-six persons for every year of her reign. Elizabeth's executions began in 1575, and averaged seven per year from that date to the close of her reign. (Pollard, *History of England*, 377, and Wand, *History of the Modern Church*.) K. M. Warren, writing in the *Catholic Encyclopedia* (V, 449), estimates that 189 Catholics were executed during her reign (or 4·2 persons per regnal year), of whom 128 (67·6 per cent.) were priests. Of this number the great majority were beyond doubt guilty of treason under the law. The laws may well be condemned, but this does not imply the Government's action to be one of persecution. Numerous instances can be adduced, as in the case of Campion, when treason was not proved, and these cases must be written down as unfortunate instances of the effect of fear on the hearts of men. The whole question has become so tangled in controversy that any conclusion must be tentative.
[5] Burleigh, *Exec. of Justice, Harl. Misc.*, II, 131–132.

and "godly" bishops of Rome followed the example of Christ and His apostles in rendering due obedience to the State. It was Hildebrand "who first beganne to vsurpe that kinde of Tyrannie, . . ."[1] Both England and France, in the long struggle against papal usurpation, have stoutly and fearlessly repelled the attempts of the papal ambitions to absorb the proper power of the State.[2] In a magnificent passage which strikingly expressed the proud nationalism of his age, he enquired, "Shall this pope Gregory, or any other pope after him, think that a soueraigne queene, possessed of the two realmes of England and Ireland, stablished so many yeres in her kingdomes as three or foure popes haue sit in their chayre at Rome, fortified with so much Dutie, Loue, and strength of her subiectes, acknowledging no superiour over her Realmes, but the mightie Hand of God: Shall she forbeare, or feare to withstand and make frustrate his vnlawful attempts, eyther by her sword, or by her Lawes, or to put his souldiers Invadours of her Realme to the Sworde martially; or to execute hir Lawes vpon hir owne rebellious subiectes civilly that are prooved to be his chiefe Instruments for Rebellion, and for his open warre?"[3]

In explicit terms the Government's definition of Catholic treason was laid down. So long as it was closely and carefully adhered to the student who appreciates the problems which Elizabeth faced, and who properly evaluates the importance of stability in the England of this period, can find small grounds for quarrel. The Queen had put to death two classes of men; those who had assumed arms in open rebellion, and the Jesuits who, in purpose and clothing, had come as spies in disguise. The Jesuits have been found traitors by "their traitorous, secret motions and practises."[4] "Their persons haue not made the warre, but their directions and counsels have set vp the Rebellion."[5] Thus when apprehended and examined concerning their attitude towards the papal Bull they have shown themselves as guilty as those who actually took up arms.[6] Thus their action in sowing discontent, communicating with traitors across the seas, their commissions from the Pope, their listing

[1] Burleigh, *Execution of Justice, Harl. Misc.*, II, 133. [2] *Ibid.*, II, 134.
[3] *Ibid.*, II, 135. [4] *Ibid.*, II, 138. [5] *Ibid.* [6] *Ibid.*, II, 139.

of potential rebels, "and not their Bookes, not their Beades, no not their cakes of wax, . . . nor other their reliques, nor yet their opinions for the ceremonies or Rites of the church of Rome," have made them traitors to England.[1] If these traitorous efforts were suspended, "all furder bodely punishments should vtterly cease."[2]

The *Execution of Justice in England* adds considerable light on the governmental position with regard to toleration, and its general Catholic policy in 1583. The tone was thoroughly Erastian and the Government plainly implied that it could tolerate just as much dissent as it desired. The Government regarded certain beliefs as false, undesirable, and even dangerous, but it pledged itself not to undertake the difficult and dangerous task of suppressing them so long as they remained purely spiritual, that is to say academic, beliefs. However, when treason was added to heresy, it must act in the interests primarily of public safety, secondarily of religion. Great pride was taken in the boast that no one had been executed during the Queen's reign for a specifically religious belief. Little or nothing was said of the State's duty to persecute unbelief or misbelief. The governmental policy was exhibited in its true political garb. It would be highly inaccurate to say, however, that the distinction which was regularly drawn between the persecution of heresy and the punishment of sedition or even of Nonconformity was without content. Religious persecution implies only the persecution of religious opinions. Henry and Mary had been frank in burning people solely for the crime of heresy.[3]

Mary kindled the fires at Smithfield for the salvation of souls, not for the safety of her throne.[4] Elizabeth's policy was in essence that opinions in religious matters were not to be punished, but that from political considerations the people must conform themselves with tolerable regularity to the established order, politically and religiously. Conformity was deemed necessary to the preservation of law and decency.[5]

[1] Burleigh, *Exec. of Justice, Harl. Misc.* II, 139–140.   [2] *Ibid.,* II, 140.
[3] Innes, A. D., *England under the Tudors*, 418.   [4] *Ibid.*
[5] Usher, R. G., *The Reconstruction of the English Church*, I, 19–20.

The policy of the Government towards its Catholic subjects had by 1583 entered its second phase. Elizabeth had by the persistent pressure of fines, short imprisonment, and gestures of conciliation endeavoured to bring her Catholic subjects at least to acquiesce in the Settlement. She and her Government displayed actual aversion to capital punishment as an instrument in achieving the desired end. This policy, contrasting so favourably with normal continental conditions, gave way in the face of armed rebellion, papal absolutions from obedience, and plots against the Queen's life. It seemed obvious that more stringent measures would have to be adopted against at least one section of Catholics.[1] In assuming this policy repeated official and semi-official utterances strove to assure loyal Catholics that their lives would not be endangered. Conscience was not to be molested, but the Government reserved the right to define that area in which the religious expression of conscience merged into political disloyalty. This definition was effective since in all treason trials in this period the Government could command sufficient agencies to convict almost anyone it desired. But the Government's actions indicated an earnest desire not to strain the spirit of its public declarations.[2] Too many eager eyes at home and abroad, and too many subtle and vigorous pens were focused upon its every action. Elizabeth, in fact, strained the letter and spirit of her own laws in her attempt to maintain the loyalty of the non-political group of Roman Catholics.[3]

[1] Klein, *Intolerance*, 49.

[2] As late as October 1583, Cobham (in Paris) reported to Beale that he had been creditably informed that the Roman Catholics boast that they have in England "the use of their sacrifices and idolatry, with masses and processions, according to the directions of the Jesuits...." *S.P. For. Eliz.* (*France*), X, 49, October 12, 1583.

[3] We find here the beginning of a conscious attempt to drive a wedge between the militant Jesuitical group and the loyal group which was interested only in the spiritual connotations of its faith. We shall consider the importance of this policy in later pages. (Cf. *post*, 202–211, C. VI, *passim*.) It has well been said that "Of the active conspirator, the enthusiast from the Jesuit Seminaries who plotted the Queen's death, or published the Bull of deposition, the fate, when detected, was certain; execution for High Treason with its attendant barbarities awaited him, but the course pursued with the ordinary recusant, who merely declined on conscientious grounds to attend

It would appear that the Government required little more than any modern Government exacts from its citizenry. Conformity resolved itself under the normal interpretation of the Government into a pledge of political loyalty to the State. Imprisonment was resorted to when a refusal was made to render this pledge of allegiance on the grounds that such an action bared a state of mind essentially dangerous to the welfare of the State.[1] The Government had attempted, in other words, to clarify and give legal content to its repeated distinction between political disloyalty and religious Nonconformity. The policy of imprisonment broke down as a consequence of the physical impossibility of confining all persons liable under the law to this punishment. The Government therefore placed an increasing dependence upon fines and confiscations. As we have noted, in 1581 the fine for absence from church was raised from one shilling to twenty pounds a month. In general, the laws against the Catholics were loosely enforced even in times of real danger. They were intolerant in spirit, but the Government's apparent purpose in the enactment of the legislation and its actual enforcement of the laws were of a very different nature. The Government was not seeking to exterminate Catholicism in England, but to insure its own safety. It might cast its laws in an intolerant mould, but a practical and able ministry used its own sane judgment in exacting conformity to them. Elizabeth acted not as one who had drunk deep at the spring of Reformation thought, but as one who had mastered Renaissance statecraft, when she demanded a compliance to the laws of religion.[2] She sought not to eradicate heresy, but to rule well and securely. She was motivated not by a pious consideration for truth, but by a profound passion for order and stability.

Burleigh, too, throughout his long and able career, sought to make State policy and not religious bigotry his guiding principle. Thus, as late as 1583, we find him urging that the

the services of the Established Church, was generous and gentle when compared with the practice in other countries. . . ." *Acts of the P.C.*, XIII, Intro., x.

Klein, *Intolerance*, 55.   [2] Osborne, C. E., *Christian Ideas*, 167.

Oath of Supremacy should be so modified as to permit a loyal Catholic to subscribe to it without violating his religious convictions. The oath, he urged, is designed to "beget despair . . . in the taking of it," since a conscientious Catholic may feel that he wrongs God in taking it and manifests himself a traitor in refusing it.[1] He therefore suggested to the Queen, "whether, with as much security of your majesty's person and state, and more satisfaction for them, it were not better to leave the oath to this sense, That whosoever would not bear arms against all foreign princes, and namely, the pope, that should any way invade your majesty's dominions, he should be a traitor? For hereof, this commodity will ensue, that those papists (as I think most papists would, that should take this oath) would be divided from the great mutual confidence which is now betwixt the pope and them, by reason of their afflictions for him, and such priests as would refuse that oath then, no tongue could say, . . . that they suffer for religion, if they did suffer."[2]

"But here it may be objected, they would dissemble and equivocate with this oath, and that the pope would dispense with them in that case. Even so may they, with the present oath, both dissemble and equivocate, and also have the pope's dispensation for the present oath, as well as the other."[3]

The policy of the Government towards its Catholic subjects was modified by the conciliatory and moderate purposes of the Government in winning the subjects to the Establishment, and by the sane realization that any serious attempt to exterminate Romanism must result in intestine religious disturbances of a serious nature, if not in civil war.

2. DISSENT AND THE MODIFICATION OF THE GOVERNMENTAL ATTITUDE TOWARDS TOLERATION, 1583–1590.

In the same year Burleigh showed his moderate spirit in his *Instructions to the Judges* about to make the Assize Circuits when he undertook to define more carefully the Council's policy towards Puritan preachers. The document, at the same

[1] Burleigh's Advice to Elizabeth, *Harl. Misc.*, VII, 57.
[2] *Ibid.*   [3] *Ibid.*

time, bears evidence to the thesis we have previously advanced that one of the most fruitful sources of toleration in England is to be found in the fact that the existence of several well defined bodies of religious opinion in England rendered impossible a definite policy of extermination of any one of them. Burleigh counted heavily upon the warm Protestantism inherent in Puritanism in the battle with the Roman Catholics and held that it was advisable on that account to deal more moderately with the Puritans. He pointed out that various "good preachers" have been indicted for "swerving from the letter of the law."[1] This "swerving" he presented as including practically every point in the Puritan demands.[2] He suggested that most of these indictments had resulted from the character of the informers of violations of the law and he therefore ordered the Justices to "sift and examine the affections of such informers touching religion." In other words, the informer should be made as uncomfortable as possible. If, nevertheless, information "creeps in," the judges should proceed against those under indictment not as rogues, felons, or Papists; "but rather giving appearance in the face of the country, what difference you hold between papists, dissenting from us in substance of faith to God and loyalty to our prince, and these other men; which, making some conscience in these ceremonies, do yet diligently and soundly preach true religion and obedience to her majesty; maintaining the common peace in themselves and in their auditors."[3]

With the elevation of Whitgift to Canterbury in 1583, however, the Government found itself less able wholly to dictate ecclesiastical policy. Whitgift was the most able and consistent opponent of Puritanism within the Church, and during the past six years had shown great energy and ability in reducing his western diocese to order.[4] He brought to his

---

[1] Strype, *Annals*, III, 268.
[2] "Namely, for not using the surplice; resorting to sermons in other parishes for want at home; leaving out some collects on the days of preaching; for using private prayers in their houses, and such like." *Ibid.*, III, 1, 268.
[3] *Ibid.*, III, 1, 268-269.
[4] *S.P. Dom. Eliz.* (1540-1580), V, cxviii, 11; Strype, *Whitgift*, 82-83, 97; Willis-Bund, J. W., *Ecc. History of Worcester*, (V.C.H.) II, 50-53.

primacy a great organizing and executive ability. As Calvinist as the Puritans in doctrine, he found himself unalterably opposed to the disciplinary demands of the Puritan party. Especially he distrusted and feared the Presbyterian organizations which had sprung up in London and the Midlands. and which he realized, had support from Leicester and Knollys, and friendly sympathy from others in the Council of the Queen.

The new Archbishop, within three weeks after his confirmation, hastened to join issue with the disintegrating forces within the Church by the publication, in conjunction with various bishops of his province, of several articles designed strictly to regulate preaching and church services.[1] The articles were placed in force on October 19, 1583, and a long and bitter conflict was begun.

The articles in reality demanded little that was new from the clergy, and the flaming hostility which greeted their promulgation clearly arose from the reiterated demand for subscriptions.[2] Thus no one was to be permitted to "preach, read, catechize, minister the sacraments, or to execute any other ecclesiastical function . . . unless he first consent and subscribe to these Articles following; . . ."[3] The first was a statement recognizing the sovereignty of the Queen over her subjects, and denying the authority of any foreign prince in the realm, with which no Puritans could be offended. The Puritans found in the subscription demanded, recognizing the book of Common Prayer, and the Book of Articles of Religion (of 1562) as containing nothing contrary to the word of God, and refusing

[1] "In the month of September (1583), divers good articles were drawn up and agreed upon by himself and the rest of the bishops of his province, and signed by them, which the Queen allowed of, and gave her royal assent unto, to give them greater authority." (Strype, *Whitgift*, I, 228.) There are really three drafts of these articles; one of fifteen arts., which was presented to the Queen; one of twelve, which is registered at Lambeth, which we have used; and still a shorter one, which bore the brunt of the Puritan assault.
[2] Thus preaching and catechizing were forbidden in private places; preaching and catechizing were inhibited for all persons who "did not" four times in the year at least say service and minister the sacraments according to the Book of Common Prayer, the legal habits were demanded, etc. *Reg. I.*, *Whitgift* (Sect. 3); Strype, *Whitgift*, I, 229.
[3] *Reg. I.*, *Whitgift*, Sect. 6; Strype, *Whitgift*, I, 229.

a pledge to "believe" and "use" them in their service, an "Inquisition as black as hell."

A flood of protests poured in from the ministers of the provinces, and the Council attempted to divert popular attention by calling upon Whitgift to deal with certain needed reforms.[1] Whitgift, however, pressed on with his programme in spite of an increasing flood of petitions to the Council by ministers who could not in conscience subscribe. Burleigh decided to take issue with the Archbishop on behalf of two Cambridgeshire ministers who had been called upon to subscribe to twenty-four articles. With their protest we are especially concerned since it is an highly illuminating evidence of the moderate temper of the Government's attitude towards religion. Burleigh especially deplored the "Romish style" of the articles and the fact that they were employed to examine all ministers "without distinction of persons."[2] He found the articles to be "so curiously penned, so ful of branches, and circumstances, as I think the Inquisition of Spain use not so many questions to comprehend and to trap their preyes."[3] He expressed his distaste of theological finesse when he declared that, although the canonists would be able to defend the articles, "this judicial and canonical sifting of poor ministers is not to edify or reform. And, in charity, I think, they ought not to answer to all these nice points, except they were very notorious offenders in Papistry or heresy."[4] The chief minister tersely outlined his own religious programme when he wrote, "I write with a testimony of a good conscience. I desire the peace of the church. I desire concord and unity in the exercise of our religion. I favour no sensual and wilful recusants. But I conclude, that, according to my simple judgment, this kind of proceeding is too much savouring of the Romish inquisition, and is rather a desire to seek for offenders than to reform any."[5]

Burleigh, in this instance, found himself obliged to support the Archbishop's policy, but the incident illustrates the essential

---

[1] Frere, *The English Church*, 227.
[2] Strype, *Whitgift, Appendix*, III, 104–107.
[3] Burl. to Whitgift, (1584), Strype, *Whitgift*, III, 106.
[4] *Ibid.*, III, 106.   [5] *Ibid.*

difference in the point of view of the State and of the Church with respect to the enforcement of uniformity. The State was motivated essentially by policy and it had determined by observation and experience that moderation and unofficial toleration of all beliefs, save rank heresy, best served its interests. Fortunately, the State was in control and, save for occasional concessions to the churchmen, it retained a firm rein upon any tendency towards driving any section of dissent into sullen rebellion.

Events of the same period, however, were to demonstrate that the attitude of the Government was not so liberal with respect to heretical opinions of an advanced nature. In general, it may be held that there was little disposition on the part of the common law courts to take heresy very seriously. Few denied that the State could and should punish heresy, but it appears to have been tacitly agreed that much might be ignored. Allen detects in this attitude a fairly general conviction that though there were doctrines essential to salvation, they must be few in number.[1]

By 1583 there had been five executions in England for heresy. In 1575 two Flemish Anabaptists had been burnt at Smithfield, the first executions for heresy since the reign of Mary.[2] The action of the Government in sentencing the unfortunates brought forward a notable protest from John Foxe, the martyrologist.[3] Foxe, in writing to the Queen in behalf of the condemned men, said he sought the mercy of the Queen for foreigners who had been judged guilty of wicked opinions. They have been sentenced to death at the stake. In such a case regard must be taken both of the gravity of the error and the severity of their punishment. He recognized the gravity of their error and the necessity for restraint in such

---

[1] Allen, *Political Thought*, 232. We shall discuss this view in later pages; cf. *post*, esp. 334 ff.
[2] These executions and the views of the accused men will be discussed in detail in later pages. Here we are interested only in the episode in its relation to the thought of the dominant groups.
[3] There are two drafts of this letter of protest, *Harl. MSS.*, 416, 151; *Ibid.*, 416, 155 ff. The latter is fuller and more tolerant, but the former appears to be in the hand of Foxe. In Fuller, *Church History*, IV, 387 ff.

cases. But to burn them for their errors is Roman rather than Christian. He would not countenance their errors, but he would spare their lives.[1] They may be brought to repentance. He suggested other modes of punishment which might serve as a commutation—*sunt ejectiones, inclusiones retrusae, sunt vincula, sunt perpetua exilia, sunt stigmata, . . . aut etiam patibula.*[2] But he does deplore that the fires of Smithfield, which have slumbered so long under Elizabeth's clement reign, may be lit once more.[3]

Shortly afterwards Foxe petitioned the Lord Chief Justice in the case.[4] The disease of heresy cannot be cured by violent means, nor may erring faith "be compelled and taught." Many have been converted from heresy and error, and some respite in the case of these men may result in their conversion.[5]

The Queen, however, was apparently uninfluenced by the stirring appeal of the great Reformation figure, and ordered the execution to proceed. In signing the writ for the execution of the two heretics she gave expression to the familiar sentiments, "that she was head of the church, that it was her duty to extirpate error, and that heretics ought to be cut off from the flock of Christ that they may not corrupt others."[6]

In 1579 another heretic, Matthew Hamont, was burnt at Norwich, and in 1583 John Coppin and Elias Thacker were hanged at Bury St. Edmunds. Coppin and Thacker were technically convicted of treason for having assailed the royal supremacy, but their heretical beliefs cannot be disentangled from their civil offence. Coppin was apparently a layman of Bury St. Edmunds,[7] and as early as 1576 had been committed to prison by his bishop for disobedience to the ecclesiastical laws.[8] Two years of close imprisonment and constant attendance by various clergymen did not suffice to bring him to conformity.[9] In 1578 he refused to permit a newly-born child to be baptized by a regularly constituted minister and

[1] *Harl. MSS.*, 416. [2] *Ibid.* [3] *Ibid.*
[4] *Ibid.*, 417, 51. [5] *Ibid.* [6] Rymer, *Foed.*, XV, 740–741.
[7] Brook, Benjamin, *Lives of the Puritans*, I, 262–263, however, says he was a minister in the diocese of Norwich.
[8] *Articles of the Bishop of Norwich against the Justices*, 1693, 89.
[9] Burghley Papers, *Lansdowne MSS.*, XXVII, 28.

declined to accept the services of a godfather.[1] In December of that year he was arraigned for having called a fellow prisoner an idolater for using the Book of Common Prayer and for having declared the Queen to be "puregid to God."[2] Coppin appears to have been detained for an additional five years and was soon joined by one Elias Thacker, who was imprisoned for unorthodox words and behaviour.[3] The two prisoners found their zeal increased by contact, and perhaps by perusal of the works of Browne, and their jailer soon petitioned both the episcopal and the civil court for their removal "for fear of infecting" the other prisoners.[4] At this point they were joined by a third prisoner, Thomas Gibson, a bookbinder of Bury, who, inspired by Browne's repudiation of the royal authority in the Church, had set up opprobrious texts in his parish church.[5] In addition he had bound and distributed some of the works of Browne, who had been preaching in the neighbourhood.[6] The three prisoners were put on trial in 1583 "for heresy and for dispersinge of Brownes Bookes and Harrisones Bookes."[7] During the trial Gibson admitted the authority of the Crown in the Church, and Chief Justice Wray at once reprieved him. Obviously the Government was pressing only this one charge. On July 6th, Wray wrote Burleigh that Coppin and Thacker "acknowledged her majesty chieffe ruler civile, for so ys ther terms, and no further."[8] Wray feared popular feeling, since Bury was a hotbed of Brownism, and Coppin was taken directly from the Court, upon condemnation, and hanged.[9] Thacker was hanged on the following day, and at the same time some forty of Browne's and Harrison's books were burned in order

---

[1] Dexter, H. M., *The Congregationalism of the Last Three Hundred Years, as seen in the Literature*, 208.

[2] Burghley Papers, *Lansdowne MSS.*, XXVII, 28.

[3] Frere, *English Church*, 204.   [4] Strype, *Annals*, III, (2) 173.

[5] Frere, *English Church*, 204. "I know thy works, etc.," from the Address to Church of Ephesus in the Apocalypse.

[6] Strype, *Annals*, III, (1), 177.

[7] It is not clear how Coppin and Thacker, being in prison, could have been guilty of distributing these books, but they made no attempt to deny the charge.

[8] *Lansdowne MSS.*, XXXVIII, 64.   [9] Frere, *English Church*, 204.

to lend further effect to the impression of severity which the Government desired to give.[1]

The Anglican definition of the nature and extent of the royal power in the Church and the purpose and theory of enforced conformity were further explained in 1584–1585. A few scattered examples from the Anglican writings of the period may suffice to indicate the development. Whitgift, in replying to Burleigh's rebuke for using inquisitorial methods in the examination of nonconforming ministers, charged that the methods of the Ecclesiastical Courts were as tolerable and equitable as those of the Civil Courts.[2] The peace and unity of the Church were posed by the Archbishop as the great end of his efforts and that could not be attained without the proper administration of discipline.[3] He declared himself unable otherwise to devise how "to deale to worke to any good effect."[4]

"Not severity but lenity hath bred this schism in the church, as it hath done otherwise many other abuses which I trust in time to redresse; but the accusation of severity is the least thing I feare. If I be able to answer to the contrary fault I shall find myselfe well repaid. . . ."[5]

Not dissimilar in tone was the speech of the Crown to Parliament in 1585,[6] in reply to the Puritan demands for correction of abuses.[7] The Queen held that religion was of fundamental importance to the State since it was "the ground on which all other matters ought to take roote, and being corrupted, might mar all the tree."[8] God had made her the

---

[1] *Lansdowne MSS.*, XXXVIII, 64.
[2] *Whitgift to Burleigh*, July 3, 1584. Strype, *Whitgift*, III, 107–112.
[3] *Ibid.*, III, 107–112.
[4] *Whit. to Burl.*, September 18, 1584, *Morrice MSS.*, LV, p. 13.
[5] *Ibid.*   [6] On March 29th.
[7] The sixth Parliament, November 23, 1584–March 29, 1585, passed an "Act against Jesuits, seminary priests, and other suchlike disobedient persons," and an "Act to ensure the Queen's safety." Otherwise the importance of the session for ecclesiastical affairs centres on the insistent demands of the Puritan party for wide reform in religion on the basis of petitions sent in from numerous counties. The agitation was unsuccessful, and was met by renewed repression by the Episcopal and Civil Courts and by restrictions on the Press. (*Order of Privy Council in Star Chamber*, June 23, 1586.)   [8] Stow, John, *The Annals of England*, 1181.

"overlooker" of the Church. She was therefore responsible for the prevention of schism and heretical errors. She admitted that some faults might have crept into the Church since that must be true of all great institutions.[1] Then, turning to the bishops, she threatened "That if you do not amend, I mind to depose you, looke you therefore well to your charges, . . ."[2] But she reiterated her high responsibility and authority, which was not shared by Parliament, when she reminded the Members who sought to meddle with the established religion that she saw "many overbold with God Almighty, making too many subtill scannings of his blessed will, as lawyers do with human testaments. . . ."[3] She declared that she did not intend to animate the Catholics, "nor yet would she tolerate newfangleness."[4] It was her steady intention to guide both parties by God's true rule.

It would be difficult to find a franker and clearer statement of Erastianism. The Queen brushed aside the parliamentary power of ordering religion by announcing the complete character of her own power in the Church. They were forbidden to scan the "blessed will of god," since they were incompetent correctly to interpret it. But it was implied that the Queen was perfectly competent to do so. She spoke reverently of her great responsibility, and of her intention to guide the English Church moderately between the rocks of Romanism and the rapids of Puritanism. Puritan extremism explains the summary character of the Queen's actions. When she saw the Establishment threatened by their intemperate demands she brusquely warned them that the State was omnicompetent in the delineation and execution of ecclesiastical policy.

In the following year the Queen enlarged her position in reply to renewed Puritan demands for alterations in the Establishment. "Her Majesty is fully resolved, by her own reading and princely judgment, upon the truth of the Reformation, which we have already; and mindeth not now to begin to settle herself in causes of religion."[5] This is especially true since foreign enemies are endeavouring to overthrow the English Church

---

[1] Stow, *Annals*, 1181; D'Ewes, *Journal*, 328.   [2] *Ibid.*
[3] *Ibid.*, 329.   [4] *Ibid.*, 328.   [5] Strype, *Whitgift*, I, 494.

and dissension and change within it would be an open admission of weakness and doubt.[1] The English Church is not perfect for some things are amiss, but "she is fully persuaded, and knoweth it to be true, that for the very substance and grounds of true religion, no man living can justly control them; to make every day new laws in matters of circumstances, and of less moment—were a means to breed great lightness in her subjects, to nourish an unstayed humour in them, in seeking still for exchanges."[2]

At the same time, the Anglican position had grown more intolerant, largely in consequence of the acrimonious literary controversy with the Puritans and the critical state of Catholic affairs. In 1585 appeared Bilson's *The True Difference Betweene Christian Subjection and Unchristian Rebellion*, which was a highly important indication of this change.[3] "Preachers," he said, "may reprove and threaten, princes may sease the goods, and chastise the bodies of such as offende, preachers may shut the gates of Heaven against non-repentants, princes may roote them from the face of the earth, and let them feele the just vengeance of their sinnes in this worlde. This is the power of prince which wee say must bee directed by bishoppes, but is not subjected to their willes or Tribunals."[4] He repeatedly argued the power of the prince in the Church, and his great responsibility in the care of religion and the rooting out of heresy.[5] He branded the teaching that the King may tolerate

[1] Strype, *Whitgift*, I, 495.   [2] *Ibid.*
[3] Published again in 1586, Thomas Bilson (1546–1616?) was a native of Winchester, and was educated there and at Oxford. He was graduated B.A. from Oxford in 1565, and became a 'most solid and constant preacher.' (Wood, *Athen. Oxon.*, II, 169.) He appears to have been a schoolmaster for a time, and was installed prebendary of Winchester in 1576. He was raised to a bishopric (Worcester) in 1596, and was translated to Winchester in the following year. He enjoyed a wide reputation for solid learning and controversial ability. (*Ibid.*, II, 169–170.) The work under consideration was perhaps his most important and was a reply to Allen's able *Defence of English Catholics*. Wood tells us that, though serving its immediate end, the book went so far in loosening the bonds of civil obedience, because of the necessity of excusing the Dutch revolt, that it contributed much to the ruin of the Stuart cause. (*Ibid.*, II, 170.) This section of the work is, as a matter of fact, insipid when compared with the Puritan writings of his own and later days.
[4] Bilson, *True Difference*, 361–362.
[5] *Ibid.*, 124, 129 ff., 198–204, 238–240, 247–250.

two religions in his realm as an invention of the Devil "whose seruice no Christian prince may so much as tolerate."[1] Princes may not "winke at corrupt and vitious religion, . . . seeing no man, and therefore no prince, can serue two masters."[2] ". . . What answere must be made for the Ruine of Faith, haruest of sinne, murder of soules consequent alwayes to the publique freedom of heresies?"[3]

Bilson and Hutchins, whose bitter sermon against the recusants appeared a year after the publication of Bilson's book, went considerably beyond their Anglican predecessors in the doctrine that Catholics and heretics should be forced to embrace the truth. Bilson bluntly stated that "heretikes of al sects and sortes may be compelled to followe truth, . . . of Christian magistrates, for dread a punishment, tempered with good instruction, to forsake their heresies, and forbeare their idolatries. . . ."[4]

Hutchins compared the recusants to the unclean, greedy and hunted fox.[5] He appeared to regard the Roman Catholics simply as obstinate and perverse. "When we doe most persecute and presse them with the truth, yet they leaue their shews and starting holes, they haue their distinctions, their shiftes, and if one serue not, yet will they coyne some other colarably for the time to credit their vntruth: . . ."[6]

The ministers of the Church, it was held, are charged to seek to recover such as are lost in heresy by mildness and patience. But the Catholics present too great a problem for the ministry to handle unaided.[7] The ministry and the magistracy must work in closest conjunction; "the one by loue the other by feare: the one by softnes, the other by sharpnes: the one by perswading, the other by punishing, if that perswasion may not

[1] Bilson, *True Difference*, 21. [2] *Ibid.*, 22.
[3] *Ibid.* [4] *Ibid.*, 16.
[5] Hutchins, E., *A Sermon preached at Westchester*, A 4. It is interesting that he employed the same text as Sandys, whose sermon on the fox and the vine is a classic of Elizabethan prose. Hutchins advanced the same arguments, but his bitterness and bigotry displayed the unfortunate effect of the Roman Counter Reformation upon English ecclesiastical thought.
[6] *Ibid.* (no pagin.).
[7] Hutchins, E., *A Sermon preached at Westchester* (no pagin.).

preuaile."[1] The prince, as God's lieutenant, is bound, not only to maintain peace between men, "but also by lawes to maintain Religiō towards God. . . ."[2]

Both Bilson and Hutchins appeared to have abandoned the early faith in the power of truth to overcome erroneous opinions. The burden of handling the Catholic problem was shifted by them to the magistracy. "Let the vine of Christ be deare vnto you, and spare not the Fox, least you lose the vine. Oh spare vs not papists: for what are they but Foxes?"[3] They must be cut down without any false feelings of charity for the sake of the stability of the Church.[4]

However, in spite of the rigorous teachings of Bilson with respect to heresy, he was far from holding that obstinate heretics should be put to death. Moderate counsels are not to be despised and correction should not be confused with murder.[5] Quoting the early writings of Augustine, he concluded, "For it neuer pleased any good men in the Catholique Church that heretiques should be put to death. Many lawes were made to punish them, but no princes law commanded thē to be slaine."[6]

Some, in his *A Godly Treatise Containing and Deciding Certaine Questions* (1588) and in his *A Godly Treatise* (1589), written in the midst of the Martin Marprelate controversy, advanced much the same view.[7] Two groups in England, he wrote, deny the validity of the Church and its orders, the Papists and the Anabaptists.[8] These persons are in reality heretics resembling the ancient Donatists.[9] A godly prince may and should compel his subjects to conform to the external

Hutchins. E., *A Sermon preached at Westchester* (no pagin.).
[2] Bilson, *True Difference*, 19.
[3] Hutchins, E., *A Sermon preached at Westchester* (no pagin.).
[4] *Ibid.* (no pagin.).   [5] Bilson, *True Difference*, 19.   [6] *Ibid.*
[7] Some, R., *A Godly Treatise wherein are examined and confuted many execrable fancies, giuen out and holden, partly by Hen. Barrowe and Iohn Greenwood : partly by other of the Anabaptisticall order, . . .* and *A Godly Treatise Containing and deciding Certaine Questions mooued of late in London and other places, touching the ministrie, sacraments, and Church.*
[8] Some, *Godly Treatise* (no pagin.). Under the latter designation he included the Brownists and the advanced Presbyterians who followed Martin Marprelate.   [9] *Ibid.* (no pagin.).

service of God.[1] Men are invited to the Gospel of their own accord, and if they will not embrace this opportunity we are obliged to compel them.[2] The godly prince is, further, not permitted to allow any but the godly religion, and, since neither Penry's doctrines nor the Catholic religion are true faiths, they should not be permitted in the commonwealth.[3] He rested his argument upon the usual premises: the responsibility of the prince for the souls of his subjects; the evils of dissension; and the necessity for attending to the execution of God's law. "Almightie God may not bee dalied with in his seruice. There must be no parting of stakes. Hee will either haue all or none," he said, resting heavily upon Ezech. xx.[4]

The great dangers which might be incurred by the State and Church by further changes in the established religion were pointed out by Thomas Cooper in his *An Admonition to the People of England* (1589).[5] Cooper urged that the safety of the realm depended upon the stability of the Establishment.[6] For that reason the governors of the realm fear to make any altera-

---

[1] "Thus Asa commanded Judah to seek the Lord God; we have the example of Jehoshaphat and Artaxerxes; Josias compelled his subjects to the true religion; Augustine at first said that an heretic should be reasoned with, but after further experience with their obstinacy recommended compulsion." (*Ibid.* (no pagin.); vide also Some, *Godly Treatise Containing*, cs. I–II.)

[2] *Ibid.* (no pagin.).

[3] Some, *Godly Treatise* (no pagin.); *Godly Treatise Containing*, 5–6.

[4] *Ibid.*, 7.

[5] The book was republished in the year of the first edition with minor alterations. A third edition was published in 1847. Thomas Cooper was born at Oxford, *c.* 1517, the son of a poor tailor. (*D.N.B.*, xii, 149.) He was educated at Magdalen College, and was elected a Fellow of his college in 1540. Later he became the master of Magdalen. (Strype, *Parker*, II, 47; III, 295.) During the reign of Mary his Protestant views prevented the assumption of orders, and he took a degree in medicine, practising for a season in Oxford. (Wood, *Athen. Oxon.*, I, 608.) Upon the death of Mary he was ordained and "became a frequent preacher," and was in 1566 made Dean of Christ Church. A year previously his monumental *Thesaurus* had appeared and he became known to the Queen for his proficiency in the humanities. He was successively Dean of Gloucester and Bishop of Lincoln. In 1584 he was translated to the rich see of Winchester. Four years later he undertook in the work under consideration to reply to the Martinist attacks on the Church. The reply, *Ha' Ye any work for the Cooper*, was one of the most vigorous of the Martin Marprelate series. He died in 1594.

[6] Cooper, *Admonition*, 117.

tions in the Church "for they knowe what danger may come in these perillous dayes by innouations: and if they shoulde once beginne, things are so infinite, that they can see no ende of alterations."[1] The Church of England is settled "in a tollerable manner of Reformation," religious truth is freely taught and error is repressed by law. There are imperfections in the Church but the State is well informed when it considers "it better to beare with some imperfections, then by attempting great alterations, in so dangerous a time, to hazard the state both of the church and of the Realme."[2]

At about the same time we find the author of the *Myrrour for Martinists* urging that the civil ruler should follow the examples of the Old Testament kings and of Constantine in the "staying and suppressing of all controuersies among the prrofessors of the Gospell, that thereby they may prouide for the peace and publike health of the church."[3] Gifford in his *A Plaine Declaration* answered the Separatists' complaint against compulsion in the organisation of a church by explaining that the prince may compel his subjects "to renounce and forsake all false worship, and to imbrace the doctrine of saluation."[4]

The clash of religious controversy had not, however, wholly destroyed the moderate and tolerant character of Anglicanism. Thus we find Edmund Bunny in his *Treatise Tending to Pacification*, published about 1585, arguing the cause of the Establishment in an admirably written book.[5] The treatise is

---

[1] Cooper, *Admonition*, 117.   [2] *Ibid.*
[3] T.T. (T. Turswell?), *Myrrour for Martinists* (1590), 33.
[4] Gifford, G., *A Plaine Declaration that our Brownists be full Donatists*, 8, 67.
[5] Edmund Bunny (1540–1619) was a native of Buckinghamshire, where his family was of considerable local importance. (Wood, *Athen. Oxon.*, II, 219–220.) He was educated at Oxford, and was sent to Gray's Inn and Staple Inn by his father. (*D.N.B.*, vii, 271.) He was determined upon an ecclesiastical career, however, and returned to Oxford, where he was graduated M.A. in 1565, and was soon afterwards elected a Fellow of Merton College. He became about 1570 chaplain to Grindal at York, and was given a prebendary in York and a rectory in the province. He was a staunch Calvinist, highly evangelical, and a unique figure. He travelled all over England, preaching and catechizing "like a new Apostle." (Wood, *Athen. Oxon.*, II, 220.) He was a "fluid" extempore speaker, and was accused of

noteworthy for its calm and reasoned spirit. Bunny was distressed by the rent in Christ's robe in England occasioned by the division of Christians between the Church of England and the Roman Catholic faith. Since the Church of Christ cannot remain divided the Roman Catholics of England should either join with the Church of England, or the reverse. Bunny sought to prove that, since England could not submit to Rome, the Roman Catholics should lend their obedience to the English Establishment. The tone of the book is most refreshing and sane when compared with the theological chatter which predominated the decade in which it appeared. Bunny, though an ardent Calvinist, assumed a rational and somewhat sceptical view of the problem of conformity. England, he argued, has enjoyed under Elizabeth the most peaceful and happy period of her national existence. The Roman Catholics might more fully partake of that happiness if they would enter the Establishment, ". . . reseruing their consciences to themselues, and conforming their outwarde demeanour no further than is needfull for the common tranquillitie of all, . . ."[1] This they could "lawfully doe . . . without impeachment to the substance of their profession."[2]

It appears fairly obvious that the bitter dispute with the Puritan party, when joined with the necessity for closer cohesion against the assaults of the Romanists, had resulted in the Church, as in the State, in a stricter and less liberal attitude towards dissent. The State was in factual control of religious policy and supported the validity of that power. The prince was urged to foster true religion and to root out heresy. It was argued that heretics and misbelievers should be forced to the acceptance of religious truth, though the unwillingness of the English thinkers to advocate the death penalty for heresy, considerably mitigated the severity of their position. In support of these opinions we hear rather more about the political necessity for order and uniformity than of arguments which urged the ideal justification of repression.

being a "divinity squirt." (*Ibid.*, II, 221.) The Treatise was first published in 1584-5, and another edition is said to have appeared in 1630. The first edition is very rare. The only copy known to the writer is in the Sion College library.   [1] Bunny, *Treatise*, 24.   [2] *Ibid.*

The long and able leadership of the Government was extracting the teeth of clerical intolerance. The bishops vindicated their enforcement of the laws of uniformity by the subject's obligation to obey the laws of his country, rather than from any essentially spiritual reasons.[1] Tillotson, in his sermons, stressed a generally held conviction when he represented the dissentients as a perverse group who refused to comply to the service simply because they were required to do so.

We shall consider in some detail in later pages the Puritan position with respect to toleration of dissent and in regard to the question of the power of the magistrate in the Church. At this point it will be well, however, to notice a neglected protest against the overweening power of the secular authorities in spiritual concerns and an interesting championship of liberty of conscience by Robert Beale. Beale had fled from England during the reign of Mary on account of his advanced Protestantism and was, in 1564, connected with the English Embassy in Paris.[2] He was secretary to Walsingham during his ambassadorship there. Returning to England, he sat in Parliament for Totnes in 1572 and was sent shortly afterwards to Germany to plead for the toleration of the Cryptocalvinists.[3] He was, after 1580, employed in numerous diplomatic negotiations of importance in Scotland, France, and the Netherlands, and on at least three occasions acted as Secretary of State.[4]

Beale belonged to the advanced Puritan Wing of the Council and in 1584 wrote a scathing denunciation of the Establishment and of the religious repression.[5] The tolerant and Erastian character of the Government was shown by the fact that a criticism which no modern Government would brook by one

[1] Neal, *History of the Puritans*, I, 103.   [2] *D.N.B.*, iv, 3.
[3] This group denied the doctrine of the ubiquity of Christ's body.
[4] In 1578, 1581 and 1583, during the absence of Walsingham. Beale was banished from court in 1592 because of his denunciation of the inquisitorial methods of the bishops. He was returned to Parliament in 1592, however, and in the year before his death (1600), was one of the emissaries appointed to treat for peace with Spain.
[5] I have been able to find no copy of the work which was commonly known as "Beale's Book." Strype prints a usable summary of the book which Whitgift had forwarded to Burleigh. (See also *D.N.B.*, iv, 6; Cooper, *Athen. Cantab.*, II, 313.)

of its members went quite unpunished; in fact, in the year of its publication he was acting in a most important capacity for the State.[1]

The Puritan official attacked at the outset the Queen's title of 'Fidei Defensor' and her ecclesiastical authority on the grounds that it was principally employed for the maintenance of "foul abuses and enormities" of a Roman character.[2] He placed the responsibility for this perversion of function chiefly upon the bishops whose jurisdiction, he held, caused "both prynces and theire lawes" to be "drawne from their true use and intention. . . ."[3] In especial, he urged that a strict enforcement of the Book of Common Prayer was not in accordance with the laws of the realm. According to Whitgift, Beale "playnlie denieth, and goeth . . . to prove, that prynces and magistrates have no authority to make lawes in things indifferent, to bynde men to the observation thereof."[4]

Beale branded as unchristian the doctrine that an earthly prince may enforce indifferent things upon the consciences of men.[5] He regarded truth as quite independent of legislative enactments: "No prynce, yea, not all the prynces in the world, have authority to ordeyne, but that indifferent things are indifferent things, and so must contynew still without any alteration, or changing of their own nature."[6] We have first to prove that God has granted any authority to earthly princes to ordain in such matters.[7] Quite magnificently he continued, "and untill then, because I fynde no suche doctrine in God's booke, your Lordship must pardon me, if I canne not be of your L. opinion, but think it verie impertinent and dangerous."[8] Beale boldly suggested that the royal authority in spiritual matters had been extended beyond the bounds of scriptural right. The regal authority is impinging upon conscience in the enforcement of these 'indifferent' matters and the magistrate "ought not to entermeddle with that case, which the Lord hath reserved to hymself. . . ."[9]

---

[1] In 1585 he was one of the agents chiefly responsible, under Walsingham, for the negotiations with Mary Queen of Scots.
[2] Strype, Whitgift, I, 284.   [3] Ibid.   [4] Ibid., I, 285.
[5] Ibid.   [6] Ibid.   [7] Ibid., I, 286.   [8] Ibid.   [9] Ibid.

The councillor then proceeded to a general condemnation of the interference of the State with Christian conscience. The Lord has not left the judgment of His doctrine to any magistrate, "either spiritual or temporal, but unto the particular conscience of evrie one of his sheepe, which *vocem ejus audiunt, et alienum non recipiunt;* so hath he done for this parcell of doctrine, touchinge the true use of indifferent things; and as well for the one as the other, the rules are to be observed."[1] The apostles sought obedience only for the sake of conscience while, he implied, the ecclesiastical policy of the Established Church outraged the sacred rights of the Christian man. This vindication of Christian individualism, much more akin to the early views of Luther, than to contemporary Puritan thought if fully extended, would embody a general theory of toleration. Doubtlessly, however, Beale would not have granted the full implications of that extension.

3. THE FINAL PHASE OF THE ROMAN CATHOLIC PROBLEM, 1583–1603

The act of 1581 had declared any attempt to convert an English subject to the Roman Catholic faith a treasonable offence, the saying or hearing of a mass to be prohibited under severe penalties, and a fine of twenty pounds a month to be levied upon recusants.[2] Events of the following year

[1] Beale continued, "They that extend the authoritie of the magistrate farther than by the Word of God it should be, which say, that the judgement of the rule of charitie, touching the usinge of indifferent thinges, dothe consist in the magistrates, and should not be left to the particular conscience of eurie man" (*Ibid.*, I, 287) are in error, "because the apostle will haue obedience for conscience sake," and "therefore no things indifferent must be commanded that is against the conscience of anye, for then no true obedience is sought." (*Ibid.*, 287.)

[2] By 23 Eliz., c. 1. The Act of 23 Eliz., c. 2, declared the utterance of seditious words to be a crime punishable by fine and mutilation; while any person guilty of publishing a seditious book, or predicting the Queen's death should be regarded as a felon and punished by death. By 27 Eliz., c. 2, all Jesuits and seminary priests were banished from the realm on pain of death; the harbouring of any such persons was declared a felony; and any English subject who was being educated abroad in a Jesuit school, and who did not return and take the Oath of Supremacy, was declared to be

conspired to increase the severity of the enforcement of the penal laws and to inculcate a deliberate attempt on the part of the Government to cripple, if not to destroy, the profession of the Roman Catholic faith in England. The Roman Catholic apologists have tended to regard this period as one of the outrageous persecution of men who were earnestly endeavouring to advance their faith and who sought only to obey the dictates of their consciences. Lamentable as the persecutions were, unwarranted as numerous instances of punishment have been demonstrated to have been, it is difficult to escape the conclusion that the Church of Rome had identified itself with a definite programme of hostility to England, which included the destruction of Elizabeth by one means or another, and that England and the Church of England had by these efforts been placed in a defensive position which rendered nice discrimination in the choice of weapons quite impossible. It has well been suggested that "There were political reasons why patriotic Englishmen should hate the pope, and from this it was only a short step to hatred of the whole religious system which the pope represented."[1]

The development of Catholic policy against the Government, culminating in the attack of the Armada in 1588, has been so thoroughly treated that there is no necessity for repetition. We shall therefore confine ourselves in this controversial period to an analysis of the attitude of the dominant groups in England towards the Catholic problem, and attempt to indicate the efforts of Englishmen to differentiate between the political punishment of Roman Catholics who had run foul of the penal laws from any policy which undertook to persecute them for the retention of dissenting spiritual beliefs.

The extension of the penal code in 1581 and in 1586–1587[2] against the Jesuits and priests from abroad had practically made

---

guilty of high treason. The Act of 23 Eliz., c. 1, was in 1587 so amended as to enable the Queen to confiscate two-thirds of the property of any recusant who did not pay the legal fine of twenty pounds a month. The Act, when enforced, was of course completely ruinous to the recusants.

[1] Tanner, J. R., *Tudor Constitutional Documents*, 142.

[2] Cf. *ante*, f.n. 2, 194.

Catholic missionary effort an offence punishable by death. The Jesuits were regarded as the spearhead of Catholic policy and a determined effort was to be made to end their politico-religious activities.[1] But even in an almost hysterical period of alarm, the laws were not given maximum enforcement. Legally, all priests from abroad were held to be evident traitors, but the Government constantly refrained from exacting capital punishment unless more tangible evidence of treason was forthcoming.[2] In every trial it sought to establish an overt act of treason. With the exception of Campion, no priest seems to have been executed without reasonable proof, under the existing laws, of political activity against the Government. The Queen was averse to religious persecution and she desisted from a wholesale policy of executions, if for no other reason, because she was sagacious enough to realize that such a programme would evoke dangerous sentiments on the Continent and that it would effect cohesion among her Catholic subjects.

It would appear that the Government was forced against its will to adopt a policy of repression. As late as 1586 the moderate character of the English policy towards Catholics was recognized even by Romanists. Thus John Foxley (Gratley)[3] wrote

[1] Elizabeth in a letter to James VI (1586) indicated this tendency. "I thanke God," she wrote, "that you beuare so sone of Jesuites, that haue bine the source of al thes trecheries in this realme, and wyl sprede, lik an ivel wide, if at the first the be not wided out. I wold I had had Prometheus for companion, for Epimetheus had like have bine myne to sone. What religion is this, that the say the way to saluation is to kil the prince for a merit meritorus? This is that the haue all confessed without tortur or menace (i.e. with respect to this particular question) I swere hit, on my worde." (*Letters of Elizabeth and James VI*, 40.)

[2] The repression was, of course, severe, and in at least three instances executions were carried out which were of dubious legality even under the existing laws. Between 1578–1585 eighteen priests and three Roman Catholic laymen were executed in London. (Sanders, Nicolas, *Rise and Growth of the Anglican Schism*, 308–333.)

[3] Foxley was the pseudonym of Edward Gratley, an English Roman Catholic who had fled the realm. He belonged to the anti-Jesuitical group, and was for some time closely connected with Walsingham. In April 1586 Stafford was seeing him in Paris, and was "secretly encouraging him." (*Cal. S.P. Eliz., For.*, 1585–1586, p. 550.) He was employed by Walsingham to "feel Dr. Allen thoroughly of all matters, and to set a faction between Parsons and him." (*Aldred to Walsingham*, April 1586; *S.P. Dom. Add., Eliz.*, xxix, 95.) Gratley was described as so eager in the venture "that with

to Walsingham that he had been informed of the clemency shown to his co-religionists and understood that the Queen "is inclined to moderation of severity and reunion of her subjects in comon society and [?] unity."[1] He regarded this as the correct policy since it removed all excuses for the invasion of England by foreign powers and would salve the wounds already inflicted, while preventing future injuries. Such a programme would be guided by the presumption "that policy teacheth no alteration to be *in instanti* whole and complete, but to proceed *per gradus discretionis.* . . ."[2]

Shortly after the execution of Campion the Government promised a statement[3] which would prove that it did not persecute religious belief "that concerneth only matters of conscience . . ." in "no ways prejudicial to her my's state and gouernment."[4] Two of those who were tried with Campion were willing to acknowledge allegiance to the Government and were accordingly spared.[5] This would indicate that the death penalty was not exacted as a means of compelling conscience. "Her mty doth mean to extend grace and mercy hoping that as it hath pleased God to prove their consciences to acknowledge towards her mty that duty of allegiance that by the laws of God an man they owe unto her as their most lawfull prince and sovereign . . ." they will not confuse conscience with sedition.[6]

Walsingham, in a memoir (1586) drawn up to define the governmental policy against foreign priests clearly distinguished between the learned and influential priests, whom he would imprison, and the "simple fellows having more zeal than wit

---

great pain he doth . . . bridle himself." (*Ibid.*, xxix, 102.) In May, Gratley wrote to Walsingham that he had "always borne as true and loyal devotion to her majesty, my country and your honour as religion and justice requireth. . . ." He attempted to point out that spiritual obedience to Rome did not exclude "obedience to the prince or governor." (*S.P. Dom., Add., Eliz.*, xxix, 110.)

[1] *Foxley to Walsingham*, April 20, 1586 (Rouen). *S.P. Dom. Eliz., Add.*, xxix, 100; *Ibid.*, June 18, 1586, xxix, 118.   [2] *Ibid.*, xxix, 100.
[3] The subject should "be hereafter answered more at large. . . ." *S.P. Dom., Eliz.*, clii, 91. (March?, 1582.)
[4] *S.P. Dom. Eliz.*, clii, 91 (March? 1582).
[5] *Ibid.*, clii, 91.   [6] *Ibid.*

or learning," whom he would banish.[1] He opposed execution save in rare instances. "For the restrained, the execution of them, as experience showeth, in respect of their constancy or rather obstinacy, moveth men to compassion and draweth some to affect their religion, upon conceipt that such an extraordinary contempt of death cannot but proceed from above, whereby many have fallen away; and therefore, it is a thing meet to be considered, whether some other remedy were not meet to be put in execution."[2]

There is likewise considerable evidence to show that recusants who were deemed dangerous enough to warrant imprisonment were treated with considerable lenity even during the critical period 1587–1590. Despite the general stringency of these years, sickness and business were often considered sufficient reasons for the release of prisoners under proper security.[3] With the passing of the Spanish danger, the Council considered that the occasion for the recent severity had been largely dispelled. Thus an order was dispatched to Ely intimating that it was the purpose of the Government to enlarge the liberties of the prisoners detained at that place. However, the Council "thought good before th' enlarginge of them that shold be treated withall to declare their conformitie in their allegeance to her majestie. . . ."[4] In general, from this time forward, recusants were given their liberty under bond upon subscribing to a declaration of loyalty similar to that used in connection with the prisoners at Ely.[5]

---

[1] Banishment was frequently employed (*S.P. Dom. Eliz.*, clxxv, 38; clxxvi, 9; *Acts of the P.C.*, xiv, 21.)
[2] Quoted in Read, *Walsingham*, II, 312–313.
[3] *Acts of the P.C.*, xiv, 27, 75; xiv, 19; xiv, 34.
[4] *Ibid.*, xvi, 313. It appears that these recusants asserted their loyalty to the Queen, for in November 1588 the Council wrote to their keeper that since they "had made a verie dutifull protestacion of ther alleageance towards her majestie, . . . he was lett to understand that her Majesties pleasure was to extend favour towardes them." They were ordered to be sent to London, where the Archbishop of Canterbury would give them "direccion and ordre for theire aboade in some convenient place within tenne myles of London, . . ." (*Ibid.*, xvi, 370); they could convince him of their resolution to remain "sincere and steadfast." (*Ibid.*, xvi, 382.)
[5] *Ibid.*, xvii, 57, 83, 351.

Even recusants who refused to sign what amounted to an oath of allegiance were treated with surprising lenity.[1] Sir Thomas Cornwallis was released from appearing in connection with his bond since he was "a very olde man, and one that besides the matter of his Religion hathe not bene knowen to have intermedled in causes of the State," and he was "suffred to Remaine and continue in the contrie where he nowe is. . . ."[2] The tendency of magistrates in certain areas to deal kindly with their Catholic neighbours was demonstrated by a preliminary list of the recusants of Lancashire and Cheshire forwarded to the Council by the bishops which revealed that no report had ever been rendered and that no proceedings had been instituted against almost a thousand recusants in that area alone.[3] An English observer pointed out to Burleigh that the Catholic countries grossly exaggerated the condition of the English Catholics.[4] Reports were abroad of a rigorous persecution, with infinite torments and intolerable deaths. On the contrary, he found "great peace, tolerance, tranquillity, and moderation, with wonderful clemency, and almost a general liberty and dismission of all."[5]

The attitude of the English Government towards its Catholic subjects was considerably clarified about 1590 by the letter of Walsingham to M. Cretoy, the French Ambassador to England, in which the English statesman sought to analyse the problem of dissent and to explain the English attitude towards its nonconforming subjects.[6]

[1] Thus John Talbot received consideration because of poor health. (*Ibid.*, xvii, 40, 198.) George Willoughby was released on bail to help "about the repayringe of the sea bankes deccied and draning the marshes. . . ." (*Ibid.*, xvii, 294.) John Townley was granted liberty until the next term "for dyspatche of some necessarye affaires of his owne, to repaier into the country. . . ." (*Ibid.*, xviii, 8.) (See also, *Ibid.*, xvii, 270, 348; xix, 34, 102, 159, 167, 194.)
[2] *Acts of the P.C.*, xviii, 170.   [3] *Ibid.*, xix, 335 ff. (July 1590).
[4] *J. Snowden to Burleigh, S.P. Dom. Eliz.*, ccxxxix, 46 (June 1591).
[5] *Ibid.*
[6] *Walsingham to M. Cretoy . . . in Defense of the Queen's Majesty, in her Proceedings in causes Ecclesiastical against Catholics.* Helmingham Hall, Suffolk. There is a slightly variant copy in the B.M.; *Sloan MSS.*, 1775, f. 75. Reprints may be found in Burnet, *Hist. of the Reform.*, III, 419 ff.;

Walsingham argued that the procedure of the Queen against both Catholic and Puritan dissenters rested upon two principles. In the first place, the Government recognized that conscience was not to be compelled but must be won and reduced by the operation of the force of truth. This process obtained assistance by the operation of time and by the agencies of persuasion and instruction.[1] But, in the second place, causes of conscience were disposed to exceed their proper limitations and to lead to factions within the State. In such instances the State was obliged to employ repression, even if the guilty persons argued the cause of conscience.

Guided by these principles of government, the Queen had dealt mildly with her Catholic subjects, "not liking to make a window into their hearts, except the abundance of them overflowed into overt acts of disobedience, in impugning her supremacy. . . ."[2]

He held, regarding the Puritans, that so long as they had confined their attacks to the abuses in the Church, "their zeal was not condemned, only their violence was sometimes censured."[3] Even their assaults on the government of the Church had been met by the peaceful weapons of discussion and debate.[4] However, their attacks on ecclesiastical discipline had eventually "opened to the people a way to government by their consistories and presbyteries, a thing though in consequence no less prejudicial to the liberties of private men than to the sovereignty of princes. . . ."[4] Still, even these attacks were borne with because the Puritans pretended to leave these concerns "to the providence of God and the authority of the magistrate."

Neal, Bk. I, c. viii; and Spedding, I, 42. The letter is to be found almost word for word in Bacon's *Observations on a Libel*, which was written in 1592. It is possible that Bacon was the author. If it was written by Walsingham, and the majority of opinion credits him with the authorship, it was written after 1589 (because of the allusions to the Marprelate pamphlets), and before his death on April 6, 1590.

[1] *Ibid.*   [2] *Ibid.*   [3] *Ibid.*
[4] ". . . Yea, when they called in question the superiority of bishops, and pretended to a democracy in the church, their propositions were considered, and by contrary writings debated and discussed; yet all this while it was perceived that their course was dangerous and very popular; . . ." (*Walsingham to M. Cretoy.*)

But more recently some of them had gone so far as to deny that the consent of the magistrate was necessary to secure the desired changes in the structure of the Church. The Protestant dissenters had combined into classes and had defiled the Church with their pasquils. Finally, they had caused many subjects to doubt the rightfulness of oaths "which is one of the fundamental parts of justice in this land and in all places; . . ."[1] In other words, Puritan sentiment had ceased to express itself in purely spiritual terms and had become seditious and dangerous to the peace and stability of the State. The State therefore found itself compelled to "hold somewhat a harder hand to restrain them than before. . . ."[2] But the Government continued to act with great moderation, seeking both with Catholic and Puritan dissent, to deal tenderly with consciences and to "discover faction from conscience."

A similar analysis of the governmental policy was made by Burleigh in 1593 in a letter to Sir Robert Cecil.[3] Catholic ministers in Paris had charged that Elizabeth had promised favour and moderation to the Catholics of England and had afterwards treated them with severity. Burleigh insisted that the Queen had pursued a perfectly consistent policy since the beginning of her reign and had carefully refrained from punishing conscience, while striking down sedition and civil disobedience, whether Catholic or Protestant.[4] Her punishments have been legally administered and have at all times been governed by political necessity.

Walsingham's explanation of Elizabethan religious policy was principally designed for foreign consumption and he therefore endeavoured to stress the similarity between the treatment of Protestant offenders against the State with that of Catholic dissenters from the Establishment. This comparison was, of course, inexact. But we have in the letter a careful statement of the Government's repeated declaration that conscience was held free in law and in practice, while faction and civil disloyalty were to be punished as belonging to a wholly different category

[1] *Walsingham to M. Cretoy.* [2] *Ibid.*
[3] *Burleigh to Cecil*, May 1593. *Hatfield MSS. (H.M.C.)*, IV, 322.
[4] *Ibid.*

of offence.[1] This distinction was at times confused but it must not be regarded as devoid of content. Both the Roman Catholic pretensions and the demands of the Puritan extremists bore ill concealed threats to the constitution of the realm; threats which no Government could ignore. If either the Puritans or the Catholics could have abandoned the political implications of their faiths, we may justly assume that their religious opinions would have been tolerated perhaps to the point of freedom of worship. One of the principal avenues by which toleration was attained was in the abandonment of political interest, at least by the Protestant sects, and by an increased emphasis upon the spiritual content of faith. These groups had first to eschew their missionary desire to impose their particular views upon others by political agencies before they could be permitted freely to win others to their convictions by the proper methods of religious conversion.

After 1590 the execution of the penal laws was less drastically enforced. During the period of stringency a division began to be apparent between those Catholics who were loyal to the Crown in political concerns and whose religion bore no evidence of complicity in seditious plots, and the extremist party led by the Jesuits. This division became especially apparent among the Catholics who had been imprisoned at Wisbeach, and by 1594 an open quarrel had developed there between the Jesuit party and the seculars who were led by Bluet. The quarrel served to accentuate the division in the country generally between the 'English party' and the 'Spanish group.' In 1596 the secular party organized an association which petitioned the Pope for the appointment of a bishop in England, and Parsons, hurrying to Rome, was able to bring pressure to bear which resulted instead in the appointment of George Blackwell, a

---

[1] Cf. *For. Pap.* (Stafford to Walsingham, June 18, 1583), *France*, xi, and *Ibid.*, xi, 57 (Nedham to Walsingham, March 18, 1583–1584) for typical examples of this declaration of policy. An interesting unsigned paper of late 1583, corrected throughout by Burleigh, stressed the contention that Roman Catholics had been punished only for political disloyalty, and that Catholic consciences were wholly free. The author emphasized the contrast between the persecutions of Mary and the continued clemency of Elizabeth. (*S.P. Dom.*, *Eliz.*, clxiv, 85.)

follower of Parsons, as arch-priest over the secular group. The seculars appealed against this appointment but it was upheld in a papal brief dated April 6, 1599, and the appellants found themselves forced to submit to his jurisdiction. Very soon, however, Blackwell charged his secular subordinates with schism, and after considerable intrigue an appeal was lodged in Rome in late 1600 by thirty of the Wisbeach priests which greatly increased the gravity of the tension.

The Government was slow to take advantage of the opportunity here offered to drive a wedge between the loyal and disloyal Catholics. It should be recalled, however, that the officials were not privy to the details of the dissension and were naturally hesitant to make any step in an issue which was so charged with explosives. By 1596, however, we may detect a warping of policy to further the friction between the two groups. Numerous recusants who were known to have no sympathy with the Jesuit party were openly favoured. Thus an order of the Privy Council commented on the case of Lord Cornwallis, "For as much as he hathe byn and so contynueth an auncyent and true seruant unto her majestie, and not with standing his difference of religion hath never byn touched with any suspicion of dysloyalty or yll affection to her majestie and the state, but hath alwayes caryed himself as a dutyfull and faithfull subject, it is therefore thought good . . . that he should be dispensed withall for anie suche straight and nedefull orders as have byn prescribed unto others. . . ."[1]

In 1598 the justices of Shropshire were reminded that "there is great difference in the disposicion of those persons," [i.e. of recusants] and that the Council considered it meet that "according to their dispocitions they be more straightly or more remissely dealt withall."[2] In the case of one Sanford, who had already lost two-thirds of his land, it now appeared that he was "a man of peaceable and quiett behauioure, not troublesome or offensive any waye . . . nor givinge himself to the perverting of others...."[3] He was to be released from all the pains of

---

[1] *Acts of the P.C.*, xxvi, 375–376 (December 19, 1590).
[2] *Ibid.*, xxix, 184 (September 22, 1598).   [3] *Ibid.*

recusancy, save that he should not proceed more than five miles from his dwelling place.[1] An action against Lady Stourton was ordered abandoned, "Forasmuche as her majesty hath bin certified that the said lady doth not in any other sorte behave herself offensively by harbouringe or maintayning any evill disposed persons towards her majestie and the state. . . ."[2] The Justices of Kent were in 1601 ordered to stay the proceedings for recusancy that had been begun against Thomas Walton of that county, "forasmuch as it appeareth . . . that (his religion onelie excepted) he is bothe forward in any her majestys seruices and very carefull that no suspected or daungerous persons do frequent his house."[3]

Many similar instances could be adduced to demonstrate that the Government was tending, during the last decade of the reign, to favour loyal Catholics by the suspension of proceedings and penalties against recusancy. This attitude, wholly unofficial though it was, served to increase the friction between the two Catholic groups and to inspire in the secular party an unfortunate hope for some measure of legal toleration. It appeared that the Government was entertaining some notion of formally recognizing what was factually true: that Catholicism which confined itself to purely spiritual ends and which recognized in full the supremacy and legality of the Crown might hope for some measure of freedom of worship.

Fisher, the secular agent for the appeal to Rome in 1598, declared in Flanders that "he was in greate hope of liberty of conscience in England as that the Jesuits might be gotten thence." Bancroft was aware of Father Mush's letter to Bagshaw (May 1599) which said, "I muse they [the Government] ar so senseless, as not to thinke upon some tolleration w[ith] conditions which might free us from this jelosye."[4]

Watson, the leader of the secular group, was highly encouraged by the interest of the Earl of Essex and of Cecil in his important book refuting Doleman. In a letter to the Attorney General he said, "The Epistle to her maty syr Robert Cicil saw in my

---

[1] *Acts of the P.C.*, xxix, 184 (September 22, 1598).
[2] *Ibid.*, xxxii, 28 (July 6, 1601).   [3] *Ibid.*, xxxii, 27 (July 6, 1601).
[4] Law, T. G., *Historical Sketch of the Conflict Between the Jesuits and Seculars*, 148.

L. of Essex hand and disliked only or rather doubted (as was told me) of this word tolleration. yt her maty wold not grant. It was sent backe to (me to) alter it, I did so and returned it againe...."[1] Obviously the Government was carefully furthering the activities of the secular group at this time. Indeed, Essex confided to Watson that "he coulde wishe wth all his hearte yt we mighte haue liberty of conscience."[2] The severity of the Government was further relaxed and every encouragement was offered to the seculars. Thus Cavalli, the Venetian ambassador, reported in late 1601 that "the queen has released a Capuchin and some other priests; as there was no proof of their having conspired against her kingdom."[3] He indicated that Elizabeth was dealing gently with her Catholic subjects at that time and reported that "this leads people to suppose that she will grant liberty of conscience."[4] Bluet declared that the Queen, at his request, mitigated the imprisonment of many priests and even instructed the judges, who were about to go on a circuit, not to take the lives of priests unless they were proved guilty of treason.[5] A number of lay priests later testified "that the Councell of Q. Elizabeth promised quietnes and tolleration, vpon priests acknowledgement of temporall obedience" to the Queen.[6]

The Jesuits, though considerably disturbed by the astute policy of the Government, did not for a moment believe that the Government could or would grant toleration to the English Catholics. In two documents of unusual diplomatic brilliancy and acuteness it was pointed out that the seculars were foolish in their enthusiasm.[7] Any concessions that might be made by

[1] *Watson to the Attorney-General*, 1599, *Archpriest Controv.*, I, 222.
[2] *Ibid.*
[3] *Cavalli to the Doge and Senate*, Paris, December 24, 1601, *Ven. Cal.*, ix, 1036.   [4] *Ibid.*
[5] Law, *Jesuits and Seculars*, xcix.   [6] *English Protestants Plea*, 48.
[7] *Memorial Setting Forth on the part of the Jesuits the Injustice of the Conditions Under which it was Proposed that Queen Elizabeth should grant Liberty of Conscience to Catholics*, and a memorandum entitled *A Discourse on the Propositions which Some English Priests are to give to His Holiness in the Name of the English Queen Regarding the Granting of Liberty of Conscience to the Catholics in England*. Both documents are unsigned and undated. They were evidently written by a Jesuit about the time of the appeal to Rome. The former may be found in *Archpriest Controversy*, II, 76 ff., and the latter in *Ibid.*, II, 81 ff.

the English Government would be dearly purchased at the expense of the Pope and the Church.[1] The policy of the seculars, it was declared, was leading directly to the exclusion of papal authority from England. Any real (utile) liberty for Catholics would necessarily involve the repeal of the penal laws and, even if the Government desired to carry out this revolutionary step, it could not do so in the face of the united opposition of the clergy and of the Puritans.[2] The writer alleged that the Queen was merely encouraging the secular party in order to extract all possible benefit from their efforts. The Queen could never admit of any papal authority in England and she realized that "by granting liberty of conscience to Catholics she cannot bind them to her sufficiently to separate them from the Supreme Shepherd."[3] The writer frankly admitted that the Catholic Church was hostile to the English State and argued that the Queen, as a follower of Machiavelli, could "never place Catholics in a position where they will not fear or undergo harm."[4] She will rather "continue to divide and disunite the Catholics and . . . persecute them under the guise of political necessity."[5] She has supported the appeal to Rome only as a means of spreading discord within the Church and in order to engender bitterness against the Jesuits. She intends, in fact, "to foment discord among Catholics in order that she may control (rovinare tutti) them all. . . ."[6]

The Pope was highly influenced by Jesuit counsels and the cause of the appellants was apparently condemned before they appeared in Rome. The interview with the Pope was arranged by the French Ambassador and took place on March 5, 1602. The Pope complained of the heresies in the books of the appellants and charged that they came to "defend heretikes against his authoritie, in that he might not depose heretical princes. . . ."[7] The Pope further charged that the appellants came at the cost of the English Government and that they were obedient neither to the authority of the Apostolic See nor to

[1] *Archpriest Controversy*, II.   [2] *Ibid.*
[3] *Ibid.*   [4] *Ibid.*
[5] *Ibid.*   [6] *Ibid.*
[7] *Mush's Diary*, in *Archpriest Controversy*, II, 6.

the Archpriest.[1] He concluded the interview by disposing of the matter of religious toleration on the grounds that "it would do harme and make Catholikes become heretikes, that persecution was profitable to the churche and therfore not to be so muche laboured for to be auerted or staied by tolleration . . . [erasures]."[2] We shall have occasion to point out in considering Roman Catholic thought that this view of religious toleration was likewise entertained at this time by the Jesuit writers.[3]

The Council and the Bishop of London lent active assistance to the appellants and the Government profited most from the incident. Bancroft, with the consent of the Queen and the sanction of the Council, provided the secular priests at Rome with printers and protected them against the Jesuits. The Bishop had, indeed, gone so far in 1601 as to assist in the presentation of a petition to the Queen for the toleration of the loyal Catholic party. The Bishop was apparently sincere in his efforts, but he was made something of a cats-paw by the Council. He had succeeded in convincing Bluet of the actuality of the Jesuit plots against the Queen and State and persuaded him that the Government had been justified in enforcing severe legislation against these men.[4] Bluet agreed and declared that the loyal Catholics "had been troubled for years, not for our religion, but for the treason of this sort."[5]

A petition, written by Bluet, was presented to the Queen requesting "some liberty of conscience" for the loyal English Catholics and protesting the complete fidelity of the secular priests and of the laity in temporal matters.[6]

The petition was not granted, but the Queen replied in a moderate and conciliatory tone. She declared that her Catholic subjects had presumed upon the clemency and moderation of her Government. She denied that the toleration of the Huguenots in France was in any way an argument for the toleration of her Catholic subjects.[7] Her honour, crown, and life were at

---

[1] *Mush's Diary*, in *Archpriest Controversy*, II, 6; *Venetian Cal.*, ix, 1061 (March 9, 1602).   [2] *Mush's Diary*, in *Archpriest Controversy*, II, 6.
[3] Cf. *post*, 382–386.
[4] *Declarationn of Bluet to the Cardinals Borghese and Aragon*, March 1602, *S.P. Dom. Eliz.*, cclxxxiii, 70.   [5] *Ibid.*   [6] *Ibid.*   [7] *Ibid.*

stake: "For their chief pastor pronounced sentence against me whilst yet I was in my mother's womb. Moreover, Pius V has excommunicated me, and absolved my subjects from their oath of fidelity, and Gregory XIII and Sixtus V have renewed the same, at the instance of the King of Spain, that he may enlarge his own borders; and so to my peril it remains."[1] She indicated, however, that her relations had been more tolerable with Clement VIII, of whom she had "nothing to complain. . . ." He has dealt wisely with France and has employed his best efforts to restore peace and prosperity where civil war and slaughter had reigned. In all these things the Pope has shown himself "worthy of his place, and worthy to be called Vicar of Christ, doctor and master of nations."[2]

The Queen expressed the same conciliatory sentiments to the French Ambassador during an interview in 1602.[3] She acknowledged, as well, the good will of the appellants, while rejecting the idea of religious toleration on the ground that no people could be well governed that owed allegiance to two faiths. She declared that she owed a great duty to the peace of her kingdom, which she could not endanger by yielding to the Roman Catholic demands. However, she proposed to treat them with great clemency and, if they would live in conformity to her laws, they would not be punished for their faith.[4]

A month later, November 5, 1602, a proclamation set at rest the rumours that were rife in London respecting Catholic toleration by expressly stating that no toleration of two religions could be allowed in England.[5] The Queen regretted that her late forbearance and clemency in relaxing the execution of the penal laws had been abused. She again called attention to the dangers to the State inherent in political Catholicism, which had endeavoured to "advance our enemies, pervert our subjects, and subvert our estate."[6] She paid tribute to the recent loyalty

---

[1] *Decl. of Bluet, S.P. Dom., Eliz.*, cclxxxiii, 70.   [2] *Ibid.*
[3] *Beaumont to Henri IV*, October 2, 1602, in Teulet, *Relat. Polit.*, IV, 264 ff.
[4] *Ibid.*
[5] *S.P. Dom., Eliz.*, cclxxxv, 52 (November 5, 1602). There are three drafts of this proclamation, all showing considerable variation. Vide also *S.P. Dom., Eliz.*, cclxxxv, 53 and 55. The latter copy was expanded and corrected throughout by Cecil.   [6] *S.P. Dom., Eliz.*, cclxxxv, 52.

of the seculars who had offered to assist in the detection and suppression of Jesuit plots. Elizabeth declared that she would gladly distinguish between the two groups of Catholics, "but we cannot, as even the latter [the seculars] concur in disobedience and disloyalty," in striving to win her subjects to an allegiance to the Pope.[1] They have, in addition, falsely intimated that the Government intended a toleration of their religion, a step which would only serve to disturb the peace of the Church, and to bring the State into confusion.[2] Emboldened by their presumption in this matter, they have illegally revived and extended their activities and have thus awakened "slumbering justice."[3] She therefore found herself obliged to order all Jesuits and secular priests from the realm within a specified time "except such as present themselves to Council, the presidents of Wales and York, or the Bishops, profess duty and allegiance, and submit to mercy. . . ."[4]

An interesting memorandum of the same period discussed the reasons for and against the extension of religious toleration to Catholic subjects.[5] It was suggested by the author that when subjects are impartially regarded they bear no envy towards one another, love their prince, and remain satisfied with their estate. But when one party is favoured and another suppressed "it breeds discontent, desire of alteration, and plots and practices to obtain it."[6] Toleration would serve to increase good living, abate dissensions, and would purge the Catholic profession in England of many evils. "The comparison of both professions, laid open to every man's eye, will enlighten the understanding to discern the best."[7] The example of France has proved that toleration is possible and that its results are not prejudicial to the State. It would be as well to imitate France in this respect as in their other fashions of public and private, martial and political, government.[8]

The writer feared, however, that the granting of toleration would induce the Catholic party to seek for more power, and that it would ultimately attempt to suppress Protestantism in

[1] *S.P. Dom., Eliz.*, cclxxxv, 52.   [2] *Ibid.*   [3] *Ibid.*   [4] *Ibid.*
[5] *S.P. Dom. (Add.), Eliz.*, xxxiv, 45.   [6] *Ibid.*   [7] *Ibid.*   [8] *Ibid.*

England. Protestants can live quietly under Protestants. But the Catholics cannot enjoy their worship without the assistance of priests who are subject to the Pope. Hence the prince would lose the command of "the best half of their vassals," and that no state can endure.[1] The author, presuming that a toleration of religion should be granted, urged that the Roman Catholic churches should be placed in the suburbs of the great towns and that under no circumstances should Jesuits or votaries be allowed in England. The priests should be required to give sufficient assurances of their allegiance and no recourse should be permitted to the Pope in any matter. With thought of the recent dissensions in mind, he held that all controversies in the Catholic ranks should be determined by persons selected from their own number and with the approval of the civil ruler.[2] He urged that there should be no alteration in the system of tithes and that the spiritual courts of the Established Church should retain omnicompetent jurisdiction in all such matters as marriages and testaments. All invectives on either side should be severely punished. Only a little liberty should be permitted to the Catholics in the beginning, and enlargement of freedom should be accorded as experience should determine.[3]

The events of the closing years of the great Queen's reign demonstrated that the problem of toleration for the loyal English Catholics was being seriously considered by the Government. The Government was principally motivated by interests of policy in promoting the cleavage between the secular and the Jesuit parties, but it had been obliged seriously to view some sort of mitigation in case the rupture became complete. The incident was closed by the Queen's proclamation announcing that the Government could not embrace the principle of full religious liberty. At the same time, however, the proclamation made a real distinction between the two groups of Catholics; it paid a high tribute to the loyalty of the secular party; and it pledged that its lot should not be rendered unbearable. The proclamation was in reality published to quiet popular feeling in London, and those who had brought the *rapprochement* so far did not abandon the continuation of a

[1] *S.P. Dom. (Add.), Eliz.*, xxxiv, 45.   [2] *Ibid.*   [3] *Ibid.*

policy of moderation and understanding. Bancroft was not wholly successful in destroying the influence of the Jesuits over the English Catholics, but he so intensified the bitter dissension in the ranks of the Catholics that the State, for the time being at least, had no real fear of the Catholic danger.[1] Under these conditions increasing moderation could be employed in dealing with the Catholic subjects. The Government had set its foot squarely in the way of toleration, but it shrank from a step which involved grave dangers to the unity and peace of the realm and which broke so violently with its traditional position and with current political theory. As we shall endeavour to indicate in our discussion of Roman Catholic thought, the rift between the seculars and the Jesuits had served a further function in creating a tolerant Catholic literature which was of considerable importance in providing a basis for further discussion of the issue and which did much to dispel the fear which was of such great importance in retarding the toleration of Catholicism in England.

4. THE RISE OF MILITANT PURITANISM AND ITS RELATION TO THE PROBLEM OF TOLERATION

The elevation of the able and iron-willed Whitgift to the See of Canterbury in 1583 marked a new stage in the conflict of the Government and the Established Church with Puritanism. Whitgift, while a staunch Calvinist in doctrine, had no sympathy with the subversive tendencies of Puritanism and checked its rising influence with a firm hand. He likewise endeavoured to suppress the developing Presbyterian organization which, with the adoption of the Second Book of Discipline in 1582, had secured an effective basis for cohesion and expansion. The Church of England appeared to him to be in grave danger of dissolution. The Separatist movement had, under the leadership of Browne, Greenwood, and Barrowe, achieved reality and a substantial English following by about 1589. The new prelate was an admirable agent for curbing these disruptive forces. He had the entire sympathy and support of Elizabeth in his efforts, but his programme met with only partial support from

[1] Klein, A. J., *Intolerance*, 48.

the Government as a whole, and with decided hostility from the Puritan section of the Council. As we have seen, Burleigh hotly criticized his efforts to detect deviations from orthodoxy,[1] and the House of Commons demanded greater leniency in dealing with Puritan ministers. The House likewise proposed that episcopal ordination should be modified by "the assistance of six other ministers at the least,"[2] and it seemed that a majority of the Commons was at this time favourable to Presbyterian modifications of the ecclesiastical system.

The Queen and Whitgift stood firm against these forces, and the wave of loyalty inspired by the Spanish War, the extraordinary virulence of the Martinist libels, and the growing respect for the ageing Queen combined to effect a reaction in favour of the governmental policy. The Government was genuinely alarmed at the Separatist doctrines, which it rightly regarded as inimical to the *status quo* in Church and State, and deemed it necessary in the cases of Barrowe, Greenwood and Penry to demand the capital penalty under a statute designed for Papists.[3] Elizabeth epitomized the position of the Government in reference to the sectaries when she wrote to James of Scotland, "and lest fayre semblance, that easely may begile, do not brede your ignorance of suche persons as ether pretend religion or dissemble deuotion, let me warne you that ther is risen, bothe in your realme and in myne, a

---

[1] Cf. *ante*, 180–181.

[2] *Petition of the House of Commons for Ecclesiastical Reform*, 1584, Sect. 4; D'Ewes, *Journal*, 357–359.

[3] The circumstances of the trials and executions need not detain us, since the Government rested its cases principally on the charge of sedition. (*Harl. MSS.*, 6848, 14, 11, 7, 9.) The case of the Separatists is fully and sympathetically treated by Dexter, H. M., *Congregationalism*, 205–252. We shall, however, treat the views of these men on toleration and on the nature of the Church in detail; cf. *post*, 277–292. It should be mentioned that Burleigh secured a reprieve for Barrowe and Goodman, and strongly opposed the executions. He pled, "that in a land where no papist was put to death for religion, theirs should not be the first blood shed who concurred about faith with what was professed in the country, and desired conference to be convinced of their error." (*Thos. Phelippes to Wm. Sterne*, April 7, 1593; *S.P. Dom.*, *Eliz.*, ccxliv, 124.) Burleigh spoke sharply both to Canterbury and Worcester about the sentence, and desired to carry the matter to the Queen, but found no support.

secte of perilous consequence, suche as wold haue no kings but a presbitiye, and take our place while the inioy our privilige, with a shade of godes word, wiche non is judged to folow right without by ther censure the be so demed."[1] She urged that if once the sectarians were able to convince men that governments err "if the[y] say so" perilous political consequences must inevitably ensue. "Suppose you, my deare brother, that I can tollerat suche scandalz of my sincere gouernment?"

Both the Queen and her great minister feared the Puritan theory which appeared to subordinate the civil power to the will of a bigoted clergy.[2] The policy of the Government was again dictated, not by religious considerations, but by a desire to strike down a force which seemed to endanger the political stability of the realm. Elizabeth invariably measured the character of dissent by its political implications. It is likewise probable that she disliked the violently anti-Catholic attitude of the Puritans, since such religious animosity ran counter to her plan, never quite abandoned, to bring the English Catholics into the comprehensive communion of the Established Church.

The mad conspiracy of Hacket, Copinger and Arthington in 1592 to murder the Queen in preparation for the establishment of the Discipline, gave the Government an opportunity further to discredit the Nonconformists and an excuse for the creation of repressive legislation against them. A Bill was first introduced in the House of Commons against Roman Catholic recusants. It passed two readings, having been somewhat reduced in stringency, and was then made applicable to Protestant Nonconformists as well. This Bill appears to have been abandoned, and in March 1593 a new Bill came from the House of Lords, covering the same ground, and in the form of an amendment to the Act of 1581. The two types of recusancy were distinguished, however, and the final enactment embodied "An act to retain the Queen's subjects in obedience,"[3] and "An act against popish recusants."[4] The former act mentioned the "seditious sectaries" in particular and any sectary who resisted the royal power,

[1] *Eliz. to James VI*, July 6, 1590, *Letters of Elizabeth and James*, 63.
[2] Strype, *Annals*, IV, 197–201.   [3] 35 Eliz., c. 1.   [4] 35 Eliz., c. 2.

seduced others, or attended services at conventicles was made liable to imprisonment without bail.[1] If such a person refused to conform, he must abjure the realm.[2] The popish recusants, on the other hand, were to be confined to their homes and were to be banished only for the violation of this limitation.[3] They were, of course, subject as well to the earlier laws against recusancy.

If the religious history of the last decade of Elizabeth's reign were to be written in the light of this legislation, it would detail the complete extinction of religious liberty in England.[4] Fortunately, however, the Queen utilized the tightened bulwark of legislation only to protect her crown, her position, and the established order. The laws were framed and used only as potential weapons. They were enforced here and there with caution and moderation for reasons of policy, but no attempt was made to secure a general application of them to dissent. A remarkable period of quiet fell over the realm during the final years of the Queen's reign.

The bill against the Separatists encountered vigorous opposition in the House of Commons from men of all religious views, and there can be no doubt that this opposition reflected the existence of a body of opinion opposed to religious persecution which was far more extensive and influential than has generally been believed. Thomas Phelippes, in a letter to William Sterrell, said that the bill passed in the Upper House only through the activity of the bishops.[5] The bill was "found so captious by the Lower House that it was thought it never would have passed in any sort. . . ."[6] He concluded, with truth, that it was finally forced through by those "who sought to satisfy the Bishops humours."[7]

During the debates, after several members had touched upon the necessity of reducing disloyal subjects to obedience, Sir Walter Raleigh pointed out numerous dangers inherent in the bill.[8] He too regarded the Brownists as dangerous to the State

---

[1] 35 Eliz., c. 1, sect. 1.   [2] 35 Eliz., c. 1, sect. 2.
[3] 35 Eliz., c. 2, sects. 1–2.   [4] Klein, *Intolerance*, 146.
[5] *Phelippes to Sterrell*, April 7, 1593, *S.P. Dom., Eliz.*, ccxliv, 124.
[6] *Ibid.*   [7] *Ibid.*   [8] Townshend, H., *Historical Collections*, 76.

and as worthy to be rooted out of the realm. But the House should consider the dangers which the State would incur by the institution of the policy proposed in the measure, "For it is to be feared, that men not guilty will be included in it, and that Law is hard which taketh Life, or sendeth into Banishment, where men's intentions shall be judged by a jury, and they shall be judges what other men meant; but that Law is against a fact, that is just; and punish the fact as severely as you will."[1]

Raleigh's keen mind had discovered the essential error underlying religious persecution: that the operation of law cannot extend to the thoughts and consciences of men, that conscience belongs to a category of phenomena into which legal procedure cannot justly intrude. If a sectary has been guilty of sedition, the court has a fact against which it may proceed; but, if a sectary should believe that the Church should not wait for the magistrate, we have an intangible concept which cannot be prosecuted because abstract ideas are not capable of correct analysis by the legal process. You may prosecute an action which is the direct result of the retention of certain ideas, but you cannot prosecute the idea. Raleigh then proceeded to expose certain technical flaws in the Bill; "If two or three thousand Brownists meet at the sea side, at whose charge shall they be transported? Or whither will you send them? I am sorry for it; I am afraid there is neer twenty thousand of them in England; and when they are gone, who shall maintain their wives and children?"[2]

The same spirit was expressed during the discussion of a bill which was introduced in 1601 for the "more diligent resort to churches on Sundayes." Mr. Owen disliked the penalty of one shilling for absence from the service because there was already a statute which imposed a fine of twenty pounds a month for recusancy and the bill simply added another penalty.[3] In addition, the Justices of the Peace were already overburdened, and the passage of this measure would make their houses "like a quarter-sessions, with the multitude of these com-

[1] Townshend, H., *Historical Collections*, 76.
[2] *Ibid.*, 76.   [3] *Ibid.*, 273.

215

plaints."[1] He charged that the bill infringed upon Magna Carta, which guaranteed trial by one's peers, while conviction was possible under the terms of the proposed law upon the testimony of two witnesses before a justice.[2] He concluded tersely, ". . . For my part away with the bill."[3]

Sir Cary Reynolds strayed from the point by citing various public and private calamities that had resulted from working on Sunday and from staying away from church.[4]

Another member, Sir George Moore, expressed the orthodox view when he urged that Christian duty to religion and to the Queen required the passage of the bill. He observed that the penal statutes already in existence had lost their force. "Let us not give such cause of comfort to our adversaries; that having drawn a bill in question for the service of our God, we should stand so much in questioning the same."[5]

The objections of Mr. Bond to the proposed statute were cast in an interesting form.[6] He disliked the power which the Bill sought to give to the Justices, whose powers were already 'luxuriant.' Magistrates, he said, are men, "and men have alwayes attending on them two ministers, libido and Iracundia. Men of this nature do subjugate the free subject."[7] He regarded it as dangerous to give authority in the handling of such important matters. "Her majesty, all the time of her reign, hath been clement, gracious, meek, and merciful; yea, choosing rather Delinquere, I know not how to term it, in lenity, but not in cruelty. But by this Statute, there is a constraint to come to divine service; and for neglect, all must pay. . . . The poor commonalty, whose strength and quietness is the strength and quietness of us all, he only shall be punished, he vexed.

---

[1] Townshend, *Historical Collections*, 273.
[2] References to Magna Carta were very rare during the Tudor period, and it is interesting that recourse should have been taken to the document in this connection.   [3] Townshend, H., *Historical Collections*, 273.
[4] *Ibid.*, 274.   [5] *Ibid.*, 275.
[6] It seems probable that the speaker was Dr. John Bond, member for Taunton from 1601–1603. Bond was educated at Oxford, graduating B.A. in 1573, and became about 1580 the master of the free school at Taunton. He was a schoolmaster for many years (*D.N.B.*, v, 339), and was a practising physician. He was a distinguished classical commentator.
[7] Townshend, *Historical Collections*, 275.

For, will any think, that a justice of peace will contest with so good a man as himself? No, this age is too wise."[1] The poor, he held, were already severely pressed by the taxes which had just been voted and this measure would only serve to increase their burdens.

The discussions disclosed an extraordinary dislike and distrust of the justices, who bore such a large burden in the administration of Elizabethan justice. Mr. Glascock declared that "our statutes penal be like the Beast called [blank] born in the morning, at his full growth at Noon, and dead at Night: So these Statutes are quick in execution, like a wonder for nine days; and that's a wonder they continue so long," for at the end of a year "they are carried dead in a basket to the Justices house."[2] The member charged that a justice "for a half a dozen chickens will dispense with a dozen penal statutes."[3]

After the Bill had been considerably altered in committee, Mr. Bond declared it to be "altogether needless . . . inconvenient, and unnecessary."[4] He wisely observed that "every evil in a state, is not to be met with in a law. And as it is in the natural, so it is in the politique body, that sometimes the remedy is worse than the disease."[5] In especial, he declared himself to be against "particular laws for particular offences." Such a law, in the case of religion, would imply, if not admit, that the ministers had preached their congregations out of the church. The law of the first year of the reign was justified because England had just emerged from Popery and superstition; but after forty-five years of the true faith and preaching no justification can be found for the proposed measure. He concluded that the Act would be quite unenforceable since "Just prosecution will be infinitely cumbersome, and partial connivance subject to quarrel."[6]

Raleigh concluded the attack on the measure. He indicated

---

[1] Townshend, *Historical Collections*, 275. [2] *Ibid.*, 276.
[3] *Ibid.*, 277. [4] *Ibid.*, 317. [5] *Ibid.*
[6] *Ibid.*, 318. After further argument a proviso was added to the Bill by a vote of 126—85, which exempted a man from its penalties if he attended an authorized church eight times a year, providing he read the divine service in his home every Sunday and Holy Day. (*Ibid.*, 320.)

his conviction that the proposed measure was highly unwieldy, since it would require the attendance of all the churchwardens in order to report to the grand juries. This would mean that from forty to two hundred churchwardens and, if say two persons were accused in each parish, from eighty to four hundred defendants would be in attendance at each session. "What quarreling and danger might happen." He then cleverly attacked the proviso as a "plain toleration from not coming to church."[1]

The debates on the two measures called forth arguments which represent the full range of the case for religious toleration, and it must be recalled that the scene of this debate was the highest judicial and legislative body in the realm. It was pointed out that matters of conscience are not properly subject to judicial examination and decision; that measures which are designed to crush a powerful body of opinion cannot effectively be enforced; that persecution, if we may employ the term, bestows an unreasonable and tyrannous power upon a small body of men against their neighbours; that the proposed measures were in essence unjust; and that the remedy which had been proposed was far worse than the evil which it was designed to correct. In particular, the view of Bond that for more than forty years the truth had been preached in England would lead us to believe that the Member would suggest that if after so long an effort by a highly privileged group, truth did not prevail of its own weight and force, then dissent would have to be tolerated as an unwanted but necessary evil. The Member did not make this position clear, but he came tantalizingly close to doing so.

5. THE CLASSICAL STATEMENT OF THE ANGLICAN POSITION

a. Gifford

The fine sentiments which were uttered in Parliament on the subject of religious dissent reflected a state of opinion which likewise extended, though to a lesser degree, in the

---

[1] Townshend, *Historical Collections*, 321. The bill was defeated in the division by a vote of 106—105.

Anglican literature of the last decade of the reign. This period was dominated by the appearance of Hooker's masterful *Ecclesiastical Polity*, and it may be argued that the fine spirit of the book was highly instrumental in securing the period of theological armistice which immediately preceded the death of the great Queen.

Four years prior to the publication of the initial books of the *Ecclesiastical Polity* appeared, George Gifford's *A Short Treatise Against the Donatists of England* which, though far inferior in its scope and style, was quite as moderate and tolerant as Hooker's more famous work.[1] Gifford's tolerance was especially exhibited in his conception of the Church and in his definition of the body of doctrine necessary for salvation. He wrote clearly, with wit and with a touch of gentle irony. The preface of his work was strikingly similar in spirit to the foreword of Acontius' more famous work.

He held that the Church of England was torn by feuds and dissensions which are the work of the devil. The Papists have assumed their position under the name of the Catholic Church and "These cry out, the fathers, the fathers, the auncient Fathers."[2] On the other side, the violent Protestants "cry alowd, that our assemblies be Romish, idolatrous; anti-christian Synagogs," and generally create dissension and ill will.[3] The

---

[1] Gifford is somewhat difficult to place. Until 1584 he appears to have been a conforming minister. At that time he refused to subscribe, and was suspended from his living at Malden by Aylmer. (Strype, *Annals*, III, 1, 354; *Whitgift*, I, 301; *Aylmer*, 71.) His parishioners petitioned in his behalf (Strype, *Aylmer*, 72), and Burleigh and Leicester interceded for his restoration. Whitgift and Aylmer deprived him of the living (*D.N.B.*, xxi, 301), but he continued in a lectureship in Essex. He was again suspended in 1587. In the work under consideration he attacked the Separatists. Barrowe and Greenwood replied, and the controversy extended to 1591. He preached in Paul's Cross in 1591, and appears to have preached in his old living in the later years of his life. We may perhaps consider Gifford as of the dominant party in this period with, however, strong Presbyterian leanings.

[2] Gifford, G., *Short Treatise*, Pref.

[3] *Ibid.*, Bancroft in his *Dangerous Positions*, published at about the same time, held that two classes of disturbers were ruining the Church. On the one hand, the Jesuits have "no other purpose, but to make a way for the pope and the Spaniards; the sworne and mortall enemies, both to the state, and to all other that doo professe the right

Church of England is caught between the waves of these opposing storms and is in grave danger of destruction.[1]

The Church, Gifford held, being composed of human creatures, cannot be perfect. But in spite of grave imperfections the spirit of Christ dwells in the Church and it remains a true Church. The sectarians did not admit this liberal view and Gifford charged them with destructive tendencies. "He that seemeth most zealous in religion, and restraineth not his toong, hath but bitter issue instead of heauenly zeal."[2]

In the most interesting section of the treatise Gifford en-endeavoured to lay down the essential doctrines of the true Church: those tenets which must be believed and adhered to in order to attain salvation.[3] There are admittedly serious abuses in the fabric of the Church of England, but have these deplorable shortcomings destroyed its character as a true Church?[4] The author held that "whosoever believeth in the Son of God, shall be saved, though he be full of errors, full of infirmities, and deformities, both in body and soul, labouring to be purged." He charged that the Brownists were unbrotherly, since they "condemne them all as Infidels and prophane, which professe the faith of Christ, because notwithstanding they doo it in some weaknesse and infirmities. . . ."[5] All the men that have received the mark of Christ and who strive to worship Him in truth are of the Church.[6] He agreed with Hooker in regarding the Roman Catholic Church as a true

---

refourmed religion of Christ." (4–5.) The Puritans, for their part, look to Scotland and Geneva for their models. The first book of Bancroft's work was concerned with pointing out the evil effects of radical Presbyterianism in Scotland and Geneva.

[1] In the will of Archbishop Sandys, which was probated in 1590, we find the view that the recent Presbyterian advances were highly inimical to both Church and State. Sandys held that "such rude and undigested platforms as have been . . . lately" set forward tend to the destruction of the English Church. For ". . . the state of a small private Church, and the form of a large Christian kingdom, neither would long like, nor, can at all brook one and the same ecclesiastical government." (Sandys, Edwin, *Proposal of Union*.)　　　　　　　　　　　　　　[2] Gifford, *Short Treatise*, Pref.
[3] This attempt should be compared with the important continental thought in this connection. The more serious and extended attempt of Acontius to reduce essential dogma to its lowest terms likewise invites comparison.
[4] Gifford, *Short Treaties*, 6–7.　　　[5] *Ibid.*, 49.　　　　　[6] *Ibid.*, 54.

Church in which salvation might be attained in spite of its grave errors and imperfections.[1]

In his consideration of the function of the magistrate in the Church, Gifford proved himself to be thoroughly orthodox. The king is the principal member of the Church,[2] and it is his duty "to procure the establishing of God's true religion . . . to destroy and abolish all false Religion, Superstition, Idolatrie, and Heresies; and to compell all states and degrees of persons within the Kingdome, to receyue the holie doctrine and rules of Christ, and to walke in the same."[3] At the same time, he recognized that God's kingdom is spiritual and that "all the power of kings in the world, cannot conuert one soule vnto Christe; that is donne by the Holy-Ghoste, through the liuelye Worde of faithe."[4] His view appeared to be that it was the duty of the Christian ruler to compel his subjects to embrace the external phenomena of worship in order that the spirit of God might work among them. The king cannot bring his subjects to goodness, but he can labour to do so.[5]

Gifford was careful to point out, however, that the king should be obeyed in his religious dicta only if they were in accordance with the will of God.[6] For "Hee whiche doeth disobeye the Prince, doth disobey God, vnto his damnation, when the Prince setteth foorth and mainteyneth Gods worde. But if there be a prince whiche maketh lawes against the lawes of God, wee must obey God rather than men."[7] The obedience which we lend to the State in matters of religion is, then, measured by the approximation of the State's policy with the revealed will of God. Clearly, the conscience of the individual Christian is the only possible criterion of the legality of such obedience. But this Gifford, like most of his contemporaries, refrained from pushing to its logical limits. His resolution of the problem of religious authority was, in fact, without conviction, especially when compared with the robust theories of the previous decade, and leaves the impression that he rounded

---

[1] Gifford, *Short Treatise*, 54–55.   [2] *Ibid.*, 104-105.
[3] *Ibid.*, 105–107.   [4] *Ibid.*, 107–108.   [5] *Ibid.*, 108.
[6] Gifford, *A Briefe Discourse*, 22–23.   [7] *Ibid.*, 23.

out his treatise with the restatement of a view which he regarded as of dubious validity.[1]

b. Hooker

The first four books of the *Ecclesiastical Polity* appeared in 1593 or 1594. The great pillar of the work, the fifth book, was published three years later, and the remaining three books appeared in a badly organized form after Hooker's death in 1600.[2] The *Ecclesiastical Polity* is not as important for the history of religious toleration as it is for the history of Political Theory and in the development of Anglican theology. In fact, its importance in the evolution of religious toleration has probably been considerably over-emphasized. The author's principal purpose was conclusively to prove that the Puritan pretensions were inconsistent with the political structure of England and that those claims involved a denial of the bases of political obedience. He was in consequence obliged to examine in detail the nature of the State and the sources of its authority. His purpose was pre-eminently political; he sought to establish a basis in reason upon which the controversialists of his party might stand. "He glossed over or passed over in silence difficulties for which he had no solution; he refused to ask questions he was wise enough to know he could not answer."[3]

Church and State were to Hooker easily distinguishable entities.[4] He suggested, however, that the Puritans went so far in distinguishing between the two in nature and definition that the one can in no wise assist the other in the discharge of its function without a breach of the Law of God.[5] He held that

---

[1] The work was answered by Barrowe's *A Plaine Refutation* . . . in 1591.

[2] The first four books were published under the title, *The Lawes of Ecclesiasticall Politie, written in defence of the present gouernment established, against the new desired discipline.* A second edition appeared in 1594. Copies of the first edition of the fifth book may be found in the British Museum, Bodleian, and the B.P.L. The eight books were published together for the first time in 1604, and copies of this edition are extant in the B.M. and Bodl. Many editions followed. We have employed the great Keble edition of 1888.

[3] Allen, J. W., *Political Thought*, 186.   [4] Hooker, *Ecc. Pol.*, VIII, i, 2.

[5] *Ibid.*, VIII, i, 2. This was scarcely accurate, cf. *ante*, 139-142, 147, 150; *post*, 243-249.

"the care of religion being common unto all societies politic, such societies as do embrace the true religion have the name of Church given unto every one of them. . . ."[1] In medieval terminology he explained that "as a politic society it doth maintain religion; as a church, that religion which God hath revealed by Jesus Christ." Nor was there anything new in his assertion that there is no one in the English Church who is not at the same time a member of the commonwealth.[2] In one capacity a man is a member of the Church; in another a member of the State. The two loyalties, or natures, are inseparably conjoined in a Christian state.[3] From this position the author began to make ground. Since the Church and Commonwealth are as one so the Parliament represents both the Church and State. When it is occupied with the passing of a civil law it may be regarded as representing the State; and, when it is framing an ecclesiastical measure it is acting for the Church.

Upon the basis of this assumption Hooker was able to accept the received theories of the royal supremacy.[4] Since the sovereign is by cession of power the representative of the whole State he is, at the same time, the representative of the whole Church, and as such he may override even the successors of the Apostles in formulating legislation for the Church and in the appointment of its officers. The Church was sustained by the civil sword in the time of the Law.[5] "I demand whether that authority, which served before for the furtherance of religion, may not as effectually serve to the maintenance of Christian religion."[6] The sword of spiritual discipline has been entrusted to the Church, but that will not suffice alone. The Church requires as well the rod of corporal punishment to keep her children in obedience.[7] Hooker made no direct suggestion as to how those Christians who stray into heresy should be treated. But his close identification of Church and State, and his conception of positive law, made it necessary for him to say

[1] Hooker, *Ecc. Pol.*, VIII, i, 2.
[2] *Ibid.*, VIII, i, 2. "No person appertaining to the one can be denied to be also of the other." [3] *Ibid.*, VIII, i, 7.
[4] Keble, *Pref. to the Ecc. Pol.*, lxxxvii–lxxxviii.
[5] Hooker, *Ecc. Pol.*, VIII, iii, 4. [6] *Ibid.* [7] *Ibid.*

223

that those who rebel against the national Church system must be punished.[1] "Schism and disturbances will arise in the church, if all men may be tolerated to think as they please, and publickly speak what they think."[2]

The power which Hooker ascribed to the magistrates in ecclesiastical affairs was conditioned by their being orthodox Christians who were in sympathy and communion with the Church of which they were the earthly head. When this intimate connection ceases, the Church is left free to set itself in order without any interference from the civil power. Hooker never squarely faced the question of the power of the Christian king to order doctrine and discipline in the Church,[3] contenting himself with the unsatisfactory formula that the ruler's power is limited by the headship of Christ.[4] This reasoning was not calculated to convince men who regarded the Church over which the magistrate ruled as evil, and who insisted upon the liberty to plant churches in which they could worship in good conscience, that they should obediently submit to the authority which Hooker sought to justify.

Hooker regarded order in human relations as of divine origin. In fact, his work began with a general discussion of the nature and variety of laws. Discipline is necessary in the Church in order to achieve an order of purpose. Hence Calvin did well when he instituted his discipline in order to restrain the fickle Genevans, but he was in error when he taught that his discipline was divinely ordained.[5] The disciplinary body, proceeding under this illusion, immediately grasped power which rightfully appertains only to the king. The Bible defines no divinely ordained discipline. Discipline is necessary everywhere, but it is not of necessity everywhere the same. In the same way, there is need of speech throughout the world, but it does not necessarily follow that all men should speak the same language.

However, it must not be presumed that men's consciences are a safe guide in the ordering of ecclesiastical affairs. When the Bible leaves to the Church a choice in the framing of its

[1] Allen, J. W., *Political Thought*, 239.   [2] Hooker, *Ecc. Pol.*, VIII, iv, 6.
[3] *Ibid.*, VIII, viii, 7.   [4] *Ibid.*, VIII, iv, 6.   [5] *Ibid.*, Pref., ii, 7.

ordinances it is not meet that "it should be free for men to reprove, to disgrace, to reject at their own liberty what they see done and practised according to order set down. . . ."[1] Such liberty would inevitably lead to complete chaos. Essentially, Hooker did not trust the doctrine of private revelation which was the advanced Protestant's ground for liberty to diverge and which, when admitted, is capable of no logical refutation. Religious toleration owed a vast debt to the increasing predominance of the theory of private revelation among the advanced Calvinists and among the Sects. Hooker's repudiation of the doctrine virtually excluded the possibility of presenting a theory of religious toleration in the *Ecclesiastical Polity*.

The great Anglican saw more clearly than anyone else in his age the spiritual, if not the civil, chaos that must ensue upon the triumph of the principle of private judgment, depending upon the acceptance of the doctrine of private revelation. He enquired, if "the Church did give every man license to follow what himself imagineth that God's spirit doth reveal unto him, or what he supposeth that God is likely to have revealed to some special person whose virtues deserve to be highly esteemed; what other effect could hereupon ensue, but the utter confusion of his Church under pretence of being taught, led, and guided by His spirit?"[2] This constituted as complete a denial of the doctrine of revelation as may be found in the century, and it arose from the fact that Hooker was at once something of a rationalist and an authoritarian. No man, he argued, has a right to defy national authority merely on the basis of a private revelation. We should not be compelled to do anything against which we are in conscience persuaded, but our persuasion must be demonstrably valid. Hooker looked askance at compulsion and found the best vehicle of control and correction to be the power of reason. If a man cannot present a valid reason for not abiding by the laws of the State (i.e. the Church), he must be punished. Otherwise the State will dissolve in anarchy.[3] The author appears to have believed that the rational decision of Parliament and Convocation on a religious

[1] Hooker, *Ecc. Pol.*, V, x, 1.　　　　　　　　　　　　[2] *Ibid.*
[3] Allen, J. W., *Political Thought*, 241.

issue was considerably more likely to be in accord with the will of God than the inspiration of the most saintly individual. His requirement that the private revelation of the individual Christian should be rationally defended was tantamount to the complete exclusion of the doctrine of revelation which in its very essence is akin to mysticism, and not to rationalism.

The finest evidence of Hooker's personal tolerance is to be found in his liberal view of the question of salvation. The doctrine of exclusive salvation had been taken over *in toto* by the various Protestant bodies and the world was confronted with the spectacle of numerous religious groups, each acrimoniously contending that salvation was attainable only within its communion. Hooker had little patience with the intolerant rigidity of orthodox Protestant thought in this particular. His view of the Church as comprehending a nation required a broad basis for its construction. The essential truths required for salvation within such a communion must be liberally and tolerantly represented.

In his earliest sermons Hooker committed himself to a view concerning the Divine Will which comprehended the salvation of all men, seeking, however, to couch this heterodox view in terms that should not clash with the current predestinarian theology.[1] He likewise trod upon the theological toes of Calvinism when, in his *Discourse on Justification*, he asserted that that doctrine did not of necessity presume the perdition of all Roman Catholics. We find in the second book of the *Ecclesiastical Polity*, as well, a remarkable definition of faith which might legitimately be held to include all the virtuous men of the pagan world as believers who may be saved.[2] Hooker was in this section disputing the Puritan teaching that good can be done only by those who have learned it from the Bible. In other words, he denied that faith is invariably impossible save by an intimate knowledge of the Word. He admitted that the Puritan view was normally true, but argued that a knowledge of the 'right way' may be obtained from other sources as well.

---

[1] Walton, Izaak, *Lives*, 184–185.
[2] Hooker, *Ecc. Pol.*, II, iv, 1; II, iv, 2; *Serm.*, I. Compare the views of Zwingli in this matter, cf. *post*, 327–329.

Thus Cicero expressed a faith identical with that of Saint Paul when he said "that nothing ought to be done whereof thou doubtest whether it be right or wrong." Hooker did not go so far as to admit that a pagan might have attained a Christian faith; he might have attained the first principles of knowledge, but that does not constitute knowledge.[1]

Hooker likewise taught that, spite its grave errors and abuses, salvation was possible in the Roman Church.[2] He probably went further than any Anglican in his century when he argued that a Roman Catholic could be saved despite error in a cardinal doctrine of faith.[3] In a noble passage he defended this position: "How many virtuous and just men, how many saints, how many martyrs, how many of the ancient Fathers of the Church, have had their sundry perilous opinions; and among sundry of their opinions this, that they hoped to make God some part of amends for their sins, by the voluntary punishments which they laid upon themselves . . . shall we therefore make such deadly epitaphs, and set them upon their graves, 'They denied the foundation of faith directly, they are damned, there is no salvation for them' . . . ?"[4] He urged that a difference must be drawn between those who err and those who obstinately persist in error; otherwise no man can hope for salvation. ". . . Give me a man," he continued, ". . . yea, a cardinal or a pope, whom at the extreme point of his life affliction hath made to know himself: whose heart God hath touched with true sorrow for all his sins, and filled with love towards the Gospel of Christ; whose eyes are opened to see the truth, and his mouth to renounce all heresy and error . . . this one opinion of merits excepted . . . and shall I think, because of this only error, that such a man toucheth not so much as the hem of Christ's garment?"[5] He concluded, " . . Let me die, if ever it be proved, that simply an error doth exclude

[1] Hooker, *Sermon on Certainty and Perpetuity of Faith in the Elect.*
[2] *Sermon II, Works,* 9, 16, 22, 27.
[3] He was speaking of the error of the Catholic doctrine of the sufficiency of works.
[4] Hooker, *Sermon II,* 35. (*A Learned Discoure of Justification, Works, and how the Foundation of Faith is Overthrown.*)   [5] *Ibid.*

227

a pope or a cardinal, in such a case, utterly from hope of life. Surely, I must confess unto you, if it be an error to think, that God may be merciful to save men when they err, my greatest comfort is my error; were it not for the love I bear unto this error, I would neither wish to speak nor to live."[1]

Obviously such a view destroyed the intellectual basis for the persecution of heresy. When it is held that the mercy of God is so infinite that error in a fundamental point of dogma may be forgiven by Him, the punishment of an individual retaining such an error by his fellow-men would be nothing less than blasphemy. Persecution would necessarily become an insult to the forgiving nature of God. Hooker was quite ready to punish men for disobedience to the Church and to the discipline which it had framed, since the proper conduct of society requires decency and order. But there was no suggestion that he would undertake to punish men for the retention of views contrary to the doctrines of that Church. In other words, Hooker expounded in the intellectual world precisely the views which the Government had been putting into practice for almost forty years.

Perhaps Hooker's greatest contribution to the development of religious toleration is to be found in his championship of the omnipotence of reason.

He earnestly taught that reason could establish the certainty of the essential truths of Christianity. When no rational demonstration of truth is possible the State or Church must erect and enforce a standard of conduct in order to prevent the dissensions which he so feared.[2] In matters of essential doctrine the Bible remains the sole authority, but reason must be employed even then in an interpretative and assisting capacity.

In matters of doctrine neither reason nor the authority of the Church can ever pretend to dogmatize when the Holy Writ is silent. But rites, customs, and discipline he held to be deductions from supernatural truth derived from Apostolic traditions and from the history of the Church.[3]

---

[1] Hooker, *Sermon II*, 35. (*A Learned Discourse of Justification, Works, and how the Foundation of Faith is Overthrown.*)
[2] Allen, J. W., *Political Thought*, 241.　　　[3] Hooker, *Ecc. Pol.*, I, xiv, 5.

By the gift of reason God illuminates everyone that comes into the world. By the exercise of its power men determine truth and error, distinguish between good and evil, and find the will of God. The will of God is not revealed, ordinarily, "by any extraordinary means" unto man, "but they by natural discourse attaining the knowledge thereof, seem the makers of those Laws which indeed are his, and they but the finders of them out."[1] The main principles of the Law of Reason are self-apparent, if they were not so it "were to take away all possibility of knowing anything."[2] Human beings have a sense of their own imperfections and desire the participation of God, which is accomplished by the direction of our will towards what appears to be good, and good is ascertainable only by reason.[3] "Goodness," he urged, "is seen with the eye of the understanding, and the light of that eye, is reason. So that two principal fountains there are of human action, knowledge and will."[4] He appears to identify the Law of Reason with the Law of Nature.[5]

There are in the Law of Reason "some things which stand as principles universally agreed upon; and that out of those principles, which are themselves evident, the greatest moral duties we owe towards God or man may without any great difficulty be concluded."[6] Reason is therefore the basis for the exposition of the Scriptures and for the propagation of the Faith among the unbelievers.[7] To the light of reason, which may be regarded as an instinctive perception of the Eternal Will, there has been added, for the Christian world, the Bible.[8] Christian faith is gained and propagated by the application of reason to the divine truths revealed by the Bible. We would deduce, too, that reason is the instrument whereby unbelief and error should be overcome. Thus Christ Himself used disputation to achieve His purposes.[9] "The light . . . which the star of natural reason and wisdom casteth, is too bright to be obscured by the mist of a word or two uttered to diminish

[1] Hooker, *Ecc. Pol.*, I, viii, 3; I, xvi, 5.   [2] *Ibid.*, I, viii, 5.
[3] *Ibid.*, I, v, 2.   [4] *Ibid.*, I, vii, 2, 3.   [5] *Ibid.*, I, viii, 9, 10.
[6] *Ibid.* I, viii, 10.   [7] *Ibid.*, III, viii, 15–16.
[8] *Ibid.*, I, viii, 5; III, viii, 12.   [9] *Ibid.*, III, viii, 17.

that opinion which justly hath been received concerning the force and virtue thereof, even in matters that touch most nearly the principal duties of men and the glory of the Eternal God."[1]

The Church has been left in possession of a rational freedom. It is to be guided by a sort of public reason. Reason is sufficient for the guidance of the Church "over and besides" the laws that are set out in the Bible.[2] The Scriptures shed supernatural light on the problems of the Church and to that illumination should be added the natural light of reason. There are many things which we may do for the glory of God which are not commanded by the Scriptures.[3] In following this natural light we should despise neither the judgment of the past nor the judgment of the present. When the private reason departs from the public judgment confusion must inevitably ensue.[4] To oppose our yea to the nay of the wise and learned is to be described only as presumptuous. Therefore, laws for the regiment of the Church may be made and followed on the basis of reason provided they are not repugnant to the express word of God.[5]

Hooker held that the Puritans and Sectarians were members of the Church and that they were denying only indifferent matters. Indifferent matters are determinable by the light of reason, and in this case by the king in Parliament. They should be enforced in the Church for the sake of decency and quietness. He deeply deplored all dissensions, since such varieties "are not only the fartherest spread, because in religion all men presume themselves interessed alike; but they are also for the most part hotlier prosecuted and pursued than other strifes, for as much as coldness, which in other contentions may be thought to proceed from moderation, is not in them favourably construed."[6] Hooker had little sympathy with the excessive zeal and bigotry of the radical Protestants, especially since he regarded the objects of controversy as quite unrelated to the essentials of Christianity.

---

[1] Hooker, *Ecc. Pol.*, III, viii, 17.
[2] *Ibid.*, III, viii, 18.
[3] Hunt, J., *Religious Thought in England*, I, 59.
[4] *Ibid.*
[5] Hooker, *Ecc. Pol.*, III, ix, 1.
[6] *Ibid.*, Ded. Bk., V, 5.

But here we have a logical impasse, for that which Hooker held to be indifferent the Puritans regarded as essential. As Professor Allen has suggested, Parliament could scarcely be regarded as competent to handle this issue.[1] Hooker taught that men must lend their conformity for the sake of public order and decency unless they could demonstrate the truth of their negative views. The Puritans, on their part, contended that they could do precisely this and quoted no less authority than the Bible. They held, further, that they could demonstrate that Hooker's non-essentials were necessary to true worship. Hooker saw the logic of the Puritan position and he did not dare face it in full frankness. He feared that full liberty of personal interpretation would lead to spiritual chaos, in which he was quite correct, and he was willing to submit private reason to public reason, legislatively determined. We cannot expect him, however, to make the step to the position that the determinations of one reason are quite as good as another. Hooker was very close at many points to the pronunciation of a theory of toleration, but he was deterred by every instinct and force of his age and by the apologetic nature of his own majestic work. One cannot avoid the feeling, however, that his work lacks, to some degree, the frank facing of difficult and hazardous matters which so characterized the less famous work of Archbishop Whitgift.

Hooker, like his royal mistress, was alternately tolerant and intolerant. They were both, at the same time, the most effective champions of toleration against those who by their bigotry and zeal had made the existence of toleration impossible.[2] Both confessed a law which binds those actions of men which are very closely related to their consciences. The operation of this law might on occasion be perverted into the coercion of opinion, but it would eventually protect one opinion from another, and serve to prevent the destruction of truth by retarding demands for liberty of opinion from groups which at the same time frankly envisaged the subversion of other opinions. Hooker's Erastianism was lightened by the knowledge that he

[1] Allen, *Political Thought*, 198.
[2] Maurice, F. D., *Modern Philosophy*, 192.

had entrusted the control of action, and to a lesser degree of opinion, to a Government which had long since disavowed the right to persecute conscience, which exercised its control judiciously, and which was able to adapt itself to the changing conditions of spiritual life in England. In every country toleration has resulted from the imposition of the will of the secular authority upon that of the clergy.[1]

Buckle, in a brilliant section, has indicated the striking difference in the point of view of Hooker and Jewel. Jewel rested his case on the Fathers and the Old Testament; Hooker on the power of reason in the interpretation of the Bible. So long as theology finds its defence in dogma, theological divergence can be regarded as nothing else but heresy. The advent of reason opens up the field of discussion and interpretation and may, if unity does not ensue, lead to the view that the opinions of one sect are quite as good as those of another.[2] When two profound and earnest minds by a reasonable examination of a doctrine find themselves at complete variance, the logical excuse for persecution has vanished. Reason will ultimately destroy intellectual authoritativism and, as it proved, will sooner or later lead to relativism. "As theology became more reasonable, it became less confident, and therefore more merciful."[3] Hooker's treatise represented the defence of a Rationalist against the Scripturalists. The Puritans, led by Cartwright, had denied the natural light of reason, in order to detect the greater glory of the supernatural.[4] His view of reason was posed against the Calvinist dictum that the Scriptures were not only all-sufficient, but that reason, save when engaged in the interpretation or exposition of the Bible, was vain. Hooker replied that by reason alone do we recognize the Scriptures as the Word of God. Reason cannot, unassisted, enable us to attain salvation, but it is able to teach us our duty as Christians and the more perfectly to live the Christ-like life.

[1] Buckle, H. T., *History of Civilization in England*, I, 337.
[2] *Ibid.*, I, 344.   [3] *Ibid.*
[4] Hunt, *Religious Thought in England*, I, 60.

6. Conclusion

In summary, the progress of political developments during the second half of Elizabeth's reign considerably modified the attitude of the dominant groups towards the problem of religious dissent.

The Roman Catholic problem especially occupied the attention of the Government during this period. The sharpening of Roman Catholic efforts to win England both by conversion and by force after 1576 necessarily resulted in a tightening of the Catholic policy and in a repression that occasionally must be described as persecution. Nevertheless, the policy of the Government was consistently secular in spirit. Professor Read has abundantly demonstrated this to be true of Walsingham, who was the chief agent of the Council in the execution of its Catholic programme. The Government had, in short, attained a singularly clear and effective definition of its religious policy. Repression was undertaken without hatred and without excessive zeal. The Council consistently adhered to the single intention of preventing civil disorder and of restraining all religious groups that sought by force to impose their particular brands of 'truth' upon the country. Thus Burleigh distinguished carefully between the priest who fostered sedition in order to achieve his religious purpose and the Catholic who desired only the right peacefully to entertain spiritual beliefs and to exercise them with proper privacy. To the one, he promised imprisonment, torture, and a horrible death under the laws of treason; to the other, he offered liberty of conscience and an undefined measure of religious liberty so long as the Government detected no political purpose in the exercise of religious rites.

The State disavowed any spiritual purpose in its policy of repression and proceeded by its own candid admission along secular and political lines in the formulation and administration of its policy. This fact represents a complete reversal of the medieval theory of the persecution of misbelief and nonconformity and attains in one bound half the distance to religious toleration.

Sufficient evidence exists both in the formal expressions of the Government and in the actual treatment of recusants to support the conclusion that the distinction between freedom of conscience and political disloyalty couched in religious terms had factual reality. The Government demanded only formal obedience to the laws of religion and professed its intention to dissociate itself from any inquisition of conscience or any attempt to dictate religious belief. Perhaps the finest and fullest exposition of the governmental policy in this period is to be found in the *Execution of Justice in England for Maintenance of Publique and Christian Peace,* which almost certainly may be attributed to Burleigh.

The Catholic policy of the Government was, in the face of plots on the Queen's life, armed rebellion inspired by papal agents, and a chronic threat of a crusade by the Catholic powers abroad, considerably tightened, but no essential difference resulted in theory or in practice. The laws of the realm were simply executed in full against one section of the Roman Catholics. The loyal Catholics whose interest in their religion was confined to the adherence to its doctrines and its worship were repeatedly reassured that their consciences would not be molested and that the Government was only concerned with the punishment of treason of which certain of their co-religionists happened to be guilty. The Government had no intention of forcibly exterminating Roman Catholicism in England; it was concerned with the first function of any Government, the preservation of civil order and of its own existence.

Even during the hysterical period which culminated about 1588, when every Catholic was regarded as a potential traitor, the Government did not abandon its position of not exacting the death penalty save only in those rare instances when a treason charge could be proved. The law of treason was in certain cases stretched to inflict terrible injustices, but Elizabeth and her Council refrained from embarking upon a policy of wholesale slaughter which the circumstances of the moment and European examples must have pressed upon them. The Government repeatedly reiterated its pledge that loyal Catholics were in no danger of their lives, and that it sought genuinely to distinguish between conscientious belief and treasonable practices which sometimes sought obscurity under religious guise. The recusancy laws were administered with surprising equity and their general enforcement was relaxed as actual danger from the Catholic powers abroad receded.

At the conclusion of the reign the Government took advantage of the quarrel between the Jesuits and the Seculars in order to win the support of the loyal group of English Catholics. The possibility of toleration for those Roman Catholics who were interested only in the free exercise of their religion and who were willing to manifest their political loyalty, was seriously entertained. The royal proclamation of 1602 announced that, while the Government could not embrace a policy of religious liberty, it would not render the lot of loyal Romanists unbearable. The incident had seriously impaired the influence of the Jesuit party over the English Catholics, and had thereby assisted in clearing, to some degree, the atmosphere of fear which had been solely responsible for the reappearance of the ugly head of religious persecution in England.

The Government likewise found itself confronted by a militant species of Protestantism which had as its aim the reformation of the English Church and the utilization of the agencies of Government for the attainment of a society which would give offence neither to God nor to the godly. The Puritan looked to Geneva for his inspiration as truly as the Catholic looked to Rome for his inspiration. The Government detected in this programme a threat to its own security and a denial of its policy of comprehension and moderation which contrived to make Puritanism only less inimical to national stability than militant Catholicism. Under the able leadership of Whitgift various expedients were undertaken in order to discipline and control the rising head of schism in the English Church. The strenuous and thorough character of his efforts evoked clamorous protests and sturdy resistance from the Puritans and excited strong Puritan sympathy in the Council itself. The dominant groups were in substantial agreement in the repression of militant Catholicism, but the attempt to repress Puritanism disclosed that no two members of the

Government shared precisely the same attitude towards advanced Protestantism. The existence of such a variety of opinions in the governing body was at once evidence that the desired end of uniformity had not been attained and that the disintegrative forces inherent in Protestantism had done their work.

Towards the conclusion of the reign, however, Puritan excesses provoked emergency legislation which was designed to arrest the further development of the movement, especially in its political aspects. This legislation was enforced with caution and was regarded as a potential weapon rather than as an instrument of consistent repression. The debates in the House of Commons upon this body of legislation, and other related proposals, were perhaps the most hopeful sign of the era. The opposition was formidable and placed its attack upon the full bases of religious toleration. The rights of conscience were declared to lie outside the province of law; persecution was held to bestow a tyrannous power upon the administrators of the law; and it was indicated that the Government had had ample time and requisite agencies to secure religious uniformity. It was intimated that the long attempt to secure even a nominal comprehension had failed and that some toleration must be granted to dissent, which had demonstrated itself to be unconquerable.

The Elizabethan Government cannot be exonerated from the punishment by death of at least five cases of genuine heresy. In all these instances the victims held views which were radical in nature and which were abhorrent to the mass of Englishmen of all shades of religious belief. In two cases the fact that the guilty men were foreigners and Anabaptists probably explains the real cause for their execution. The political beliefs which Anabaptists held, or were supposed to have held, were regarded with universal horror in the sixteenth century. Earnest attempts were made to secure a recantation and the unfortunate victims found no less a supporter than Foxe. The other martyrs to Elizabethan intolerance were technically convicted under civil charges and the procedure testified to the unwillingness of the Government to demand the death penalty for heresy no matter how flagrantly the belief of the accused might violate the tender religious conscience of the age. The evidence with regard to the last three heretics disposes one to the conclusion that the Justices were considerably more expert in the law than in the symptoms of acute religious psychosis.

Anglican thought in this period was the reflection of governmental policies and difficulties. Whitgift regarded severity as the only instrument capable of sealing the widening fissure in the Church, and his unsystematic reflections in this busy period of his life would indicate that he had abandoned to some degree the nobler sentiments of his earlier writings. The State was in factual control of religious policy and Anglican thought tended to support the validity of that power. The writers argued the duty of the prince to support true religion and to extirpate heresy. They held that unbelievers might be forced to embrace religious truth though their disinclination to admit the justice of the death penalty for refusal softened the point of their argument. They dwelt at length upon the political necessity of order and uniformity and had surprisingly little to say for the ideal necessity for uniformity of belief. They stressed uniformity of worship, having lost faith in the possibility of attaining uniformity of opinion. Half the case for religious toleration had been conceded.

At the close of the century Hooker set forth in the calm sunset of the Queen's reign the essence of forty years of Anglican thought on the manifold problems which relate themselves to the question of religious toleration. He was unwilling to allow complete freedom to reason and to private judgment since he detected the spiritual anarchy which must ensue from the free play of these agencies. He preferred to raise a law and an interpretation of the law which would turn religious thoughts and actions into a broad and comprehensive stream which would, however, have restraining banks. He envisaged a law which, while checking disintegrating tendencies, would guarantee a large measure of freedom and toleration within the majestic Church which his mind created. He held with reason that the Elizabethan Government, having, through a long and difficult

237

period, guarded the rights of conscience, having erected an establishment in which men with many shades of religious opinion had found a spiritual home, and having prevented that spiritual fractionization to which Protestantism is by nature inclined, might safely be entrusted with the definition and the preservation of English religious life. He posed reason as the bulwark of his conception and left reason free to alter the structure of the Church as it bit deeper into the spiritual requirements of a rapidly changing order. He did not open the door of toleration, but he did not permanently debar the opening of that door when it would become necessary to release the pressure of the ever-mounting weight of solidifying religious groups even now beginning clearly to formulate and forcibly to state their claims for some guarantee of religious freedom.

IV

THE MINORITY GROUPS DURING THE REIGN OF ELIZABETH

A.—Puritan Thought and its Relation to the Development of Religious Toleration

1. General Characteristics of Puritan Thought in Relation to Religious Toleration

The Puritans, during the reign of Elizabeth, made no direct contribution to the development of religious toleration.[1] Their theological system, its social and intellectual implications, and their attitude towards the Church of England, towards the Government, and the Sectarians, may be described as highly intolerant. "It was an awkward position for Puritan Independents, because they had to claim for themselves liberty from the State to worship God in their own way and to interpret the Bible according to their own ideas, and yet they themselves were most unwilling to tolerate any serious divergence from what they believed to be the truth."[2] Perhaps the accusation that T. T. laid against them was not without some justice: they charge that "the present State is anti-Christian"; while the Apostles laboured in an humble and helpful spirit to effect unity and peace in religion, the contrary is true of the reformers. "How many heads, so many opinions."[3] But in the fact that where there were so many heads there were so many opinions the Puritans by their sturdy championship of the right of individual interpretation were to make by a process of indirection a highly important contribution to the development of religious liberty.

The Puritan saw in the Bible a complete repository of divine

---

[1] We are considering the Presbyterian movement as part of the Puritan system of thought. Certainly, with respect to our problem, any effort to distinguish between Puritanism and Presbyterianism during the Elizabethan period would be misleading.   [2] Gow, H., *The Unitarians*, 27.
[3] T.T. (Turswell, T.?), *A Myrror for Martinists*, 11.

truth and from its pages he received a religious commission which was at once powerful and intolerant.[1] This literalism sought in the Bible the precise outline of civil and ecclesiastical policy and refused to accept the milder persuasions of reason and of tradition. The hand of God rested upon the Puritan, and he observed a world of sin and ignorance which could be saved only by the imposition of the order of society, civil and religious, which God had revealed to him. The Puritan was vigorous in his religious outlook and despised the moderate leaders in Church and State as 'neuters'; "they reckon a singular witty part, that they can craftily cloak and dissemble themselves in all other affairs after such sort, as if a man were familiarly linked to both parties: not altogether gone from the papists, lest he be counted a stubborn fellow; not altogether divested from the Gospellers, lest he be called an Apostate: and by that shift to walk, as it were, in the middle and the most safe way: to be indifferent to both sides: to keep peace, substance, honour, and doctrine safe."[2]

The comprehension and easy tolerance of the English Church appeared feeble when compared with the Church of Geneva, which constantly rose before the Puritan's eyes as the ideal towards which the Church of England must strive.[3] He despised the English ecclesiastical structure as a creature of governmental policy, which he regarded as governed by the unworthy ends of political expediency. A Puritan author expressed neatly the predominant attitude of his party when he admonished the reader to "start not one inch from the word of God."[4]

As the Puritan efforts to reform the 'corruptions' in the Church were repulsed, as the Government regarded their zeal with increasing impatience, the Puritan spirit grew sterner and more intolerant.

The system of compromise by which the Tudors cemented

[1] *Zurich Letters*, clxxvii; Cartwright, *Sec. Rep.*, 5; Whitgift, *Works*, I, 180–181, 187–8, 190–191; 195, 196 ff.
[2] *A godly and necessary admonition concerning Neuters, and such as deserve the gross name of Jack of Both Sides.* (2nd ed., 1585.) Digest in Strype, *Annals*, III, 1, 517 ff.
[3] Fairbairn, A. M., *Studies in Religion and Theology*, 207.
[4] Strype, *Annals*, III, 1, 518.

England became more and more distastful to his literal spirit.[1] To men who regarded themselves as soldiers of God, and as soldiers on the defensive, the struggle with the papacy was no matter for compromise.[2] It was a struggle between the powers of light and darkness, and the peril of the children of God was too great to admit of any moderation or toleration. The Anglican Church had, under the able guidance of Elizabeth, enlarged the possible sphere of toleration by regarding the Church structure as unessential, mutable, and subject to reasonable variations.[3] Whatever intolerance the Government and the Church may have displayed in enforcing conformity was, therefore, designed not to secure a conformity necessary for salvation but a conformity necessary for decent and orderly worship. The difference is, of course, vast.

The apparent tendency of the Government to advance an Erastian toleration of dissent was rudely checked by the appearance of militant Puritanism, shading off in one of its important branches into Presbyterianism. Puritanism aroused Elizabethan England and succeeded for the first time in English history in making the English a theologically disputationous nation.[4] The Puritans demanded the formulation of an unqualified line between absolute truth and absolute error, both of which they announced themselves capable of defining. This dogged determination, while forcing Puritan theology into the fixed moulds of which Lecky and Tulloch complained, presented an unyielding front against which governmental persuasion was useless. The Puritans, as has well been said, thereby indirectly rendered their most important contribution to the development of religious toleration. They refused to permit the Government to reduce the kingdom to a state of uniformity.[5] They opposed one rigid group of opinions to another. Toleration ensued when a wise Government declined to permit the increasing friction of opinions to pulverize the social and political structure. The

[1] Green, *History of England*, IV, 100–101.   [2] *Ibid.*
[3] ". . . That any one kind of government is so necessary that without it the church cannot be saved, or that it may not be altered into some other kind thought to be more expedient, I utterly deny. . . ." (Whitgift, *Works*, I, 184.)
[4] Haynes, E. S. P., *Religious Persecution*, 102.
[5] Pearson, A. F. S., *Church and State*, 115.

counsels of moderation proving of no avail, pressure which could scarcely be called other than persecution had to ensue. The eyes of the Puritans were fixed entirely upon the purging of the Church so as to concentrate its energy more effectively on the struggle with Rome. They were equally intolerant of the Establishment, the Catholics, and the Protestant sectarians.

Cartwright and the Presbyterians insisted that their organization was the only true Church and that no salvation could be found outside it. Indeed, all persons outside the Church were regarded as heretics, and Cartwright's ideal solution for the problem of heresy was capital punishment.[1] The Word of God had ordained a particular form of organization before which all false forms must give way. Theocratic, exclusive Calvinism must be substituted for the expedient, moderate, and comprehensive structure of the Establishment.[2] The Church of England may be regarded as an attempt to nationalize the religious organization with loyalty to the Queen as its fundamental article. Cartwright, and his followers, insisted upon a structure which was, in comparison, narrow and sectarian and founded exclusively upon Biblical authority. The Puritan, "absorbed as he was in the thought of God, craving for nothing less than a divine righteousness, a divine wisdom, a divine strength, grasped the written Bible as the law of God and concentrated every energy in the effort to obey it."[3] A policy of comprehension seemed to him simply a policy of faithlessness to Almighty God.

The central position of the doctrine of predestination in the Puritan dogmatic system likewise contributed to the intolerance of the group. It would appear that the doctrine that only the elect are to be saved, that a vast number of men are irretrievably damned, and that no human effort can possibly alter the process of election would lead to a tolerant view of the problem of heresy.[4] Indeed, in so far as Pietism grew out of Calvinism this was to be the case, but Pietism was a sectarian

---

[1] Cf. ante, 142–145, 146–147.
[2] Klein, A. J., Intolerance in the Reign of Elizabeth, 163.
[3] Green, J. R., History of England, IV, 105.
[4] Knox's opponent dealt critically with this point, cf. ante, 76.

phenomenon rather than an essentially Puritan development. Had it not been for the highly positive nature of Calvinism, moderation might have developed from the doctrine. We might conceivably have seen the communion of the Saints quite indifferent to the sins of the hosts of the damned. But Calvinism was highly moralistic in its psychology. The world must be moulded into a proper abiding place for the elect. The damned might not be saved by human efforts but they must so live as not to give scandal to the elect. It was from this point of view that the liberality and tolerance of the Elizabethan Government scandalized the Puritans. They attacked the comprehensive nature of the Established Church as proceeding from lack of zeal for the Lord.[1]

2. THE PLACE OF THE MAGISTRATE IN THE CHURCH

We shall now examine in some detail the Puritan views with respect to the place of the magistracy in the Church, the attitude which the State should assume towards error, and the proper solution of the Roman Catholic problem, in order to analyse more closely the bases for the extreme intolerance of the Elizabethan Puritans.

Spite the Puritans' continual stress upon the absolute authority of the Bible and their insistence upon the power which the true preaching of that Word had upon the hearts of men, they did not propose to erect a kingdom of God solely by these instruments. Truth conquers but slowly and the necessity for the purification of the Church they declared to be most urgent. Hence the civil power was called upon to enforce the obvious will and requirements of God. Imbued with a hatred of vice and with a sense of true holiness, the Puritans proposed an active campaign of vice suppression. They did not, as a Church, propose to carry out the necessary penalties, having drawn a sharp line between the functions of Church and State. The function of the Church ended with

[1] Thus they attacked the prayers of the service which "pray that all men may be saved without exception; and that travelling by sea and land may be preserved, Turks and traitors not excepted. . . ." "In all their service there is no edification, they pray that all men may be saved." (*First Admonition to Parliament*; Hooker, *Ecc. Pol.*, V, 27, 1.)

the awful sentence of excommunication.[1] The function of the magistrate should properly begin at this point. The Puritan assertion of loyalty to the Elizabethan supremacy postulated the enforcement by the Crown of the determinations of the ecclesiastical body.[2] Thus, they held that it was the duty of the magistrate "to assist and maintaine the discipline of the kirk, and punish them civilly, that will not obey the censure of the same. . . ."[3] Godly princes will further "heare and obeye" the voice of the true ministers and will "reverence the majestie of the son of God speaking in them."[4] The ideal Calvinistic state presumed a civil power controlled and directed by the ecclesiastical organization; a system which approached a theocracy and whose obvious model was Geneva.

The *Admonition to Parliament* denied that the civil ruler should be called the head of the churches in his dominions and strictly limited his ecclesiastical powers. The leadership of the Church, it was held, should be placed in the hands of ecclesiastics and the prince should not meddle in functions not appertaining to his jurisdiction. The Church, Cartwright explained in the *First Reply*, exists for the sake of the inward man and the State for the outward man. These formulae were ancient, but they obtained vital content when considered in the light of the moralistic aims of Puritan thought.

The *Second Admonition to Parliament* further explained that the Queen should take the defence of God's cause upon her shoulders. She should "fortifie it by law, that it may be received by common order throughout her dominions."[5] The proper order for the Church should be drawn from the Bible, pre-

[1] "But in their hands excommunication was not merely the merciful prohibition of the partaking of a Christian sacrament; it carried with it the exposure of the guilty person to an intolerable isolation amongst his fellows, and it finally necessitated a public and degrading ceremonial before he could again be received into favour." (Gardiner, S. R., *History of England*, I, 25.)
[2] Allen, J. W., *History of Political Theory*, 214.
[3] *Second Scottish Booke of Discipline*, 84.   [4] *Ibid.*, 85.
[5] *Second Admonition (Puritan Manifestoes)*, 130 (1572). The two *Admonitions* were reprinted together without date in 1589 (?), and again in 1617. Copies of the first edition of the *Second Admonition* may be found in the B.M., Bodl., and Lambeth Collections. The *Second Admonition* was reprinted in the valuable collection *Puritan Manifestoes* (1907) under the editorship of W. H. Frere and C. E. Douglas.

sumably by the clergy, ". . . yet in it hir majestie that by hir princely authoritie shuld see every of these things put in practise, and punish those what neglect them. . . ."[1] The cause of God will never be advanced without the effective co-operation of the civil and spiritual forces of the kingdom.[2] Travers taught that the authority of the ruler should secure the free discussion of theological matters by ecclesiastical assemblies so that they may be authorized "which should be most agreeable to God's worde."[3] The ruler must not interfere, however, in the formulation of doctrine, discipline, or policy. ". . . the magistrates haue this proper and peculiar to themselues aboue the rest of the faithfull. To set in order and establishe the state off the Churche by ther authoritie and to preserue and mainteine it according to Godds will being once established.[4] But he made it plain that the "establishment of that will" is properly the task of the clergy, and that the civil ruler finds his highest function in maintaining and executing the discipline of the Church under the direction of its officers.[5]

Finally, Travers urged, "their civill power would enforce all men to honour God, and live in duetie one towardes another as they ought, defending the godlie against the mightie oppressours, . . . and punish the iniquitie of the wicked according to their desertes in iustice and equitie. . . ."[6] By submitting

[1] Second Admon. to Parl. (Puritan Manifestoes), 130 (1572).
[2] The prince should give the ecclesiastical decisions force of law, "for the Churche maye keepe these orders, but never in peace, expect the comfortable and blessed assistance of the states and governors linke in to see them accepted in their countreys and used." (Second Admon. to Parl. (Puritan Manifestoes), 130.)
[3] Travers, Walter, A Defence of Ecclesiastical Discipline, 177.
[4] Travers, Full and Plaine Declaration, 187. In 1574, Travers published in Latin at Geneva The Holy Discipline of the Church described in the Word of God. An English version under the title A full and plaine Declaration of Ecclesiasticall Discipline owt off the Word of God . . . appeared in the same year, probably at Geneva. A second edition appeared in 1580 at Geneva. The work was translated and revised by Cartwright, and was being printed at Cambridge when it was discovered and burned by order of Whitgift. Another copy appeared from Leyden (H.C.L. copy) in 1617; and a copy of an earlier translation, which was found in Cartwright's library, was reprinted under a variant title in 1644 (?).   [5] Ibid., 186–187.
[6] Travers, Def. of the Ecc. Disc., 177.

themselves to the Church and by bowing before the unearthly authority of Christ, the civil ruler may carry out "all faythfull duetie, seruice, and obedience vnto him. The performance whereof is to renounce in them selues and to abolish from amongst their people, all false worship and idolatrie, . . . and to establish in all partes the trew worship of God. . . ."[1]

Travers reduced the function of the prince in spiritual matters to the mere execution of the requirements of the Church, for " . . . the regiment and gouernment [of the Church] dependenth not uppon the authoritie of princes, but uppon the ordinaunce of God. . . ."[2] This regiment may succeed with or without his assistance,[3] the co-operation of the prince ensuring its more rapid predominance. "For the Church craueth helpe and defence of Christian princes to continue, and goe forwarde more peaceably and profitably, to the setting vp of the kingdome of Christ; but all hir authoritie she receyueth immediately frō God."[4] The prince is a useful adjunct to the policy of the Church, but is by no means necessary to the ultimate attainment of its perfection.

Dudley Fenner, writing in 1590, was even more explicit in regard to the power and function of the prince in the Church. He held that it was not only lawful but necessary that the prince should perform his duty in caring for the Church and in reforming religion.[5] But the office of pastor and prince must not be confounded, "for, as it is not lawfull for the prince to preache nor administer the Sacramentes; no more is it lawfull for him to make laues in ecclesiastical matters contrarie to the knowledge of his learned pastors."[6] To the pastors are granted by God the duties of preaching, ministering the Sacraments, and ecclesiastical government. It is as iniquitous for the prince to usurp the last function as the other two.

However, the Puritans would impose upon the prince grave spiritual responsibilities. A Puritan writer of 1590 regretted that after thirty-two years of the true religion in England

---

[1] Travers, *Def. of the Ecc. Disc.*, 197–198. [2] *Ibid.*, 224.
[3] Travers had shown (*Ibid.*, 165–176) that the government of the Church was wholly perfect before the days of Christian princes. [4] *Ibid.*, 224.
[5] Fenner, Dudley, *A Defence of the Godlie ministers*, etc. (no pagin.)
[6] *Ibid.*

there remained so much sin and false worship.[1] He clearly held the prince responsible for these shortcomings and endeavoured to arouse the magistrates to a realization of their "awful task" to reform the kingdom following "the most singular example of Iosiah the annoited of the Lord. . . ."[2] It is the special duty of the prince to see that God is glorified in his dominions.[3] To that end he ought "to make civill lawes to binde the people vnto the confession of true faith, and the right administring and receyuing of the Sacramentes" and to punish infractions of the same.[4] But in these capacities the prince should be guided by the advice of his clergy.

The Puritans, further, were frank in their conviction that the magistrate was subject to the spiritual censure of the Church. "Neither let the magistrates think . . . that in this behalffe (ecclesiastical discipline) they are to be exempted from his precept and commaundment off the apostle who chargeth euery one to be subiect to those who in Lord are set ouer them for seing they ought to be carefull as well off the saluacion off the magystrate as off others and that the sowle of the magystrate as well as of the rest is committed to theyr charge."[5] The spiritual censure of the magistrate might include the serious penalty of excommunication.[6] The Church should not be bound by the remnants of the canon law.[7] Christ should become truly King in England, "to prescribe lawes vnto them, whereby they may be ruled."[8] The Church represents a province of life over which the State has no spiritual control, and the highest officers of the State are as amenable to its censures as the humblest subject.[9] The officers of the Church represent

---

[1] *Reformation of Religion of Iosiah*, etc., Pref. [2] *Ibid.*
[3] *Confession of Prisoners*; signed by Field. Neal, *Puritans*, I, 192.
[4] Fenner, *Defence of the Godlie ministers* (no pagin.).
[5] Travers, *Full and Plain Decl.*, 185.
[6] "To this position, that princes should be excepted frō ecclesiastical discipline, and namely from excommunication, I vtterlie mislike." (Cartwright, *Rest of Reply*, 65, 92.)
[7] Udall, John, *Demonstration of the Truth of That Discipline* . . ., Pref.
[8] *Ibid.*
[9] "They must also as well as the rest submit themselues and be obedient to the iust and lawfull authoritie of the officers of the Churche." (Travers, *Free and Plain Decl.*, 185.)

the majesty of Jesus Christ, and "Is it not meete that euen kinges and the highest magystrates should be obedient vnto them"[1] just as he should submit his body to the subjection of a physician in case of sickness?[2]

These claims bit deeply into the royal supremacy, and when the full portent of the Puritan demands was comprehended it is entirely explicable that the Government brought considerable pressure to bear on the party. The Puritans were wholly honest, and they left no doubt in the minds of men as to what their attitude would be towards dissent if they should attain power. They would have made of the secular Government an agency for the extermination of what they deemed heresy, i.e. beliefs which happened to conflict with their own dogmatic system. In so far as the interests of religious freedom were concerned, it was fortunate that the secular power was able to keep the zealots in all parties in check until they had learned, by tasting of repression for themselves, something of the lesson of moderation.

3. THE QUESTION OF HERESY

The Puritan literature displayed considerably more uniform and vigorous unanimity on the question of the duty of the State to suppress and punish heresy than did the Anglican literature of the same period. The Puritan theory of State discipline was quite admirably summarized in the *Admonition to Parliament*: "This regiment consisteth especially in ecclesiastical discipline, which is an order left by God unto his church, whereby men learne to frame their wylles and doyngs accordyng to the law of God, bye instructing and admonishing one another, yea and by correcting and punishing all wylfull persones, and contemners of the same."[3] If State (publique) discipline were restored it "wolde be very necessarie and profitable for the building up of God's house. The final end of this discipline, is the reforming of the disordered, and to bryng them to repentance, and to bridle such as wold offend."[4]

[1] Travers, *Free and Plain Decl.*, 185.
[2] Bradshaw, William, *English Puritanism*, 29.
[3] *Admon. to Parl.* (*Puritan Manifestoes*), 16–17.   [4] *Ibid.*, 17.

Punishment of erroneous views was regarded as a means of bringing men to a perception of their duty to God.[1] The magistrate must at once advance the preaching of the Gospel, and see that "all superstition and idolatry" are rooted out of his dominions.[2] In fact, the principal duty of the Christian Ruler is to see "that the true God be worshipped according to his Worde, that Idolatrie be cast out, and Idolaters and heretikes be punished according to God's word by the sword of iustice."[3] The pleas of conscience which will be aroused by such a meritorious policy must not be heeded. If such pleas were regarded in the execution of the civil laws, the Government would soon perish.[4]

When we compare the attitude of the Puritans towards the Roman Catholic Church, or even towards the Anglican Church, with the fine tolerance of Hooker, we are driven to the conclusion that a far greater hope of toleration resided in the comprehensive folds of the Church of England than in the Puritan ranks.

There appears to be no instance of a Puritan denunciation of the Church of England as a false Church in which salvation could not be found during the sixteenth century, but some of the indictments ranged close to that mark. The *Admonition* charged that "We in England are so fare off from having a church rightly reformed, . . . that as yet we are not come to the outwarde face of the same."[5] The government and discipline of the Church of England were called "both anti-christian and devilish." Even more severe was the stricture of the *Supplication to the Parliament* which charged that "The established gouernment of the church, is trayterous against the maiesty of Jesus Christ; it confirmeth the pope's supremacie, it is accursed. It is . . . an vnlawfull, a false, a bastardly government."[6]

The denial that salvation could possibly be found within the Roman communion was, of course, a Puritan common-

[1] Travers, *An Answer to a svpplicatorie Epistle*, etc. (1583), 18–19 (pagin. irreg.).   [2] *Confession of Prisoners*; signed by Field. Neal, I, 192.
[3] *Reform. of Rel. of Iosiah* (no pagin.).
[4] Travers, *An Answer*, 24 (pagin. irreg.). We have already noticed *in extenso* the view of Cartwright on this matter. Cf. *ante*, 142–145.
[5] *Admon. to Parl.*, 9.   [6] *Suppl. to the Parl.*, 56.

place.[1] But the Puritan hatred of the Roman Catholics far exceeded this rather academic, though intolerant, view. Many Anglicans would have agreed to that point, but the advanced Puritans held that they might lawfully be put to death as heretics, a position which the Government had denounced since its formation. It would be interesting to know how many Puritans would have agreed "That papistrie be condemned by law for heresie, that without further ambiguitie of tearmes, if the law canon be now English and not Romish, it may easily appeare which part is comprehended within the compasse of that law, and that accordingly thei may be proceeded against as sectaries that erre in faith. . . ."[2] The Martinist pamphlets were virulent in their hatred of the Catholics and, in general, regarded them as both traitors and heretics.

It is encouraging to be able to point to instances of hesitation on the part of the more moderate Puritans in connection with the problem of the treatment of obstinate heretics. Dering, when questioned as to the validity of the Judicial Law of Moses, professed uncertainty when Cartwright had stubbornly stood by his Scriptural guns. Dering held that these laws were "an absolute patterne of most perfect iustice," but directly afterwards confessed to their relativity when he agreed that they should be followed with due regard to time and place.[3]

Travers appeared to be even more uncertain. In the early pages of *An Answer* he appeared to boast that, though English Catholics were in reality dangerous heretics,[4] ". . . no one of all their catholickes, for cause of his conscience and religion onely, . . . hath lost either life or limme, since the happie day of her m. coronation, vntill this time."[5] England has been compelled, in order to prevent civil war, to punish sedition and treason rigorously, but this does not imply that these persons have been punished for their faith.[6] But later in the

---

[1] S.C., *A Brief Resolution of a Right Religion* . . . 1566, presented a typical statement of the Puritan view in this matter.
[2] *Morrice MSS.* (Dr. Williams' Lib.), No. 224, 1586. *Articles for Reformation of the Ministers. Seconde parte of a Register.*
[3] *A Parte of a Register*, etc., 80.   [4] Travers, *An Answer*, 26.
[5] *Ibid.*, 27, 37.   [6] *Ibid.*, 28–29.

book Travers indicated that the Old Testament lays down a general law which obliges "the magistrate . . . to put an heretique to death."[1] The parable of the tares had always been urged against this view, but Travers explained that the parable refers to the wicked in general and not to the heretics in particular. He admitted that compulsion could not bring a man to a knowledge of saving faith, but "he may be occasioned to vse such meanes whereby after he may beleeue."[2] He recognized the predicament that follows when the Roman Catholic Church adjudged one man an heretic, and the Protestants another. With Calvin, he adopted the unconvincing explanation that since Protestantism was in possession of the truth its judgment was correct.[3] In keeping with the Biblical injunction, national legislation has been framed to secure conformity to this truth.[4]

4. The Doctrine of Private Judgment and the Claim of Liberty of Conscience

Intolerant as the Puritans may have been in their actions and in their expressed theories, they evidently made a highly important contribution to the development of religious toleration. The Puritans, as ardent Calvinists, were profoundly influenced by the belief in the imminence of God and in the actuality of private revelation. They retained to a peculiar degree those tenets of the early Reformation which had stressed the importance of individual judgment in matters of faith. These factors combined to convince the Puritan not only of the rightness of his views but of his right in conscience to hold and exercise them.[5] The Puritan was disposed to contend that

---

[1] Travers, *An Answer*, 35 (pagin. irreg.).   [2] *Ibid.*, 54.
[3] Calvin, in the *Defensio*, carefully argued against the validity of Catholic persecution of his followers by a curious extension of the doctrine of election. The Elect know that they are right, and therefore persecution of them is insupportable. This view represents an amazing extension of what Troeltsch has called the sectarian sense of monopoly of truth. It is with difficulty that logic can penetrate such a revelation of 'rightness.' Calvin urged that the Catholic prince, not being of the Elect, persecuted not from a false conviction of right but from mere greed and superstition.
[4] Travers, *An Answer*, 56.   [5] Neal, *History of the Puritans*, I, 160.

it was the natural right of every man to judge for himself in matters of faith and to profess that doctrine which his conscience and intelligence dictated without the interference of the civil magistracy or of the ecclesiastical power.[1] Unfortunately this principle was subverted by his accompanying insistence in forcing his fellow-men to adopt the beliefs which by indisputable authority he regarded as true. Until the conviction that absolute truth could be imposed upon a nation by Bible reading, preaching, and properly applied compulsion had been weakened by the discouragement of experience and the stubborn refusal of the civil power to accept such a position, the Puritan's defence of the liberty of the Christian conscience could not bear its true fruit.

Most of the Puritan protests that conscience could not be forced resulted from their own persecution. The Puritans secured an opportunity to test in person the efficacy of religious coercion. Their pleas extended, in general, no further than the merits of their own case, or the merits of their party. We will seek in vain for any plea for the liberty of all sects and of all consciences. None the less, their defence of the inviolability of the Christian conscience could not have been without effect, and it may be well to examine a number of such instances occurring in a selected period—1564–1590.

In 1564 Sampson and Humphrey found themselves cited before the Ecclesiastical Commission and unable to return to their colleges because of their refusal to conform to the regulations relating to vestments. They protested that they professed the same doctrine as their conforming brethren and that they differed only in non-essentials of the faith. It appeared to them that "where there might be a room for liberty often, . . . there ought to be for charity ever."[2] They recalled the fact that the Church had in the past frequently differed on indifferent matters which had in no way destroyed the unity of the faith. They were moved then to address the Commissioners since "conscience is a tender thing, that ought not to be touched nor

---

[1] Neal, *History of the Puritans*, I, 160.
[2] Sampson and Humphrey, Letter to the Archbishops and Commissioners, 1564. Strype, *Parker*, I, 324.

angered," and "They were taught by conscience, that things in their own nature indifferent do not always seem indifferent to the opinions of men, and are changed by times and accidents."[1]

A year later the fellows of Saint John's and other colleges at Cambridge apologized for the disorder that had occurred in the University, following an attempt to enforce the rule regarding the wearing of the surplice. They pled with Cecil that their consciences should not be compelled to accept the ceremonies which they had laid aside,[2] and that he would not permit that most bitter yoke of slavery to be imposed upon them again.[3] They protested that "the slavery of the body is grievous, but that of the mind, tormented with the daily racks of conscience, is more sharp than the most exquisite torments."[4] They pled that they had not refused the ceremonies from contempt, but from the dictates of reason and "that they might enjoy the peace of their consciences before God."[5]

In the same year Humphrey petitioned the Queen to abrogate or suspend the edict which required the wearing of the hateful vestments. They were admittedly indifferent matters, and compulsion in respect to them was, in his opinion, a blemish on the reformation of religion. The "liberty of conscience ought by no means to be restrained" in such matters.[6] He urged that he and his brethren were wholly loyal to the Queen. Since their doubts were honest and the decrees were of doubtful validity, he held that mercy should dictate a suspension of the letter of the law. If she could not abrogate the law, she might at least grant a toleration of it. He concluded, "it is most fit and equal not to force the minds of men."[7]

These petitions were concerned with matters which the Government had defended as indifferent in character and therefore enforceable for the decency and good of the Church. The Puritan protest, though seizing the obvious advantage of this fact, proceeded from the reason that to the Puritan these

---

[1] Sampson and Humphrey, Letter to the Archbishops and Commissioners, 1564. Strype, *Parker*, I, 324.   [2] *Ibid.*, I, 390.
[3] "Acerbissimum illud conscientiæ servitutis jugum."
[4] Strype, *Parker*, I, 390.   [5] *Ibid.*, I, 390–391.
[6] *Humphrey to Elizabeth*, 1565. Strype, *Annals*, I, 2, 517.
[7] *Ibid.*

matters were not indifferent. It was a short step from the vindication of the rights of conscience in these matters of secondary importance in religion to a general vindication of the sacred character of the human conscience.

A Puritan, about 1568, urged that no authority could compel a man to believe anything contrary to the Word of God, and that conscience could not be forced. He held that it was beyond doubt "that the Quenes highnes hath not authoritie to compell anie man to beleeue any thing contrary to Gods word, nether may the subiect geve her grace the obedience, in case he do his soule is lost for ever without repentance. Our bodyes, goodes, and liues be at her commandement, and she shall haue them as of true subjicts. But the soule of man for Religion is bound to none but unto God and his holy word."[1]

The conclusion of the *Exhortation to the Bishops* (1570) demanded that the prelates should expound the truth. The Word is the armour of spiritual warfare and should be "practised."[2] "Let not Newegate be the onely meanes to stay false proceedings: If you do so, where error is redressed by the magistrate, you shal be judged because you did not your duety, and bring them into the way if they be out, or bi such good conference they bring you home."[3] Persecution was severely condemned by the Puritans, at least when it concerned their own group.[4] The view that the Christian should not be compelled to believe anything contrary to the Bible was, when conjoined with the Puritan insistence upon the validity of personal interpretation, a powerful force in the direction of religious freedom. The ultimate weight of such a contention must be in the direction of toleration.

The Confession embodied in the order of prophesying of the Northampton Church extended this principle.[5] "We condemn as a tyrannous yoke (wherewith poor souls have

---

[1] *Seconde parte of a Register. Morrice MSS.* (Dr. Williams' Library), 33 (*c.* 1568), author unknown.
[2] *Exhortation to the Bishops to deal mildly*, Part II (*Puritan Manifestoes*), 78.
[3] *Ibid.*
[4] *Admonition*, 6; *Unlawful Practise of Prelates* (no pagin.); Udall, J., *State of the Church of England*, F. 1–3.
[5] Strype, *Annals*, II, 1, 139 ff. (1571).

been oppressed) whatsoever men have set up of their own invention, to make articles of our faith, or to bind men's conscience by their laws and institutes."[1] Upon this basis all of the accretions of custom, tradition, and human legislation were denied. The authors confessed themselves as "content with the simplicity of this pure word of God, and doctrine thereof, a summary abridgment of which, we acknowledge to be contained in the confession of faith, used by all Christians, which is commonly called the creed of the Apostles . . . and to try and examine, and also to judge thereby, as by a certain rule and perfect touchstone, all other doctrines whatsoever."[2]

Edward Dering, in 1573, brilliantly denied the validity of secular interference in spiritual affairs.[3] "The minister is appointed for another defence, where horsemen and chariots will do no good. . . . He must frame the heart upon which you cannot set a crown; and edify the soul, which flesh and blood cannot hurt."[4] Dering would apparently limit the function of the minister to that of spiritual guidance and correction. He concluded, "and to these things, what availeth either sword or spear? God asketh but a tongue that is prepared to speak; and he ministereth the power that is invisible."[5]

Two years later Laurence Humphrey likewise urged the ecclesiastical authorities to abandon the use of force in religion, especially in regard to non-essentials. Both the Puritans and the bishops confessed one faith in Jesus; both preached one doctrine, both acknowledged one ruler upon earth; and, he concluded, "in all these things we are of your judgment." "Shall we then be used thus for the sake of a surplice? Shall brethren persecute brethren for a forked cap, devised for

---

[1] *Confession in Order of Exercises* (prophesyings), Strype, *Annals*, II, 1, 139.
[2] *Ibid.*, II, 1, 139–140.
[3] Dering was a reader at St. Paul's, and had in his sermons reproached the power of the civil magistrate in religious affairs. (Strype, *Annals*, II, 1, 398.) He was, in consequence, forbidden to preach by the order of the Privy Council in 1573. In order to vindicate himself he addressed a long letter to Burleigh which was, in the main, a masterful attack on episcopacy. It was in connection with this view that he dealt with the problem of secular interference.   [4] Strype, *Annals*, II, 1, 405.   [5] *Ibid.*

singularity by our enemy?"[1] Certain Norwich ministers protested to Burleigh in the same vein against the removal of ministers who could not in conscience conform to the ceremonies required by law.[2] They declared that "For our owne parts, although we do and fullie will yield unto our Souereigne prince our bodies, goods, and liues, yet herein we dare not yeld to this conformitie of ceremonies, for feare of that terrible threat of the Lord Jesus, who saieth it were better that a millstone . . ."[3]

An anonymous Puritan writer in 1584 expressed indignation that any man "woll take vppon hym to make any interpretation of the Scriptures according to the private opynyon of hymselffe and som others, to bynde his poore bretherne" to subscribe to such an interpretation.[4] The bishops continually practise this species of spiritual tyranny. This document was almost unique as a clear vindication of the right of the private judgment to determine religious matters and, at the same time, in implying that such judgment should not be imposed upon other men.[5] In the latter respect the writer was not typically Puritan in his sentiments.

The rigours incident to the enforcement of the *Oath ex officio* evoked in 1586 a noble protest against it as a species of spiritual tyranny and a document which sought to vindicate the rights of conscience.[6] The petitioners complained that the process was employed to interrogate ministers concerning their use of the Book of Common Prayer. The oath was condemned as more violent "to a conscience that feareth God . . . than anie racke . . ."[7] Such procedure and the punishment which followed conviction under it was declared to be against the law of God and the law of the land, "and of all nations in Christendom except it be in Spaigne by the Inquisition and

---

[1] Humphrey, Laurence, *Fresh Suit*, Pt. II, 269.
[2] *Petition of six Norwich ministers to Burleigh*, 1576. *Seconde parte of a Register. Morrice MSS.* (Dr. Williams' Library), 94.   [3] *Ibid.*
[4] *Lansdowne MSS.*, XCVII, 15 (B.M.) (1584).
[5] The *Dialogue concerning the Strife . . .*, 16–18, 66–67, came close to the same position.
[6] *Petition of Puritan ministers against the Oath ex officio* (November 1586). *Seconde parte of a Register. Morrice MSS.* (Dr. Williams' Library), 204.
[7] *Ibid.*

fathers of that bloudie house caled yet by them the holie house, and where the Anti Christian tirrany of the Bishop of Rome prevaileth."[1]

These examples, selected from a great mass of similar statements, will perhaps suffice to indicate the nature of the Puritan vindication of the rights of conscience. Conscience, it was asserted, cannot be forced and any attempt to do so is contrary to the expressed will of God. The Puritan's defence of the rights of conscience rested essentially in his conviction that the truth contained in the Word of God was readily ascertainable and that the individual Christian constituted, because of his immediate relationship with God, a higher court in matters of faith than Parliaments and Ecclesiastical Commissions. Into the sanctity of that miraculous relationship the arm of authority should not intrude. Perhaps the stubborn insistence of the Puritan upon this principle compensates for the generally bigoted and intolerant character of his moral philosophy.

The survey of Puritan thought in its relation to the problem of toleration may well be concluded by an examination of the *Triall of Subscription*, published anonymously in 1599. The treatise was apparently written by a Puritan, but it departs from the normal Puritan view of the treatment of religious dissent and is one of the most soberly and calmly written books of the century. Its moderate character may be due partly to the fact that it was written late in the reign in a period when the bitter controversies which had marked so much of Elizabethan theological discussion had for the time being worn themselves out. A reading of the book leaves an impression, as well, that the author had drunk deeply at Hooker's moderate spring, and that his general theory had been profoundly influenced by the Anglican's championship of reason.

The treatise was addressed to "such ministers of the Gospell as would seeme desirous of Reformation; and yet haue sub-

---

[1] *Petition of Puritan Ministers against the Oath ex officio* (November 1586). *Seconde parte of a Register. Morrice MSS.* (Dr. Williams' Library), 204; see also the *Letter of the Puritan Ministers in Prison to the Queen* (1592), which denounced the oath for similar reasons.

scribed to the arch-bishop of Canterberie his articles."[1] The author lamented the recent subscriptions of Puritan ministers who were not in conscience favourably disposed towards the articles to which they swore their assent, and who in part signed under a formal protest. One should be able either to make a full and free subscription or refuse to subscribe.[2] After a lengthy discussion of the evils of subscription, the author pled that "resolved consciences are vncompellable. . . ."[3] Thus the Queen permitted the Roman Catholic Heath to continue as Lord Chancellor when his conscience made it impossible for him to subscribe to the established religion. In a similar fashion the faithful ministers should not be deprived simply because of their inability to subscribe.[4]

He admitted that the Puritans might be in error in their judgment of these matters, but the discipline and service of the Church are admittedly of rational origin and a Christian should not be removed from the Church because of his inability to conform in such matters.[5] The author denied that the Puritans might legally be punished for their refusal to lend conformity against the dictates of their consciences. The statute of subscription was intended only "to keepe papistes and other heretiques out of the ministrie. . . ."[6] Even if such punishments were permitted under the law the ecclesiastical courts have been far too harsh in their enforcement of them.[7]

The inconveniences which arise from a rigorous enforcement of conformity should move the authorities "to allowe or consent to tolleration or mitigatiō in their cases."[8] The enforcement of conformity is specially reprehensible since it may induce or compel men to subscribe against their true beliefs.[9] The policy of the ecclesiastical courts is dividing and weakening the Church. He pled for the "Brownistes, to whō these ceremonies are great stumbling blocks, and therefore to be remooued, or not so grieuouslie vrged, least the rent of our

---

[1] *A Triall of Subscription, by way of a Preface vnto Certaine Subscribers* . . . It was printed at Middleburgh in 1599, and copies are preserved in the Bodleian and in Dr. Williams' Library.   [2] *Ibid.*, Preface.
[3] *Ibid.*, 9.   [4] *Ibid.*, 9–10.   [5] *Ibid.*, 11.   [6] *Ibid.*, 13.
[7] *Ibid.*, 16–17.   [8] *Ibid.*, 17.   [9] *Ibid.*, 17–18.

churche prooue greater and greater . . ."[1] "For if by contention we byte one another, let us take heede least we be cōsumed one of another."[2]

The treatise held that conscience which has found resolution in the spiritual nature of man is inviolable, and that attempts to compel it are both fruitless and wrong. The author appeared to applaud a moderate action towards a Roman Catholic and urged the extension of such action as a national policy. His appeal for the Brownists was unique in the Puritan literature of the period, even if his pleading had his own party chiefly in mind. The general thesis of the book was a proposal for the toleration of a quiet Nonconformity, and his brief treatise foreshadowed the more highly developed conceptions of toleration advanced in the next century.

5. CONCLUSION

The Puritan intelligence, in summary, was repelled by the tolerant and comprehensive philosophy of the Elizabethan Settlement of Religion, while the Puritan conscience was scandalized by the retention of dubious rites of service in the Anglican worship, and by the inclusion in its communion of men and women who were obviously not of the elect of God. The Puritan opposed a rigidly defined faith and worship to the generous and flexible construction which Anglican thought was disposed to put upon organized religion, and by his opposition encouraged and necessitated an unfortunate hardening of the Anglican conception of the Church and its government, which began to show ill effects as early as the closing years of Elizabeth's reign. The high place of the doctrine of election in Puritan thought assisted in heightening the intolerance of the system by regarding sin and false worship from a moralistic point of view.

The Church, as the moral instrument of God, should define and ferret out instances of evil and false worship which the State, under the guidance of the clergy, should punish and exterminate. The more advanced Puritans were prepared to recommend that the State was obligated by the Judicial Law

[1] *Triall of Subscription*, 21.   [2] *Ibid.*, 22.

of Moses to exact the death penalty in instances of stubborn heresy.

Especially intolerant was the attitude of the Puritans towards the Roman Catholic Church. They denied that salvation could be attained within its communion and left little doubt of the nature of their treatment of its members in the event of their predominance in English life and politics. The Church of England was likewise intolerantly condemned by the more radical members of the group. There was, however, among the more moderate of the party, pronounced hesitation in interpreting too literally the mandates of the Judicial Law.

Puritan thought in the Elizabethan period leaves no doubt that the cause of religious toleration was greatly assisted by the exclusion of the group from power and by the brilliant and steadfast determination of the Government to disregard, in so far as possible, religious differences in national life. Elizabeth's interest resided essentially in the State, and religious policy was warped and modified to accommodate the greatest benefits to the greatest possible number of her subjects; the Puritans, on the contrary, viewed life in all its aspects from the sole basis of spiritual welfare and perfection, and they proposed to bring every agency of national life under discipline in order to achieve the realization of their ideal.

At the same time, however, Puritanism contributed powerful forces to the ultimate development of religious liberty. Profoundly swayed by his belief in the direct guidance of God in his life; stubbornly devoted to that most powerful dissolvent of religious tyranny—the right of private judgment; and jealous of the interference of the secular power in his personal beliefs and worship, and in his purpose to erect a Kingdom of God upon earth, the Puritan remained untouched by the steady erosion of the governmental policy of comprehensive uniformity which operated so successfully in other sections of English religious life. By successfully maintaining his peculiarity he made necessary, in the end, some compromise which would ensure the right of his position in the religious life of the nation.

The Puritan likewise nobly defended the right of freedom of

260

conscience. His plea, in general, extended no further than his own case, but his arguments were easily adaptable to a more general defence of the inviolability of the human conscience. In the conviction that "the soule of man for religion is bound to none but unto God and his holy word" is to be found the germinal concept upon which the case of religious freedom must of necessity reside. Puritan thought, by a logical extension of the view, was disposed to exclude the civil power from any interference in spiritual affairs. Had it not been for the related disposition to view the secular arm as the executor of religious policy, Puritan theory might have enunciated a complete distinction between civil and spiritual functions which would have embraced the idea of religious toleration. The Puritan vindication of the rights of conscience rested upon the conviction that absolute truth and error are accurately ascertainable by the individual. The individual Christian, as one of the elect of God, is directed by an organic relationship with the Divine Will, and the secular arm cannot rightfully invade the sanctity of that relationship.

B.—SEPARATIST THOUGHT AND ITS RELATION TO THE DEVELOPMENT OF RELIGIOUS TOLERATION

1. GENERAL CHARACTERISTICS OF SEPARATIST THOUGHT IN ITS RELATION TO RELIGIOUS TOLERATION

The most important contribution that the Separatists made to the development of toleration during the reign of Elizabeth lay in the very fact of their separation. The theory of a uniform, national religion, which had been the ideal to which practically all opinion adhered at the accession of Elizabeth, had by the conclusion of the reign ceased to have much actual content. The Government had itself contributed most largely to the disappearance of the Catholic concept of religion by its moderate attitude towards dissent and by its disinclination to endanger the civil peace by attempting to exterminate dissenting groups. The Roman Catholics, though their influence steadily declined under governmental pressure and because of the disgust of many with the political implications of the Jesuit programme, continued to exist as a large body of dissentients. The Church itself could lay no legitimate claim to unity within its own communion. The Puritans had carried their criticism of its institutions and worship to such a degree of severity that large masses of the group were sloping towards separation. Finally, the Separatist groups, notably the Congregationalists, had from small beginnings established by the conclusion of the reign an independent Church structure, a literature, and binding traditions enhanced by the martyrdom of some of their founders. The fact that the Separatists were able, despite the laws of the land, to make good their separation is a fact of outstanding importance for the development of toleration. The existence of several religious bodies within a country for a continued period of time not only belies the doctrine of enforced uniformity but renders its claim absurd. Separatism had not, in the reign of Elizabeth, attained a degree of influence requisite to this effect, but sturdy foundations had been laid.

In addition, the Separatists were to make notable contributions to the theory of toleration by opinions and by points of view embedded in their creed, Church government, and general attitude towards spiritual life. Toleration was, in fact, implicit in the act of separation and dissent from the orthodox and dominant group. The act of separation served as a denial that the dominant ecclesiastical organization had the authority of divine sanction and that any one ecclesiastical system could pretend to monopolize the loyalty of Christians.[1] Psychologically, the act of separation was also a vindication of the right of individual decision on what constitutes the beliefs requisite to salvation, and the dissenter could not for long deny the same right to other men. Any claim to the arbitrary suppression of dissent by a separatist body would be a denial of the right of its own communion to exist. Unfortunately, these principles were often slow in expressing themselves and the normal reformation sect was disposed to seek to enforce an exclusive system upon all men. In England such tendencies were curbed by the Erastian policy of the State and the Sectarians were restrained to their fundamental teaching that

[1] Clark, H. W., *History of English Nonconformity*, I, 9.

divine truth should be spread abroad by preaching and teaching.

We shall now examine the thought of the Congregationalists, or Brownists, in its relation to the problem of toleration, and notice the beginnings of Baptist thought.

2. ROBERT BROWNE

English Congregationalism appears to have been to some degree influenced by the Church covenant idea of Anabaptism, but its inception must properly be related to the effects of Pietism and the searching of the Bible for the true pattern of ecclesiastical organization.[1] Strype noted the meetings of secret congregations at a date as early as 1550, but these meetings probably had little organic relationship with the later Congregationalism. Burrage has shown that as early as 1561 a confession had appeared in London which embodied the essentials of the congregational idea.[2] The more vigorous efforts of the ecclesiastical authorities to secure religious uniformity resulted in the private gatherings of nonconforming Protestants from 1565 onwards, but in the absence of literary remains it is quite impossible accurately to determine their religious views beyond what the evidence of separation indicates. These groups, after 1568, secured spiritual leadership from a number of deprived ministers, and by that time a body of about two hundred persons appears to have separated from the Church along the lines later formulated by Browne. There was, however, no noticeable growth in this unorganized body and no clear definition of its position prior to the appearance of Robert Browne.

The Brownist conception of the Church at least suggests a principle of toleration.[3] Browne held that since the civil society was unlikely to bring about a reformation, the task should be left to each congregation. He strongly asserted the indifference of the State to religion. The Presbyterian sought to

[1] The contention that Browne derived the doctrine of the separation of Church and State from the Anabaptists (Campbell, *Puritans* . . ., II, 179, 180, 200) has never been proved satisfactorily. Selbie seems disposed to allow of considerable influence. (Selbie, W. B., *Congregationalism*, 20.)

[2] Burrage, C., *The Church Covenant Idea*, 43, n. 1.

[3] Allen, J. W., *Political Thought*, 225.

secure his Church-State polity by the assistance of the State, while Browne completely dissociated the Church and State as having no functional similarity. He denied that the State could command conscience or coerce reason and urged that religion was gravely endangered in its spiritual character by too intimate an identification with the State.[1] He merely claimed the right of any body of Christians, however small, to set up a true Church, and denied the power of the magistrates to interfere in this process. In so far as the Congregationalists followed the leadership of Browne, they founded their system on the principle of a separation of the spheres of religion and government, which logically leads to the toleration of dissent.[2]

Browne and his followers recognized the legitimate authority of the civil magistrates in all civil causes.[3] But Browne sought to limit the jurisdiction of the magistrate by a denial of his competence to erect a Christian Church. The effect of this limitation was a complete dissociation of the spheres of government and religion.

Browne held as accursed those who would wait for the Parliament and the magistrate to form a true Church.[4] "They want the ciuill sworde forsooth, and the Magistrates doe hinder the Lordes building and kingdome, and keepe awaye his gouernment." The magistrate is incapable of such a function, and to hold such a view is to confuse the civil and spiritual powers. Faith cannot be compelled by law, and force will only serve to erect a fictitious Church. "They would make the magistrates more than Goddes, and yet also worse than beastes."[5]

The magistrate, as a Christian, is subject to pastoral charge, and is under the "scepter of Christe." "Howe then shoulde the Pastor, which hath the ouersight of the magistrate, if hee bee of his flocke, bee so ouerseene of the magistrate, as to leaue his flocke, when the magistrate shall uniustlie and wrongfullie

[1] Fairbairn, A. M., *Studies in Religion and Theology*, 229.
[2] Figgis, J. N., *C.M.H.*, III, 756.
[3] Browne, Robert, *Treatise of Reformation*, 18–19.
[4] *Ibid.*, 18.   [5] *Ibid.*

discharge him."¹ The slackness of the clergy of the Church of England is due to the fact that they shift responsibility to the magistrates and because they bend every effort to retain his favour rather than to carry out the will of Christ. "They leaue their owne burthen, and crie out that it is not caried by faulte of the magistrate."² The Church of England, he held, confesses that Christ should reign over it, yet it depends upon the order of the magistrate.³ It waits for Parliament to decree and enforce the discipline which Christ has ordained for His Church. He enquired, "Is not this to make the kingdome of God to come with obseruation? To be an arme and strength, and not by his Spirite: To be by Boue and by Battle, by horses, and by Horssemen, and not by the Lorde. . . ."⁴ He charged that the English Church refused "Christ Jesus to raygne ouer them, except he come by ciuile laues and decrees of parliamentes. . . ."⁵

The recognition that it was no part of the duty of the ruler to establish and maintain the true religion was a long step towards toleration. The establishment of such a system would divest the secular arm of any interest in the persecution of heresy and would rob persecution of its theoretical justification. Browne sought to vindicate his removal of the ruler from the sphere of religious affairs by an able exposition of Old Testament texts in order to prove that the Prophets and not the Kings governed the Church of Israel. Within the Church the civil rulers have no power. They may "doo nothing concerning the church, but onelie ciuile, and as ciuile Magistrates, that is, they haue not that authoritie ouer the Church, as to be prophetes or priestes, or spiritual kings, as they are magistrates ouer the same; but onelie to rule the commonwealth in all outwarde iustice, to maintain the right welfare and honour thereof, with outward power, bodily punishment, and ciuille forcing of mē."⁶ Since the Church is of the Commonwealth the magistrates should make outward provision for it, "but to cōpell religion, to plant Churches by power, and to force a

¹ Browne, *Treat. of Reform.*, 18–19.   ² *Ibid.*, 19.
³ Browne, *Treatise vpon the* 23 *of Mattheue*, 35.   ⁴ *Ibid.*
⁵ *Ibid.*, 38.   ⁶ Browne, *Treat. of Reform.*, 26.

submission to Ecclesiastical gouernement by laues and penalties belongeth not to them. . . ."[1]

The purpose of the exclusion of the civil rulers from any share of the setting up of the Church was, of course, to make possible a theory of separation. The Church should not tarry for the magistrate. If the magistrate is a Christian, he will gladly submit himself to the government of the Church, and if the ruler is not a Christian, the welfare of men's souls cannot wait upon his courtesy.[2] In fact, the Church flourished most when it was undergoing the trials of persecution.[3] A finer argument could not be found for the separation of Church and State than Browne's plea that ". . . The outwarde power and ciuil forcings, let vs leaue to the Magistrates; to rule the common wealth in all outwarde iustice, belongeth to them: but let the church rule in spirituall wise, and not in worldlie manner; by a liuelie laue preached, and not by a ciuill laue written; by holinesse in inwarde and outwarde obedience, and not in straightnesse of outward onelie."[4]

Browne came in the *Treatise of Reformation* close to the enunciation of a theory of toleration. If the State were deprived of any power in the Church, and if the Church existed as a voluntary organization for purely spiritual ends, persecution would be quite impossible. Unfortunately Browne was not interested in a toleration that extended beyond his own group and with peculiar inconsistency he alienated the power of suppressing heresy to the magistrates in a later book.[5] The book is confused, rambling, and obviously incomplete. It was written soon after he conformed and may be regarded as the work of a man whose spirit had been crushed, and should not be given the weight of the earlier treatises in an estimation of his thought. In this work Browne admitted the civil magistrate to a large share in the maintenance of true discipline and religion.[6]

[1] Browne, *Treat. of Reform.*, 26–27. See also Browne, *A Booke which Sheweth*, Def. 117.   [2] Browne, *Treat. of Reform.*, 27.
[3] *Ibid.*, 28–29.   [4] *Ibid.*, 29.
[5] Browne, *Letter to Mr. Flower*. The identity of Mr. Flower is not clear. First published by C. Burrage in 1904 as *A New Years Guift*.
[6] "If then it be demaunded who shal call and consecrat ministers, excommunicat, depose, and put downe false teachers and bad fellowes, and iudg in a number of ecclesiastical causes, let the word of God answere, which

The magistrate likewise should assist in restraining heresy and licentiousness.[1] We should be interested to know how Browne would have had heresy tried. The punishment of heresy presumes a body competent to determine between absolute right and error and we infer that Browne would have had the civil ruler follow the dictates of the clergy in this matter. Were it not for this greatly inferior work, we would be willing to acknowledge with Dr. Dexter that Browne pronounced a fairly full theory of toleration. But it appears that Browne felt that he and his followers had attained truth and that they demanded only the toleration of that truth.[2]

Browne's insistence that the Church may avail itself only of spiritual weapons in its struggle with evil and in its efforts to establish itself has been somewhat neglected. In this respect his theory, though not so well developed as that of some earlier English writers,[3] was unquestionably on the side of toleration. The kingdom of Christ is spiritual in character and cannot be advanced with the assistance of the sword.[4] The English clergy, he urged, have given up their only weapons, which are found in spiritual leadership, and are hence divested of authority. Nor is the civil ruler able to carry out the will of Christ in the erection of His kingdom. Hence the spiritual kingdom of Christ must be set up without waiting on the magistrate.[5] The kingdom of God cannot be achieved without great effort, "and yet they will have it with ease and the ciuill sworde must get it them."[6] The clergy give to the civil ruler the first place in spiritual authority, "yet haue they no ecclesiastical authoritie at all, but onely as anie other Christians, if

appointeth the chiefest and most difficult matters to be iudged by them of chiefest authoritie and guifts, and othe matters of inferior gouernours. If it be asked who be of cheifest guifts or ought to haue cheifest authoritie, I answere that the ciuil magistrates have their right in al causes to iudge and sett order, and it is intollerable presumption for particular persons to skan of euerie magistrats guifts or authoritie or to denie them the power of iudging ecclesiastical causes." (*New Years Guift*, 30.)   [1] *Ibid.*, 30–31.
[2] See Professor Allen's Remarks. Allen, *Political Thought*, 228–229.
[3] Cf. *ante*, esp. 57–58, 61–64, 66–67, 73–76.
[4] "For the Scepter and Kingdome of Christ is not of this worlde, to fight with dint of sworde. . . ." (*Treat. of Reform.*, 19.)   [5] *Ibid.*
[6] *Ibid.*, 19–20; *Treatise vpon the 23 of Mattheue*, 35.

so be they Christians."[1] It is difficult to see how such a conception of Christianity would have permitted the persecution of heresy by the magistrate even upon the authority of the ministry.

Browne's conception of the Church as a voluntary organization was not only a theoretical contribution of great importance to the development of toleration, but in forming the central pillar of the Congregationalist structure it proved to be a practical contribution of the first rank. Religion, Browne held, consists essentially in the establishment of a spiritual relationship between God and the individual soul.[2] The civil power is manifestly incompetent to bring about such a relationship and, since the Church consists of a voluntary association of men and women who have achieved this contact, the State cannot possibly set up a true Church.

The English clergy err in their conception of the nature of the Church.[3] They desire the immediate creation of the Kingdom of God by legislative enactment and "are offended at the basenesse and small beginnings, and because of the troubles in beginning reformation."[4] But the Kingdom of God is not attained "by swarde, and by battell, by horses and by horssemen, that is, by ciuill power and pompe of Magistrates; by their proclamations and Parliamentes. . . ."[5] The Kingdom of God dwells only in the human soul. These men take the inheritance of Christ and give it to the magistrate;[6] ". . . The magistrates haue the ciuill sworde, and least they should strike them therewith they giue them the ecclesiasticall also."[7]

But to wait for the pleasure of the magistrate is disloyalty to God. The magistrate cannot possibly form a Church. Christ and the Apostles did not sue to Parliament when they

[1] Browne, *Treat. of Reform.*, 20.
[2] Fairbairn, A. M., *Studies in Religion and Theology*, 237. The importance of regeneration and of the direct relationship existing between God and the individual Christian cannot be over-emphasized in estimating the Independent's conception of religion. The immediacy of that relationship constitutes the basis for the Brownist conception of the Church and the firm denial that the State can organize a Church or interfere in spiritual affairs.
[3] Browne, *Treat. of Reform.*, 21. [4] *Ibid.*
[5] *Ibid.*   [6] *Ibid.*   [7] *Ibid.*

planted the Gospel.[1] Fear of the disapproval of the civil ruler does not exempt the pastor from the discharge of his spiritual duty. "The magistrates commaundment must not be a rule vnto me of this and that duetie, but as I see it agree with the Worde of God."[2] The command to preach and the duty to preach did not come as a dispensation from the magistrate, but from "God by consent and ratifying of the church, and therefore as the magistrate gaue it not, so can he not take it away."[3] The minister and the Christian are answerable only to God for the performance of their divine charge, and any commandment of the magistrate that is against the will of the Lord should be ignored. The magistrate is simply one of the flock, and it is not proper that the sheep should guide the shepherd.[4]

These preliminary remarks formed a worthy preface to Browne's definition of the Church. Christians are defined as "a companie or number of beleeuers, which by a willing couenant made with their God, are vnder the gouernment of God and Christ, and keepe his Lawes in one holie communion. . . ."[5] A true Church is formed by the voluntary association of such Christians into a body to worship God. "The church planted or gathered, is a companie or number of Christians or beleeuers, which by a willing couenant made with their God, are vnder the gouernment of God and Christ, and kepe his lawes in one holie communion; because Christ hath redeemed them vnto holines and happines for euer, from which they were fallen by the sinne of Adam."[6] The Separatist always insisted upon the volitional character of the association. In describing the formation of his church at Norwich, he said: ". . . a couenāt was made and ther mutual cōsent was geūe to hould to gether. Then vvere certain chief pointes proued vnto them by the Scriptures, all vvich being particularlie rehersed vnto them with exhortation, thei agreed vpon them and pronoūced their agrement to ech thing particularlie, saing: to this vve geue our consent."[7] Or again, a true Church

[1] Browne, *Four principal and weighty causes of separation.*
[2] Browne, *Treat. of Reform.*, 22.   [3] *Ibid.*   [4] *Ibid.*, 24.
[5] Browne, *Booke which Sheweth*, A. 2.   [6] *Ibid.*, C. 3.
[7] Browne, *True and Short Decl.*, 20.

is formed, "first, by a couenant and condicion made on God's behalfe. Secondlye, by a couenant and condicion made on our behalfe. Thirdly, by using the sacrament of Baptisme to seale those condicions, and couenantes."[1]

The insistence of Browne upon the idea of the voluntary Church, which can be constituted only without any interference from the secular power, was of the utmost importance in the development of religious freedom. The conception had earlier been vigorously asserted by the Anabaptists, and it is not improbable that Browne owed something to them.[2] The

[1] Browne, *Book which Sheweth*, C. 3. See also the important description of the formation of a covenanted Church in Browne's *True and Short Declaration*, 20.

[2] As Trechsel has pointed out, Hans Denck regarded force as incompatible with Christian freedom and equality, since the sword can only be an instrument of external compulsion. Force cannot affect the mind or heart. His view of regeneration swept away the very bases of ecclesiastical authority. He urged that salvation was wholly a matter of the spirit, and therefore that the external characteristics of religion have no real significance. (Denck, H., *Widerruf* (Confessions), 7, 1527. In Jones, R. M., *Spiritual Reformers*, 27–28.) Denck denied the efficacy of any form of compulsion, and he extended the right of private judgment to its logical limitation by eliminating ecclesiastical forms as useless encumbrances.

The Anabaptists held that the Church is composed only of those who, after the personal and spiritual experience of conversion, voluntarily seek the binding and testifying sacrament of Baptism. Thus the Church is constituted of those who have found God, who have been saved by His mercy, and who testify to that experience by the act of Baptism. It is therefore patently impossible to create a Christian by force, and the true Church must of necessity be a voluntary association. Thus a State Church would be regarded as an essentially wicked manifestation of the civil power. (Allen, *Political Thought*, 40.) Allen holds that the Anabaptist doctrine of toleration is secondary to their general views; i.e. that they denied the power of the magistrate to punish heresy because they denied his power to punish anything. It may be urged, however, that the two concepts have no organic relation. Their view of the Church precluded the possibility of the coercion of the human being in a matter of faith by any human agency. Their contempt of the magistracy, on the other hand, proceeded from their dislike of the institutions of this world because the elect are directly ruled by God and belong to the new dispensation.

Schwenckfeld likewise regarded the true Church as the totality of that spiritual community of which Christ is the head. "We maintain that the Christian church according to the usage of the Scriptures, is the congregation of believers, or assembly of all or of many who with heart and soul are believers in Christ." (*Corpus Schw.*, I, 295.) The true Church bases all of its doctrinal beliefs upon the Bible. Further, the true Church cannot possibly be identified with any earthly organization. No outward unity or conformity

doctrine obtained its inception from a variety of influences. It can scarcely be denied that the facts of the English religious situation constituted a powerful influence in the formulation of the notion. The State was obviously determined to lend permanent support to the Establishment and the formation of a reformed body would have to forego the assistance of the State, and probably constitute itself in the face of political opposition. For that reason the ancient theory of the relations of Church and State have to be restated.

In addition, Browne and his followers were genuinely convinced that true religion consisted only in an intimate relationship between the Christian and God. That relationship could not be effected by the civil power, and hence the interference of the magistrate in spiritual affairs was condemned. The Church should govern itself on the basis of a common faith and a true perception of the will of its Master. It required the power to govern and discipline itself, but it required no assistance from the secular power.

Finally, the voluntary Church had its origin in the development of the doctrine of election. This view is not stressed by Browne, but we shall find it emphasized by his followers, especially in the next century. Election was a miracle which God alone could work. The mass of men were sinful and lost, and the elect suffered by association with them in worship, the true Church consisting of a company of the elect or regenerated. We see in Brownism an excellent example of the tendency of groups of the elect to draw away from the sinful and to construct themselves into a true Church for the true worship of God. Browne emphasized this conception when he urged that the Church, if persecuted by a wicked civil power, should flee.[1] He was not nearly so much impressed with the mission-

can conceivably make a Christian Church. (Schw., *Schriften*, II, 785.) The Church rests upon the bond between God and man which lies beyond the province of compulsion.

These examples of early Anabaptist thought might be considerably expanded. It is evident that the Brownist theory of the Church as a voluntary organization of believers who had set themselves in an intimate relationship with God bears striking resemblance to the Anabaptist notions on the subject.

[1] Browne, *Treatise vpon the 23 of Matt.*, 26.

ary aspects of Separatism as with the necessity of maintaining intact the purity of doctrine and worship of the true Church. Hence, in England, "thoughe the magistrates shoulde give vs leaue to worshippe God rightlie," the true Church should seek to depart because of the danger inherent to the faith in ecclesiastical and public opposition.[1] He denied that the argument that the true Church should not flee because it may hope to win others to the faith had any efficacy.[2] He feared that the Church might suffer contamination in its contacts with the unregenerate.

The argument is of importance. It is difficult to say precisely what Browne did demand of the State. He seems to have envisaged the body of the faithful as hermetically sealed against contact with the world which was evil and spotted. His was the most unmissionary of all the evangelical faiths. He was primarily interested in the edification of the elect and in the maintenance of doctrinal purity. He would not persecute because he denied the efficacy of it in principle and because he had no great interest in the unregenerate. From such a view a national Church composed of good and bad, elect and damned, was an absurdity if not an insult to God. The Church of England he regarded as false principally because it attempted to serve two masters. "Haue they not open abominations and wicked men amongst them, which they say must be tolerated, because they are incurable: can they then haue anie parte of Church gouernment when neither by Rebuke, nor by separation, they can cleanse the Church . . ."[3] The Regenerated should form a group apart, stamped with the hall-mark of Election, and living directly under the sway of God's will.

This important influence operated powerfully upon the Puritans and Presbyterians as well, and was, in the next century, to have important consequences. But for the time being, both groups were imbued with the idea of predominance and with the necessity of gaining power in order to cleanse the realm of vice.

This tendency brought into prominence the view that the true Church cannot be erected by any worldly power. It

[1] Browne, *Treatise vpon the 23 of Matt.*, 26.   [2] *Ibid.*   [3] *Ibid.*, 31

was highly individualistic in temper and led to the introduction of flexibility in the structure of the Church. In other words, it tended to emphasize the spiritual character of religion and to discount the importance of the ecclesiastical structure. And, when we consider that most persecution resulted from the efforts of powerful ecclesiastical structures to prevent their own dissolution, it will be apparent that the concept is of vast importance for the cause of toleration.

The voluntary Church ideal made it logically impossible for the State to advance true religion by the weapons of intolerance.[1] The State was not able to save a single soul by its instruments of compulsion. The great emphasis placed upon the communion of the elect made it intolerable that the State should attempt to dictate ecclesiastical policy, and especially to appoint or to share in the appointment of the clergy. The Establishment had shown that the State tended to appoint men who could evidence formal training without much regard for evidence of election.[2] Calvin's idea that the damned should be subjected to the Church for the glory of God gradually gave way to the idea that it was blasphemy to partake of the Eucharist with the rejected of God.[3] Thus the true Church could only be a voluntary association of the regenerated. The logical result of Congregationalism is the toleration of one Church community as to another.[4] The chief impediment to the triumph of this concept was the stubborn survival of the doctrine of exclusive truth.[5] The Elizabethan Congregationalists were so imbued with this concept that they would still exclude all heretical groups from the Christian State.[6] But the force of "voluntarism" was greater than that of "exclusivism" and the true contribution of the Brownists to toleration came ultimately to prevail. As Troeltsch has taught us, the voluntary idea has its roots in the liberal theory of the inviolability of the inner personal life from the authority of the

[1] Weber, M., *The Protestant Ethic*, 242.
[2] *Ibid.*   [3] *Ibid.*, 242–243.
[4] Troeltsch, *Die Soziallehren der Christlichen kirchen und Gruppen*, 758–759.
[5] We shall deal with the decay of this concept in later pages. See 323 ff.
[6] Troeltsch, *Die Soziallehren der Christlichen kirchen und Gruppen*, 759.

State.[1] The triumph of this idea, and it was in this particular that Sectarianism made its greatest contribution, brought to an end the medieval ideal of a civilization based upon the compulsory leadership of an effective Church-State, and represents the attainment of individual freedom.[2]

Closely connected with Browne's conception of the Church as a voluntary institution was his teaching that the Church cannot be erected by ulterior force and that physical compulsion has no place in the discipline of the Church. It is the anti-Christ that "forceth his religiō by civil power, or by binding their consciences; whereby he hideth and shifteth away their guiltiness, which the world doth bewray."[3] But the religion and Church of Christ cannot be forced upon men.[4] He branded the punishments of the magistrates in spiritual matters as a "continuall plague."[5] The cries for discipline are principally an excuse for the wrongful forcing of the people. The true Christian cannot be forced, for ". . . The Lord's people is of the willing sorte. They shall come vnto Zion and inquire the way to Ierusalem, not by force nor compulsion, but with their faces thitherward . . . and they themselues shall call for the couenant, saying, come and let vs cleave faste vnto the Lorde in a perpetuall couenant that shall neuer be forgotten. For it is the conscience and not the power of man that will drive vs to seeke the Lordes kingdome. . . ."[6] Such a conception clearly teaches that the civil power can under no conditions rightfully use force to compel any man to become a member of the Church or to conform to its practices, nor should the Church make any claim to control or discipline the lives of those who are outside its covenant. "We leaue it free to them to follow or not to follow our ways and doctrines, except they see it good and meet for them."[7] This is probably as close as

[1] Troeltsch, *Protestantism and Progress*, 125.   [2] *Ibid.*
[3] Browne, *Book which Sheweth*, D. 3.   [4] Browne, *Treat. of Reform.*, 24.
[5] ". . . There is no ende of their pride and crueltie which ascend vp and sit in the Magistrates chaire and smite the people with a continuall plague, and such of them as haue not yet gotten the roome, do crie for Discipline, . . . that is for a civill forcing, to imprison the people, or otherwise by violence to handle and beate them, if they will not obeye them." (*Ibid.*, 25.)
[6] *Ibid.*   [7] Browne, *Book which Sheweth.*

any English religious leader had come to an expression of complete toleration by this time.

Browne likewise rebuked the harsh internal discipline of the Church of England and of the Presbyterians which could on occasion approach persecution. Many confuse the true discipline of the Church with the discipline of the State.[1] It does not permit "bodelie punishing, nor outward forcing of good and bad. Neither is it a violence, outward power, maiestie, dignitie, or honour of the world. . . ."[2] The true discipline of the Church is simply a reflection of the power of Christ in His Church, and is hence purely spiritual.[3] We may detect false discipline in those "whose dealing and whole endeuour in the ministrie for reformation is alltogether by extremitie, crueltie, violence, force, and civill penalties, and neuer by lenitie, gentlenes, patience, mercie, kindnes, and charitie."[4]

3. ROBERT HARRISON

The tolerant theory which Browne had laid down did not, unfortunately, obtain to a general acceptance by his followers. It was only gradually that the tolerant principles inherent in the Congregational system asserted themselves. Indeed, it is doubtful if the early Brownists realized the full implication of their own principles. The thesis that the Church could not be erected or coerced by the State may be regarded as a fundamental tenet of their thought. But they were not yet prepared to disclaim the assistance of the magistrate in enforcing the policy which the true Church might desire to establish.[5] While the State might not coerce the true Church, the Brownist leaders were all too prone to argue that it might assist the Church in the coercion of those who were outside it; at least to the extent of forbidding the open practice of infidelity and blasphemy. While the State could not make the Church, it might preserve the honour of the Church when it was once erected.[6] This teaching was drawn from Calvin rather than from the older traditions of the Church and resides at bottom in the Calvinists' hatred of evil.

[1] Browne, *Letter to Mr. Flower*, 36. [2] *Ibid.* [3] *Ibid.* [4] *Ibid.*, 39.
[5] Clarke, H. W., *English Nonconformity*, I, 199. [6] *Ibid.*, I, 200.

Robert Harrison, next to Browne the earliest Congregational writer, displayed these intolerant tendencies at their worst.[1] He followed Browne in insisting that the Church must not await the pleasure of the prince in erecting itself. This delay is in fact the gravest sin of the present ministry of the Church of England.[2] He held that instead the "Kings and princes should waite what the Lord should say unto them by the mouth of the prophets and priests, but never the contrarie, that the prophets or any mynisters, should waite what God should say to them by the mouth of magistrats. . . ."[3] The ministry of the Church of England wait for Reformation "as the wicked people of England waited for death. . . ."[4]

Harrison would have the Church of God erected by the same free and voluntary process that Browne had outlined. Harrison, however, appears to have been attracted by the problem of what policy should be pursued when his Church polity should gain dominance in the State. The result of these reflections constituted one of the strongest defences of coercion that appears in the century. He recognized the power of the magistrate over Christians in civil causes.[5] But the power of the

---

[1] Harrison matriculated at St. John's College, Cambridge, in 1564, but received his B.A. degree from Corpus Christi in 1567. In 1572 he received his M.A. from that College. (Cooper, *Athenæ Cantabrigiensis*, II, 177–178.) In 1573 he was appointed master of the grammar school at Aylsham (Norfolk), despite the objections of the Bishop of Norfolk to his advanced reformed views. (Strype, *Parker*, II, 335.) But he was dismissed shortly afterwards as a result of a protest against the rubric in the administration of the ordinance of Baptism, and sometime later he appears as the master of a hospital in Norwich. (Dexter, *Congregationalism*, 69.) He now returned to Cambridge, where he fell under the influence of Browne, whom he had known previously. He and Browne retired to Norwich about 1580, where they lived together. (Browne, R., *True and Short Declaration*, 8.) Browne won him to his views on Church Government, which had now reached clear formulation, and they were associated in the formation of the first Congregational body at Norwich. (Dexter, 70.) He followed Browne into exile and assisted in the financing of the older man's books. (Dexter, 75.) Harrison removed to Holland after Browne's departure for Scotland (1583), and appears to have joined Cartwright's English Church with his followers. However, the association was incompatible and Harrison assumed the pastorship of the remnant of the Brownist Church in Middleburgh, retaining the position until his death at an early age.

[2] Harrison, *A Treatise of the Church*, 49.   [3] *Ibid.*, 50.   [4] *Ibid.*, 51.
[5] Harrison, *Little Treatise on 122 Psalm*, 119.

magistrate should extend for the edification of the Church into spiritual causes as well. "Therefore I am thus persuaded that as the Kinges of Juda did reforme by their civile power, those things which outwardly were sett up for abominations; namely as they did break downe the altars, cutt downe the groves, burne the images with fire, slaye the preistes of Baal, and suche like thinges: so also it appertaineth to the magistrates now, to break downe the idolitrous altars, plucke downe their buildinges, burne their images with fire, and to slaye those who have revolted from Christianity to open idolatrie."[1] In another place, however, he limited the punishment of spiritual crimes by the civil ruler to those who are in the Church.[2]

4. HENRY BARROWE

The writings of Barrowe demonstrate that he was confused with regard to the question of force in religious affairs. Barrowe, indeed, clung to Puritanism with one hand while grasping after Separatism with the other. In the main his writings retrace the ground which Cartwright had already covered in a more able fashion.

Barrowe on numerous occasions recognized the civil authority of the ruler and went farther than Browne in recognizing the authority of the prince over the property of the Church. In his examination in 1586 he testified that the Queen was "supreme gouernour of the whole land, and over the church also, Bodies and Goods, but I think that no prince . . . may make any lawes for the Church, other than Christ hath already left in his Worde."[3]

When examined by the Chief Justice (Sir John Popham) and Anderson in 1592 he used practically the same words[4] He added, "that the prince ought most carefully, above all

---

[1] Harrison, *Little Treatise on 122 Psalm*, 120.
[2] ". . . The ciuil magistrates may and ought also to strike with their sword every one which being of the chuich, shal openly transgresse against the Lord's commandements." (*Ibid.*)
[3] Barrowe, Henry, *Examination of 1586*, Harl. Misc., IV, 333.
[4] *Examination of Barrowe, 1592*, Egerton Papers, 169–170.

other, to revyve and inquier oute the lawes of God which are commaunded in his worde, and cann make noe neue."[1] He testified that the confusion of the English Church was so great that he could not tell whether the existing ecclesiastical structure was legal or not, ". . . but of those I knowe, sundrye of them are ungodly and contrary to his Word."[2]

In his *Brief Discourie of the false Churches* (1590) he enlarged his condemnation of the Anglican ecclesiastical structure by a comparison of its form with that of the primitive Church. He attacked the orthodox argument that the primitive structure of the Church was accidental, holding that its form and discipline were essential to the true Church in all ages. No true Church, he held, can be planted without this arrangement. In particular, he criticized the religious policy of the Government because it presumed that the magistrate might "Keep out Christ's governement, and . . . erect and establish another, after their wills."[3] He adroitly pointed out that the claims of the true Church were denied in England "by Machiavel's considerations, and Aristotle's politics" being used as examples rather than the New Testament. There are alleged, "I know not how many politic inconveniences, in way of bar."[4]

Barrowe likewise contributed a highly interesting criticism of the repressive policy of the Government. No one that writes against Episcopacy, he urged, should be put to death as a felon. The most the Government can charge in such a case is an error in religion.[5] The Catholics are not put to death in England for the heretical opinion that the Pope has spiritual authority over them and that he has episcopal authority over the whole Church. They are put to death for the treason of "giuing him an externall dominion ouer this realme and prince. This is that the execution of iustice doeth duely respect, which is farre from any matter of faith and religion . . . the Papistes haue not nor doe not suffer for Religion and heresie, but onelie

---

[1] *Examination of Barrowe, 1592, Egerton Papers*, 169.   [2] *Ibid.*
[3] Barrowe, *Brief Discourie of the false Churches*, 187. Reprinted with certain changes in 1707. This edition has been used.   [4] *Ibid.*, 191.
[5] Barrowe, *A Petition Directed to her most Excellent Maiestie*, 31.

for treason."[1] Much less should those who strive for the reformation of religion be put to death, "whose offences both to God, the prince and realme, are nothing matcheable with the detestable heresies and practises of the traiterous Papistes."[2]

Barrowe's contribution to the advancement of toleration resided principally in his theory of the Church and the method of its establishment. He denied the authority of the ruler in ecclesiastical affairs on the grounds that such authority had no basis in the Scriptures. In especial, he urged that it was a false doctrine "That a Christian prince, which publisheth and maintaineth the Gospel, doth forthwith make all that realm, which with open force resisteth not his proceedings, to be held a Church to whom a holy ministry and sacraments belong."[3] This power has been reserved by God for Himself and any attempt on the part of the prince to exercise it is a usurpation. The prince may by good government further the work of the Church, and he may comfort and assist the faithful, but he can in no wise exercise spiritual functions.[4] A man can only become a member of the Church by personal faith, and by the open confession and profession of that faith.[5]

Barrowe's denial that a national Church could be erected by the civil ruler rested, with Browne, on his conception of the phenomenon of conversion and his realization that any but a willing profession of membership was vain. As we shall see, Barrowe was likewise deeply convinced of the sinfulness of communion with the unregenerate. It was he who first among the Separatists stressed this factor which was to be of so much importance in the development of religious toleration.

Religion cannot be advanced by force nor can the true Church be founded by the agencies of compulsion. Hence the prince cannot "compell any to be a member of the church, or the church to receive any without assurance by publique

---

[1] Barrowe, *A Petition Directed to her most Excellent Maiestie*, 31.
[2] *Ibid.*, 32. [3] Barrowe, *Brief Discourie*, 13.
[4] "They may by their godly gouernment greatly help and further the church, greatly comfort the faithfull, and advance the gospell. But to chuse or refuse, to call or debarr, these are things, which the eternal and almighty ruler of heauen and earth keepeth in his own hands. . . ."
[5] Barrowe, *Brief Discourie*, 13.

profession of their owne faith: or to reteine any longer, then they continue and walk orderly in the faith."[1] The general application of such a rule would lead directly to the toleration of dissent. He held that the Church in England had erred seriously in attempting to set up a Church by the instruments of repression. For "no prince can make any a member of the church." He branded as "a most false and pernicious doctrine" the teaching that a Christian prince who upholds the Gospel "doth forthwith make all that realm, which with open force resisteth not his proceedings, to be a church."[2] In addition, he argued, "We are also taught in the Word, that the Kingdome of God commeth not by observation, neither is brought in by the arme of flesh, but by the spirit of God, and by the power of his Worde working in the harts of all Christs faithfull seruantes. . . ."[3] Our Christian duty is to do the will of God and to refrain from the repressing of all men. "We are to obey God rather than men, and if anie man be ignorant let him be ignorant stil: We are not to stay from doing the Lords commaundement vppon the pleasure or offence of anie."[4]

The true Church, he taught, is formed by the voluntary actions of men who have, by their unfettered judgment, been convinced through conversion of the truth of its teachings. No compulsion may accompany its organization. There is a pressing need for the Church and, if the magistrate should be unwilling to permit its erection, "the churche need not to staye for the prince in reforminge of any abuse, but may reforme it, though the prince saye noe."[5] The true Church is composed only of the faithful who are under the leadership of Christ, and that body has in the New Testament an accurate pattern wherewith it may be organized.[6] The primitive Church "sued not to courtes and parliaments, nor wayted upon princes pleasures, when the stones were in redines, but presently having received the faith of Christ, received likewise the

---

[1] Barrowe, *A Plaine Refutation of M. Giffards Booke*, Pref., A. 3; *Brief Discourie*, 190.   [2] *Ibid.*
[3] Barrowe, *A Collection of Certaine Sclaunderous Articles*, Art. vi (no pagin.).
[4] *Ibid.* (no pagin.).
[5] *Examination of Barrowe, 1592, Egerton Papers*, 170.
[6] Barrowe, *Plaine Refutation*, 6.

ordinances of Christ, and continued in the same. . . . If they should tarie princes leisures, where were the persecutions you speak of?"[1]

The Church of God, then, is composed of individual Christians whose redemption has been won by personal religious experience. The Church was conceived by Barrowe not in terms of a nation but in terms of the individuals who composed it. Hence he lent to the member of the Church a great deal of influence in the administration of its affairs. Every Christian has a personal interest in the actions of the Church and in the maintenance of the purity of its doctrines: "Every particular member hath power, yea, and ought to examine the manner of administration [of] the sacraments: and also, the estate, disorder, or transgressions of the whole church."[2] Every man should look to his private estate and should not seek to meddle with the affairs of other men.[3]

If the civil magistrate should prohibit the erection of the Church, true Christians will none the less obey the command of God. Barrowe carefully sought to distinguish between the duty of the Christian to God and to the ruler. In order to attain salvation he and his followers must abandon the false Anglican ecclesiastical structure.[4] Nor were they able to conform to its practices, even if the civil ruler should demand it: "no, herein, we shew no disobediēce to magistrats, vvhose displeasure vve must rather vndergoe, then fall into the hands of the euerlyuing God vvho vvill abide no halting."[5] The private subject may not break into revolt or employ violence against the magistrate if he imposes a false worship, but he must refuse to obey.[6]

The influence of the 'election' factor in Congregational thought was well demonstrated in the writings of Barrowe. The Church of England was condemned not so much because of the faults of its ministry as for the fact that its ministry had been forced upon it.[7] "I thinke," said Barrowe, "that these

[1] Barrowe, *Plaine Refutation*, 6.
[2] Barrowe, *Brief Discourie*, 35. [3] *Ibid.*, 36.
[4] Barrowe, *Collection of Sclaunderous Articles*, xv; see also Art. viii; xiv.
[5] *Ibid.*, xv. [6] Barrowe, *Mr. Henry Barrowes Platform*, F. 2.
[7] Barrowe, *Plaine Refutation*, Pref., 12.

parish assemblies, as they stand generally in England, are not the true established churches of Christ; and that the People, as they now stand in disorder and confusion in them, are not to be held the true and faithful people of Christ."[1] Men are intoxicated and held by the magnificence of the false Church, especially those who exercise authority in it. "They will neuer endure to see fire cast into her" or "suffer loss of their dainty and precious merchandise."[2] They will, indeed, seek to suppress those who speak against the false Church and strive to reform it. But, nevertheless, the false Church will be consumed by the light and fire of the Gospel: "For as there is but one truth, so whatever is (divers), more or less, than that truth is faulty and to be repented."[3] He held that the Church of England erred particularly since it was composed of a nation which had been brought into the Church by indiscriminate compulsion. "They be rather of the reffuse, common pibble chalke stones, which cannot be vsed to any sownd and sure building, euen al the profane and wicked of the land; Atheistes, Papistes, Anabaptistes and heretikes . . . and who not, that dwelleth within this Iland, or is within the Queenes dominion."[4] They have repeated the mistake of Calvin who "at the first dash made no scruple to receaue al the whole state, euen al the profane ignorant people, into the bozome of the church, to administer the sacramentes vnto them. . . ."[5] The true Church, on the contrary, is composed of stones which have been shaped and hardened by the fire of religious experience and which are cemented into the edifice by voluntary profession of faith in the sacrament of baptism.

Spite the tolerant implications of Barrowe's general position, he spoke far more clearly than Browne for the persecution of error by the magistrate, we presume under the direction of the true Church. In this respect his thought was identical with the Puritan group from which he had sprung. In the course of his examination in 1586, he confessed, "I cannot see it lawful for any prince to alter the least part of the Judicial law of Moses, without doing injury to the moral law, and opposing

---

[1] *Examination of Barrowe, Harl. Misc.*, IV, 332.
[2] Barrowe, *Brief Discourie*, 7.   [3] *Ibid.*   [4] *Ibid.*, 9.   [5] *Ibid.*, 33.

the will of God."[1] He acknowledged that "the prince ought to compel all their subjects to the hearing of Gods Word, in the public exercises of the Church,"[2] though in the same preface he uttered a noble defence of freedom of conscience. He appears to have lent his support to the opinion that blasphemy and open idolatry should be punished by death.[3] "It is the true office and duty of princes most carefully to advance and establish in their dominions the true worship and ministry of God and to suppress and root out all contrary." In his *Platform*, written in the last months of his life, he held that the prince "ought to proclaime and publish the Gospel of Christ, with the true preaching and sincere practise thereof in all things that God shal give knowledge of: and to forbid and exterminate all other religions, worship, and ministeries within her dominions."[4] The Christian prince must advance and establish within his dominions the true worship of God and root out all that is false.[5]

These expressions clash violently with the general character of the author's theory of the Church and the spiritual character of religious experience. He envisaged the operation of these repressive forces in the ideal kingdom of separate congregations, in which the ruler was but a Christian layman. The ruler would in this case be guided by the divinely inspired wisdom of the ministry in the cleansing of his kingdom. Barrowe, with his Congregational contemporaries, did not see the full implications of his own theories and could not free himself of conceptions which had been current for a full millennium. Time was to see the erection of a powerful Church along the lines suggested by Browne and amplified by Barrowe, and the experience of that body with neighbours that rubbed conflicting theological elbows was to release the operation of the inherent principles that made for the toleration of other religious points of view. First, however, the hope that by some method the truths of the party might secure a predominance in the nation must be reduced by the experiences of time to

---

[1] *Examination of Barrowe, 1586, Harl. Misc.*, IV, 326 ff.
[2] Barrowe, *Plaine Refutation*, Pref.   [3] Barrowe, *Brief Discourie*, 290.
[4] *Mr. H. Barrowes Platform*, E. 4.   [5] *Ibid.*, F.

a hope that it and other religious groups might go their several ways in peace and with some measure of mutual assistance.

5. CONGREGATIONAL THOUGHT IN THE LAST DECADE OF THE CENTURY

The writings of the last decade of the reign indicated that the Separatist position was rapidly undergoing clearer definition. The writers of the period were not so quick in their profession of loyalty as Barrowe or as precise in their separation of the spheres of Church and State as Browne. Penry, writing in 1590–1591, in a manuscript addressed to Parliament, begged that body to consider that he made a complete distinction between the Queen's civil power and the ecclesiastical authority of "these Corahs, these Dathans, these Abirims."[1] He urged that his denunciation of the eccelsiastical government should not be interpreted as a denial of the secular authority of the Queen. He did not deny the legitimate power of the Queen, but he did protest at the wrongful exercise of the secular authority in the setting up of a false ecclesiastical system.[2] "What kinges and princes do establish in one thing, their authoritie and power whereby they do this, is another."[3] The secular authority may by error or oversight set up a false religion without impairment to the legitimate quality of that power, but for the abuse of it they will answer to God.[4] However, if the prince should set up a false worship, Christians may not lend obedience to his laws in that respect, and we may assume that the individual Christian is the court of decision in the matter. Christ has commanded true Christians "to keep and observ" all that He has commanded of them without any allowance for the orders of princes.[5] The "comaundement or permissiō of the magistrate maketh not the way of God any whit more lawful but onely more free from trouble."[6] To withhold our obedience to the will of Christ until that will shall be enacted in terms of law is to be forced by man to lend obedience to God.[7] The ordering of religion is not properly

---

[1] Penry, John, *The Historie of Corah, Dathan, and Abiram*, 27.
[2] *Ibid.*   [3] *Ibid.*   [4] *Ibid.*
[5] Johnson, Francis, *Treatise of the Ministery*, 32.   [6] *Ibid.*, 71.   [7] *Ibid.*

a function of the ruler. Such a view is tantamount to placing the civil state above the kingdom of Christ and exalting the prince above Almighty God.[1] In such cases the conscience of the Christian must be the final guide, "For as true obedience to the magistrate is alwayes in the Lord: so is [it] disobedience rather than obedience vnto them, to obey them against the Lord."[2]

If the civil ruler is not disposed to erect or to permit the erection of the true Church, the Christian must nevertheless strive to obey the commandment of God. It is a great comfort and blessing if God disposes the magistrate to protect and foster true worship;[3] "But if God withhold the magistrates allowance and furtherance herein, yet must wee notwithstanding proceed together in Christian covenant and cōmunion thus to walke in the obedience of Christ and confession of his faith and gospell," in spite of all sufferings and pains which may follow upon the pursuit of that righteous course.[4] Christ must not be made to "attend vppō princes, and to be subiect to their lavves and gouernment."[5] Among the false teachings of the Church of England is the view that "the planting or reforming of Christ's Church must tarrie for the civill magistrate, and may not otherwise be brought in by the Word and Spirit of God in the testimony of his servantes, except they have authoritie from earthlie princes."[6] Johnson likewise condemned the doctrine that a true Church may embrace an entire nation of saints and sinners alike. The growing sense of 'apartness' on the part of the elect operated as the mainspring of the Congregational theory and this doctrine must be designated as of great importance for the development of toleration. The separation of "righteous men and women, from the idolaters

---

[1] "What were this els, but to make euery State and Kingdome such an Idoll as was Nebuchadnezars golden image, ād to exalt earthly princes above the heauenly King, and to annihilate the Testamēt of Jesus Christ confirmed in that this precious blood." (Johnson, Francis, *Treatise of the Ministery*, 133; see also, *Ibid.*, 136.) [2] *Ibid.*, 49.
[3] *The Confession of faith of certayn English people* (1602), 60–61.
[4] *Ibid.*, 61–62.
[5] Quoted from an unnamed Brownist pamphlet by Alison, Richard, *A Plaine Confutation of Brownisme*, 114.
[6] Johnson, *Answer to Jacob*, 158; 22, 27.

and open wicked of the world," they held to be an essential attribute of the true Church.[1]

The Brownists made the Bible the ultimate standard for the definition of the Church with regard to both its doctrine and government. The Biblical injunctions with respect to the Church were held to provide a complete and authoritative standard for the Church in all ages. Thus, they held that the Church was not composed of the whole body of the baptized inhabitants of a kingdom, but was a company of men and women who could lay claim to a personal religious experience, and who were joined to Christ and one another by the sanctity of that experience.[2] In this Church the truth is perfectly taught and surely kept.[3] The writers conceived of the Church as the exclusive organ wherein salvation might be attained since all true Christians would be drawn into its fold. "Into this temple entreth no uncleane thing, neither whatsoever worketh abhominatiō or lyes, but the which are writē in the Lambes Book of Life. But without this church shalbe dogs and enchauntres, and whore mongers, and murderers, and Idolatours and who soeuer loveth and maketh lyes."[4] The Church of England has erred so far in an attempt to embrace the entire realm that it has become a false Church in which there is no salvation. Thus the framers of the *True Confession of 1596* testified that by word and writing they have proved the Anglican structure "to bee false and counterfeit, deceyving hir children with vain titles of the Word, Sacraments, Ministrie . . . having indeed none of these in the ordinance and powre of Christ emongst them."[5]

[1] Johnson, *Answer to Jacob*, 158.
[2] *A True Description out of the Word of God of the Visible Church* (Confession of 1589). Three years before the full organization of the first Separatist congregation was achieved by Francis Johnson (Dexter, *Congregationalism*, 234, 258–262), two of its members published this confession. The creed was written by Barrowe and Greenwood, who were then in the Fleet.
[3] *Ibid.*, 1, 7.   [4] *Ibid.*, 8.
[5] *True Confession*, iv. This Confession was the work of Johnson's Church. The London Church was organized in 1592 with Johnson as pastor and Greenwood as teacher. Greenwood was soon afterwards arrested and executed. Johnson was likewise arrested, and in 1593 about fifty-three members of his Church appear to have been in prison. (Dexter, *Congrega-*

Gifford correctly held that an essential teaching of the Brownists was the view "that the people were all by constraint received immediatlie from capital idolatrie into our Church without preaching of the Gospell, by the sound of a Trumpet at the coronation of the Queene, that they bee confused assemblies, without any separation of the good from the bad."[1] The basic error of the English Church was, in fact, held to be that it comprehended the entire land.[2] At the beginning of the reign Papists, sinners and all were compelled by force and law to become communicants in the one Church.[3] They were "receved and compelled to the Lords Supper, had their ministery and service (which now they vse) inioyned and set over thē, and ever synce they and their seed remayne in this estate, being all but one body commonly called the Church of England."[4] The true Church, on the other hand, must be marked by the voluntary separation of the regenerated from the sinful and evil people of the world. It is a body set apart, hedged against evil by the immediacy of its obedience to the leadership of God, and must be formed without any other force than the

---

tionalism, 266–268.) After the passage of the Act of that year, which called for the abjuration of the realm by stubborn Nonconformists, a group of the congregation migrated to Holland. A small Church was organized there in 1594 under the leadership of Henry Ainsworth, Johnson being still in prison. After some consultation with the Separatist leaders in London (Dexter, 270) this Confession appeared. The Preface was probably the work of Ainsworth, and he had much to do with the drafting of the entire document. (Walker, Williston, *The Creeds and Platforms of Congregationalism*, 43.) The Confession, as we shall see (cf. *post*, 293), was the most intolerant expression of sixteenth-century Separatism. The exiles were now free from danger, and they gave full expression to their hatred of the system which had driven them from England. The creed consists of forty-five articles, but it is of no especial interest since it is thoroughly orthodox in its advanced Calvinism. *A true Confession of the Faith, and Hvmble Acknovvledgment of the Alegeance, vvich vvee hir maiesties subiects, falsely called Brovvnists, doo hould tovvards god, and yield to hir maiestie and all other that are ouer vs in the Lord. Set dovvn in Articles or positions, for the better and more easie vnderstanding of those that shall read yt:* . . . was published in 1596, probably at Amsterdam. There is a copy at Yale and two copies are preserved in the Huntington Collection. *The Confession of faith of certayn English people* . . . (N. Pl. 1602; Amsterdam, 1607) is a variant.

[1] Gifford, George, *A Plaine Declaration that Brownists Be Full Donatists* . . ., 7.   [2] *Confession of faith of certayn English people* (1602), 9.
[3] *Ibid.*, 9–10.   [4] *Ibid.*, 10.

inner compulsion or desire of the true Christian to worship God in spirit and in truth.[1]

This attitude is emphasized in Johnson's concise definition of the true Church as "a company of faithfull people by the Word of God called out and separated from the world and the false wayes thereof, gathered and ioyned together in fellowship of the Gospell, by a voluntary profession of the faith and obedience of Christ."[2] Hence, if true Christians are required by law to "resort unto the publick assemblies of the land, and so to enter . . . into the tents of the anti christian land, and continue therein; I answer againe, that this is against the written Word of God, and therefore that her Majesty hath no power, no authoritie from the Lord to require this at our hands."[3] If the redeemed are punished for their obedience to the Word of God, the Government will have abused its authority.[4] Such quiet determination based upon the deepest sentiments of the human mind boded ill to any attempt seriously to prohibit dissent from established order.

Stressing the spiritual and personal character of religious experience, the Separatist leaders denied that religion could be compelled, and denounced as sinful any attempt of the secular arm so to do. Penry sought to distinguish between the inward worship of God and the external formulae of devotion. The inward worship of God is solely personal and may be described as "the worship of the spirit, when the heart and soule is by Gods spirit so directed, that in trueth and sinceritie it yeeldeth to the Lord, the worship whiche he requireth according vnto his Word."[5] This spiritual, or inward, worship alone enables man to attain salvation. It is formed "in spirit and trueth" and "is not in the power of man to give or to take away at his pleasure, but the Lorde must and doth worke it, when and where he pleaseth . . ."[6] The arm of compulsion would completely fail

---

[1] Cf. *True Description*, 1–3. [2] Johnson, *Answer to Jacob*, 196.
[3] Penry, *History of Corah*, 30.
[4] "We are punished for it: we answer againe that the sword is given for our wealth, and not for our hurt, that it ought not to be drawn against vs for well doing. . . ." (*Ibid.*, 30.)
[5] Penry, *A Treatise wherein is manifestlie proved* (no pagin.).
[6] *Ibid.* (no pagin.).

to affect the intimacy and strength of this spiritual tie between man and God since it arises from the fact of election rather than from persuasion or force. The external service of God was regarded by Penry as of secondary importance, stimulating the spiritual devotion of the Christian if properly organized.[1] Penry charged the Establishment with having hindered the true exercise of outward worship.[2] The prelates have usurped jurisdiction, which belongs properly to the civil State.[3] The weapons of the true Church are spiritual, and the spiritual agencies of preaching and teaching are "the onely weapons that are graunted vnto ministers, to ouer throw the gaynsayer."[4] This conception emphasized the spiritual character of worship and would seem to minimize the importance of the Church as an agency of salvation. It reduced to an absurdity the thesis that persecution could be of any possible assistance either in the attainment of salvation or in the construction and functioning of the true Church.

The Separatists of the period gave expression to noble sentiments against religious persecution which could not have been without effect either upon the England of their day or the Church whose organization they were founding. It was pointed out that the study of the Bible was quite useless, and that Christianity could not hope to develop if thinkers and seekers after truth were not permitted to hold and advance the truths which they found in the Bible. The only weapon of this cause, they held, is the Word of God.[5] "Imprysonment, yndytements, arraignments, yea death yt selfe, are no meet weapons to convince the consyence grounded upon the Word of the Lord, accompanied with so many testimonies of his famous seruantes and Churches."[6] They pled that even if their cause was erroneous, "yet prisons and gallows were no fit means to convince and persuade our consciences; but rather a quiet and godly conference, or discussing of the matter by

[1] Penry, *A Treatise wherein is manifestlie proved* (no pagin.).
[2] Especially by the discouragement of preaching and edification.
[3] Penry, *A Treatise wherein is manifestlie proved* (no pagin.).
[4] *Ibid.* (no pagin.).
[5] Penry, *Confession of Faith and Apology* (1593), in Burrage, C., *The Early English Dissenters*, II, 87.   [6] *Ibid.*

deliberate writing before equal judges."[1] Religion cannot be built upon force. God adds to his Church those whom He would save and "it is not in the power of princes or anie man what soever, to persuade the conscience and make members of the church: but . . . this must be left to God alone, who onelie can do it."[2] The prince should establish the true worship, and, as Johnson would have it, prohibit the false, "yet must they leave it vnto God to perswade the conscience, and to adde to his church from tyme to tyme such as shalbe saved."[3]

Penry called that State miserable which permitted men to be punished "against whome the Lord doth not commaunde the sworde to be drawne," and where "lawes are in force, which commaund them to be smitten, which are not euil doers, of which nomber non are to be accounted, saue those only who by violating human positiue lawes, break also the lawe of God."[4] Any man who holds a contrary view is not worthy to live in a Christian state.[5] Such persecution was condemned as evil by every test, and Parliament should not permit "this bloodie and tirannous inquisition" of men's consciences to be practised any longer. "What can the murthering inquisitors of Spaine do more, then by this snare, inueigle mens consciences, and constraine them to spill their owne blood?"[6] The repressive religious laws were declared to violate the laws of God and of the realm.[7] The dissensions and evils of religion in England will never be healed by such means. The attention of the magistrates should rather be fixed "vppon some holie and mercifull meane (whereby) this our too much heate may be cooled and tempered . . . as it becometh Englishmen to deale with Englishmen, Protestantes with Protestantes, Fathers with their Children, and briefly Christians with Christians."[8] The petition of the imprisoned Separatists in 1593 pointed

---

[1] Letter of Francis Johnson to Burleigh, January 8, 1593, in Strype, Annals, IV, 190.   [2] Johnson, Answer to Jacob, 199.   [3] Ibid.
[4] Penry, Th' Appelation . . . Vnto the Highe Court of Parliament, 36.
[5] Ibid.   [6] Ibid., 47 (mispaged).   [7] Ibid.
[8] The humble petition of the Imprisoned Barrowists to the . . . magistrates of our most mercifull soueragin Lady Queene Elizabeth in their severall places (1593). (In Burrage, II, 117.)

from the time of the Patriarchs to the present ...d in matters of doctrine. It has been demon-... cannot be put down and that truth cannot be w... ...loyment of force: "as for dungeons, Irons, clos... ...ent, honger, cold, want of meanes whereby to main... ...eir famulies, theise may cause some to make shipwrack of a good consyence are to lose their life, but they are not fitt wayes to perswade (honest men) to anie truth or diswade them from errors."[1]

The century gave rise to no finer sentiments in favour of religious freedom than these. The theological system of the Separatists permitted the extension of their plea for toleration beyond the limits of their own group to the inclusion of all men. First, however, the chastening rod of repression had to weaken their resolute desire to impose their system upon other men before the inherent principle of toleration could strongly manifest itself. They performed a noteworthy service to the cause of religious toleration when they urged that the kingdom of God is spiritual and that the power and the weight of the Word are the only possible means for the advancement of the cause of religion. Calm persuasion, they taught, can alone move the conscience of the man who is honestly convinced of the truth of his opinions. The primary error of persecution was rightly declared to be the view, whether expressed or unexpressed, that men may thereby be saved. This position, the Brownists pointed out, is rendered untenable by the fact of election. A persecuting system is unworthy of a Christian State, and violates the laws of God and man. Persecution is contrary to the very essence of the Christian faith; it is useless in advancing truth, and helpless in overcoming error.

If we could summarize the Congregational thought of the period at this point, we could in justice say that the early leaders of the movement had given expression to the first tolerant theory of religious practice in England. But when the Separatist viewed the sin and false worship of the nation and when he

[1] *The humble petition of the Imprisoned Barrowists to the . . . magistrates of our most mercifull soueragin Lady Queene Elizabeth in their severall places* (1593). (In Burrage, II, 123.)

envisaged his party in control of the public opinion of the nation he was motivated by those principles of persecution which had for so many centuries impeded the progress of religious freedom. The magistrate in a Congregational community was reduced to the onerous duty of executing the sentences of the godly. The comprehensive theory of the Church of England and the moderate policy of the Government had advanced far beyond that conception of religion by this time. However, the repressive tendencies of Brownism were patently an illogical and contradictory supplement to the generally tolerant character of its theory of the nature of religion and the purpose of Church government. The inheritance of Calvinism was too heavy in the Brownist system immediately to eliminate the vision of a world which should be ordered by and for the elect of God.

Thus Penry in his *An Exhortation vnto the gouernours, and people of hir maiesties countrie of Wales*, a book which is, however, hardly typical of his thought, urged that the responsibility for the true teaching of the Word in Wales rested upon its governors. "For you ought to acknowledge your selfe ruler ouer none, that doe not subiect themselues at least outwardly vnto the true religion. . . ."[1] Conscience cannot be forced, nor can religion be compelled, but "if anie Turke, Papist, or other pagan idolatour remaine in any our cities or townes, he ought to be compelled to conforme himselfe to the outward seruice of the true God, or expelled."[2] Penry, then, would have subjected dissentients to the precise penalty which his own party incurred five years after the publication of the book.

Johnson, spite his refusal to grant to the civil ruler any power over conscience and his fine defence of Christian freedom, represented the normal position on the subject of the treatment of error. He urged that the Catholic priesthood erred so greatly that the prince should banish them and their religion from his dominion.[3] Penry declared that the errors of the Catholic Church were so grievous that anyone who died in its communion was lost to salvation, so far as "is made knowen vnto

[1] Penry, *An Exhortation vnto the gouernours, and people of hir maiesties countrie of Wales*, 15. [2] *Ibid.* [3] Johnson, *Treatise of Ministery*, 105, 25.

man."[1] Johnson "unfeynedlie" desired "that God would put into the heart of her maiestey and all other princes, within their dominions, to commaund and cōpell a Reformation according to the Word of the Lord"[2] His reasoning appeared strange when he wrote, "for the receyving and profession of the faith of Christ giveth not to princes and rulers any power to refuse chaunge or break his lawes and ordinances, . . . but it rather byndeth them so much the more, both themselves in theyr own persons to obey and by theyr authority to commaund and draw theyr subiects also to yield obedience to the Lord Jesus in his own ordinance, and no other."[3]

We have already had occasion to indicate that the *True Confession* represented Congregationalism in its most intolerant stage.[4] The Separatists had just been imprisoned and then banished under the severe legislation of 1593. In the safety of exile they gave full expression to the hatred which they bore for the Establishment which had dealt so harshly with them and their leaders. Article XXXIX of their Confession dealt with the relation of the civil ruler to the Church in a truly Christian State. It was declared to be the duty of the ruler "to suppresse and root out by their authoritie all false Ministries, voluntarie religions, and counterfeyt worship of God; to abolish and destroy the idol temples, Images, Altares, Vestments, and all other monuments of idolatrie and superstition . . ."[5] In addition, the civil ruler has been invested by God with a positive function "to stablish and mayntein by their lawes every part of Gods Word, . . . His Christian religion, pure worship, and true ministery . . .; to cherish and protect all such as are careful to worship God according to his Word, and to leade to godly lyfe in al peace and loyaltie. . . ."[6] The ruler should compel all his subjects to perform their duty to God. The good should be cherished and maintained and the evil should be punished and restrained according to the commandment of God.[7]

---

[1] Penry, *A Defence of that which hath bin Written*, 15; see also, 23, 24–26.   [2] Johnson, *Answer to Jacob*, 199.
[3] Johnson, *Treatise of Ministery*, 134.   [4] Cf. *ante*, 286–287.
[5] *True Confession*, Art. XXXIX; see also Ainsworth, *Confession of Faith* (1598).   [6] *True Confession*, Art. XXXIX.   [7] *Ibid.*

If we may regard these expressions of the early Brownist leaders as unworthy and contradictory appendages to the main principles of their system, it may be held that Congregationalism had as early as 1600 established a theory of Christian and civil relationship in which religious toleration might develop. The very fact that they had been able to establish themselves as a Separatist body must be regarded as an important step in the dissolution of the theory of a nationally imposed uniform religion. The claims of the State to the power and the right to establish a Christian Church had been vigorously repudiated by a counter-claim that the Christian Church found its origin in the voluntary action of a group of regenerated Christians, a phenomenon which the State could not influence and which lay entirely outside its functional capacity. Faith results from an immediate and personal contact between God and man. Hence the magistrate can neither compel conscience nor dictate the erection of a Church. The claims of national uniformity disappear before the highly individualistic and spiritualistic religious conceptions of the Brownists. The Anabaptist insistence upon the impotency of any but spiritual weapons in the erection and maintenance of pure religion was followed with varying conviction by the Brownist leaders. Numerous factors combined to produce the Congregationalist conception of the voluntary Church, which was in itself a highly important contribution to the development of religious liberty. The comparative isolation and weakness of such companies of believers would render any systematic persecution in a Brownist commonwealth unlikely. The Brownist system was highly individualistic, and persecution is normally to be found in a close-knit, well-organized, and arbitrarily directed Church-State. The logical result of Congregationalism would be the toleration of one Church community by another.

The generally tolerant principles enunciated by Browne did not obtain full acceptance by his successors. It is possible that the tolerant attributes of a Congregational system loom large only in the historical light of the later developments of the theory. By 1600 the structure of Congregationalism was fairly laid, and it was disposed towards a denial of the rightfulness and efficacy of compulsion in religious matters; a disposition which the circumstances of its history were happily to enhance and enlarge.

6. EARLY BAPTIST THOUGHT IN RELATION TO THE PROBLEM OF RELIGIOUS TOLERATION

The English Baptists, during the reign of James I, were to make notable contributions to the literature of religious toleration. However, there are few clear evidences of any organized Baptist congregation in England during the reign of Elizabeth, and such examples of their thought as we shall be able to produce will consequently be fragmentary and unsystematic.[1] Anabaptist opinions had been condemned by royal proclamation as early as 1536, and in 1538 a man and woman belonging to the sect were burned. Hooper informed Bullinger in 1549 that his public lectures had been disturbed by Anabaptists, and Latimer spoke of them as worshipping in separate bodies as early as 1552. There can be no doubt that several Anabaptist communities flourished during the reign of Elizabeth, especially in London and Kent.[2] The most important member of these groups appears to have been Robert Cooche, a writer and controversialist of ability.[3] The confusion and uncertainty which enshrouds the status of the Baptists during the late sixteenth century arises principally from the fact that there were many who held Baptist views in the Brownist congregations. It may be presumed that their separation from the Congregational bodies awaited the able leadership of John Smyth, who first gave the English Baptists identity as a Separatist body. The English Baptists owed the inception of their doctrines to the Dutch and Flemish emigrants who began to arrive in England in considerable numbers as early as 1559.[4] Elizabeth gave these refugees assur-

---

[1] Burrage has noted (*Early English Dissenters*, I, 221–225) references which would appear to indicate that numerous Baptist secessions took place between 1594–1600 from the Brownist congregations. However, nothing has been clearly proved, and the literary remains are, of course, from the opponents of the Baptists.

[2] *Acts of the P.C.*, VIII, 369, 389.   [3] Cf. *ante*, 74 ff.

[4] Dixon, R. W., *History of the Church of England*, V, 356.

ance that they would be protected in the exercise of their religion, and permission was granted to them to settle in England under the authority of the Bishop of London. Complaints were filed almost at once against the Anabaptist tenets of a number of the group and a proclamation was set forth on September 22, 1560, in which the danger of corrupting the realm and the evils which would follow the multiplication of sects was declared.[1] The Ecclesiastical Commission was hereupon ordered to visit all suspected towns and to try all who were tainted with the Anabaptist heresy. Those who could not be reconciled were to abjure the realm within twenty days.[2]

The Commission appears not to have shared the alarm of the Government for it was 1562 before the first case was presented: that of a Dutch minister named Hamstedius, (or Hamsted), who was tried before Grindal for favouring Anabaptist doctrines.[3] He was found guilty and was excommunicated by Grindal and by the Dutch Church, and was required to leave the realm.[4] The Dutch migration had evidently served to sow the seeds of Baptist doctrines in England. As Strype observed, "With these [the Dutch] came our Anabaptists also and sectaries holding heretical and ill opinions; . . . and doctrines sprung from some of these foreigners; begin now, if not before, to be dispersed in the nation, dangerous to the established and orthodox religion and civil government."[5]

Whitgift in 1573 had accused Cartwright, quite wrongly, of holding certain Anabaptist tenets. In describing the teachings of the Anabaptists, Whitgift observed that "They taught that the civile magistrate hath no authority in ecclesiastical matters, . . . that he ought not to meddle in causes of religion and fayth. That no man ought to be compelled to faithe, and to religion. That Christians ought to punish faultes, not with imprisonment, not with sworde, or corporall punishments,

[1] *Grindal's Remains* (Parker Society), 297–298.
[2] *Ibid.*, 297; *A proclamation against the Anabaptists* (Bodl. Lib.).
[3] Cf. *post*, 316.
[4] Dixon, *History of the Church of England*, V, 357.
[5] Strype, *Annals*, I, 2, 271.

but only with excommunication."[1] This simple statement of the Anabaptist position presented in advance the skeleton of the extended Baptist defences of liberty of conscience in the reign of James I.[2]

The Queen had, since her first proclamation against the Anabaptists, issued two additional warnings to them to abjure the realm. At the suggestion of Grindal, a careful investigation was undertaken in London in order to ascertain from every householder the names of all foreigners under their roofs, their occupations, character, and religious views.[3] In 1574 Sandys handed over sixteen Anabaptists to the Mayor of London to be transported out of the realm, and on Easter day, 1575, a number of Flemish Baptists were arrested at a meeting at Aldgate.[4] They were brought to trial before Sandys, the Bishop of Rochester, the Master of the Rolls, and two magistrates, for heresy. The examination disclosed that they rejected the baptism of infants, taught that a Christian should not take an oath, and held blasphemous opinions concerning the nature of Christ's body.[5] Four or five of the group carried faggots at Paul's Cross, recanted and were pardoned.[6] Eleven of the number were declared guilty of obstinate heresy and were accordingly condemned to death. However, the Government had no intention of carrying out such a wholesale piece of persecution. Every effort was made to secure a recantation and finally nine (or eleven) were banished.[7] Two of the number, Pieters and Terwoort, refused to recant and were, after lengthy consultations and considerable efforts to secure a recantation, handed over to the sheriffs.[8] Even in the case of

---

[1] Whitgift, John, *An Answere to a Certen Libell Intituled an Admonition to the Parliament*, 15. Poinet had earlier observed, 1556, that the Anabaptists would destroy all political power because of their emphasis on Christian liberty, and hence refusing all obedience to the State. (Poinet, *A Short Treatise of Politike Power*, 22.)

[2] Compare the views of Knox's adversary, 74 ff. *ante.*

[3] Strype, *Grindal*, 180–183.

[4] Oldmixon, 459; Carlile, J. C., *English Baptists*, 38.

[5] Lingard, Jno., *History of England*, VI, 345.

[6] Stow, John, *Annales of England*, 1149.   [7] *Ibid.*, 1151.

[8] Vide Rymer, *Foedera*, XV, 740–741. Pro Nicholao Bacon milite custode magni sigilli Angliae, de commissione speciali pro Haereticis comburendis.

the execution of these men, Froude has suggested, with good proof, that possibly this severity was employed because the Queen at the moment desired to parade her orthodoxy before Spain.[1]

Pieters and Terwoort apparently believed that religious persecution was wrong in principle, and finely denied the right of physical compulsion in spiritual matters. Unfortunately, very little is certainly known about their views. Evans and Crosby quote a letter said to have been written by the Anabaptists to Foxe, thanking him for his efforts to persuade the Queen to mitigate the capital sentence.[2] Neither writer indicated his source, and the letter has an apocryphal flavour.[3] The Anabaptists declared that they were willing "to submit to the instruction of all those who are able to prove to us, by the Scriptures, something that is better, but that men should constrain us with fire and sword, appears to us to be vain, and to militate against reason—for it is possible to constrain us, through fear of death, to speak differently from what we understand; but that we should understand differently from our belief, you are well aware is an impossibility."[4] We are told, as well, that a number of the group seized with Pieters and Terwoort refused to sign a statement admitting "that a Christian magistrate may with propriety punish obstinate heretics with the sword."[5]

The condemned men, in an effort to clarify their views, communicated a confession of their faith to the authorities which dealt briefly with the problem of toleration.[6] They demonstrated that they did not belong to the Terrorist group of Anabaptists by their full recognition of the civil power of the magistrate and the religious requirements of obedience to his authority.[7] It is significant that the plaintiffs dealt only with

[1] Froude, J. A., *History of England*, XI, 25–27.   [2] Cf. *ante*, 181–182.
[3] The writer knows of no other source for this interesting letter.
[4] Quoted in Evans, B., *Early English Baptists*, I, 158.   [5] *Ibid.*, I, 162.
[6] *Het Bloedig Toonel*, 704–706; translated in *Broadmead Records, add.*, 507 ff.
[7] *Ibid.*, Art. x. "We believe and confess that magistrates are set and ordained of God (Wisd. vi. 4, Sirach xvii. 18, Rom. xiii. 1), to punish evil and protect the good; which magistracy we desire from our hearts to obey,

the question of the civil power of the ruler: the ecclesiastical power of the magistrate was left unmentioned.

Terwoort amplified his views somewhat more fully when he wrote: "observe well the command of God; Thou shalt love the stranger as thyself. Should he who is in misery, and dwelling in a strange land, be driven thence with his companions, to their great damage . . . oh!, that they would deal with us according to natural reasonableness and evangelic truth, of which our persecutors so highly boast."[1] He urged that Christ and His disciples persecuted no one but taught a doctrine of love. This doctrine was left with the Apostles, as they testify: "From all this it is clear that those who have the true Gospel doctrine and faith will persecute no one, but will themselves be persecuted."[2]

Pieters and Terwoort condemned religious persecution without reservation as devoid of scriptural warrant. Persecution they held to be contrary to the spirit and teachings of the Christian faith. They urged that repression could only lead to the apostasy of the accused man and that it was not a fit instrument to convince one who is in doubt.

The English Baptists were to be profoundly influenced by the Anabaptist view of the wrongfulness of persecution, and the obscure teachings of Pieters and Terwoort were to find clearer and more forceful expression in the writings of Murton, Busher, Smyth, and other Baptist leaders of the next century.

as it is written in the first of Peter, ii. 13, submit yourself to every ordinance of man for the Lord's sake. For he beareth not the sword in vain (Rom. xiii. 4). And Paul teaches us that we should offer up for all prayers, intercessions and giving of thanks for all kings and magistrates; that we may lead a quiet and peaceable life in all godliness and honesty. For this is good and acceptable in the sight of God, our Saviour, who desires that all men should be saved. (1 Tim. ii. 1, 2, 3, 4.) He further teaches us to be subject to principalities and powers, to obey magistrates, and to be ready to every good work. (Peter iii. 1.) . . . We likewise do not approve of those who resist the magistrates; but confess and declare with our whole heart that we must be obedient and subject unto them, as we have here set down."

[1] *Het Bloedig Toonel*, III, 694, 712.   [2] *Ibid.*

V

LAY THOUGHT DURING THE REIGN OF ELIZABETH AND ITS RELATION TO THE PROBLEM OF TOLERATION

1. The importance of lay thought in the development of religious toleration

We have had occasion to examine in some detail the thought of several roughly classified groups in relation to the problem of toleration. All these groups, and likewise the Catholics whom we shall consider in the following chapter, were influenced by special factors in their public pronouncements with regard to the proper policy to be undertaken in the case of stubborn religious dissent. Their opinions, therefore, must be viewed with considerable hesitation and with the reflection that each group was pleading a special case. Their utterances were, on the whole, motivated from practical considerations rather than from pure theory. Experience has taught, as well, that the historian must view with considerable scepticism the pronouncements of clergymen in theological debate. No field of controversy inspires such extreme bigotry and so many acrimonious accusations. In addition, theological discussion tends to express itself in crystallized terminology which has often lost its content. For example, we may find a meek Anglican cleric savagely recommending the destruction of the rotten branch, when in point of fact his rhetorical thunder does not presume a desire to burn his theological opponents. We have noted, too, that when men speak of liberty of conscience in the noblest phrases they subjectively desire its benefits only for their own party.

It is pleasant, therefore, to escape from the realm of the professional theologian and to consider the attitude of the layman towards the problem of religious dissent. We have considered the attitude of the Government in connection with Anglican thought because the two together comprised the dominant thought of the period. Elizabeth, Burleigh,

300

Atkinson, Raleigh, and the others were laymen, but they regarded the problem of toleration through the somewhat coloured glasses of State policy. The governmental position had, on the whole, none of the animus and bigotry of clerical thought. It was, indeed, essentially anti-clerical and thoroughly Erastian. The Government was faced with a difficult task and, while remarkably tolerant, it had little inclination to consider the theoretical aspects of the problem of toleration. This attitude was well expressed in a letter from Francis Johnson to Burleigh in which he described the examination of Wroth and Smith who were with him in prison. The examining commissioner, when the Separatists protested that subscription on their part would be to dissemble, said, "Come to the church, and obey the Queen's laws, and be a dissembler, be a hypocrite, or a devil, if thou wilt."[1] The Government was inspired by lay and not by theological considerations in the formation and execution of its policy.

More strictly, however, lay thought may be regarded as having been held by a group which was chiefly influenced neither by ecclesiastical nor political considerations. The period was one of deep religious conviction and we shall find that these laymen regarded the problem of toleration from a religious background. There was surprisingly little scepticism in English thought before the outbreak of the Civil War. The views of such men have the rare virtue of objectivity and for that reason especial importance may be attached to their thought. They tended to discern the essential catholicity undergirding all creeds and they were disposed to discard the encrusted shell of dogmatic opinion in order to emphasize the spiritual nature of Christianity. The mass of laymen were, of course, wholly inarticulate, but the scattered fragments of lay thought which we are able to present will serve to indicate the character of the public opinion which impelled the Government so fre-

---

[1] *Johnson to Burleigh*, January 8, 1593. Strype, *Annals*, IV, 188. The Erastian and lay character of the governmental policy was also well shown by an order in Privy Council regarding Field and Wilcox. The Bishop of London was instructed "to cause some dealing to be donne with Wilcocke and Field to bring them to conformitie, and thereupon to shew them more favour." (*Acts of P.C.*, March 1572, VIII, 90.)

quently and so clearly to define the distinction between the persecution of conscience and the prosecution of sedition.

Cabot, in his *Ordinances of 1553*, had urged that explorers and settlers should not endanger themselves by insisting too vigorously upon their religion. He held that it was well "not to disclose to any nation the state of our religion, but to passe it over in silence, without any declaration of it, seeming to beare with such lawes, and rites, as the place hath, where you shall arrive."[1] This astute advice demonstrates that there were few missionary impulses connected with English exploration and it expresses the conviction that even 'truth' should not be too vigorously imposed upon other people. The Ordinances summarized quite accurately the later position of the English Government toward its Roman Catholic subjects.

Somewhat more than a generation later Dallington in his interesting travel book advised the English voyager in the same spirit.[2] He urged the traveller " not to alter his first faith."[3] "Wherefor if my Traveller will keepe this birde safe in his bosome, he must neither be inquisitive after other mens religions, nor prompt to discover his owne. For I hold him vnwise that is in a strange country will either shew his mind or his money. . . ."[4]

Without doubt the great increase in Continental travel by Englishmen during the reign of Elizabeth did much to break down English prejudice and bigotry, especially against the Roman Catholics.[5] The wider outlook which travel inspired and the observation of nations living commendably under different ecclesiastical and dogmatic systems served to introduce an element of 'relativism' into English religious life. The intimate contact with the Netherlands which began about 1580 had its fruits in the next reign in the Arminian controversy. Travel must have confirmed the observation of Castellion, that in this day there were numerous sects (*sans nombre*) each one of which

[1] *Ordinances of 1553*, in *Hakluyt, Voyages*, II, 202.
[2] Dallington, Sir Robert, *A Method for Trauell. Shewed by Taking the View of France*. . . . Preliminary to his *The View of France*, 1604.
[3] *Ibid.*, B. 2.   [4] *Ibid.*
[5] This was certainly true of Edwin Sandys, cf. *post*, 367 ff.

considered the others heretical. Thus in a given town one might be truly faithful, but in an adjoining town an heretic.[1] There have become as many truths, he urged, as there are sects, and in travelling through the country one should change his faith as he changes his money.[2] A tour of Europe in Elizabethan times would have confirmed Castellion's vigorous condemnation of this patently absurd 'exclusivism.'

2. JACOBUS ACONTIUS

The lay thought of the century received its finest and fullest expression in the writings of Jacobus Acontius Tridentinus (Jacapo Aconcio). Acontius was the first man in England to enunciate a systematic and philosophical defence of religious toleration in the *Satanae Stratagemata libri octo*, published in 1565.[3]

---

[1] Castellion, Sébastien, *Traité des Hérétiques*, 25.   [2] *Ibid.*

[3] The bibliographical history of the work is not entirely clear. The following list of editions, with the libraries in which copies may be found, is suggested:

LATIN EDITIONS

1. *Satanae Stratagemata libri octo, J. Acontio authore, accessit eruditissima Epistola de ratione edendorum librorum, ad Johannem Vuolfium Tigurinum eodem authore.*
   Basle, P. Pernam, 1565 (with many errors).
   (Berlin, Breslau, Brown Univ., Göttingen, Halle, Königsberg, Paris, Tübingen, Vienna, Zurich.)
2. *Stratagematum Satanae libri octo, etc.*
   Basle, 1565, in a different type and corrected.
   (Basle, Breslau, B.M., Edinburgh, Munich, Oxford, Paris, Rostock, Tübingen, Vienna.)
3. Reprint, Basle, 1582.
4. Reprint, Basle, 1610.
   (Amsterdam (Univ.), Berlin, Bonn, B.M., Frankfort-on-Main, Göttingen, Greifswald, Kiel, Lausanne, Vienna.)
5. Reprint, Basle, 1616.
6. Reprint, Basle, 1618.
7. Reprint, Basle, 1620.
8. Reprint, Amsterdam, 1631.
   (Amsterdam (Univ.).)
9. Reprint, Oxford, 1631.
   (B.M., Göttingen, Greifswald, La Hague (Royal), C. H. McIlwain, Cambridge, Mass., Oxford, Dr. Williams' Library, London.)
10. Reprint, London, 1648.

303

a. Early Life and Associations with the Italian Academicians

All that is known concerning the life of Acontius may be

11. Reprint, Oxford, 1650.
(H.C.L., Oxford.)
12. Reprint, Amsterdam, 1652.
(Amsterdam (Univ. and Mennon. Lib.), Basle, Berlin, Breslau, B.M., Königsberg, Munich, Paris, Rostock, Vienna, Zurich.)
13. Reprint, Hoogenhuyse, 1661.
(B.M., H.C.L.)
14. Reprint, Amsterdam, 1664.
(Göttingen.)
15. An edit. by G. Koehler on the basis of the second Basle ed. of 1565. Monaci, 1927.

TRANSLATIONS
French

1. *Les Ruzes de Satan recueillies et comprinses en huit liures* . . .
Basle, 1565.
(Bibl. Natl., B.M., Oxford, Wolfenbüttel.)
2. Reprint, Delf (?), 1611.
(Rostock.)

German

1. *Acht Bücher Hn. Jacobi Acontii Tridentini, von den listigen Kriegs-Rencken dess Satans* . . .
Basle, 1647.
(Breslau, Königsberg.)

Dutch

1. *De Archlisticheden Des Satans, Begrepen in acht Boecken* . . .
Graven-Haghe, 1611.
(Amsterdam (Univ. and Mennon. Lib.)
2. *VIII Boecken van de Arglistigheden des Satans* . . .
Gravenhague, 1660.
(Amsterdam.)
3. Reprint, Amsterdam, 1662.

English

1. *Satans Stratagems, or the Devil's Cabinet Council Discovered. Whereby he endeavours to hinder the Knowledge of the Truth, through many delusions . . . and also the testimonies of some Ancient Divines: with an Epistle written by Mr. John Goodwin and Mr. Durie's letter touching the same* . . .
London, 1648.
(Only the first four books were translated. The translation was free but correct. Copies are preserved in the B.M., Bodl., and in the library of the late George Brinley, Esq., Hartford, Conn.)
2. *Darkness Discovered. Or the Devils Secret Stratagems laid open. Whereby he labors to make havock of the People of God, by his wicked and Damnable designs for destroying the Kingdom of Christ. Wherein*

sketched in a brief compass.[1] He was born about 1500 at Ossani, near Trent.[2] He studied law for some time, and tells us that he devoted years to the study of Bartolus and Baldus.[3] He appears to have been engaged in the practice of law for a number of years. His writings display an intimacy with the works of Aristotle, Plato, and Archimedes. He was for a period in the service of the Marquis of Pescara, and he probably gained his knowledge of engineering while in this service. He was later a member of the Court of the Viceroy at Milan, where he became acquainted with Francis Betti, son of the Intendant of the Viceroy. Acontius and Betti had left the Catholic faith at an uncertain date,[4] and, due to the increased activities of the authorities, they, with numerous Italian Protestants, fled from Italy to Switzerland. Betti appears to have gone to Basle in August 1557, and he was joined there by Acontius in October of the same year. Acontius was at this time almost sixty years of age, and the fact that he had left the Catholic faith at so late an age displays a remarkable flexibility of mind. It is likewise impressive that his very considerable literary achievements are all dated after 1558.

Acontius and Betti became acquainted with Celso, Curio, and other Italian Academicians while in Switzerland. Acontius' first publication, the *De Methodo*, appeared in 1558 while he

is contained an exquisite Method of Disputation about Religion, and putting an end to all controversies in matters of conscience . . .
London, 1651.
(A duplication of the first English edition with a new title page. Very rare. This edition is unique in having a fine portrait of the author which, however, has been questioned as to authenticity (*D.N.B.*, art. "Acontius"), but see the *B.M. Cat. of Engr.* Copies may be found in the B.P.L. and the B.M.)

This catalogue of Acontius' works should be compared with the list suggested by Dr. G. Koehler in his valuable edition of the *Satanae Stratagematum*, praef. edit., ix–xv.

[1] The biographical notice by H. R. Tedder in the *D.N.B.* remains the best summary of his life. (*D.N.B.*, I, 63 ff.)
[2] The *Nouvelle Biog. Général*, I, 197, gives the date of his birth as 1492 (September 7th), but quotes no authority for the date.
[3] *Satanae Stratagemata*, Edit. 1653, Letter to J. A. Wolff.
[4] *Nouv. Biog. Gén.*, I, 197.

was at Basle.[1] The two friends left soon afterwards for Zurich where they were warmly welcomed and entertained by Ochino. Acontius likewise met his life-time friend Woolf and Lelio Socinus while at Zurich. He seems to have visited in Strassburg during the same year and there he met the leading German reformers of the period and several of the English refugees.[2] It is certain that he knew Jewel and Grindal while in Strassburg.

Acontius' association and warm sympathy with the Italian Academicians can scarcely have failed to influence his views on religious toleration. They, like Acontius, were among the finest products of the humanism and free thought of Renaissance Italy. This little group of 'academic sceptics,' as Calvin called them, presented a united stand against bigotry and persecution; rejected the doctrine of the Trinity; and may be regarded as the founders of Unitarianism.[3] As laymen they had a deep-seated aversion to excessive theological severity and as humanists they rejected many of the 'coarser dogmas' of the Reformation. They did not hesitate to apply rational tests to dogmas and the first result of this tendency was a denial of the divine character of Jesus and of the doctrine of the Trinity.

Following their expulsion from Italy, most of the group settled in Switzerland, but their advanced theology soon resulted in persecution and expulsion from that country.[4] Several of the leaders of the group migrated to Transylvania and Poland where they enjoyed great favour and success for a time under the leadership of Acontius' friend Lelio Socinus (1525–1562).[5] After his death, however, dissensions broke out in their ranks as a result of the infiltration of Anabaptist doctrines and in

---

[1] Cf. *post*, 317–318. Buisson believes that he brought several manuscripts which he had been unable to print in Italy to Basle, among them the *De Methodo*. (Buisson, F., *Sébastien Castellion*, II, 291–292.)
[2] *Jewel to Martyr* (January 1559), *Zurich Letters (First Series)*, III.
[3] Bury, J. B., *Freedom of Thought*, 93.
[4] Robertson, J. M., *History of Free Thought*, II, 67.
[5] Lelio Socinus came from a long line of patrician jurists of Siena. The family was allied by blood and marriage with some of the noblest houses of Tuscany. He was trained in the law, but had little interest in what he regarded as a barren subject. He removed to Venice in 1546, and his advanced religious views appear to have developed shortly afterwards. (Gordon, A., *The Sozzini and Their School*, 300 ff.)

1578, Faustus Socinus (1539–1604), the nephew of the early leader, was called upon to settle the controversy. He spent the remainder of his life in completing the *Catechism of Rakau*, which attempted to systematize the teachings of the group and which must be regarded as a great landmark in the history of religious toleration.[1]

[1] There is a remarkable similarity between the views of Acontius and Socinus; a connection which early critics of Acontius did not fail to notice. (Voëtius, *Disput.*, I, 500–501, *et passim*.) Socinus was willing to embody as a principle of faith the idea that there were other Christian Churches than his own. (Harnack, *Hist. of Dogma*, VII, 138.) Side by side with the definition which restricted the Church to those who have and hold the sacred doctrines of his Catechism, stood the full recognition of other communions. Socinus, like Acontius, sought to reduce the doctrines essential to salvation to a few broad and easily comprehended principles of the New Testament upon which all men could agree. He had the laudable courage to simplify the question of the nature and import of religion, to glorify the freedom of the individual in forming his private judgments, and to emphasize the spiritual nature of worship. (Harnack, VII, 166.) The reason of the individual Christian was enthroned as the supreme judge of the Bible and of faith. He held that it was impossible for any two minds to arrive at identical judgments in spiritual matters and thereby cleared the way for the position that the opinion of one man is worth precisely as much as that of another in such matters. (Buisson *Sébastien Castellion*, II, 313 ff.) He repeatedly expressed his attachment to the principle of religious toleration, and his reply to those who asked him if they should condemn sectaries who did not agree with them is classic in its noble tolerance. Nine years after the publication of the *Satanae Stratagemata* the first Socinian confession of faith expressed a position which displays a remarkable similarity in point of view. The Socinians specifically condemned all temporal punishment and persecution of heretics. The use of Old Testament texts as a support for the theory of persecution was branded as 'spurious.' "Christians ought to conquer not by arms but by the persuasive force of truth." This point of view was retained and expanded in the *Catechism of Rakau*, which was promulgated in its final form in 1609. The principle of religious toleration has well been described as the mainspring of the document. They declared: "In giving to the world the Catechism of our Church it is not our intention to make war on anybody. With good reason pious people complain that the various confessions or catechisms which the various Churches are publishing at the present time are apples of discord among Christians because it is sought to impose them upon other people's consciences and to regard those who dissent from their teachings as heretics. Far be it from us to commit such a folly: our intention is not to proscribe or to oppress anyone. Let each be free to judge of religion: this is imposed by the New Testament and the primitive Church." (Compare Acontius, *Satanae Stratagemata*, and *Confession of the Remonstrants*.) Acton has well said of Socinus, he "was the first who, on the ground that Church and State ought to be separated, required universal toleration." (Acton, *History of Freedom*, 52.)

The system of thought which the Sozzini and other Italian Protestants had planted at Vicenza, and had by 1570 propagated over most of Europe, was the natural result of the humanistic philosophy of the Renaissance. A group of philosophers had in the fifteenth century undertaken philosophical and logical speculations quite as daring as any of the eighteenth century, and had habituated a small but influential group of thinkers to the close criticism of all dogmatic questions.[1] These men, as philosophers, elaborated theories of unquestioned scepticism, though, as Catholics, they continued to lend formal obedience to the Church. Their acceptance of a particular doctrine on the basis of faith did not in the least prevent the simultaneous rejection of it on the score of reason. The sixteenth-century school, affected as well by the Reformation, proceeded with courageous logic to disregard tradition; to deny the claims of the Church to compulsion of conscience; and to an interesting and valuable attempt to simplify and secularize religious doctrine. Acontius was in the *Satanae Stratagemata* to provide the first systematic and in many ways the classical expression of this development.

The execution of Servetus in 1553 was still fresh in the minds of men when Acontius arrived in Switzerland. This event was largely responsible for Castellion's important condemnation of religious persecution and for his noble defence of religious liberty which appeared in 1554. The connection between the *De Haereticis* and the *Satanae Stratagemata*, which was published eleven years later, is of such importance as to deserve special consideration.[2]

Castellion had been profoundly influenced by the Italian group and the Academicians were unanimous in their condemnation of the execution of Servetus. Camillo Renato wrote a long poem condemning Calvin's action under the title *De iniusto Serviti incendio*. Matteo Gribaldi Mofa, who was in Geneva at the time, expressed his disapproval of punishment for religious belief during the period of the trial. Curio, a friend

[1] Lecky, W. E. H., *Rationalism in Europe*, I, 370.
[2] Cf. *post*, 310–315, 363.

308

of Acontius, is said to have written a violent apology for Servetus which he apparently did not publish.[1]

Bernardino Ochino (1487-1565), whom Acontius knew at Zurich, likewise spoke in favour of religious toleration. Especially important were his *Dialogues*, published two years prior to the *Satanae Stratagemata*.[2] This book was the chief cause for his banishment from Zurich at the age of seventy-eight, and the translation of the *Dialogues* completed the ruin of Castellion's cause. The twenty-eighth dialogue was dedicated to Sigismund of Poland, with the declaration that he had opened his kingdom to the Gospel, but it was understood that he now feared that Satan would introduce heretical notions into his realm.[3] Ochino proceeded to a discussion of the matter. Pius II and Cardinal Morone are supposed to be conversing. The latter was kept in prison for a long period because of supposed heretical connections. Ochino makes him argue that the true Christian seeks to lead those who have erred back to the true faith.[4] The Pope presented the usual Old Testament passages which permit the use of force;[5] to which Morone replied that the moral laws of the New Testament have swept away the ceremonial laws.[6] Heresy is very difficult to ascertain and accurately to judge.[7] Morone was persuaded to admit that instances of obstinate blasphemy are conceivable and that in such cases the community may be compelled to exact the death penalty in order to provide a warning to the weak. But his admission of the death penalty was hedged by twelve conditions which reduced it to a purely formal concession. He placed persecution in the category of a ceremonial law. He cited the humility and tolerance of Jesus and held that persecution tended to destroy good rather than to cure evil. The thoughts here expressed by Ochino, and his general point

---

[1] The writer has not been able to examine or to locate these works. Hallam knew of them only indirectly, and Schaff was able to ascertain little concerning them. They are said to be in private hands.

[2] Ochino, B., *Dialogi xxx in duos libros divisi, quorum primus est de messia continetque dialogos xviii. Secundus est cum de rebus varis tum potissimum de Trinitate. Quorum argumenta in secunda utrivsque pagina invenies.*

[3] *Ibid.*, 378.   [4] *Ibid.*, 380 ff.   [5] *Ibid.*, 390 ff.

[6] *Ibid.*, 393-395.   [7] *Ibid.*, 388-389.

of view, have become commonplace in the course of time, but they were revolutionary and daring in his day.[1]

Mino Celso in the *In haereticus coercendis quatemus progedi liceat, Celsi Mini Seninsus disputatio. Ubi nominatim eos ultimo supplicio affici non debere, aperti demonstratur* (1559) likewise sought to prove that persecution could not be justified by the Bible.[2] He held that the fining and banishment of the heretic was sufficient punishment for the most grievous error.

The greatest luminary of the Academicians was Sébastien Castellion, whose *De Haereticis* was the most important work favouring religious toleration to be published on the Continent during the century. We should consider his thought with some care in order to compare his work with the somewhat later contribution of Acontius. Acontius probably knew Castellion at Basle, and he had certainly read his book. But there is surprisingly little in common between the two great works. Castellion and Acontius arrived at the same general conclusions, but the methods by which they did so were quite unrelated.[3] The difference in their attack of the problems of dissent and heresy rested essentially in the differences in the temperaments of the two men.

Castellion was born in 1515 at Chatillon in Savoy of poor and bigoted parents.[4] He acquired a sound classical training

---

[1] "Die Gedanken, welche Ochino hier aüssert und der Standpunkt, welchen er vertritt, sind im allgemeinen im Laufe der Zeit demeingut unserer Anschauungen geworden. Aber über das Gesamtbewusstsein seines eigenen Zeitalters gingen sie weit hinaus." (Benrath, K., *Bernardino Ochino von Siena*, 332.)

[2] A reprint was made in 1584 with no place of publication indicated, and a third edition appeared in Amsterdam in 1662. Hallam would appear to err (I, 551) in giving the date of the first edition as 1584. The argument of the book was principally drawn from Castellion, and was, on the whole, undistinguished.

[3] Buisson, however, regarded the inspiration of Castellion and Acontius as "absolument identique" and would consider their treatises as highly similar in content and in contribution. (Buisson, F., *Sébastien Castellion*, II, 293.) It would appear, however, that Buisson over-estimates the debt of Acontius to Castellion and errs in some degree in making the brilliant contribution of the Italian group revolve too completely around the figure of Castellion.

[4] His French name was Bastien de Chatillon. He assumed the classical name of Castalio, alluding to the Castalian fountain.

by hard study, and with a rare genius for languages mastered Latin, Greek, and Hebrew. In 1540 he was teaching Greek at Lyons and there published a manual of biblical history under the title of *Dialogi Sacri* which attained great popularity. In the same period he composed a Latin and a Greek epic which are said to have delighted the critical Melanchthon. Shortly afterwards he began his translation of the Bible which was completed in 1551. The object of the translation, according to Bayle, was to present the Bible in classical Latin according to the humanist taste. Castellion was a man of wide ability, a philologist, orator, critic, and a poet of merit. He had the temperament of an artist and the soul of a mystic. He was repelled by the harshness of the Calvinist doctrine of predestination, which he had an opportunity to study at close range during his stormy stay at Geneva, and this fact without doubt assisted in bringing him into close relation with Ochino and the Socinians. In the closing years of his life he published a translation of Ochino's *Dialogues* in which numerous passages favour Unitarianism.

The preface to the Bible, published in 1551, contained the core of his argument for toleration. Here he urged caution in dealing with matters of faith since accurate judgments in such concerns are difficult to attain. He conceived of religion in a spiritual sense and the employment of temporal weapons in a religious cause appeared to him to be stupid, if not criminal. The preface, written some time before the execution of Servetus, shows that Castellion had been arriving at his conception of toleration by slow degrees and there are clear indications of Socinian influences even at this early date.[1] However, the execution of Servetus with circumstances of so much cruelty and for no other cause than error of opinion so profoundly affected his sensitive intelligence that he was moved to consider at length the problem of the legitimacy of the persecution of error.[2] In March 1554, eleven years before the appearance of the *Satanae Stratagemata*, was published the Latin edition of

[1] Trechsel, F., *Die Protestantischen Antitrinitarier vor Faustus Socin*, I, 211–213.
[2] Hallam, H., *Literature of Europe*, I, 549.

the *De Haereticis* under the false name of Martinus Bellius.[1] Castellion's argument for religious liberty may be briefly summarized. Most quarrels over doctrine, he held, are concerned with non-essentials and do not warrant the bitterness which they engender among Christians. Every phase of Christian theology is in serious dispute and men seek to persecute all those who do not agree with them. He detected that the basis of this attitude was a desire for supremacy on the part of each sect.[2] The logical extension of this view would lead to the complete extermination of all sects save one. We must, as followers of Christ, exercise forgiveness in viewing doctrinal dissent.[3]

Castellion likewise held that the difficulties in accurately

[1] The title of the Latin edition was *De haereticis an sint persequendi, et omino quo modo sit cum eis agendum, docterum vivorum tum veterum tum recentiorum sententiae.Liber hoc tam turbulento tempore per necessarius. Magdeburgi, per Georg. Rausch,* 1554, *Mense Martio.* Castellion was promptly accused of the authorship of the book, and denied any share in the compilation of the work. Calvin and Beza were deceived neither by the pseudonymity of the book nor by the false place of publication. They concluded that the book had been printed at Basle by an Italian refugee named Pietro Perna, and that it was the work of Castellion and the Italian Academicians. (Calvin, *Opera,* XV, 95–97, 134–136.) In the same year a French translation appeared at Rouen under the printer's name of Pierre Freneau. It seems probable that this edition was actually printed at Lyons by Castellion's brother. Castellion's close relationship with the Italian Academicians seems definitely established. (Ruffini, 75–77.) He "found great comfort" in his friendship with Socinus. (Lecky, *Rationalism in Europe,* II, 55–56.) He was a friend and translator of Ochino and the death of Castellion was solemnly observed by the Socinians of Poland. Calvin wrote to Bullinger in the month of its publication, "a book has just been clandestinely printed at Basel under false names, in which Castellio and Curio pretend to prove that heretics should not be repressed by the sword. Would that the pastors of that church at length, though late, aroused themselves to prevent the evil spreading further." (Calvin, *Opera,* XV, 96.) A few days later Beza wrote to Bullinger with regard to the book and expressed the opinion that it had really been printed at Basle, and that Castellion was the author: "he treats of the articles of faith as useless or indifferent, and puts the Bible on a parity with Aristotle." (*Ibid.,* XV, 97.)
[2] Castellion, *Traité des Hérétiques,* 15.
[3] "For certainly when I consider the ways of Christ, and his doctrine, ... for He has always pardoned iniquities and sin and has commanded we pardon them, even up to seven times seven. ... I do not know how we can retain the name of Christian if we do not follow Him in His clemency and forgiveness." (*Ibid.,* 17–18.)

determining and punishing heresy made persecution unthinkable. Persecution has spread as a sort of contagion as a consequence of the multiplicity of sects. Heresy is a matter of grave concern, but there are serious dangers in the present rage against it. Heresy is wholly spiritual in its nature and is therefore difficult to determine. It should be recalled that Christ Himself was punished unjustly in precisely this fashion.[1] Indeed, if an accused man is actually guilty of heresy, there is danger that he may be punished more severely than Christian discipline requires or permits.[2] The present age accounts as heretical any opinion which is not in agreement with our own. Actually, the word heretic occurs but once in the Bible,[3] and there refers to an obstinate man who persists in his error. Those who "obstinately hold to some vicious sect or opinion are properly called heretics."[4] The severest punishment permitted by the Bible for such offenders is rejection from the community of believers. Heresy relates to an opinion, and since an opinion may not be judged as easily as an action, we should be very slow in condemning men as heretics. He argued that the essential doctrines are set out with sufficient clarity by the Bible to prevent dissension. Thus all the Christian world agrees that Christ is the Son of God, but here agreement ends, "for concerning baptism, the Eucharist, adoration of saints, freewill, justification by faith, and many other questions, there is much argument and debate." His implication is plain. The only doctrine necessary for salvation is a belief in Christ as the Son of God. This attempt to narrow Christian dogma to a few incontrovertible essentials of faith, though not developed, is an interesting introduction to the more serious efforts of Acontius and Socinus to find a common rallying point for all Christians.

Finally, Castellion held that persecution represented a misapprehension of the essentially spiritual character of the Christian religion. The lives of Christ and His Apostles indicate that the more we know of truth the less likely we are to persecute

[1] Castellion, *Traité des Hérétiques*, 18–19. [2] *Ibid.*, 20.
[3] Titus, ii. 10–11. Compare the words of Christ, Matt. xviii. 15–17.
[4] Castellion, *Traité des Hérétiques*, 27.

our fellow men. If we govern ourselves by their example, we will be able to live together in peace and concord.[1] The strife and persecution which is rampant in Christendom prevents the effective propagation of the truth.[2] The fundamental truth of Christianity is to be found in the law of love. Men should examine their own lives and beliefs as critically as possible and treat those of other men with charity. He held that we have no other guide than the Gospels which give us the record and example of Christ's life.[3]

Castellion's defence of religious toleration was brilliant rather than systematic. His approach to the problem was that of the mystic rather than that of the layman who is impressed with the stupidity and illogical nature of persecution. His treatise was the reflection of the effect of persecution upon a sensitive spirit, and in this psychological reaction is to be found the reason for his stirring pleas against religious bigotry. The book gives the impression of having been written in the heat of a deep persuasion, rather than from a calm analysis of the complex motives underlying religious repression. Thus he failed to make his position clear on several important points, and passed over others in silence. Acontius, on the other hand, approached

---

[1] Castellion, *Traité des Hérétiques*, 30. [2] *Ibid.*, 30–31.

[3] Mr. Allen regards the assertion of the principle that we have no other guide than the Gospels and the record of Christ's life as verging towards scepticism. (Allen, *Political Thought*, 94.) In a sense, it is true, but this point of view must be regarded as the keystone of the entire Protestant system of theology and thought. The distinction between Castellion and the Protestant Reformers of his age lay in the fact that Castellion viewed the body of truth at the heart of religion as capable of several interpretations, all of which were probably valid for salvation; while the Reformers, employing the same body of truth, cast it into a systematic and unyielding mould according to their own interpretation. Nor does it appear that Mr. Allen is wholly correct in his assertion that Castellion says that there is no heresy (*Ibid.*, 94), which, if true, would place him among the sceptics. He plainly says that there is heresy, and that it is not a matter of inconsequence (Castellion, *Traité des Hérétiques*, 26–27, 18–19), but that the Christian religion does not permit brutal repression of stubborn error. He defines an heretic as an obstinate man who persists in his error. Then, following the Bible, he pointed out the two classes of heresy. (*Ibid.*, 26–27.) He did not deny the possibility or the fact of heresy, but he would limit its punishment to excommunication, and he sought to impress men with the great difficulty in accurately judging religious opinions.

the problem calmly and judiciously. His argument accumulates proof upon proof, his denunciation penetrates into the false motives and the warped psychology of the persecutors. His treatise is systematic—complete. Castellion is the Luther of the literature of toleration; Acontius the Calvin.

Acontius was one of the remarkable group of thinkers which was led by Castellion, and it is difficult to believe that he was not considerably affected by their teachings.[1] The *Satanae Stratagemata* cannot be justly appraised out of the intellectual setting in which the author had lived. The short time which he spent in Switzerland must be regarded as highly important in the formation of his views on the subject of toleration. His work may well be regarded as the greatest and most systematic of a considerable number of pleas for religious freedom which were induced by the lay point of view, the philosophical inclinations, and the highly spiritual religion of the Italian Academicians. The execution of Servetus was the inspiration which resulted in the crystallization of their views on religious liberty and the guilt of the punishment of error by temporal means.

b. *Acontius' Career in England*

Acontius finally left this circle when he proceeded from Strassburg to England in November 1559.[2] He was by no means an obscure man and soon secured an introduction to

---

[1] Beza likewise mentioned Clebergius as being a prominent supporter of Castellion's views. (Beza, *Vita Calvini* (no pagin.).) Unfortunately, his writings have been lost, and we know of his opinions only from the prejudiced pages of Beza. He appears to have objected to all forms of persecution, and to have based his arguments upon the interesting grounds of the absolute innocence of the heretic from error in case his belief were honest. (Compare Acontius, 215–216, 231.) He rested his teaching upon the impossibility of absolutely ascertaining religious truths. (Compare Acontius, 87–90, 21, 6, 10, 77.) This fact he held to be demonstrated by the continuance of religious controversy. The following quotation from Beza indicates the nature of his position. "De controversiis nondum certo constat; si enim constaret disputari defuisset. . . . Nonne Deus eos amabit qui id quod. Verum esse putant defenderint bona fide? Etiam so forte erraverint, nonne eis veniam dabit?" (Beza, *Vita Calvini*, 63, 95.)

[2] *Jewel to Martyr*, November 16, 1559, *Zurich Letters (First Series)*, XXIV; *Ibid.*, May 22, 1560, *Ibid.*, XXXIII.

the young Queen. Shortly afterwards he petitioned Elizabeth to grant him a patent of protection for numerous mechanical inventions.[1] He was not successful in his suit, but on February 27, 1560, he was granted an annuity of £60, probably on the basis of his engineering ability. On October 8, 1561, he was granted letters of naturalization.

He took a keen interest in English religious affairs and appears to have become a member of the Dutch Church in London shortly after his arrival. In 1559 the minister of his church, Hamsted, was excommunicated by Grindal for favouring certain Anabaptists in his congregation and for refusing to renounce their errors. Acontius intervened in the controversy as a champion of toleration for the Anabaptists. He appears to have been technically excommunicated by Grindal in 1562 as a result of his share in the affair. Hamsted soon retracted his views, but Acontius refused to withdraw his opinions and urged that those doctrines which are not essential to salvation should not be imposed upon Christians.[2]

It is a fine tribute to the moderate and secular policy of the Queen that his espousal of the cause of a proscribed sect and his avowal of the principle of toleration in no way affected his relations with the Government. His annuity appears to have been continued until his death. In 1563 he undertook to drain and embank about two thousand acres of lowlands in the Thames Valley.[3] An Act of Parliament of the same year

[1] *S.P. Dom. Eliz.* (*Add.*), ix, 39, December ?, 1559. *Jacobus Acontius to the Queen.* Nothing is more honest than that those who by searching have found out things useful to the public should have some fruit of their rights and labours, as meanwhile they abandon all other modes of gain, and are at much expense in experiments, and often sustain much loss, as has happened to me. I have discovered most useful things, new kinds of wheel machines, and of furnaces for dyers and brewers, which when known will be used without my consent, except there be a penalty, and I, poor with expenses and labour, shall have no returns. Therefore, I beg a prohibition against using any wheel machines, either for grinding or bruising or any furnaces like mine, without my consent. (Latin.)
[2] Hessels, J. H., *Eccl. Lond.*, II, 224 ff.
[3] *S.P. Dom. Eliz.* (*Add.*), xi, 99, May ?, 1563. *Petition of Jacobo Aconty to the Queen.* The Thames has so overflowed as to inundate lands near Erith. He understands the means of preventing serious damage therefrom. But when land has many owners, they will rarely combine to bear the expense, unless someone will assume the risk. He cannot do it alone, but

awarded him one-half of all lands which he should be able to recover within a period of three years. On June 24, 1563, a licence was granted to him enabling him to take up workmen to amend the Plumstead Marshes.[1] He and his company appear to have recovered a tract of six hundred acres by January 8, 1566, but a portion of the gain was soon lost to the river. Acontius entered into an agreement with other enterprising spirits to attempt further efforts. Among these men was G. B. Castiglione, who was to be his literary executor.

c. Minor Writings

Acontius enjoyed the friendship and patronage of the Earl of Leicester, to whom he dedicated his manuscript work on the *Use and Study of History* in 1564.[2] He appears to have been defending himself on a charge of Sabellianism in 1566. He probably died in the same year,[3] leaving several treatises and poems unfinished. His papers were left in the custody of Castiglione, who published in 1580 his *Una Essortatione al timor di Dio*, with a dedication to the Queen.

A clearer understanding of Acontius' analysis of the problem of heresy and its treatment will follow a brief survey of his first literary work, *De Methodo, hoc est, de Recta investigandarum tradendarumque scientiarum ratione*, which appeared at Basle in 1558.[4] Bonet-Maury and Bayle have paid high tribute to the method for the investigation of scientific and philosophical questions which is here delineated.[5]

According to Acontius, method is the means by which we study the sciences. The first condition of a correct method is

has friends who will help. Suggests that Henry VIII offered half the land near the Tower to anyone who could reclaim it. (Latin.) (The licence for amending the Plumstead Marshes was allowed June 24, 1563.) See also Ruffini, *Religious Liberty*, 82.   [1] *Ibid.*, 83.

[2] *S.P. Dom. Eliz.*, xxiv, 53, August ?, 1564. MS. treatise in Italian on the *Use and Study of History* by Giacopo Acontio. (32 pp.)

[3] *D.N.B.*, I, 64; *Nouv. Biog. Gén.*, I, 197. Deslandes gives the date of his death as 1567. (Deslandes, M., *Histoire Critique de la Philosophie*.)

[4] There are copies of this edition in the B.M., Berlin Public Library, Göttingen, Königsberg, Bibl. Natl., Vienna Public Library.

[5] Bonet-Maury, G., *Des Origines du Christ. Unitaire Chez les Anglais*, 196–197; Bayle, *Dict. Hist. et Crit.*, Art. "Acontius."

to attain a just spirit in order to distinguish between the true and false. One's judgment should be checked by a comparison with "*summorum hominum*." The source of method is to be found in the science of mathematics. We are especially struck by his principle that correct method seeks to determine a small number of principles; which should be clearly defined. This view was carried over into his examination of the variety and complexity of Christian dogmas, and his scientific and practical intelligence turned naturally to an attempt to simplify those doctrines into a few fundamental and incontrovertible tenets of faith.

Method consists both in the search for truth and in the exposition of truth. We should seek first to learn those things which are best known, passing from this step to those things which are less clearly evident.[1] We should likewise proceed from the singular principles to the general.[2] When all of the characteristics of a thing have been determined, we may proceed to a division of it into all of its parts.[3]

The logical, systematic, and fearless approach of Acontius to the complicated and delicate problems of persecution and toleration was like a breath of fresh air in the damp chambers of sixteenth-century theological debate. He cut across the empty formulae of discussion and erected a logical and philosophical defence of toleration on the basis of the absence of sufficient guilt on the part of the heretic to warrant persecution. He did for this question the service that Machiavelli had done for politics, though the minds and points of view of the two men were essentially dissimilar.

d. *The Psychology of Persecution*

Acontius sought to analyse and explain the psychology which underlies all religious persecution and his contribution in this regard has probably never been equalled. Satan, always anxious to promote violence and discord among men, finds religion the easiest way to accomplish his ends. The root of the evil is to be found in the mind of man. The devil's stratagems have only one end in view, the turning of men from

---

[1] Acontius, *De Methodo*, 40.   [2] *Ibid.*, 48–49.   [3] *Ibid.*, 50–56.

"whatever may prove conducive to their salvation."[1] Salvation depends upon our lending obedience to God, and Satan seeks to turn men from that high obedience.[2]

In order to achieve the undoing of man, Satan takes advantage of certain psychological weaknesses in his character. Acontius then proceeded to an examination of those weaknesses. In the first place, man loves himself immeasurably and esteems himself as a kind of deity.[3] Directly he has attained a little dignity or has scraped together a parcel of earth he feels that everyone should lend him all respect. Indeed, so presumptuous is man that he shapes his conception of God to fit his idea of what God ought to be. Man is naturally jealous of the profit and benefit of another, and seeks in every possible way to hinder the attainment of those benefits by another.[4] As a consequence of this selfish and arrogant nature of man, "if he is resisted ever so slightly, he is exceedingly prone to anger." All sorts of "bloody vengeance" then ensue.[5] "Et pour le couper court, la nature de l'homme . . . est bien peu dissemblable de l'impure et ordre nature des Diables."[6] This evil disposition is, of course, relative among men, but it is present to a degree among all men. Custom and study are able either to induce a man towards these vices or to draw him away from them.[7]

Acontius, like Machiavelli, based his view of persecution upon a very low opinion of human nature. But the spectacle of persecution, bloodshed and repression which Europe presented to him as a result of the attempt to extirpate religious dissension almost justified his position. Acontius' analysis of the motives underlying persecution rests squarely upon this psychological basis.

The disposition in man to persecute his fellow men for holding views contrary to his own may be said to arise chiefly from a species of intellectual arrogance. Arrogance is especially instrumental in bringing about bitter disputes when it is accompanied "by riches, offices, great benefices, great reputa-

---

[1] ". . . de le desbaucher de tout ce qui peut profiter et seruir à son salut." (Acontius, *Les Ruzes de Satan*, 1.) [2] *Ibid.*
[3] ". . . il s'estime cõme Dieu." (*Ibid.*, 2.) [4] *Ibid.*, 4.
[5] *Ibid.* [6] *Ibid.* [7] *Ibid.*, 4-5.

tion, and the like."[1] An arrogant man does not deign to hear his opponent through. He believes that he can reduce him with a word.[2] "Yes, rather with one laugh, one wry look, one gesture or other, thou wilt imagine thou hast abundantly confuted him. . . ."[3] If your opponent has the effrontery not to be convinced, you will regard him as guilty at least of treason: "Car d'autant plus que quelqu'vn est en authorité, et qu'il parle de plus haut degré, il estime qu'il en doit estre tenu plus sage, tellement qu'il veut que son authorité soit recue pour raison."[4] The author astutely observed that wisdom is not necessarily the attribute either of wealth or of authority.

Arrogance is especially heightened when a man believes that he has full possession of the truth:[5] "puis si on s'estime auoir fait suffisante preuue et comme chef d'œuure de sagesse et iugement. . . ."[6] This often befalls those who always or usually emerge triumphant from disputations and those who frequently speak in public.[7] This intellectual arrogance should be tempered by the knowledge that error is the most prevalent evil in the world, and, at the same time, the most difficult to detect, especially in one's self.[8] A man always regards himself as the exception to all rules. Truth may be ascertained only by the exercise of patience and as a result of careful enquiry. But men are prone to form opinions hastily and with very little reflection. Men arrive at their convictions in this casual fashion yet presume that they are direct from God.[9]

Acontius regarded the clergy, for whom he had very little

---

[1] Acontius, *Les Ruzes de Satan*, 68. The English version of 1648 includes also "magistracy" as contributing to an arrogant attitude in spiritual controversies. (57.) In this it follows the Latin text, "Hosce autem spiritus addunt saepe opes, magistratus, ampla sacerdotia, nominis celebritas, atque alia id genus."

[2] Et si de telle fantasie ton esprit est vne fois ensorcelé, tu ne bailleras à homme viuant le loisir de prononcer vne sentence entierement. Tu estimeras qu'auant qu'il ouure la bouche, tu entends tout ce qu'il veut dire, et te semble qu'en vn mot: en vn mot? (*Ibid.*, 68.)   [3] *Ibid.*   [4] *Ibid.*

[5] *Ibid.*, 11.   [6] *Ibid.*, 12.   [7] *Ibid.*   [8] *Ibid.*, 68.

[9] He pointed out that human beings dislike admitting defeat, and will in consequence actually contend against the truth after their error has been demonstrated. (*Ibid.*, 64–65.) As a matter of fact, men are as quick to applaud the vanquished who admit their mistake as the victor. (*Ibid.*, 65.) One party must be in the wrong in every argument.

respect, as pre-eminently guilty of the intellectual arrogance that leads directly to the persecution of dissenting views. In fact, this presumption is so characteristic of the group that few men dare contradict them.[1] When diversity exists in a country the ministry presumes that its position is threatened and seeks to engender hatred and bitterness. Satan prompts and encourages these discords. His aim is to enlarge a debate into general dissension, "to inflame men's minds, to rend the church into sects . . . in a word, he aims at nothing but mighty combustions and dissensions."[2] Satan's strategy is especially forwarded when the magistrates consider it their duty to carry out the whims of the jealous and embittered clergy in the suppression of views contrary to their own.[3]

Persecution may be said to result essentially because men violently resent being contradicted. A man is astounded, when he has advanced an opinion, to find that other men do not immediately concur. Experience demonstrates that when a man is convinced he has rational support for a belief "he is astonished that it is possible to find a man in the world who is not able to see eye to eye with him, and unless at the first blow his adversary does not throw down his arms," as if it were obvious that he had refused assent out of sheer obstinacy, he grows angry.[4] Thus persecution proceeds from anger and from what we presume to be the perverse obstinacy of our opponents.[5] Satan works directly from this mental state. If the error of our opponent is a real one, Satan will first attempt to make the heresy attractive to us. That failing, he approaches from another tack. "What wickedness," he will say, "this man deserves to be engulfed in an abyss, that dares utter such words; he is a man worthy of consumption by the fire from heaven. . . ."[6]

[1] Acontius, *Les Ruzes de Satan*, 12–13. [2] *Ibid.*, 67.
[3] *Ibid.*, 236. [4] *Ibid.*, 13. [5] *Ibid.*
[6] "H'a meschāt (dira-il) homme digne d'estre englouty aux abysmes, quel parolle t'est eschappée? homme digne sur lequel le feu descende pour estre consumé. . . ." (*Ibid.*, 40–41.)

e. The Evils of Persecution

After establishing the psychological basis from which religious persecution proceeds, Acontius endeavoured to demonstrate that persecution was psychologically wrong. Error cannot be overcome in the heat of passion; in fact, error is the more deeply implanted by anger.[1] The more heated the mind becomes, the more difficult it will be to convince an opponent by reason and equity.[2] When a discussion is conducted in anger, the man who is in error not only clings frantically to his reasoned views, but will defend his position with such foolish and inept "reason as rashness and a maddened mind could collect. . . ."[3] Hence, such discussions, even if undertaken to defeat the designs of the devil, actually assist him in the attainment of his purposes. "For they do not destroy errors, but make them invincible; they do not pluck them up, but they propagate them; they do not destroy them, but they multiply them in great abundance."[4]

Inevitably such a state of mind results in the threat of force to accomplish the overthrow of the error. Such a gesture convinces the man who is in error that his opponent does not find his own position defensible in reason and he is in consequence the more deeply convinced of the verity of his own belief. Such bitter contention can only result in brawls and in the dissipation of Christian unity into countless sectarian groups. He urged nobly that some "will as much disapprove of the means used to resist error . . . as of the error itself." Men are driven by the fury of religious contention to abandon all faith and hope in religion.[5] The comparative importance of doctrines is distorted, and all perspective is destroyed. It is a sad commentary upon Christendom that the Gospel had almost mastered the world when its advance was dissipated by contentions and disputes.[6] Little by little the Christian gains of the past are slipping away.[7]

This keen and clear analysis of the psychology of persecution cut through the tendons of the outworn theological justification

---

[1] Acontius, *Les Ruzes de Satan*, 13–14. [2] *Ibid.*, 14. [3] *Ibid.*
[4] *Ibid.*, 14–15. [5] *Ibid.*, 17. [6] *Ibid.*, 19. [7] *Ibid.*

of religious repression as with the sharp knife of the spiritual surgeon. The Church of the Middle Ages could advance a logical basis for its persecution because it could demonstrate a real spiritual and social Catholicity. The Protestant Reformation, by its very nature and by the central dogma of the right of private judgment, rendered the logical adoption of the Roman Catholic theory impossible. Acontius laid bare the ugly impulses which motivate persecution. He displayed in convincing style that persecution rendered impossible the very remedies which it proposed to introduce. He made use of that highly utilitarian character, Satan, to bear the onus of these disagreeable traits of the human mind. But his Satan was a thinly disguised symbol for the arrogance of the human mind. Indeed, he detected much in the psychology of the clerics which would identify that group with the Angel of Darkness. There was very little superstition and almost no employment of outworn terms in his analysis; it moved forwards to an inevitable conclusion with that precision which the *De Methodo* had sketched as proper to correct philosophical and scientific discussion.

f. The Attack on the Doctrine of Exclusive Salvation to 1600: Renaissance Philosophical Thought; Zwingli; Castellion; Acontius; the Early Arminians

One of the greatest contributions of the *Satanae Stratagemata* to the development of the theory of religious toleration was the denial that absolute truth could be attained by any doctrinal system, and the view that truth may be only relatively ascertained. It followed that Acontius by his relativism weakened the doctrine of exclusive salvation, which must reside at the heart of any persecuting system. Lecky has brilliantly reflected upon the vital connection between the doctrine of exclusive salvation and the Roman Catholic theory of persecution.[1] This doctrine, as moulded by orthodox hands, had been in the early period of ecclesiastical development the principal weapon for quieting controversy and bringing order out of dogmatic and administrative chaos. It may be said to have been finally crystallized by S. Thomas Aquinas. The reformers retained

[1] Lecky, *Rationalism in Europe*, I, 379 ff.

the doctrine of exclusive salvation and in turn utilized it as the central pillar of their system for enforcing uniformity of belief. Tulloch has well complained that this readaptation of the Catholic doctrine was highly responsible, not only for intolerance, but for the extinction of the original spirit of free enquiry; the increasing bitterness of reformation controversy; and the consequent impossibility of the various Protestant groups effecting a united resistance to the Counter-Reformation. In some form or other the doctrine is stated in almost all of the Protestant creeds.[1]

It will be well at this point to trace the growth of opposition to the notion of exclusive salvation, and to indicate the place which Acontius holds in the development of the conception of dogmatic relativism. Only a small group of thinkers had advanced to the point of relativism before 1600. A denial of the doctrine of exclusive salvation implies that the truth essential to salvation is not as easily ascertained in the absolute sense as the Dogmatists contended. The denial of the doctrine is likewise apt to be associated with the view that salvation proceeds from a direct spiritual union of God and man which may or may not occur within the prescribed limits of creed, i.e. a denial of the assumption that faith can be fettered by the rigid formulae of dogma. Such a view will, sooner or later,

[1] *A.* The Lutheran Confession (Arts. vii, viii) clearly implies this view of the Church. Luther repeatedly emphasized the teaching, especially in the *Catech. Majori*, Part II, art. iii, ed. Recheub, 503.

B. The Scotch *Confession of 1560* stated the opinion very specifically, "Estra hanc ecclesiam nulla est vita. Nulla aeterna faelicitas, iaciro plane ex diametro abhorremus ab eorum blasphemiis, qui asserunt, cujusvis sectae, aut religionis professores fore salvos, modo vitae suae actiones ad justitiae et aequetates normam conformaverint. . . ."

C. The Belgic *Confession of 1561*, Art. 28, says, "We believe, since this holy congregation is an assemblage of those who are saved, and out of it there is no salvation. . . ."

D. Chapter XXV of the *Westminster Confession* states the view with typical Calvinist rigidity.

E. The Anglican Confession is not clear on the point. One is tempted to believe that the assertion of the point was consciously avoided. The Athanasian Creed was given a high place in the formularies of the Church during the sixteenth century, and most of the clergy appear to have asserted the doctrine of exclusive salvation. But it is not to be found in the Thirty-Nine Articles.

lead to a relative attitude towards religion and the holder will be disposed to tolerate the convictions of other men if they appear to be serious and genuine. Emphasis will be placed upon the validity of private judgment, and formal devotion to creed forms will be criticized.

This development may be observed in an uncritical form in certain aspects of Renaissance thought. Thus Boccaccio's famous story of the "Three Rings" contrasted the three great religions in a philosophical and tolerant spirit which completely excluded sentiments of bigotry.[1] Boccaccio, in opening the story, made a half apologetic aside for the benefit of the orthodox: ". . . as enough has been said concerning God and the truth of our religion, it will not be amiss if we descend to the actions of men."[2] The dialogue was put in the mouths of Saladin and the rich Alexandrian Jew, Melchizedeck.[3]

To Saladin's question of which of the three great religions was the true one, the wise Jew answered by a parable. A very rich man had among his treasures a ring of great rarity. In order to keep the ring in his family he willed that the son whom he should favour with the ring should likewise inherit his house and all of his possessions. This was done for several generations until a father and heir of the family found himself with three sons "all virtuous and dutiful to their Father, and all equally beloved by him."[4] The three sons, all of whom were aware of the priceless value of the ring, began, each in turn, to entreat the Father for the ring. The Father, loving all alike, thereupon ordered an artist to prepare two rings exactly like the genuine one. He secretly gave a ring to each son and upon his death all three produced a ring. They immediately fell into a violent dispute about the authenticity of the rings and the disposition of their Father's possessions and "no man could distinguish the true ring." They went to court in great bitterness and the question has not yet been decided.

[1] Owen's comments on the story in relation to religious toleration are valuable. (Owen, J., *Skeptics of the Italian Renaissance*, 29.)
[2] Boccaccio, *The Decameron*, Kelly ed., 27.
[3] It is significant of Renaissance breadth of view that Saladin was taken by many writers as the finest example of the feudal ideals of chivalry and honour.　　　　　[4] Boccaccio, *The Decameron*, 28.

"And thus," the Jew concluded, "it has happened . . . with regard to the three laws given by God the Father, concerning which you proposed your question: everyone believes he is the true heir of God, has his Law, and obeys his Commandments; but which is in the right is uncertain, in like manner as the rings."[1]

It would be difficult to find a more subtle and forceful denial of the claims of the Church to the totality of religious truth. God has given the world three great religions because He loves mankind equally well. Only God knows which is the true religion, and, indeed, the implication is that they are all sufficiently true for human needs. The bitterness and the contentions which characterize religious discussion arise from bigotry and jealousy. Every man considers his belief to be the true one, but truth is not so easily ascertainable.

At the close of the High Renaissance, Luigi Pulci (*c.* 1431 to *c.* 1487) in the *Morgante Maggiore* gave expression to much the same point of view. The imaginary world which formed the canvas of the epic was divided between the Christian and Mohammedan camps. The medieval and orthodox technique would have been to have made the Christians victorious in the great battle, and in the end to have staged a reconciliation crowned by the conversion and baptism of the infidels—the battle being the test, apparently, of the relative truths of the two faiths. Pulci burlesques the traditional treatment. The appeals to God, Christ, Mary, and a large assortment of saints which preface every canto testify to the author's disgust with the current conceptions of the exclusive merits of Christianity. The faith of the infidels collapses in the middle of the battle and they are baptized on the spot. Pulci confesses quite as clearly as Boccaccio that he believed in the relative merits of all religions.[2] In similar fashion Galeottus Martius held that any man who walked uprightly and who followed the dictates of the law which was born within him would attain Heaven without respect to his particular nation or religion.[3]

[1] Boccaccio, *The Decameron*, 28.   [2] Pulci, *Morgante Maggiore*, xxv, 276 ff.
[3] Martius was saved from the Inquisition by his former pupil, Sixtus IV.

The relativism of the Renaissance, however, must be related to scepticism rather than to a tolerant view of religion. The sceptic views all religions objectively because he is deeply attached to none. Scepticism has great value as a dissolvent of the bonds of authority, but it has no constructive contribution to make towards a philosophy of religious toleration.[1] It is far more difficult to view other faiths with a generous and tolerant spirit when one is genuinely attached to a particular creed. We must regard as considerably more important, therefore, any evidences of relativism among men who were themselves religious in character, and who were members of a particular faith.

Zwingli was unique among the great reformers in clearly denying the principle of "*extra ecclesiam nulla salus*." In the *Articuli sive conclusiones, LXVII*, of 1523, he criticized the emphasis upon the saving character of the Church and its doctrines to the exclusion of the Gospels which contain everything essential to salvation. "All who say that the Gospel is nothing without the approbation of the Church, err, and cast reproach on God."[2] He went further and expressed the view that the essential requirement of belief necessary for salvation is to be found in "the sum of the Gospel" which "is that our Lord Jesus Christ, the true Son of God, has made known to us the will of his Heavenly Father, and redeemed us by his innocence from eternal death, and reconciled us to God."[3] The teachings of Christianity may be reduced to the belief that "Christ is the only way to salvation, for all those who were,

---

[1] Belasco, *Authority in Church and State*, 23.
[2] Zwingli, *Articuli sive conclusiones*, LXVII. "Alle, so Redend, das Euangelium sye nüt on die beuernus der kirchen, irrend und schmädend gott." (*Sämtliche Werke*, I, 458.) (Quicunque Evangelion nihil esse dicunt, nisi ecclesiae calculus et adprobatio accedat, errant et deum blasphemant. Niemeyer, *Collectio*, 1.)
[3] *Ibid.*, II. "[Die] Summe des Evangelium ist, das unser Herr Christus [Jesus] wahrer Gottessohn, uns den willen seines himmelischen Vaters Kind gethan, und uns mit seines Unschuld vom Tode erloset und gott versöhnet hat." (Summa des euangelions ist, das unser herr Christus Jhesus, warer gottes sun, uns den willen sines himmlischen vatters kundt gethon unnd mit siner unschuld vom Tod erlöst und gott versunthat. *Werke*, I, 458; Niemeyer, *Collectio*, 1.)

who are, and who shall be."[1] Zwingli held that salvation might be found only in the belief in the Gospels;[2] he said nothing about the necessity for attaining that belief within the communion of the Church.

The *Articles*, as well as the subsequent *Ten Theses* of Berne (1526), laid emphasis upon the sufficiency of adherence to the truths of the Gospels and faith in Christ for salvation.[3] Even more striking were his views as expressed in the *Expositio Chr. Fidei* addressed to Francis I.[4] He warmly contended, toward the close of the address, that God has His elect among the Gentiles as well as among the Jews. Zwingli, in a tone that is strangely reminiscent of the days of Pico and Ficino, said that he expected to find in heaven the saints of the Old Testament from Adam to John the Baptist. Even more tolerant was his view that good and faithful men of all races (and we

[1] *Articuli sive conclusiones*, III. "Daher ist Christus der alleinige Weg zur Seligkeit aller, die Waren, sind, und sein werden." (Danneher der einig weg zur säligkeit Christus ist aller, die ie warend, sind und werdend. *Werke*, I, 458; Niemeyer, *Collectio*, 1.)

[2] "Denn in dem Glauben an daselbe steht unser Heil, und im Unglauben daran unsere Verdammniss, denn alle Wahrheit ist klar in ihm." (*Articuli sive conclusiones*, XV.) (Dann in dess glouben stat unser heyl, und unglouben unser verdamnus; dann alle warheit ist clar in im. *Werke*, I, 459; Niemeyer, *Collectio*, 4.)

[3] Vide Theses I, III, IV of the *Theses Bernenses*, Niemeyer, *Collectio*, 14–15.

[4] The work was written in 1531 at the request of Maigret, the French Ambassador in Switzerland. The work was published by Bullinger with an enthusiastic preface in 1536. (Niemeyer, 36.) Somewhat later (exact date uncertain) Leo Judae published a free German translation from Zurich. Niemeyer, in his *Collectio*, gives what is probably the most accurate text now extant. "Deinde sperandum est tibi visurum esse sanctorum, prudentium, fidelium, constantium, fortium, virtuosorum omnium, quicunque a condito mundo fuerunt, sodalitatem, coetum et contubernium. Hic duos Adam, redemptum ac Redemptorem; hic Abelum, Enochum, Noam, Abrahamum . . . Baptistam, Petrum, Paulum; hic Herculem, Theseum, Socratem, Aristidem, Antigonum, Numam, Camillum, Catones, Scipiones; hic Ludovichum pium antecessoresque tuos Ludovicos, Philippos, Pipinnos, et quotquot in fide hinc migrarunt maiores tuos videbis. Et summatim, non fuit vir bonus, non erit mens sancta, non est fidelis anima, ab ipso mundi exordio usque ad eius consummationem, quem non sis isthic cum deo Visurus." (Niemeyer, *Collectio*, 61–62.) (Compare text in Schaff, *Creeds of Christendom*.) This is not, as has been held, an isolated and perhaps propagandist statement for the consumption of the humanistic French king. See Zwingli's *Commentaries*, and especially the whole of his *Tract on Providence*.

might add of all creeds) will be saved by a merciful God from the beginning to the end of time. This noble and tolerant view was regarded as a dangerous heresy by Zwingli's contemporaries; for in this period the Catholic, Calvinist, and Lutheran damned each other with abandon, while the heathen were totally assigned to perdition by common agreement. So long as Christians adhered to the doctrine of exclusive salvation, it was necessary for the peace of mankind that their religious tenets should consist of absolutely ascertainable doctrinal truths; and in order to be so certain of truth, it was necessary to suppress all adverse views—if one were powerful enough so to do.[1] The triumph of Zwingli's relativism would inevitably mean the relaxation of the bonds of ecclesiastical discipline and the growth of a spirit of enquiry within the Church. In such a medium alone could an objective and religious theory of toleration develop.

Zwingli's views failed to exert an appreciable influence upon the development of the Protestant theory of the Church. The reformers, while exercising the right of private judgment for themselves, refused that right from the necessity of solidarity to members of their own communion. Protestantism under the unrelieved pressure of Catholicism was forced almost immediately to harden its doctrinal position into an exclusive system. However, the continued dissipation of the Protestant body into an ever-increasing number of sects had inevitably to convince thinking men that the Protestant claims to exclusive truth were not demonstrated by the facts of the case. As in England, the very fact of repeated sectarian dissensions weakened the vitality of the theory of uniformity and impelled men to a more spiritual and tolerant view of religion.

Castellion touched only indirectly upon this important question. He noted that Christendom had been split into numerous sects and that each considered the other as heretical.[2] He observed that there had become as many truths as there are sects. In the *Contra libellum Calvini*[3] he criticized Calvin

[1] Lecky, *History of Rationalism*, I, 395–396.
[2] Castellion, *Traité des Hérétiques*, 25.
[3] The work was written in 1554. Castellion was unable to secure its publication, and it remained in manuscript until 1612.

for having asserted the right of private judgment for himself and for his bigoted denial of that right to other men.[1] Calvin, he held, regarded his particular sect as the true one, but all the other sects have made the same assertion. Calvin and the other reformers have asserted that the truth of their doctrines is made manifest by the Bible. But, he enquired, if this is true, why has Calvin written so many books to prove an obvious fact?[2] This 'truth' has not been self-evident to the 'heretics' who died for opposing it.[3]

Acontius further developed the criticism of the doctrine of exclusive salvation and his work in this connection, especially when considered with his attempt to reduce Christian doctrines to the smallest possible number of truths, ranks first among the thinkers who displayed this tolerant tendency in the sixteenth century. Acontius had little reverence for creed and little respect for the bigotry which the clergy displayed in formulating and enforcing their doctrinal tenets.

The multiplicity of sects and creeds has caused many men to cast aside all care for religion since they despair of finding truth.[4] He regarded with extreme disfavour the insistence of the various religious groups upon their monopoly of truth. No one would deny that truth ought not to be opposed, but the carrying out of that assumption involves great difficulty: "For if one has once drunk down some abuse, he cannot consider it as anything but true, and that anyone who differs from him is in error," and that his view must be opposed.[5]

It is true that men are always found in the light of either truth or error; "or nous n'entendons pas que iamais il y ait tāt de lumiere, qu'il ne reste quelque petite nué d'erreurs."[6] But men and nations cannot hope to attain the fullness of truth. Always a haze of darkness hangs about. In addition, seducers are always at hand to lead men from the truth. These seducers can be opposed only by reason or by authority,[7] and Acontius lent the entire weight of his argument to the side of reason.

Religious truth, he would say, can never be fully ascertained.

[1] Castellion, *Contra libellum Calvini*, Pref.   [2] *Ibid.*, H.
[3] *Ibid.*, H. ff.   [4] Acontius, *Les Ruzes des Satan*, 76.
[5] *Ibid.*, 21.   [6] *Ibid.*, 6.   [7] *Ibid.*, 10.

Men have made a complex problem and an arid science of the simple teachings of Christ. He was moved, therefore, to attempt to strip Christianity of the manifold accretions of doctrinal 'truth' and to reduce it to its simplest possible terms. We shall be deeply interested in that attempt.[1]

Before continuing with the discussion of Acontius' views on religious toleration, it will be well to conclude the examination of the development of opposition to the doctrine of exclusive salvation to the close of the sixteenth century. The weakening of that doctrine was to play a highly important rôle in the dissipation of the philosophy which underlies a persecuting religious system. The Rationalism of which Acontius was the first considerable exponent in England was in the seventeenth century to attain important proportions and was in the following century to attain mastery. Following Acontius, the next important exposition of opposition to the doctrine of exclusive salvation appeared in Holland and it is certain that the Dutch thinkers of the period were considerably influenced by the teachings of Acontius.

The revolt of the Arminians in Holland against the rigid absolutism of Calvinism was inspired by much the same sentiments as those which Acontius had dwelt upon. The exactness and rigidity of Calvinism left little room for the free play of thought.[2] The keystone of the system was absolute predestination which Calvin alone, among all Christian thinkers, had dared to pursue to its logical conclusion. Against the presumption of Calvinism purely intellectual logic was of no avail.[3] The Dutch brand of Calvinism was an accurate replica of the Genevan model. However, the very rigidity of the system repelled many minds "more Christian than logical" and led to a revolt which found its academic ground in a denunciation of the doctrine of predestination, and which was characterized by a noble defence of religious liberty.[4] We have already had

[1] Cf. *post*, 334–342.
[2] Tulloch, *Rational Theology*, I, 8.
[3] Giran, E., *Sébastien Castellion*, 483.
[4] The Arminians and the Remonstrants were undoubtedly acquainted with the works of Castellion, and were probably influenced to some extent by Acontius. A Dutch translation of the *Satanae Stratagemata* appeared as

occasion to refer to the Arminian controversy in its relation to the important tendency to narrow and simplify dogma, and we shall endeavour to separate, in so far as possible, that development from the denial of the possibility of proclaiming and enforcing a system of absolute truth.[1]

Coornhert declared himself flatly opposed to all compulsory confessions of faith and sought to assume an objective and philosophical position outside the pretensions of any sect. He held that the Calvinists had ignored the intensely personal and spiritual character of Christianity which may be attained only through faith, which he defined as the soul's free acceptance of the Living Word of God.[2] All creeds, save as they embody this conception, he held to be of value only as they prepare the heart for the entrance of faith. Thus all systems of dogma have but partial validity, and should be regarded merely as directing the soul to salvation. The Church has been torn by controversies over creeds, having incorrectly ascribed to them an internal virtue in attaining salvation. Man is, when saved, bound to God by ties which transcend the empty letter of the creed. He especially criticized Calvin and Luther for having presumed to claim exclusive truth for their respective systems of theology. The harshness engendered by their attempts to enforce a system of thought upon other men has only served to militate against the formation of the true Church.[3]

In 1582 Coornhert's valuable *Critique* of the *Belgic Confession of Faith* appeared. He criticized both the emphasis on predestination and the intolerance of a creed which persecuted those who ventured to question it "in so inhumane a manner,

---

early as 1611, and a Latin edition was published in Holland in 1631. In the next generation no less than five editions of the work appeared in Holland. Giran (488–489) probably overstates the influence of Castellion on the Dutch groups. Their position was evidently an adaptation to the requirements of a particular situation. Their arguments for toleration resemble those of Castellion, but, after all, the arguments for religious liberty may be reduced to a few general principles—all of which Castellion had touched upon, and which were to be implanted in men's minds only by constant reiteration until, finally, we have come to accept them as axiomatic.

[1] Cf. *ante*, 124–125.
[2] Coornhert, D. V., *Wercken*, III, 413–427; I, 1 ff.
[3] Jones, R. M., *Spiritual Reformers*, 112.

that the people's patience was exhausted by their bloody tyranny."[1] The introduction of an exclusive Catechism was branded as a forcing of conscience and a "poisoning of the minds of youth" which was "more pernicious than that of a hostile invasion, or setting a town on fire."[2] In his Preface to the *Abridged Critique* he posed the most forceful argument that had yet appeared against the doctrine of predestination.[3] He pointed out the emphasis which Calvin and Beza had placed on the doctrine as an article of faith essential to salvation.[4] He denied that the doctrine had anything to do with salvation which is attained by seeking life in God and through the invitation of Christ.[5] Coornhert regarded the consideration of doctrinal intricacies as a profitless dispute about matters which were known only to God.

Similarly, C. P. de Hooft, the Burgomaster of Amsterdam and a member of the Arminian group, attacked the doctrine of exclusive salvation on the grounds that each group held that it enjoyed absolute truth and on this basis sought to persecute all who differed from it.[6]

From this position Arminius and Episcopius proceeded to a further denunciation of the doctrine of exclusive truth and a denial that any dogmatic system should or could be enforced upon the Church. Their contribution in this connection will

---

[1] Brandt, G., *History of the Reformation . . . in . . . the Low Countries*, I, 393.
[2] *Ibid.*
[3] Buisson has pointed out the importance of the Preface as an agency for the expression of controversial opinions in this period. (Buisson, *Sébastien Castellion*, I, 301.) In a period filled with ideas and disputes about ideas, and when no periodical Press was in existence to serve as a vehicle of opinion, the writer aired his feelings in his Preface. It is to be recalled that Castellion's Preface to his translation of the Bible, which contained the gist of his theory of toleration, exercised in at least six countries a profound influence, while his actual treatise on the subject had a small circulation.
[4] *Abridged Critique.* (Coornhert, *Wercken*, III.)   [5] *Ibid.*
[6] This great figure should be studied thoroughly. His speeches were eloquent pleas against religious bigotry and intolerance. See especially his *Speech to the Magistrates of Amsterdam*, 1598. (Brandt, I, 468–473.) *Memorial to the Magistrates of Amsterdam* (1596) against persecution. (*Ibid.*, 463–468.) *Discourse on the Conduct and Designs of some of the Clergy*, 1611. *Speech to the Council in 1615 on the Differences about Matters of Religion.* (*Ibid.*, II, 149–151.)

be considered in the survey of the literature of toleration in the seventeenth century.

g. The Attempt to Simplify the Essential Doctrines

Closely connected with Acontius' denial of the possibility of attaining a doctrinal system which embodied absolute truth, was his effort to simplify the body of truth which must be received in order to attain salvation. In other words, he endeavoured to set forth a common ground upon which Christians might meet in unanimity of belief. The chief danger in religious discussion is found in the fact that there are few people who, when in an argument, will seek to express themselves simply and clearly. Most men prefer to appear as speakers or writers, rather than as mediators.[1] But we must seek for a common ground on which we can meet our opponents. Thus it is of no avail to quote Origen to a man who has no regard for the Father, or to quote the Bible to a Turk.[2] This remarkable rationalism can scarcely be duplicated in the sixteenth century. Acontius detected the difficulty which is involved in all theological discussion. Men base their religious views upon doctrines which they conceive as having been directly revealed by God and which cannot, therefore, be assailed by rational means. As William James observed, reason is not a sufficient instrument for denying faith. Reason cannot claim the ability to penetrate into the immediacy of a contact between man and God. Thus when, for example, the Calvinist and the Lutheran are in dispute with regard to the doctrine of the Eucharist and each pretends to a divine authorization for his view, a logical impasse is reached. The issue in the sixteenth century was usually determined by the persecution of the weaker by the stronger.

---

[1] Acontius, *Les Ruzes de Satan*, 57.
[2] ". . . Comme si tu prise tant l'authorité d'Origene, qui'il te semble qu'on y doyue adiouster foy: si tu apporte quelque passage. Auquel Origene s'accorde du tout à ton opinion, il te semblera que ce tesmoignage est fort bien à propos: mais si celuy auec qui tu as à faire ne tient conte d'Origene, tu ne proufiteras de rien par ce tesmoignage: comme aussi ne feras tu auec le Turc, au quelque autre ennemis de nostre religion par les tesmoignages de lettres diuine." (*Ibid.*, 57.)

334

Christian logic was apt to extend revealed truth by means of force since reason was not an effective instrument of persuasion. Acontius proposed as good an answer to this problem as has ever been offered. The only solution, he urged, is to "agree with reasons which are not only true and indubitable in thy faith, but also in his."[1] We must endeavour to understand the point of view of our adversary and to hear him through.[2] Desire of conquest and victory should be banished from all Christian disputation; "let all thy care be, that truth may prevail. . . ."[3] Truth does not have to find support in arrogance and harshness which are in reality tantamount to an admission of weakness. Thus, "the mathematicians use most sure and infallible demonstrations, but nevertheless, you will find in their works nothing of such outrageous character, for [such speeches] neither add clarity nor certainty to the demonstrations."[4]

Acontius' precise and scientific mind was distressed by the variety of the conflicting doctrinal systems which he saw about him. His analytical mind turned naturally to an attempt to reduce these clashing systems to their lowest common doctrinal denominator. He suspected that there was much truth in all of the Christian systems and likewise much that was either wrong or unessential in them. His was an *"humanistische Ideal,"* simple in character, practical in its nature.[5] He saw a simple and practical ideal interlacing the historical differences of the various creeds and sects. He sought to advance the noble conception of a common meeting-ground for Christianity, to set forward what Seeberg has called a *"heilsnotwendigen Kern"* which might override the minor differences in dogma. In his opinion, the various sects were persecuting each other chiefly over non-essentials, psychologically because they inwardly acknowledged the doubtful validity of their contentions.

The elevation of doctrine to a sacrosanct position among the various Protestant bodies had been largely responsible for so much confusion and bitterness.[6] With this tendency Acontius had no patience. There may be beliefs necessary for salvation

---

[1] Acontius, *Les Ruzes de Satan*, 57.   [2] *Ibid.*, 58.
[3] *Ibid.*, 62.   [4] *Ibid.*, 63.   [5] Seeberg, E., *Gottfried Arnold*, 303.
[6] Gow, H., *Unitarians*, 12, comments interestingly on this tendency.

but they are very few. He regarded most dogma as mere formal speculation, and as wholly vain. Hence the practice of exacting confessions of faith from men is wholly reprehensible.[1] The emphasis on creed is merely thinly disguised tyranny.[2] The exaction of subscriptions and confessions causes men to confess doctrines which they regard in their hearts as false to God, simply from the instinct of self-preservation;[3] "and if a man has the courage to speak that which seems good and agreeable to God, he is punished by death."[4] He urged that this species of tyranny drove men from the Church, solidified them into sects, and caused them to flee with their families and goods to foreign lands.[5] "It is necessary," he contended, "to desist from such laws and ordinances as serve only as shells (*laqs*) to conscience and to be content with a simple faith comprehending the principal articles of our religion."[6] The pastors should leave the secrets of conscience to God Almighty.

Throughout the treatise it is apparent that Acontius was deeply interested in the formulation of those religious truths which were necessary to salvation and upon which all men could agree. He deplored the elevation of confessionals to a position which placed the judgment of men above the Word of God.[7] The number of sects has increased in direct relation to the multiplication of confessions of faith.[8] He held, therefore, that nothing would operate more advantageously to the Church than the abolition of the variety of confessions and the substitution of a single symbol.[9] He enquired whether "there is not one thing, to which all doctrine and religion relate themselves . . .";[10] whether there is not some essential and fundamental truth necessary to purity of doctrine and for the attainment of salvation? If such an agreement could be attained it would "suppress much of the cackle of men" and would eliminate many of the scandals which impede the course of the Church.[11]

---

[1] Acontius, *Les Ruzes de Satan*, 239.   [2] *Ibid.*, 240.
[3] *Ibid.*, 241.   [4] *Ibid.*   [5] *Ibid.*, 241–242.
[6] *Ibid.*, 242.   [7] *Ibid.*, 265.   [8] *Ibid.*
[9] *Ibid.*, 265–266. It is to be noticed that he employed, like Coornhert and Arminius, the word 'symbol.' A confession should not have a binding character.   [10] *Ibid.*, 31.   [11] *Ibid.*, 266.

Endless controversy has ranged around the doctrinal formularies. Some contend that a point of faith is of such great importance that salvation depends upon receiving it, while other men ascribe less importance to the doctrine in question. In such a clear-cut issue one side or the other must be in error. Acontius proposed that we have no certain knowledge of any point of doctrine unless there is some clear prescription for our guidance in the Word of God.[1]

The author then sought to define that body of faith which is necessary for salvation. But, in so doing, he made plain that he did not "endeavour to introduce by force and to authorize our judgment . . . but rather that the truth itself may be brought to light."[2] The end of religion is the attainment of eternal life and whatever is necessary for that end ought to be counted profitable, and whatever is unnecessary to that end should not be regarded as binding.[3] If anything is added, even if it is in itself profitable, it will only be a source of schism and argument.[4] It is quite possible, he urged, to distinguish weighty from indifferent matters if we will only observe a given doctrinal issue coolly and objectively. Directly controversy begins with regard to a doctrine every point assumes great importance to the two sides. He pled, in fine, that we should keep our sense of proportion.[5] If teachers, preachers, and writers would confine themselves to the earnest consideration of the important problems of religion, most contentions would immediately cease.[6] Their perpetual argument has had the dire effect of "reducing the study of religion into sophistical vanities."[7] Thus every professor feels obliged to set out a commentary, but usually adds little or nothing to our knowledge of the sub-

---

[1] Acontius, *Les Ruzes de Satan*, 77. Compare the view of Episcopius. (Calder, F., *Episcopius*, 499–500.)

[2] Acontius, *Les Ruzes de Satan*, 86. Compare, Arminius, Jacob, *Works*, I, 408; *confessio . . . Remonstrantes, Pref.* (Episcopius, Simon, *Works*, II, pt. 2, 97 ff.); *Episcopius to Grotius*, Calder, *Episc.*, 500 ff.; and Episcopius, Simon, *Lectiones Sacrae, Works*, II, 1, 437–439; 2, 289–291.

[3] "Donques il faut dire que tout ce qui sert pour l'obtenir (salut) est necessaire à croire: et tout ce qui ne tire à ce but, doit estre obmis sans aucune fatigue et rōpement d'esprit." (Acontius, *Les Ruzes de Satan*, 31.)

[4] *Ibid.*, 267.   [5] *Ibid.*, 34–36.   [6] *Ibid.*, 36.

[7] ". . . de changer l'estude de theologie à vne vanité de sophistes." (*Ibid.*, 38.)

ject. He regarded these contentious persons as the *plus venimeuses pestes* in the Church.[1]

Acontius laid down the following interesting rule for the avoidance of contention and bitterness; "Douques selon mon iugement il n'y a riē meilleur, que de mettre peine à ce que la confession de foy, laquelle on veut tenir pour vn symbole, non seulement ne comprent rien, qui ne soit necessaire de cognoistre, tres veritable . . . et tres approuué par le tesmoinage des lettres diuines: mais aussi qu'elle ne contienne rien, qui ne soit couché en mesmes termes, et manieres de parles . . . desquelles l'esprit de Dieu a vsé. . . ."[2] The ideal confession should reduce doctrine to its simplest possible terms in order to avoid controversy.

In framing his confession, Acontius first presented the familiar words of John 3, "That whosoever believeth in Him should not perish, but have everlasting life."[3] He showed that controversy may easily develop over such a clear and simple statement as this: "For one may ask, 'What does it mean to believe in the Son of God or in His Apostles?' "[4] He denied the possibility of every Christian obtaining the same meaning from every passage.[5] It is beyond all controversy, however, that every man ought to hold as true whatever Christ taught by Himself or by His Apostles.[6] It is by no means necessary to

---

[1] Acontius, *Les Ruzes de Satan*, 39.   [2] *Ibid.*, 268–269.

[3] There is a possibility that the Confession of Faith which follows is an interpolation. It does not appear in the first two Latin editions, the first of which is so full of errors that it may be disregarded. However, the Confession appears in the French edition of the same year, which was contemporaneous, published with Acontius' approval, and which is in many ways the best of all the editions. The Confession, so far as the writer has been able to ascertain, appeared in every subsequent edition. Since the argument in at least three sections of the book was clearly designed to lead to an attempt at simplifying dogma, since such an effort was in accordance with the systematic temper of the author, and since the text of this section is in no way dissimilar in its structure to the remainder of the book, it may be held with reasonable certainty that the confession is genuine. However, the expanded confession which appears later (271–272) has all the earmarks of an interpolation. The expression of this section is different, and there is a suspicious air of Trinitarianism which is totally lacking in the confession beginning p. 94. (Cf. n. 1, p. 340.)   [4] *Ibid.*, 87.   [5] *Ibid.*

[6] "Or la question, est assaueir non, s'il est necessaire d'auoir vne droite cognoissance de toutes les choses, lesquelles le Seigneur à enseignées tãt en sa personne, que par ses apostres." (*Ibid.*, 87–88.)

understand or to believe all the doctrines enunciated in the Bible in order to attain salvation, even though certain texts appear to imply that requirement.[1] If this understanding were necessary, it is doubtful if any man could be saved; "But it is indeed certain that an infinite multitude will be saved; it must needs therefore follow, that men must be saved," though they do not rightly understand some part of that which the Lord has delivered and though they are contaminated with some errors.[2] Christ taught His Apostle such things as were necessary for their salvation, but Himself said they had not attained a full knowledge of that which He had taught them. Hence "it may be concluded, that all those things which Christ taught, are not so necessary to salvation, so that, though one were ignorant of part of them, he could not be saved."[3] Some of God's truths may remain unknown to man without endangering his salvation.

The author confessed that he had never been able, despite diligent search, to find "any general note or mark" for the determination of the body of doctrine which is necessary for salvation.[4] It is quite fruitless to say that "the principal heads of doctrine" must be believed, for such a statement would in itself lead to endless controveries.[5] He laid out for consideration numerous passages from the Bible which would appear to define the 'belief content' necessary to salvation, and presented several passages showing "unto whom in Scriptures salvation is denied in respect of unbelief."[6]

Acontius concluded that "we have found only these very few passages in the Scriptures, which are necessary to the belief of every man in order to be saved." In the first place, we must "acknowledge the one only true God, and Him whom He hath sent, Jesus Christ His Son, being made man,[7] and that by His Name [we] shall obtain salvation, and that [we] place not [our] righteousness in the works of the Law, but that [we] be truly persuaded, that there is no other name under heaven

---

[1] Acontius, *Les Ruzes de Satan*, 88–89.   [2] *Ibid.*, 89.   [3] *Ibid.*
[4] *Ibid.*, 90.   [5] *Ibid.*   [6] *Ibid.*, 90–91.
[7] The English version of 1648 inserts here, "and that he believe that God hath raised him from the dead." (81.)

339

whereby we can be saved."[1] Acontius likewise presented a few additional beliefs which he regarded as essential to the Christian faith. Thus one should believe that we are subject to eternal damnation, and we should trust that we are freed from that sentence by Christ and are by His benefits ordained to eternal blessedness.[2]

About a year after these words were written Acontius again testified to his conviction that Christian doctrine could be reduced to terms of such simplicity that contention could scarcely arise with respect to it. In a letter of June 7, 1566, he wrote, "One sole thing is demanded of us, that we believe in Christ as the Son of God; that is to say, not that in thinking or in speaking of Him we should employ this term, but that we should admit the notion that it comprehends."[3]

"I confess frankly," he wrote, "that I find no other points, that I can demonstrate from the Scriptures, as necessary to

---

[1] Later in the book this portion of the Confession varies slightly: "Qu'il y a vn seul vray Dieu et celuy qu'il a envoyé Iesus Christ, et le sainct Esprit; et que on ne doit nyer que le pere et le fils ne soyent personnes distinctes; pourau tant que Iesus Christ est vrayement le fils de Dieu." (*Ibid.*, 271.) ("I believe in the one true God, and that He has sent Jesus Christ and the Holy Ghost; and that one should not deny that the Father and the Son are distinct persons, but that Jesus Christ is truly the Son of God.") This has the odour of an interpolation. Acontius certainly had unitarian sympathies, according to Strype (*Grindal*, 66) he was technically excommunicated for having denied that the birth of Christ from the womb of the Virgin Mary was a fundamental article of faith, and the variant article of confession gives a Trinitarian polish to the simple statement as given above.

[2] "Mais seulement s'ensuit que ceste cognoissance est necessaire, assauoir, que nous sommes subiects à damnation eternelle, et que nous ayons ceste ferme fiance, que nous sommes deliurez par Christ et predestinez à la beatitude eternelle par le benefice d'iceluy." (Acontius, *Les Ruzes de Satan*, 95.) The dubious confession, 271–272, adds: (2) "That man is subject to the wrath and judgment of God; and that the dead shall be resurrected; the just to eternal happiness, and the unfaithful to eternal torments." (3) "That God has sent His Son Christ into the world and being made man He has died for our sins, and has been resurrected for our salvation (iustification)." (4) "That if we believe in the Son of God, we will obtain eternal life in His name." (5) "That there is no salvation other than in Christ; not in the Blessed Virgin, nor in Peter, nor in Paul, or in any other names whatsoever; that justification does not consist in the law, nor in the commandments, or in any invention of men." (6) "That baptism is only in the name of the Father, the Son, and the Holy Ghost."

[3] See also Crenius, Thomas, *Animadversiones*, II, 30–31.

the attainment of salvation."[1] He disclaimed any desire to impose this or any other confession upon the Church. However, he suggested that if someone could draw up a confession comprehending the entire Church, an inestimable blessing would be conferred upon Christendom. Such a contribution would at once assist in the eradication of heresy and would help to heal the bitterness and contention which are despoiling the Church. All those who found themselves in accord with such a simple statement would needs regard themselves as brothers in the same Church.[2]

As an illustration of the tragic consequences of the over-emphasis on dogma, he cited the long and bitter controversy over the meaning of the words, "Take, this is My body."[3] He regarded the entire controversy as unnecessary. Both parties, according to his formula, were members of the true Church. Hence, neither party "should condemn the other or account it guilty of heresy."[4] The bitterness which has resulted from the controversy has ensued from a difference in the interpretation of the phrase and not of the truth which it embodies. "But you will say, that the words are clear, evident and manifest, and that it is impossible to mistake their meaning. They are manifest to you who understand them, they are not so clear to them who lend them another meaning. Therefore, it must be granted, that the difference lies in the interpretation of the words and not in their truth."[5] He denounced the actions of Christians who brand as heretics those who hold opposite views with regard to the Eucharist: "Le Seigneur promet salut à tous ceux qui inuoquent son nom: qui croiront le fils de Dieu: qui en luy mettront leur asseurance. . . ." This faith and this hope are constantly professed by those who are branded as heretics. "By what Testament of God's Word art thou induced by thy judgment to deny them salvation?" he enquired.[6] Not one word may be adduced from the Bible to prove that they may not inherit eternal life.

The sixteenth century did not afford a more comprehensive and tolerant view of religion than that sketched by Acontius.

[1] Acontius, *Les Ruzes de Satan*, 96.   [2] *Ibid.*, 273.
[3] *Ibid.*, 97–98.   [4] *Ibid.*, 99.   [5] *Ibid.*, 99–100.   [6] *Ibid.*, 100.

He swept aside the differences of creed and dogma to arrive at the conclusion that all groups of Christians in reality worship God in a faith which meets the requirements demanded by the Bible. He regarded the bitter controversy over the Lord's Supper as idle and foolish. It would be difficult to find another writer in this period who would so boldly discard as unessential an article of faith which had been most highly responsible for the bigotry and persecution which marked the century. His formula would include the Roman Catholics, and, in fact, every Christian body. He obviously envisaged no corporate Church united along the lines which he had laid down, but he did stress the possibility of the various religious groups abandoning their hatred and persecuting zeal, under the realization that they were united in a worship that had a common basis and a common purpose despite striking external differences. It was a high and noble ideal, before which the vaunted tolerance and comprehension of Hooker is dimmed and incomplete. "One party may be in error, yet they are both in the way of salvation," he urged.[1] They are therefore "bound purely to the commandment of the Lord, by which they ought charitably to reverence and honour one another, as brethren and servitors of God, and as members of Christ. And if they shall mutually annoy one another with outrages, furious words . . . and shall exercise hatred against another, they shall not escape the severe and rigorous judgment of God."[2] Men have clothed the simplicity of Christ's religion with complicated and obscure formulae which have all but choked out its spiritual content.

h. The State, the Church and the Problem of Error

No writer in the century made a clearer distinction between the affairs of Church and State than Acontius. He regarded spiritual life as residing within the soul of man and bravely denied that the State possessed any legitimate authority to interfere in spiritual concerns. The evils and dissensions which beset the Church he held to be of its own creation, and they could be corrected only by an internal purging, with which

[1] Acontius, *Les Ruzes de Satan*, 102.   [2] *Ibid.*

342

the State had no concern. He denied without any reservations that the State had any authority to correct or to punish heresy. This portion of his thought would alone entitle him to first rank among those who upheld religious toleration in the six-teenth century. It is important to recall, in addition, that his theory of toleration found its basis in the essential wrongfulness of persecution of religious beliefs, rather than on the grounds of expediency.

He regarded the interference of the State in religious affairs as evil and stupid. He condemned the punishment of error as a species of brutal tyranny.[1] He declared that the interference of the civil power in the settlement of a religious controversy was a confession that truth is helpless in the face of error. He urged that the very word 'heresy' was an invention to cloak the tyranny of persecution. This species of tyranny opposed Luther and at the present time hinders the progress of the Reformation. The ecclesiastics play upon the fears of the prince, convincing him that heresy is dangerous to the stability of the realm.[2]

The author did not confine himself to a rhetorical denuncia-tion of persecution; he sought to analyse the motives which underlay the interference of the magistrates in cases of heresy, and to demonstrate that such interference could find no support in justice or in religion.

The question, he admitted, is "full of controversy, involved, and of very grave importance." He pointed out that the natural disposition in a case of error is to employ force in order to secure its eradication. Acontius proposed "to consider diligently that which appears convenient and most agreeable to divine law" in the treatment of religious error.[3]

Toleration, he admitted, is a difficult policy for the ruler to embrace. For all conditions of men argue confidently about the chief heads of faith, engender doubt, deceive the ignorant, and create innumerable scandals.[4] If we should imagine ourselves

---

[1] Acontius, *Les Ruzes de Satan*, 247.   [2] *Ibid.*, 251.   [3] *Ibid.*, 107.
[4] ". . . et que tous les iours il y agès sans doctrine: de nul iugement, n'ayants zele aucun, impudēs, eshontez qui ne cessent de t'importuner et rompre la teste mesme, qu'il n'ya patissier, cousturier, pescheur, bouchier, cuisinier,

343

in the place of the magistrate, it would be easy to see why a policy of restraint of such licence seems necessary. This is especially true since the Scriptures can be used to support such a policy.

Let us presume, he suggested, that those persons who oppose a commonly accepted body of doctrines are put to death as a consequence of a repressive policy.[1] This, of course, presumed nothing beyond the accepted governmental theory of his day. Directly such heretics are put to death, he held, the Church "attains peace and tranquillity, discipline is relaxed and enfeebled, devotion is chilled, and an extraordinary and most stupid forgetfulness of God and His law develops."[2] Craft and sophistry will creep in and though the same doctrine will appear to be present, it will be by degrees changed and corrupted. He appeared to hold that heresy might be a positive benefit to the dominant ecclesiastical body by inspiring zeal, by compelling attendance to doctrinal purity, and by engendering a helpful competition with the heretical sect.[3] Such a view appears bold and strange only twenty-six years after the publication of the *Institutes*.

Acontius urged that the term heresy was an invention, a sort of legal fiction, which the dominant ecclesiastical body employed to damn its opponents. The meaning of the term has been determined solely by the construction which the ecclesiastical authorities and the magistrates have seen fit to give to it. In those places where spiritual controversy is settled by the sword, whoever opposes the commonly accepted doctrines, whether he be right or wrong, is accounted an heretic, "and whatever testaments he may produce or arguments he may draw from the Holy Scriptures" the hangman alone will answer

si petite famelette, qui ne vueille hardiment en toute liberté disputer et caqueter des principaux points de la religion: tellement que toutes choses sont reuoquées en doutes, les simples abusez, bref que tout est rempli de scandale." (Acontius, *Ruzes de Satan*, 107–108.)

[1] *Ibid.*, 108.   [2] *Ibid.*

[3] This essentially modern view would appear to be sound. The electrical effect of the Protestant Reformation on the Roman Catholic Church and the invigorating consequences of the Wesleyan Movement on the moribund structure of eighteenth-century Anglicanism are compelling evidences of the psychological correctness of Acontius' position.

him.[1] In a short time what appeared at first to be just severity will have degenerated into "savage and barbarous cruelty."[2] "Imagine yourself, then, to have fallen in such times, when it is not permitted to those who are of sound doctrine, to oppose the errors which are sown and received by the ignorant, then if you speak at all, the sword, the gallows, and the fire are pressed upon you. . . ."[3] This tyranny had its origin in the punishment of true heretics, and one is led to wish that no heretic had ever been molested rather than that such tyranny should have come into the world.[4] He concluded, "Unhappy are you who have your eyes fixed only upon the dignity of your own reputations, holding yourselves as Gods among men and contemning your brethren; usurping a certain tyranny over their consciences. . . ."[5]

Nor was Acontius convinced that the capital punishment of heretics accomplished the purpose for which the penalty was designed. He regarded free discussion as a safety-valve which was perfectly competent to destroy error by exposing it to the healing rays of evangelical truth. But, if discussion and opinion are driven underground, a sect will take root before the public authority is cognisant of its existence.[6] The Church would, in such a case, be in possession of no certain knowledge of the error and would be quite unprepared to combat its tenets. In fact, if the pastors come to depend upon the civil sword to destroy error, they would probably be too indolent and ignorant to offer effective opposition in any case. The persecution of the sect will have the psychological effect of making martyrs of those who suffer and will place the dominant party in the unenviable rôle of tyrants.[7] "By which means," he astutely observed, "it comes to pass that they [the heretics] are irritated the more, are confirmed in their error, and are rendered wholly incorrigible. There is no need to search for these instances in ancient histories. For we have enough examples before our eyes, which, if one considered carefully, he would have no cause to desire the use of the sword for the extirpation of heresies."[8]

Acontius' frank and bold handling of the relation of the

---

[1] Acontius, *Les Ruzes de Satan*, 109.   [2] *Ibid.*   [3] *Ibid.*   [4] *Ibid.*
[5] *Ibid.*, 310–311.   [6] *Ibid.*, 109.   [7] *Ibid.*, 110.   [8] *Ibid.*, 110–111.

Mosaic Law to the problem of heresy was refreshing. The defenders of religious oppression had for centuries found their strongest entrenchment in the Mosaic Law and the orthodox interpretation of the Code had caused considerable inconvenience to those literalists who had none the less been forced to plead for the toleration of their own sect or group. Acontius frankly admitted that under the Old Law heresy and idolatry were punished by death. Nor was there any doubt that the "reason" or the essence of the Law still remained in force, and that the magistrate might legally erect a new law which prescribed similar punishments for such offences. He professed to regard Christ's parable of the tares as the solution of the problem and argued that it definitely forbids the capital punishment of heretics and idolaters. The parable has been variously interpreted, principally because men have desired the predominance of their particular opinions, without regard for the truth which the parable conveys. Christ did not command us to be tolerant in inconsequential matters or to punish only grievous errors, but said without any reservation that ". . . Veut que le froument et l'hyuroye croissent iusques à la moisson."[1]

Likewise the argument that Christ has reserved the general purging of the Church to Himself, but does not prohibit the cleansing of particular Churches may be regarded as a strained interpretation of the passage.[2] Acontius' logic was tight; if particular Churches were all cleansed, and ideally they would be, then the Church in general would likewise be purged and Christ's Commandment would be violated.[3] The magistrate, in endeavouring to purify the Church, resists the expressed Will of God.[4] Only heretics are comprehended by the meaning of the parable, since alone they are "sown among the wheat,"[5]

---

[1] ". . . That both the tares and the wheat should grow until the harvest." (Acontius, *Les Ruzes de Satan*, 113.)

[2] *Ibid.* It would be interesting to know who was originally responsible for this ingenious interpretation of the parable.   [3] *Ibid.*, 113–114.

[4] He pointed out that the parable does not mean that all kinds of ungodly persons are to remain unmolested by the magistrate. (Acontius, *Les Ruzes de Satan*, 114.) The magistrate has an express commandment to destroy persons who are guilty of civil crimes, whether they are of the wheat or of the tares. (*Ibid.*, 114–115.) The parable refers solely to the Church, and distinguishes between pious and impious persons.   [5] *Ibid.*, 116.

and since the tares are nothing more than imperfect grain. Hence, it is evident that the punishment of heresy by death is expressly forbidden by the Bible.

In general, Acontius regarded the Bible as obscure on the problem of heresy, holding that the term had received its importance principally because of the arrogant bitterness of the orthodox Churches. But, admitting that the Bible lacks clarity on the point, we would be wholly unwarranted in "shedding blood by the authority of a dubious law," especially when we recall the general prohibition of killing.[1] The confusion with regard to the scriptural injunctions in the case of heresy results principally from the interpretation which the civil authority has chosen to make of it,[2] "For how few of hose who exercise the office of magistrate, though they profess the [rule?] of the Gospel, affect the study of the divine Word as they should? How many of them are eminent for piety and prudence?" In fact, we expect unjust and rash judgments from them as a matter of course. The author appears to have had as little respect for the competence of the magistrate in spiritual concerns as he had for the clergy.

However, for the sake of his argument he presumed an ideal case of a truly pious and just magistrate confronted with a manifest heresy. He reflected, in presenting this case, that any ruler will, because of his authority, be *ipso facto* accounted just, and that we brand as an heretic whoever opposes our own view.[3] Heresy, he said, is almost always that opinion which conflicts with our own.

In his ideal situation an admittedly difficult problem arises if the heretic, having been warned, persists in spreading the infection of his error.[4] In considering the problem, Acontius declined to take refuge in the doctrine of predestination which might be used to support the view that the magistrate may not punish an heretic because God may ultimately intend him

---

[1] Acontius, *Les Ruzes de Satan*, 118. [2] *Ibid.*, 119.
[3] ". . . Mais qui est celuy, lequel ayāt la puissance du glaiue, qui ne vueille estre tenu pour homme de bien? Et ne tiendra pour heretique quiconque luy contredit en la religion?" (*Ibid.*)
[4] *Ibid.*, 119–120.

347

for salvation. Acontius rightly regarded this position as theologically untenable, for "if he is among God's elect, he will not be put to death, before all that which is necessary for his salvation will be revealed to him; and, if he is not [of the elect], any hope of his repentance is in vain."[1] The real danger, in his view, is that the magistrate may be quite mistaken in his judgment of what constitutes an heresy. Acontius was as distinctly sceptical of the possibility of accurately determining heresy as of the possibility of accurately determining religious truth in the absolute sense. God has declared that the magistrate is not a fit judge of heresy or of its punishment, and He has forbidden him any jurisdiction whatsoever in the matter.[2] Law, he acutely observed, is "a guesser rather than an expositor," and is accordingly not a fit instrument for the determination of such a case.[3] The possibility of an error of judgment on the part of the magistrate and the consequent execution of a man who is not an heretic, is too probable "and consequently . . . judgments of this nature pertain not to the magistrate, nor to any man, but to the son of God alone. . . ."[4]

If we admit that the magistrate is incompetent to judge an heretic, it must follow that he is also incompetent to determine what constitutes the offence of heresy, and to forbid the teaching of heresy. The author enquired, "Car qu'est ce cognoistre vn heretique, sinō cognoistre la cause, laquelle rent l'hōme heretique?"[5] It is preposterous to argue that the magistrate should determine points of doctrine. The interference of the State in religious issues can only mean that spiritual matters will be determined by force or by man's opinion. The intervention of the magistrate must result, sooner or later, in the suppression of truth.[6] He brilliantly urged that for the magis-

---

[1] Acontius, *Les Ruzes de Satan*, 121. Acontius did, however, point out the fact which should have been evident that the doctrine constituted a strong reason for refraining from persecution. No one can say that God has not permitted one of His elect to fall into error in order to raise him up again for some great purpose. (*Ibid.*, 41.) God's purposes are inscrutable, and the secret of election resides in the mind of God alone. There is an awful danger that a man may be condemned and punished for whom God has reserved a future greater than that of any earthly king. (*Ibid.*, 53–54.)

[2] *Ibid.*, 121.   [3] *Ibid.*, 122.   [4] *Ibid.*   [5] *Ibid.*   [6] *Ibid.*, 123.

trates to constitute themselves "as judges of the differences of such men as submit to the Word of God, and employ the testimonies thereof; that by force and opinion of fact they should advance and maintain one doctrine, and repress another; they should rather consider seriously what it is which they assume, and how much liberty they allow unto themselves."[1] He rebuked the view that the preservation of the Christian Church and of pure faith depends upon the weight of the civil sword, "As if the Word had no mettle or force." He proposed that heresy should be permitted freedom of discussion and that it should be permitted to test itself with truth. "Allow the truth to come into discreet combat with imposture, and she will necessarily emerge the victor."[2]

The attempt to defend the Church by temporal weapons actually redounds to the benefit of Satan.[3] Satan has no cause to fear worldly force; he is only put to rout by the Word. The employment of force ensures the complete overthrow of the very weapons by which Christianity alone may be advanced. In the fine words of the English translation, "As soon as the ministers shal have obtained thus much, that whosoeuer shal dare to mutter anything against their doctrine, the executioner shall presently be called for, which by his halter or ax alone shal resolve all doubts, and unty all knots: what great study of the scriptures will they then use. . . . Woe be to us and to our posterity, if we shall cast away this weapon wherewith alone we are allowed to fight; wherewith fighting we are alwayes sure of victory."[4] We must hold fast to the weapon with which God has endowed us, and with which alone we may destroy Satan and his followers.[5] He condemned the employment of force in the defence of the Gospel without reservation. Force in such instances, he well pointed out, is really employed to avenge hatred; "certenement il faut qu'vn chacun soit diligent à examiner ses affectiōs à fin qu'on ne s'abuse, et qu'en pensant seruir à Dieu, on ne s'estudie du tout a soy mesme."

[1] Acontius, *Les Ruzes de Satan*, 124.   [2] *Ibid.*, 124–125.
[3] *Ibid.*, 125.   [4] English translation of 1648, 105.
[5] "Plustost tenons comme a belle dēts ce glaiue de la parolle de Dieu, efforcons nous d'esgorger et saccager les auant—coureurs de satan, et le satan mesme. . . ." (*Ibid.*, 126.)

Acontius, having demonstrated that it is not the proper function of the civil ruler to constitute himself a judge of heretics or of heresy, advanced the view that it is much less his duty to employ violence in enforcing a body of doctrine which has been adjudged correct by other men.[1] It naturally follows that his subordinates will be unable to assume a task for which he is not fitted. The employment of the civil sword in religious matters by the magistrate and by his subordinates stands or falls together.[2] How is it possible for the magistrate to commit a charge of enforcement which he is not competent to understand?[3] As a parting blow he reminded the civil magistracy that Christ was legally executed by a civil magistrate who had presumed an ability to render judgment in just this particular.

The writer concluded his examination of the relation of the civil magistracy to heresy by an attack upon the time-honoured custom of exerting mental and physical compulsion on an heretic in order to extract a formal recantation from him. He urged that the practice was "entirely devoid of reason."[4] "A persuasion must indeed be lightly entertained, if it may be so easily removed."[5] Such a recantation proceeds from fear of punishment rather than from the heart. The magistrate places himself in a very bad state of grace if he destroys not only the body of the heretic but endangers his soul. "Are we so poorly equipped in the Word of God for the destruction of errors, that we must needs defend ourselves with a lie, and counterfeit retractions?"[6] The mind can be touched neither by punishment nor by the fear of punishment. Nor can bodily punishment cause what seemed true to appear false. "Wherefore," he concluded, "if an heretic is not able to cast off his error, even if he would do so, why trouble him and constrain him . . . and thus give more and more offence to God?"[7]

Acontius had outlined a systematic and reasoned theory of the complete differentiation of the functions of Church and State which prevented any interference of the ruler in matters of conscience. Since, at the same time, he denied any authority

[1] Acontius, *Les Ruzes de Satan*, 126–127.
[2] Acontius seems to have had the ecclesiastical authorities in mind.
[3] *Ibid.*, 128.   [4] *Ibid.*   [5] *Ibid.*   [6] *Ibid.* .   [7] *Ibid.*, 131.

to the clergy over religious freedom, his system of thought represented a complete vindication of the idea of religious toleration. He denied that the guilt of heresy was the concern of anyone save the heretic, so far as any correction beyond moral suasion and ecclesiastical discipline were concerned. The interest of the State in the punishment of misbelief, he accurately observed, is derived from political considerations rather than from any real concern with the welfare of the soul of man. Heresy is, in general, a term with which we reproach our opponents and it has never been absolutely defined. The presence of heresy in the spiritual commonwealth may well be an actual incentive to a closer application of the Church to its spiritual duties. He proved that the temporal punishment of heresy was expressly forbidden by Christ, and that any attempt on the part of the ruler to effect a cleansing of the Church contradicted the will of God. Even if we admit the exceptional case of a wholly just ruler confronted with a wholly evil heresy, no excuse may be advanced for the persecution of that belief. The magistrate is not competent to judge either the heresy or the heretic since the civil law cannot penetrate into the mind and conscience of man. Persecution will sooner or later result in the triumph of sheer force and will destroy the spiritual weapons wherewith Christianity must effect its entrance into the hearts of men. The use of force may work an external change in men but it is powerless to affect either the mind or the heresy with which the mind is affected. Acontius held that the sole weapon of the Church was the power of truth and he finely denied that it might employ any form of compulsion.

i. Acontius' Programme for the Handling of Error

The author did not content himself with a mere denial of the right of the magistrate to punish heresy. He made a considerable positive contribution to the theory of religious toleration by seeking to discuss in full the ideal way of handling the difficult problem of misbelief.

In considering the problem of error, he sought to distinguish between minor errors and fundamental heresies. As he had previously indicated, all the doctrines of the Church are not of identical importance. Some are of such great importance that they must be adhered to in order to gain salvation, while the denial of others does not break the unity of the Church.[1] With his definition of essential doctrine in mind, it will be seen that he would condemn as heretical no doctrine that could be called Christian, for his doctrinal formula was sufficiently comprehensive to include all Christian faiths. Presuming a man errs in a doctrine which is essential to salvation, he should be condemned for his view only if he seeks to seduce others and will not repent. The gravest punishment which he would allow in such a case was excommunication and if the heretic were willing "to hold his view quietly," Acontius was disposed to refrain even from that penalty.[2]

His hesitation was based upon his doubts as to the ability of the Church to determine heresy with accuracy and his conviction that excommunication would be an incentive for the formation of a sect. He pointed out that a triple error may easily be perpetrated by excommunication, "first, the person or his doctrine may be unjustly condemned; second, the condemnation may be beyond reason; third, it may be made by persons who are not qualified to do so."[3] Certainly, no person should be cast out from the Church withuot a patient effort to win him from his error, and a careful explanation to the congregation of the nature of his heresy. The more ill-will the Church arouses in the man, the more he will endeavour to injure the Church after his separation.[4] He concluded, ". . . It is my judgment, that the heretic should be condemned with a simple declaration: without injury and reproach: with an intimation of sorrow, [and] without any anger or hatred: in such way that the judgment may have an honest gravity,

[1] Car tous les points de la vray doctrine ne sont pas de mesme importance. Il y en a aucuns lesquels il est si necessaire de cognoistre et qu'ils doiuët estre sichez, emprains, et grauez en nos esprits sans en douter aucunement. Il y en a d'autres, lesquels sont en disputes entre les eglises: toutefois n'en troublent pas l'vnion." (Acontius, *Les Ruzes de Satan*, 74.)
[2] *Ibid.*, 106.   [3] *Ibid.*, 73.
[4] "Il est tout manifeste, que d'autant que celuy, qu'on retranche est mal affectionné enuers l'eglise, qu'il sera plus importür et dressera force embusches contre icelle à fin d'en seduire tous ceux qu'il pourra. . . ."

but may be void of all passion and cruelty."[1] This far, and
no farther, would he go in dealing with a man guilty of the
most flagrant heresy and the active dissemination of those views.

He regarded excommunication as a matter of the utmost
gravity. When a man is guilty of disseminating errors the Church
immediately condemns him without attempting to learn whether
the heretic is motivated by ignorance or lust.[2] The heretic
at once regards himself as having been sorely injured.[3] "He
will then be moved and inflamed with anger, and will determine
to defend his error, despite the consequences . . . thereupon
people will assume sides, and all will be confused and disquieted
with contentions, disorders, and clamours, so that no good, but
much evil will follow."[4] The excommunication of an heretical
faction he regarded as particularly dangerous because they will,
"as persons who are lost . . . form a sect to themselves, a thing
more dangerous than the pestilence. For we see what cruel and
bloody enmity is exercised and practised by one sect against
another. Then hatred and rancour determine, that that which
is affirmed by one [sect], is likely to be suspected by the other
. . . and whatever has one time been affirmed, whether good
or not, pride and affection of contrariety . . . will not permit
it to be retracted . . . and when once it has grown into custom,
that for every difference of judgment, one man will condemn
another, you shall see sects develop out of sects daily."[5] He
wisely observed that it is far easier to begin a contention than
to terminate one.[6] Controversies of small beginnings may well
up into an overpowering deluge which can sweep away the
very foundations of religion. Even if a man is in error, we
should carefully consider all aspects of the matter before rushing
into controversy. Men dispute quite as acrimoniously over a
trifle as about matters of the gravest importance. We must
carefully distinguish between unimportant errors and really

---

[1] Acontius, *Les Ruzes de Satan*, 106.   [2] *Ibid.*, 43.   [3] *Ibid.*
[4] ". . . ce qui sera cause qu'il se troublera, enflambera de courroux, et se
resoudra de defendre son erreur. . . . Puis les contraires affections des
hommes si ioindront à la cause tellement que tout sera confus, et brouillé
de contentions, rioteries et clameurs, en sorte, qu'il n'en sortira rien de
bon, et en viendra beaucoup de mal." (*Ibid.*, 43–44.)
[5] *Ibid.*, 76.   [6] *Ibid.*, 30.

pernicious heresy, difficult as that distinction may be.[1] The disposition towards unconsidered severity in ecclesiastical discipline, and the consequent multiplication of sects delights Satan and assists in the fulfilment of his designs.

Acontius' sympathy appears in every case to be with the heretic. He reminds us that most men are quite sincere when they endeavour to bring forward a new doctrine. It would indeed be a strange man who would deliberately incur hatred and danger if he were not sincere in the beliefs which he proposed.[2] In a surprising and discerning sentence he suggested that to condemn a man who errs through ignorance is virtually equivalent to condemning God for His failure to endow the man with greater insight and intelligence.[3] Even when a man spreads error through deliberate malice, the punishment of his great sin may not be expedient to the Church.[4] We must be careful in reproaching men for heresy. The term has been too lightly bandied about. No man can be won from error by the injury of his reputation or by the wounding of his sensibilities. He concluded with a noble phrase, "and if you see nothing in the man deserving of your love, consider what there is in God, and His only begotten Son whose workmanship he is, which may command thy affection . . . regard not his person: but look upon the person of Christ, whom he represents, and recall how great His love hath been to thee. . . ."[5]

Acontius regarded excommunication as the last resort of the Church. He held that its only purpose was to save the communion from the infection of heresy, and that its effect was entirely negative since it was not a proper instrument for combating error. The extreme penalty of the Church must be regarded as a sad admission of its failure to overcome heresy with truth, and the employment of that penalty testifies to a lack of spiritual vitality in the Church.

[1] Acontius, *Les Ruzes de Satan*, 30–31.   [2] *Ibid.*, 44.
[3] "Dieu ne luy a fait ceste grace de luy donner meilleur esprit, ou iugement: si donques tu te courrouce, ce n'est pas tant contre luy, que contre Dieu, qui ne le muny de meilleur iugement." (*Ibid.*, 44.)
[4] "Et encor que quelqu'vn soit digne de grande punition, si n'est il pas expedient de le punir incontinent selon la grauité de son peché." (*Ibid.*, 45.)
[5] *Ibid.*, 53.

Reason and a sympathetic understanding of the heretics' point of view were proposed as the only effective cures for heresy. He held that reason was the handmaiden of truth, and that when it was brought to bear on error fruitful results may ensue.[1] But, unless reason and the speech of the righteous "shall have power to lead the adversary to such a disposition and such a tranquillity of mind" as is conducive to a quiet consideration of the error, the designs of Satan will be forwarded.[2] The rational conversion of an opponent is psychologically difficult. Men lose their dignity and self-esteem in changing their views in the face of reason. Then too, the attachment to his own doctrines will make the heretic short of patience and lacking in ability to endure logical contradiction.[3]

Because of these facts reason must be accompanied by a sympathetic understanding of the heretical point of view. The scientist spoke when Acontius suggested that we must learn to listen patiently and especially to suspend our own judgment while considering the views of our opponents.[4] One must learn carefully to weigh the beliefs of every other man. We must reflect that many men fall into error, and that error is by no means a prerogative of the unlearned.[5] In fact, no one can ever be certain that he is not himself in error, and hence should lend full attention to the opinions of other men.

Acontius was obviously urging suspension of judgment to the point of toying with scepticism. He arrested his train of thought quickly with the reflection, "Mais il ne faut douter . . . en la doctrine de la religion."[6] Scepticism being out of the question, the Christian is confronted by a serious difficulty. He must acquire a faith and a knowledge of faith which is as certain as possible.[7] When the Christian comes into knowledge of a new doctrine he must think carefully and suspend his

---

[1] Acontius, *Les Ruzes de Satan*, 10.   [2] *Ibid.*

[3] "A quoy sont fort subiecte ceux qui enseignent: car on ne peut rien changer à la doctrine qu'ils n'y mettent beaucoup de leur dignité et bonne reputation, côme s'ils auoyent enseignee et maintenue fause doctrine. Aussi l'amour qu'on porte à la doctrine fait qu'on n'a point de patience d'ouyr celuy qui la veut corrompre." (*Ibid.*, 11.)

[4] *Ibid.*   [5] *Ibid.*, 22.

[6] *Ibid.*, 23.   [7] *Ibid.*

judgment before condemning it as heretical.[1] Thus one should consider whether the heresy is a perfectly clear and evident error; whether the author of it is possessed of a stubborn and perverted heart; and whether he is willing to acquiesce to reasonable consideration. One should likewise reflect "whether if he does not prostrate himself at your feet and adore you as God, you will become angry, and resort to injuries and defamations, thereby rendering his disease incurable, [and] compel the man to create sects. . . ."[2] One should, in other words, by a careful self-scrutiny, exclude from one's mind and actions that psychology which undergirds all religious persecution and which has brought the Church to ruin.

The proper treatment of heresy, in addition to the necessity of understanding the point of view of the heretic, and confuting his position by careful reasoning, requires a charitable attitude on the part of the orthodox. Charity may be regarded, in fact, as an attribute of true faith.[3] We are disposed to minimize and excuse our own faults and rigorously to judge the shortcomings of others.[4] Charity, Acontius held, follows from a realization of our own sinfulness which makes it impossible for us harshly to judge our fellow Christians.[5] We must first correct our own faults and then attempt to assist those who are in error.[6] A man is moved by the spirit of God when he acts from motives of kindness and charity.[7]

A rational attack on heresy must find its weapons in truth as revealed by the Bible. The Bible constitutes the only sure guide to what is true in matters of religion and by it alone are we able to confute error. In all matters of faith the Scriptures constitute the sole foundation upon which we can erect our faith and trust.[8] Doctrines change almost impercept-

[1] "Think with thyself what certain knowledge thou hast of this thing." (Acontius, *Les Ruzes de Satan*, 23.)
[2] "Afin donques que tu ne face iamais sascherie à celuy qui est prest de t'enseigner: ou il est necessaire que tu aye vne tresacomplie et certaine science des choses qui peuuent venir en querelle et debat . . . ou certain emētsi quel que fois il te sonne aux aureilles quelque chose estrange, auant que de la condamner, il te faut subsister: surfeoir et pēser quelle sciēce tu en peu auoir." (*Ibid.*, 25.)   [3] *Ibid.*, 167–168.   [4] *Ibid.*, 169.
[5] *Ibid.*, 180–171 (mispaged).   [6] *Ibid.*, 171.   [7] *Ibid.*, 178–179.
[8] ". . . la parolle de Dieu est ce, ou il se faut asseurer cōme sur un rocher, qui ne bouge aucunement." (*Ibid.*, 77.)

ibly from truth to falsehood.[1] This tendency may be attributed
to our "over-curiosity," especially in the interpretation of
figurative texts. The power of the Bishop of Rome has been
consolidated by this means. Then, too, the difficulty in trans-
lating the Bible through and into numerous languages has
been a fruitful source of error and misunderstanding.[2] Purity
of belief may be maintained only by the critical comparison
of the doctrines of a given period with those given in the
Bible and accepted by the Apostolic Church.[3] He would re-
institute the Puritan Exercises in order to assist in the maintenance of doctrinal purity, and he lent a guarded support to the
doctrinal decisions of General Councils.[4]

Acontius was a true son of the Reformation and correctly
detected that the evangelical system must be based on a free
interpretation of the Bible as the sole standard of religious
truth. He regarded the Bible as the only rule of faith and the
sole repository of that truth which must be mobilized for the
assault on error. But his discerning mind appreciated the fact
that Bible study and biblical authority had not and were not
likely to produce the uniform and absolute truth which the
early reformers, and to a lesser degree the Elizabethan Establishment, had envisaged. The typical writer of the period
would have rested content with the argument we have just
outlined. But Acontius in complete intellectual honesty admitted
that the solution was not only inadequate but not likely to be
effective.

We must grant that nothing can be held as certain in matters
of faith that is not found in the Bible. But the difficulty comes
in reaching a uniform interpretation of the standard of truth.
We may observe a variety of judgments even among the learned.[5]
Indeed, many persons are honestly convinced that they can
demonstrate the truth of their opinions by biblical authority
when they manifestly err.[6] The attainment of religious truth
has also been complicated by the variety of opinions, the
dissensions and the bitterness of ecclesiastical controversy.
There are so many conflicting points of view and such an

---

[1] Acontius, *Les Ruzes de Satan*, 133–134.   [2] *Ibid.*, 137–138.
[3] *Ibid.*, 147.   [4] *Ibid.*, 147–148.   [5] *Ibid.*, 26.   [6] *Ibid.*

innumerable quantity of books that the opinion has developed that religious enquiry should be relegated to the scholar and the specialist. But this view endangers the vitality of the Christian faith and may lead to a dangerous authoritativism in the Church. Acontius expressed himself as distressed with the growing tendency to take refuge, in the face of so much variety, in the authority of the learned and in the sacrosanct character of doctrinal formulae.[1]

The author was so sceptical of the possibility of attaining an absolute body of truth by which error might be judged that he was disposed to minimize the importance of heresy. The necessities of salvation, as he had pointed out, are in the Bible and are clearly expressed. The people should be exhorted to read the Bible and to attain an understanding of its message. The people may be somewhat excited as a result of their study and dissensions may arise, but the effect will be salutary if it stirs the pastors to leadership.[2] We must be infinitely cautious in accusing fellow Christians of misbelief. Even if a man is convinced of the truth of his opinion and is certain that he is led by the spirit of God, he must carefully search a suspected error by the tests of reason and the revealing insight afforded by prayer before assailing it as false.[3] Even then we must take great care that we are not deceived by that "crafty fox . . . Satan";[4] i.e. by the arrogance of our own opinions. We must hear and consider the opinions of those who err, seeking first to understand before we condemn. Nobly he enquired, "Quoy? Vne chose souuent examinee, sera elle moins esclarcie? et non pas de plus en plus descouuerte et manifestee?"[5]

Acontius' defence of religious toleration reached its highest plane when he argued the case of the complete independence of private judgment and the right of freedom of enquiry. In the last analysis people must determine religious truth for themselves. They have long trusted too much to their pastors to see that true doctrine is maintained.[6] People are all too prone to accept whatever their pastors tell them without independent examination. This trust in the specialist, in the professional

---

[1] Acontius, *Les Ruzes de Satan*, 228.   [2]*Ibid.*, 223.
[3] *Ibid.*, 28–29.   [4] *Ibid.*, 29.   [5] *Ibid.*, 29–30.   [6] *Ibid.*, 144.

man of religion, he regarded as fatal to the vitality of the Christian faith. Religion belongs to the people. The essentials of the faith are simple and do not require learning in order to be understood.[1] He based his plea for complete religious freedom on the inherent capacity of the ordinary layman to understand the essentials of religion and upon a conviction that men love truth and hate error by their very nature.[2] Men naturally love what they consider to be true in religion because they regard it as the way to salvation; and they hate what they consider false since they believe it leads to eternal damnation.[3] Herein we have at once the key to religious hatred, because men seek to rescue by any possible means those whom they believe to be damned;[4] and the basis of religious freedom, because a man's convictions in a matter of such gravity will be honest. For that reason Acontius would leave men to their doubts; he would give them a free opportunity to work out their own salvation. The search for truth may well begin with doubt and error and the attainment of truth lies by the way of free discussion and enquiry. If freedom is established,

---

[1] Acontius, *Les Ruzes de Satan*, 144.

[2] "Il est tout certain, que l'hõme ayme tellemēt la chose vraye: et hayt le mēsonge, qu'il ne veut qu'on luy propose l'vn pour l'autre: et ne veut chopper, estre deceu, ne surpris. D'ont aduient, qu'il ayme ceux, desquels il a opinion qu'ils disent la verité: ayant en horreur, et refuyant ceux qu'il estime enseigner choses fauses: . . ." (*Ibid.*, 229–230.)

[3] Compare Hooker, *Ecclesiastical Polity*, I, v, 2 ff. Acontius would go much further in permitting freedom of investigation than would Hooker. Indeed, it may be held that the 'sweet reasonableness' of Hooker has been considerably over-emphasized. Hooker taught that reason could determine the essential truths of Christianity, but he avoided the task of defining what those truths were when the doctrinal confusion of his age demanded just that contribution. Hooker allowed reason a certain scope of freedom, but it was curbed by the authority of the State and of the Church arbitrarily to dictate in matters which, though non-essential to him, might appear "reasonably" essential to others. Acontius would permit of no such interference of authority with freedom of thought. In brief, Hooker taught that the Church and not its members enjoyed rational freedom. Dissent could be permitted only if the dissentients showed rational grounds for their position, but the judge of those grounds was the Church. Hooker's championship of reason, when closely analysed, redounded to the authority of the Church, and may, in fact, have been motivated by the urgent necessity for presenting a case for the suppression of the Puritans by the Church.

[4] *Ibid.*, 231.

truth will be found and will come ultimately to prevail. It is only when the sword of persecution intervenes to disturb the operation of this refining process that God's purpose is thwarted and Satan's designs promoted.

The man who is in doubt or who entertains scruples of conscience is in reality inspired by a desire and an appetite for truth,[1] and so long as men seek diligently for truth they are likely to find it in the end.[2] The attainment of religious truth depends to a considerable degree, therefore, upon the "franchise et liberté de mettre en auant son opinion touchant le fait de la religion."[3] Acontius, like Franklin, whom he resembled in so many ways, pled for an extension of the range of free enquiry and deplored religious controversy as arising "for want of knowing how to differ decently. . . ."[4] Any law which prevents liberty of religious opinion is fanatical, and it is not difficult to determine what usually motivates the denial of such liberty.[5] The multitudes of debates and dissensions are inspired by Satan, both when doctrine is pure and when it is corrupt. Those who are in authority will be moved by Satan to bring an end to free enquiry and discussion. Since man is naturally possessed of an ability to discover the truths of religion, Satan will endeavour to destroy the only possible means for its attainment by stimulating the substitution of force for the power of reason.[6] "Since the occasion of seeking comes from this appetite for knowledge, and since enquiry is a means for attaining the cognizance of truth," it is expedient that Satan should do all in his power to prevent religious freedom.[7]

j. Summary

Acontius, in summary, brought to the discussion of the problem of religious toleration a scientific point of view which

---

[1] "Celuy qui est en doute ou scruple de conscience est aiguilloné d'vne desir et appetit de cercher la verité." (Acontius, Les Ruzes de Satan, 215.)
[2] Ibid. [3] Ibid., 215–216.
[4] "I hope the disagreements in our Royal Society, are compos'd; quarrels often disgrace both sides; and Disputes even on small matters often produce quarrels for want of knowing how to differ decently, an art which they say scarce anybody possesses but yourself and Dr. Priestly." (Franklin to Dr. Price, August 16, 1784. Letter in R. N. Carew Hunt collection.)
[5] Acontius, Les Ruzes de Satan, 216. [6] Ibid., 217. [7] Ibid.

he had outlined in the *De Methodo* and which the *Satanae Stratagemata* demonstrates to have had more than academic value. He was without doubt influenced by the Italian Academicians, but his point of view was his own, and his defence of toleration went considerably beyond their more sentimental efforts. In particular, Acontius laid bare the psychology of arrogance and hatred which was fundamentally responsible for religious persecution. He showed that the Protestant sects, at least, enjoyed no tenable grounds for a theory of persecution. Nor can there be any doubt that his teachings had a far-reaching effect upon Protestant thought.[1]

No less important was his denial that absolute truth and absolute error may be exactly ascertained. The general acceptance of such a view would, of course, sweep away at one stroke the possibility of enforced uniformity. He regarded salvation as depending upon a simple doctrinal formula which all communions professed, and he expressed the conviction that heresy could result only from the denial of the fundamental tenets of Christianity. He looked forward to the day when all religious groups might become aware of the identity of their basic beliefs and of the fact that they all sought the same goal —salvation. If corporate union were not possible as a consequence of such an understanding, at least the bitter friction which had for so long characterized their relations might disappear following the acceptance of such an objective view. He invited the religious groups to face outward rather than inward.

Moreover, Acontius presented a theory of religion which completely separated the spheres of Church and State, and which effectively denied the right of the State to interfere in the punishment of error either from a mistaken conception of its moral purpose or at the command of the clergy. The guilt of the heretic was a matter which God alone could determine and judge. The Church could exert moral suasion and in extreme instances protect itself by the execution of the penalty of excommunication, but that was all. In both of these instances the State was completely debarred from participation. He held

[1] Seeberg, R., *Dogmengeschichte*, IV, 2, 670–671.

that the State had long cloaked political motives in ecclesiastical garb. Heresy has become a legal fiction which the State and Church employ to curb their enemies. Persecution will sooner or later obliterate truth and destroy the avenues by which truth may be attained. The Church alone may dispose of cases of heresy, and Acontius obviously doubted, not its right, but its capacity accurately to define and judge heresy. He regarded excommunication as a serious measure since a grave injustice may be done to the excommunicate and the heresy may be fanned into a schism. His solution was rather to use moral and rational persuasion and to leave the heretic to the working out of his own salvation. He looked upon excommunication as the last desperate resort of the Church.

Acontius extolled reason and free enquiry as the solutions for the evils which beset the Church. Religious problems must be approached objectively, and with a cool, impartial suspension of judgment. The Bible is the sole source of religious truth and the author candidly admitted that no absolute system of doctrine may be gained from its pages, except those "saving essentials" which he had previously outlined. Every Christian should be permitted full liberty to construct his own belief and any authority which attempts to dictate the form or content of that opinion is tyrannous. Men will be led into doubt and error, but he regarded these intellectual states with complete equanimity. Doubt is a stage on the road to truth and men must labour up that difficult ascent by their own efforts. These axioms may sound worn to-day, but they were bold and revolutionary in 1565. Acontius was a deeply religious man, but he was so completely tolerant that he had abruptly to check his reasoning when he found himself in his defence of religious freedom on the verge of supporting honest agnosticism. If Acontius had been a sceptic or indifferent to religion, his treatise would have an important but a formal value; enhanced as it is with a rich spiritual ardour and an earnest and stalwart piety, it may be held to rank as the foremost philosophical and religious justification of religious liberty. A careful examination of the book conveys the unmistakable impression that Acontius believed that heresy should be left entirely unmolested.

Heresy must work its way to truth by the laborious but sure way which he termed the innate desire of man for truth. His comments on heresy and the practical impossibility of accurately determining it would not be lacking in value as a treatise to be digested prior to heresy trials in our own age.

The point of view expressed in the *Satanae Stratagemata* was remarkably dispassionate and objective. The book has especial value because it was the work of a man who was not himself persecuted. The sects provide us with numerous pleas for toleration, but their statements were marred by the fact that they pled for a cause whose limits were those of their own communion; or, if they pled for a general toleration, there remains in the mind of the reader a suspicion that their tolerance might give way in the event of their dominance to the current philosophy of enforced uniformity. Acontius, on the contrary, pled the case of toleration from the point of view of pure theory and objectivity. He was deeply distressed by the stupidity and tyranny of persecution and its obvious failure to effect the end it proposed to attain, but his feelings never mastered him. His treatise was cool, calm, detached and philosophical. Hence, as a literary composition, it may not be compared with the *De Haereticis* which glows with the sustained heat of conviction and personal feeling. Castellion was a sentimentalist; Acontius a philosopher. Castellion touched upon the dramatic and addressed his plea to the hearts of men; Acontius sought to present the case for toleration in all of its aspects and appealed to the minds of his readers. Castellion's treatise moved with quick and liquid ease; Acontius' arguments mounted up with that slightly heavy accumulation which marks the style of the philosopher. Castellion spoke from the heart; Acontius from the mind. As a pure and philosophical justification of religious toleration his book was not equalled before the appearance of Locke's famous *Letters*, if indeed then. Of him, the judicious Selden was able to apply the term which has been used of Origen, "Ubi bene, nil melius; ubi male, nemo pejus."

Quite as remarkable as the book itself was the fact that Acontius was able to publish it and escape censure and punishment. He denied the very bases of the Elizabethan religious structure and struck at authority which the Government guarded with a jealous hand. He was himself under the sentence of excommunication for upholding the rights of conscience for an exceedingly unpopular religious belief. Yet he appears to have continued in the Queen's favour and there is no evidence that he encountered any difficulty as a consequence of its publication.[1] This is a remarkable evidence of the moderate and tolerant character of the English Government in this period. Great as Acontius' book was, its influence in the ultimate securing of religious toleration in England was infinitely small when compared to the salutary and moderate moulds into which Elizabeth and her great Council had cast the Establishment. Religious liberty resulted from the realization of practical men and able rulers that the continuance of persecution and the over-arduous application of the bonds of enforced uniformity must inevitably result in the dissipation of the State's authority in the most disastrous of all species of internecine struggles. Toleration was attained as a consequence of the necessities of policy, and not as a result of the triumph of a noble theory in the hearts of men. The State yielded ground and sacrificed the ideal of a unified spiritual community, an ideal which had ceased to have content in the variegated complexion of national religious life.

This wary and politic course, though ignoble, was necessary for the preservation of national life. The Elizabethan Settlement had meant the triumph of the lay point of view and the sub-

[1] The first formal condemnation of the *Satanae Stratagemata* seems to have occurred in 1648. Cheynell called the attention of the Westminster Assembly to the book in a session in March of that year. Cheynell regarded the teachings of the book as a pestilent heresy. The considerations of the body were, of course, directed to the English translation which had appeared earlier in that year, and which contained a letter by Dury. Dury was present in the Assembly, and when questioned answered vaguely and excused himself on the remarkable grounds that he had not read the book. A committee, headed by Cheynell, was appointed to examine the work, and concluded that the author was an heretic. The book was interdicted on the grounds: first, there was no mention of the divinity of Christ or of the Holy Spirit; second, because Acontius regarded Christ as the "true Son of God" and not as the "natural Son of God." The Assembly concurred in the judgment of its committee.

ordination, or at least the control, of the ecclesiastical sphere by men whose interests were primarily secular. Religion had, to a larger degree than the hierarchy of the period would have cared to admit, become a curtain "for ye parliament windowes" and a "stalking house to temporal ends. . . ."[1] Only an Erastian point of view would have framed a bill to "allow and oblige" the full and free publication of all religious controversies in order better to control the acrimonious disputes of the time.[2] The growing Erastianism of the governmental policy was resented by all the religious groups. It was consistently repressive of religious zeal and vitality and it was occasionally tyrannous in its control. But toleration owes the policy two great debts: in the first place, the very stringency of governmental control called forth an ever-increasing body of protest against its interference in spiritual affairs and resulted in an attempt definitely to dissociate the secular and spiritual spheres; and, in the second place, the very Erastianism of the Government provided the greatest assurance that the annals of England would not be marred by a holocaust of religious strife, and that the policy of moderation and partially recognized toleration would in the very nature of things be gradually extended.

This point of view was not inaptly expressed by O. C. in his justification of Burleigh's conformity under Mary:

> How wary in Queene Maryes daies,
>   he did himselfe behaue,
> And sailes which hung aloft at mast,
>   to windes relenting gaue,
> Because it better is, to yeeld, to rough
>   and mightie force,
> Of raging floud, then stand against,
>   and to resist his course,
> Which doth a deadly perill prest, and
>   certaine harme procure;
> By iudgement plaine, apparent doth
>   expresse his wisdome sure. . . .[3]

---

[1] A brief discourse of the seueral parliamentary alterations and contrary changes of religion in the sixteenth century. (*Tanner MSS.*, Bodl., cciv, 86, temp. Chas. I.)   [2] *Ashmole MSS.* (Bodl.), 831, 258. Temp. Eliz.
[3] O. C., *Elizabeth Queene* (no pagin.).

3. ALBERICO GENTILIS

The tolerant attitude of the laity was likewise indicated by the incidental comments which the great Elizabethan legist, Alberico Gentilis, made on religion in his *De juri belli*[1] and in his *De Legationibus*.[2] Gentilis sought to divorce International Law from the fetters of theological consideration. Thus he declared in the *De juri belli* that differences in religion constituted insufficient grounds for war.[3] No one can or should be compelled to accept the faith of another unwillingly.[4] Complete liberty should be permitted in spiritual matters, for religion is an affair between God and man. He accused Baldus of having confused the temporal motive which largely influenced the Church in its wars on the infidels, and held that infidel princes enjoy unlimited sovereignty over their territories.[5] "Religion," he held, "is not properly a right of men towards God, religion is concord with God"; a divine right and tie between God and man. Since it is not a human right, having no sense of relationship between man and man, it is governed solely by Divine Law. Human law cannot interfere in the relationship which appertains between God and man. Thus a prince may not compel his subjects to adopt his religion.[6] However, the prince and his people may lawfully change their religion if the State suffers no injury thereby.[7] Gentilis was too much a legist, however, to admit the spiritual anarchy of complete religious freedom. Religion constitutes no just cause for the rebellion of subjects. The prince may, from the divine order of obedience, change the religion of the State. Gentilis would not, however, admit the right of the prince to persecute or to compel faith. Those subjects who cannot conform to the change have no alternative in such a case but to leave the country.[8]

[1] The first complete edition of the *De juri belli libri tres* was published in Hanau in 1598. A second edition appeared in 1612, and a third edition was published in Naples in 1770. A definitive text was published in London in 1877.　　[2] *De Legationibus, libri tres.*
[3] Gentilis, *De juri belli*, Bk. I, c. ix.　　[4] *Ibid.*
[5] Nézard, H., *Les Fondateurs*, 52.
[6] This was a distinct step beyond the principle of International Law expressed by the Treaty of Augsburg. (*De juri belli*, Bk. I, c. x.)
[7] *Ibid.*, Bk. I, c. iv.　　[8] *Ibid.*, Bk. I, c. xi.

The Law of Nations takes no cognizance of religious differences. It includes both heretical and infidel nations. Thus in the *De Legationibus* he pointed out that the excommunication of a ruler or of a State was no bar to normal diplomatic intercourse. Diplomatic relations may likewise be maintained with the Turks. In conclusion he wrote, "Religion is an affair between God and man, not between man and man; . . . others have proved it and I consider the proposition as established."

4. Edwin Sandys

Somewhat more important for our consideration is the *View or Survey of the State of Religion in the Westerne parts of the World* by Edwin Sandys, the son of the great Archbishop of York.[1] Sandys had been a pupil of Hooker and travelled abroad from 1593–1599, bringing back the manuscript of the book as the fruit of his observations.[2]

Sandys stood almost alone in the breadth of his view of the religious situation in Europe. He pointed out that the two great religious groups were so equally balanced in strength that neither could hope to subdue the other. Nor was there any hope that either side could enforce any sort of unity on Christendom. Unity, he urged, could only be attained by the tolerant efforts of thoughtful men who "expect the same finall reward of glory" and who will endeavour to lay aside controversy in order to strive for peace and unity.

[1] Allen, J. W., *Political Thought*, 242. Professor Allen's excellent discussion of Sandys has restored him from a long obscurity.

[2] The history of the book is confused. The first edition seems to have appeared anonymously in 1605 under a variant title. There are copies of this edition in the British Museum and in the Huntington Library. It is probable that two other editions appeared in the same year. There is a copy in Sir R. L. Harmsworth's Library which differs from the other two editions of 1605, and may probably be regarded as a specimen of the second edition. The third edition of 1605 (Hunt, Camb.), however, bears the printer's name, and may in reality be the first edition, the other two editions being reprints with false dates. The book was published without leave, and was burned in November 1605 by the High Commission at the request of the author. A fourth edition bearing the title *Europae Speculum, or, A View or Survey of the State of Religion in the Westerne parts of the World*, appeared in 1629. We have used the fifth edition of 1637, of which there are copies in the Harvard College Library and the McAlpin collection. It has been urged, however, that this is in reality the seventh edition.

Sandys proposed a rational agreement on central religious teachings between the various religious groups and the generally tolerant attitude of sect towards sect. The possibility of this desired end is to be found in the fact that there is agreement among all Christians on the "general foundations of religion," which he defined as the Apostles Creed.[1] He regarded the bitter religious feuds which were engulfing Europe as stupid and as dangerous politically and spiritually. These controversies serve only "to the encrease of atheisme within, of Mohametisme abroad . . ." to "taint the better minds with acerbity, and load the worst with poyson. . . ."[2] Unity may be attained only by the exercise of charity on both sides, by the recognition of faults, and by stressing the good points of the other group. He suggested that it was quite possible that God has removed absolute truth from the reach of man. Hence Christians should endeavour to unite on the essential doctrines of Christianity.

The writer appears to have envisaged a loose and general system of dogmatic and ecclesiastical organization which might prove acceptable to Christians, whether Catholic or Protestant. Difference in point of view and in conscience need prove no effective impediment to such unity; "For all other questions, it should be lawfull for each man so to beleeve as hee found cause; not condemning other such peremptorinesse as is the guise of some men of over-weening conceipts: and the handling of all controversies for this final compounding, to be confined to the Schools, to Councells, and to the learned languages, which are the proper places to try them, and the fittest tongues to treat them in."[3]

A universal Church to which any Christian might belong was clearly envisaged by Sandys. But his ideal broke down when he passed to a consideration of the means for its accomplishment. He suggested that the proper instrument for healing the wounds of Christendom and for resorting the Christian unity would be a General Council, chosen impartially by Catholics and Protestants.[4] If the obstinacy of the Pope and of the Protestant

---

[1] Sandys, *View of Religion*, 195. [2] *Ibid.*, 196.
[3] *Ibid.*, 199. [4] *Ibid.*

clergy should prove an impediment to such a procedure, his only suggestion was that the secular arm should intervene and force the recalcitrant group to accede in the interests of religion and peace.

However, Sandys was forced to confess that though "any kind of peace were better than these strifes," his hope had but slender prospects of realization. He regarded the Roman Catholic Church as the greatest impediment to Christian unity. He charged that the papacy had shown that it was incapable of the slightest compromise.[1] The Church is dogmatic and highly intolerant in its denial of the possibility of salvation for those who die outside its communion. The Pope will never consent willingly to such a programme and it therefore remains for the princes to "take the matter in hand, and constraine the Pope and others to yeild to some such accord."[2] But he could see no such champion at hand, for there are no princes who "will breake their sleepe for such purposes."[3] They are wholly concerned with civil affairs and are themselves promoters of faction and dissension. Sandys looked with longing eyes to the reforming emperors of the Middle Ages.

The author was accordingly driven to the hope that necessity might compel the attainment of some sort of unity. Thus the constant and increasing pressure of the Turks may "leave no hope for Christendome to subsist but in their inward concord. It is true that a forreigne enemy is a reconciler of brethren, and that common danger holds them together, so long as it lasteth, who else would flee asunder upon every light occasion."[4] But this danger, or hope, he discounted because of the probability that the Turkish Empire would fall to pieces as a consequence of its huge size and inefficient administration.

Therefore, the only hope remaining is that liberty may be achieved by peaceful persuasion. The Protestants, in this connection, find it to their advantage that they have "the unity of truth" on their side which is in itself able to win men.[5] The Catholics, on the other hand, trust to their superior historical

---

[1] Sandys, *View of Religion*, 202. [2] *Ibid.*, 205.
[3] *Ibid.* [4] *Ibid.*, 207. [5] *Ibid.*, 211-212.

and administrative position for the attainment of ascendancy. Sandys would appear to welcome the leadership of either of the two great branches of Christianity in the attainment of unity. But he regarded the zealous character of Calvinism and the firm devotion of England to the Protestant cause as insuperable barriers to union.[1] He was driven in the end to leave his cherished dream to the providence of God. "This is all I can say for any hope or meanes of this generall unity, and so must I leave and recommend it to God: as being both our best and now remaining onely policy, to addresse our united and generall supplications to His divine power and majesty: that it may please him by that ever springing fountaine of his goodnesse and gracious mercy, even beyond all human hope . . . to effect those things which to man's wit may seeme impossible, to extend his compassionable and helping hand over his miserable, defiled, disgraced Church . . . and to engraft" in all Christians "a pure and single Eye, to behold that eternall truth, which seen breeds love, and loved conduces to happiness; to root out all gal and acerbity on both sids, and to bend their hearts to charity. . . ."[2]

Sandys regarded European Christianity with rare objectivity, and saw beyond the claims of his own group and the somewhat boisterous national character of English Protestantism to a vision of a united Christendom. His ideal lay partly in the past, but he realized that the Reformation was a *fait accompli* and that any future unity of European Christendom must find its basis in a loose agreement on the essentials of faith. He believed that the intolerance of his day was sapping Christianity of all its vitality. He vigorously denied that absolute truth might be attained and suggested that all the Christian groups were already united in the essentials of religion, if they could only be brought to a realization of the fact. Force has no place in religion and the Government usurps its function when it seeks to advance the pretensions of a particular sect by its power. In fact, he held it to be the duty of European governments to force the various sects to tolerate each other.[3] Sandys' magni-

---

[1] Sandys, *View of Religion*, 213–215
[2] *Ibid.*, 215–216.   [3] Allen, *Political Thought*, 245.

ficent ideal broke down when he was obliged to discard one means of securing it after another. But the fact that he had such an ideal and that he could seriously propound it warrants the conviction that much progress had been made towards religious toleration during the reign of Queen Elizabeth.

VI

ROMAN CATHOLIC THOUGHT DURING THE REIGN
OF ELIZABETH AND ITS RELATION TO THE
DEVELOPMENT OF RELIGIOUS TOLERATION

1. GENERAL CHARACTERISTICS OF ROMAN CATHOLIC THOUGHT
   IN ENGLAND

Roman Catholic thought made no highly important contribution to the development of the idea of religious toleration,
despite the fact that the Catholics were the most severely
repressed of the several nonconforming groups in the realm.
This fact may be held to be the natural consequence of the
Roman Catholic theory of heresy and the generally intolerant
character of Romanist thought with regard to misbelief.
Catholic thought, in this particular, was obliged to confine
itself to the moulds which had been forged in an age when
the Church exercised universal spiritual dominion, and it did
so with remarkable consistency. The tendency of a persecuted
minority, as we have observed, is to lay down theoretical
and practical reasons for its own toleration and these arguments
may be expanded into a general plea for the toleration of all
minorities. The Catholics, however, were so deeply convinced
of the truth of their religious convictions and so filled with
abhorrence at the prospect of the multiplying Protestant sects
that they steadfastly refused to propound a plea for the general
toleration of error.

Catholic thought under Elizabeth was marked by at least
two peculiar characteristics which sharply differentiated it
from the Protestant thought of the period. It became, in the
first place, increasingly un-English and was disposed to be in
the crisis of the reign anti-English as well. It appears that most
of the clergy and the vast majority of the laity were soundly
Catholic at the time of the Queen's accession to the throne.
But so subtle was the change; so able and consistent the
pressure of the Government; and so difficult the proper educa-

372

tion of the young and the effective administration of the spiritual requisites of sound faith, that, as the reign wore on, the majority of Englishmen adjusted themselves to the new order. It was conclusively demonstrated that patience, tact, and moderation could accomplish what blind force had failed to achieve. The consciousness that Catholicism was being stifled under the astute policy of the Government and the untiring missionary zeal of the ultra-Protestant clergy was chiefly responsible for fanning the ardour of the Jesuits to the point of treason. One of the fairest provinces of the Church was rapidly slipping into irretrievable infidelity. The increasing rigour of English laws tended to force the more zealous and vigorous of the priesthood and laity into exile. They were touched on the Continent by the tremendous enthusiasm and the self-sacrificing aims of the Counter-Reformation, just as the Marian exiles had earlier drunk deep at the Rhenish sources of radical Protestantism. This group cast its lot with the Jesuits and developed a distinctly Continental point of view. Their solicitude was for the Church rather than for their country, and for the triumph of their Church they were prepared to sacrifice the stability if not the identity of England.

Elizabethan Catholic thought was marked, in the second place, by a far-reaching difference in the point of view of the Jesuit, or missionary, party and the English, or lay, party. The missionary party proposed to recover England for the Church at any cost and it utilized any weapons that came into its hands in order to achieve that purpose. Hence we find the Jesuits at once urging the toleration of English Catholicism on grounds not dissimilar to the Separatist pleas, persuading the Pope that toleration would mean the ruin of the Catholic cause in England, supporting the political designs of Spain, and entering into treasonable conspiracies. The apparent inconsistencies of the Jesuit party are resolved into a simple pattern when we bear in mind that they used all weapons with high but unscrupulous skill in their effort to achieve their end. We may applaud the courage and the singular devotion of the Jesuits to a high purpose, but we cannot commend either their honesty or their methods. The utterances of the Jesuits in

373

favour of religious toleration must consequently be regarded with care and scepticism.

The direct result of the Jesuit policy was a considerable increase in the suffering of their co-religionists in England. Only a small minority of the laity appears to have had any sympathy with or interest in their programme. The majority of the laity remained loyal to the Crown and acknowledged the civil overlordship of the Queen, denying the right of the Pope to alienate their allegiance to her. They were exercised only by a desire to translate the freedom of belief which they enjoyed into freedom of worship. As we have seen, they realized that the Jesuit programme was making that goal increasingly unattainable and towards the end of the reign a bitter quarrel divided the Catholics into two well-defined parties. The utterances of the non-political group on the subject of toleration are of great importance and merit full respect. Unfortunately, however, the missionary party was more active and articulate and most of the Catholic literature of the period was the product of the facile pens of that group.

A survey of Catholic literature during the period 1558–1603, with reference to the development of toleration, throws interesting incidental light on the moderate character of the governmental policy during most of the reign. Thirty-eight pleas for toleration or indictments of the repressive laws against recusants were consulted for the purposes of this study. Not one of this number appeared before 1580; i.e. before the concentrated Jesuit invasion of that year.[1] Fourteen books and pamphlets appeared between that date and the fresh penal laws of 1585. With the slackening of repression after the defeat of the Armada the literary efforts disappear until 1592 when four protests were made, inspired no doubt by the severity of the years 1591–1592. The Archpriest controversy and the association of the Government with the appeal to Rome called forth ten titles relevant to our subject in the two closing years of the reign.[2]

[1] Frere, *English Church*, 216 ff.
[2] This analysis makes no claim to completeness, and was suggested only by the striking grouping of the titles considered around certain dates. The

ROMAN CATHOLIC THOUGHT

English Catholic thought, in so far as it was tolerant, must be regarded as differentiated through the pressure of momentary circumstances both from the historical teachings of the Church and from the normal theory expounded at Rome on the question of heresy during the sixteenth century and thereafter. Even the pleas of the persecuted lay group for toleration were in a real sense repudiated by the Pope. The Church had turned a steadfast front against misbelief at the Council of Trent and its authorities could not recognize the implicit relativism in the supplications of its English communicants.

2. THE HISTORICAL ATTITUDE OF THE ROMAN CATHOLIC CHURCH TOWARDS HERESY

A perception of the peculiar difficulties involved in the toleration of the Catholic faith in England requires a brief survey of the historical attitude of the Church towards heresy. The early tolerance of the Church when it was under persecution and when it was dominated by a highly spiritualized conception of religion has been frequently and well commented upon.[1] But with the attainment of a dominant position in the western world the early tolerance of the Church rapidly disappeared. The heretic came naturally to be regarded as a possible focal point of a new sect which could rend the uniformity so recently and so laboriously acquired. He might be regarded as a menace both to purity of doctrine and to the solidarity of the ecclesiastical structure. The Church had by the fourth century acquired power, dignity, and traditions, and the preservation of these attributes became its first concern.

number of titles and the years in which they appeared follow: 1580..2; 1581..1; 1582..1; 1583..2; 1584..4; 1585..4; 1592..4; 1595..1; 1597..4; 1598..1; 1599..2; 1601..2; 1602..8.
[1] See especially Lea, H. C., *History of the Inquisition of the Middle Ages* I, 209 ff.; Creighton, *Persecution and Tolerance*, 74 ff.; Tertullian, *ad Scapulam*, c. ii, *Apologet.*, c. xxiv; vide, however, *adversus Gnosticos Scorpiace*, ii, iii; Lactantius, *Div. Instit.*, V, xx; Sulp. Severus, *Hist. Sacrae*, in *Migne*, xx, 155-159, for Martin of Tour's noble protest against the execution of the Priscillians. Lea has thoroughly searched the patristic writings for utterance in this connection, and his references (esp. I, 211 ff.) are of great value.

375

The Church no longer sought to discriminate between motives; it was primarily concerned with the fact of heresy. Compulsion came naturally to be regarded as necessary for the preservation of the unity of faith—to prevent the dissolution of the spiritual and social structures. This essentially political attitude received reinforcement from the close contact of the Church with the civil power and from the fact that it was in this period carrying so much of the burden of the State. The preservation of the purity of doctrine could be urged by churchmen as the prime duty of the civil ruler.[1] The basic doctrine of the Christian theory of missionary effort, that the Church is a spiritual body seeking to spread its influence by the persuasive power of truth, was forgotten.

Christian persecution of heresy would appear to have arisen, in part at least, from the close conjunction of State and Church and from the emphasis upon the integrity of the ecclesiastical structure. The excellent machine thus forged, as has been urged, may have saved the Church from dissolution in the period of the Barbarian invasions. It may well be argued that without the instrument founded for the beating down of internal dissensions the task of converting and civilizing an untutored society could never have been achieved. But for a uniform, well-knit ecclesiastical and dogmatic structure a great price had to be paid by the Church in the coin of spiritual values.

It will now be well briefly to notice the theory which was formulated by the Fathers to support the practice of persecution. Chrysostom taught that heretics should be suppressed and their meetings broken up in order to prevent them from contaminating others.[2] He did not admit, however, that heresy should be punished by death. Jerome, when Vigilantius forbade the adoration of relics, expressed his surprise that the bishop of the diocese had not destroyed him for the benefit

---

[1] Lea, *Inquisition of the M.A.*, I, 215. Thus the African Church urged the suppression of the Donatists; Leo the Great sought to impress upon the Empress Pulchina the importance of destroying Eutyches; Pelagius persuaded Narses that the suppression of heresy was in reality a work of love and not of persecution.

[2] Chrysostom, *Homil. XLVI on the Gospel of Matth.*, cs. i, ii.

376

of his soul. Zeal for God's truth, he held, cannot be regarded as cruelty. In fact, rigour is the most merciful treatment since it may prevent the soul from incurring the pains of eternal damnation. Cyprian cited the Levitical Laws in order to justify the doctrine of coercion.[1]

As the doctrinal position of the Church became more clearly defined, severity towards heresy tended to increase. It remained for the doctrine of persecution to receive systematic justification, and that was supplied by the genius of Saint Augustine. As Lecky has so well said, "He made it his mission to map out her [the Church's] theology with inflexible precision, to develop its principles to their full consequences, and to co-ordinate its various parts into one authoritative and systematical whole."[2] The struggle of the Church with the Arians and the Donatists served to spread as well as to solidify the theory and practice of persecution.[3] These conflicts supplied the impetus for the development of Saint Augustine's views on the subject of heresy. Graced by the weight of his name, the theory of persecution survived to permeate all of the schools of Christian thought during the Middle Ages. It nourished the bitter enmity of the sixteenth century and his writings were employed both by Protestants and Catholics as a cloak to shelter their intolerance.[4]

Augustine was descended from a pagan Numidian family and had himself vacillated for a period between the attractions of philosophy, Manichaeism, and Christianity. The tolerant expressions of his early career may probably be ascribed to the memory of that spiritual indecision. His early attitude was well expressed in his famous letter against the Manichaeans.[5]

---

[1] Cyprian, *Epist.*, Bk. I, epist., ii.

[2] Lecky, *Rationalism in Europe*, II, 29.

[3] Augustine stressed the rights of conscience so long as the Donatists had the advantage in Africa. He was quick to change his views when the situation was reversed. (Saint Augustine, *Epist.*, xciii, 17 (*ad Vincentius*, 408).)

[4] Janet ably stresses the powerful influence of Augustine in this connection. (Janet, P., *Histoire de la Science Politique*, I, 332–333; see also Lecky, *Rationalism*, II, 31.)

[5] *Contra Epistolam Manichaei quam vacant Fundamenti* (397). He urged that the correction of heretics is best accomplished by kindness and quiet discussion. (c. i.) "Let those storm against you who do not know how hard

377

In this letter Augustine displayed himself as a man of thoroughly tolerant conceptions.

This leniency was soon definitely abandoned and repeated expressions in favour of the rigorous suppression of heresy occur throughout his works. He retracted repeatedly all he had ever written in his earlier days about tolerance.[1] He said of his early views, "My first opinion was that no one should be compelled into the unity of Christ, that we must cut only by words, fight only by arguments, and prevail by force of reason. . . . But this opinion . . . was overcome not by the words of those who controverted it, but by the conclusive instances to which they could point."[2] In the same letter he said that he was finally persuaded that force should be employed against heretics by the advantages which accrued to the Church from the imperial laws against the Donatists.[3] He urged that when the ruler persecutes for the good of the Church he does so through piety and mercy. Thus Pharaoh's persecution of the Jews was evil since it was motivated by tyranny and cruelty; while the rigour of Moses was just since it proceeded from love.[4] This conviction was to be re-expressed in a variety of ways during the Middle Ages and throughout the period of the Reformation, and from it the Church was able to justify its repressive actions. It would appear to have been the principal basis for Augustine's theory of persecution.

The great Father's arguments for persecution were the obvious ones, and his Scriptural sanctions for them were naturally principally drawn from the Old Testament.[5] It was

---

it is to avoid error." (c. ii.) He recalled the days when he was hopelessly mired in error (c. iii), and "I must bear with you now as formerly I had to bear with myself, and I must be as patient towards you as my associates were with me, when I went madly and blindly astray in your beliefs." He expressed his desire to seek the truth with them "as if it were unknown to us both." (c. iv.) This offer is strikingly similar to Acontius' view of suspension of judgment.

[1] Coulton, G. G., "Protestant View of Toleration," *Contemp. Rev.*, 777, September 1930.

[2] *Epist.*, xciii, 17. The entire letter is valuable in setting forth Augustine's mature opinion on the question of toleration. Vide also *Ibid.*, clxxxv.

[3] *Epist.*, xciii.   [4] *Ibid.*, cxiii, 8, and clxxxv, 8.

[5] Augustine, *Epists.*, xciii, cxxvii, clxxxv.

merciful, he held, to punish heretics even to the extent of death, if this action might possibly save them or others from eternal punishment. Heresy must be regarded as soul murder, the worst species of murder. The New Testament provides no instances of persecution, but this was explained by the fact that no priest had yet embraced Christianity.

Augustine often compared the repression of heresy with the restraints which were imposed upon lunatics. Insane and delirious persons must be controlled in order to prevent them from harming themselves and others. Thus, if we saw an enemy possessed with the fever about to precipitate himself off a cliff, every instinct informs us that it would be better forcibly to restrain him than to permit him to destroy himself.[1] He likewise gave a literal interpretation to the Gospel parable *compelle intrare*, which Lecky rightly regarded as the most important argument advanced for medieval persecution.[2] The torment of Jesus was even cited by Augustine in his search for materials with which to fortify his position.[3] Persecution, he concluded, since it is motivated by charity and since it is salutary for the erring, is righteous. "Better all the wounds of a friend than the proferred kisses of an enemy. It is better to love severity, than to deceive with goodness."[4]

Little could be added to these arguments.[5] Later writers

---

[1] Augustine, *Epist.*, xciii, 2.

[2] This thesis is a complete denial of the spiritual nature of Christianity. Bayle answered this position in detail and with devastating logic in his brilliant *Commentaire Philosophique sur ses Paroles de Jesus Christ contrain les d'entrer.* . . .   [3] Augustine, *Epists.*, clxxxv, clxxv.

[4] *Ibid.*, xciii, 2; clxxv.

[5] As Professor Coulton has ably pointed out, Augustine's general and mature position on the subject of heresy makes it difficult to understand the Encyclical *Immortale Dei* of Leo XIII: "Nor is there any reason why anyone should accuse the Church of being wanting in gentleness of action or largeness of view, or of being opposed to real and lawful liberty. The Church, indeed, deems it unlawful to place the various forms of divine worship on the same footing as the true religion, but does not, on that account, condemn those rulers who, for the sake of securing some great good, or of hindering some great evil, patiently allow custom or usage to be a kind of sanction for each kind of religion having its place in the State. And, in fact, the Church is wont to take earnest heed that no one shall be forced to embrace the Catholic faith against his will; for, as St. Augustine wisely reminds us: 'Man cannot believe otherwise than of his own free

placed greater emphasis upon the contagious nature of heresy, its evil consequences to the State and to Society, and erected a legal case for the repression of heresy, but they added little more to the ethical and religious bases which were supposed to undergird the coercion of religious dissension.

Somewhat more than a quarter of a century after the Inquisition had been fully launched, St. Thomas restated and amplified the theory of persecution with calm and judicial logic. His teachings in this matter formed the basis of Roman Catholic theory in the sixteenth century and, ideally at least, represent the position of the Church on error to-day. Granting his premises, that the Church contains and controls the full body of truth necessary for salvation and that there can be no possibility of salvation outside the Church, it is difficult to escape the logic of his conclusions. Resting his arguments upon Augustine, he declared that heretics deserved not only to be separated from the Church by excommunication, but to be excluded from the earth by judicial death.[1] Errors in geometry, he declared, do not constitute mortal guilt, but errors in the faith do. The Church, in its infinite mercy, should extend two warnings to the heretics. If this cannot break the stubborn core of heresy, the guilty man must be despaired of by the Church and relaxed to the secular tribunal for execution. He urged that this procedure demonstrated the abounding charity of the Church, since it is infinitely more evil to corrupt the purity of the faith upon which depends the eternal welfare of every soul than to be guilty of a crime that threatens only the temporal structure. Hence, if the violator of a civil law may be justly slain, it is incomparably more just to slay one who threatens the spiritual welfare of generations yet unborn. Nevertheless, the Church in its mercy will one time receive the penitent heretic back into its communion. But charity

will.' " (*Contemp. Rev.*, 777, 310.) The quotation quite ignores the mature opinion of the Father, and, if taken as representing his historical view and influence on the subject of the persecution of error, would lead to an entirely erroneous impression.

[1] ". . . merverent non solum ab Ecclesia per excommunicationem separi, sed etiam per mortum a mundo excludi." (S. Th. Aq., *Summa*, II, ii, q. xi, art. 3.)

must not be permitted to become a menace to the spiritual welfare of the many. If the repentant heretic again relapses, he must be executed, though he may be admitted to penance for his soul's sake.[1] No one, Aquinas taught, may be compelled to enter the Church, but once having entered its communion, he must, if necessary, be forced by violent means to lend obedience to its faith,—"haeretici sunt compellendi ut fidem teneant."[2] The sin of heresy, since it completely separates man from God, is the worst of all sins and hence deserves the worst possible punishment.[3]

We have endeavoured to show that the Protestant sects were disposed to take over this theory *in toto*, but that in consequence of the fact that their own separation constituted a vindication of the right of heretical secession from the Universal Church, and because of their emphasis upon the right of private judgment and the spiritual nature of religion, the spirit of philosophy and persecution was being rapidly dissolved in all Protestant quarters within three generations from the beginning of the Reformation movement.[4] In England the doctrine of religious persecution for the sake of the preservation of doctrinal purity had been completely devoid of content since the accession of Elizabeth. The doctrine fitted only the structure of a Universal Church and the Protestant communions could claim that title only in the rhetorical flourishes which headed their formal confessions of faith.

[1] S. Th. Aq., *Summa*, II, ii, q. xi, arts. 3–4.
[2] Augustinas Triumphas was the first theologian strongly to assert the power of the papacy over unbelievers. In the late thirteenth century Innocent IV claimed certain powers over infidels as well as over the Christian flock (*Apparatus ad quinque libros decretalium*, iii, 34, 8), but the claim was not fully expounded at that time. Generally speaking, Jews, Saracens, and other infidels, who had never received the faith, were regarded as wholly outside the fold of the Church and hence as incapable of heresy. It would seem that a logical extension of Augustine's interpretation of 'compel them to enter' would have resulted in forcible proselytism, at least among infidel groups residing within a Christian State. Such a doctrine was, however, never officially admitted. It was necessary that an unbeliever should be baptized before the Church claimed spiritual authority over him. (S. Th. Aq., *Summa*, II, ii, q. x, arts, 8, 12.)
[3] *Ibid.*, II, ii, q. x, arts. 3, 6. It was stated at the Council of Constance that if a belief were Catholic in a thousand points and false in one, it must be regarded as wholly false. [4] Cf. *ante*, 31–40.

3. ROBERT PARSONS AND THE JESUIT POSITION

However, the Roman Catholic Church had receded not one step from its historical position in the matter. In certain sections it had become 'inexpedient' to enforce the practice of persecution, but 'inexpedient' was a synonym for 'impossible.'[1] The Jesuits were inexorably wedded to the principle of coercion. No observing Englishman had any doubt but that the restoration of Roman Catholicism as the religion of the State with control of policy and with power to execute that policy would result in an attempt completely to exterminate Protestantism in England. This fact was openly admitted by the Jesuit leaders. England was now thoroughly Protestant and such an attempt would have resulted in a miserable fiasco, but this could not be appreciated at the time. England was afraid, and so long as that fear persisted the toleration of Roman Catholics was a political and a social impossibility. Toleration is possible only

[1] For the present Roman Catholic position on the question of religious toleration see the excellent article by J. Polile in the *Catholic Encyclopedia*, XIV, 763 ff. He would say that 'theoretical dogmatic tolerance' is impossible in a truly religious man. Philosophical tolerance implies scepticism in philosophy and indifference in religion. He would define dogmatic intolerance as the 'objective intolerance of truth towards error.' However, 'practical civic tolerance' is commended as 'requisite for the maintenance of friendly intercourse and co-operation among a people composed of different religious denominations. . . .' It is necessary, however, that the Church, as the sole repository of truth, should present a 'firm front to untruths,' and its 'fundamental idea' is to be found in the term 'extra Ecclesiam nulla salus.'

We would gather that the Church assumes a tolerant attitude in countries in which it does not wield a dominant influence from a policy of expediency. It may be argued that the members of the Protestant bodies have in the course of centuries become not so much misbelievers as unbelievers. They might, indeed, be regarded by the Church as the Jews and Saracens were viewed in the Middle Ages and, consequently, reside beyond the coercive jurisdiction of the Church. But, presuming Catholic dominance, with continued missionary effort towards a Protestant group which met every effort at conversion with a stubborn refusal to accept 'the truth,' at what point would unbelief become heresy? At what point would the formal (dogmatic) intolerance of the Church acquire factual character? Historically, Catholic intolerance has become formal because it has become impossible to persecute heresy in a world in which the secular policy dominates to the exclusion of ideal but dangerous spiritual ends. An authoritative statement of the Roman Catholic position on these important questions would be valuable and timely.

when the dominant groups observe no danger involved to their institutions, property, and security in the teachings and activities of a minority group which desires liberty freely to exercise its tenets. The militant Catholics had set their goal at the complete recovery of England to the fold by the quickest and most rigorous means at hand. They asked for no compromise, for no toleration, and they got little. Between the millstones of a resolute purpose to conquer England for the Church and a high resolve that England should not suffer the pains of an internecine struggle such as was proceeding in France, the lay Catholics, whose only interest in the issue was confined to the spiritual implications of their faith, suffered cruelly and their faith in England came into grave danger of extinction.

The Jesuits believed that the extension of religious freedom to the English Catholics, under conditions which would require complete political fidelity to the Crown and debar their missionary efforts, would result in the impairment of their plan to win a dominant position for their faith in the realm. They were able to persuade the Pope to a partial acceptance of this position, and we shall find the leaders of the Church condemning an effort to secure some measure of religious freedom for the lay group. The Jesuits had determined on a struggle which made no compromise possible; they expected no quarter and gave none.

Thus their greatest leader, Robert Parsons, with his keen and reasoned analysis, pointed out the futility and impossibility of compromise in his *A Conference about the Next Succession to the Crowne of Ingland*. He was discussing the succession to the English throne and asserted as his basic principle that religion was the most important factor to be considered in the choice of a monarch.[1] The cultivation of the spiritual well-being of his subjects is the highest duty of the prince.[2] For the "highest and chiefest end of every state is cultus Dei, the seruice of God, and religion, and consequently that the principal care and charge of a prince and magistrate euen by nature it selfe, is to looke thereunto. . . ."[3] Since the end of

---

[1] Parsons, Robert, *Conference*, I, 203.
[2] *Ibid.*, I, 204.   [3] *Ibid.*, I, 207.

man extends beyond his temporal requirements, "it followeth that what souerer prince or magistrate doth not attend vvith care to assist and helpe his subiects to this ende, ommiteth the first and principal part of his charge, and commiteth high treason against his lord and master, in whose place he is, and consequently is not fitt for that charge and dignity, though he should performe the other two partes, neuer so well, of temporal iustice and valor in his person. . . ."[1] Religion, in other words, should be the test of political loyalty. This doctrine denounced the effort of Elizabeth to differentiate between the temporal and spiritual spheres and to convince men that political loyalty had its roots in other soil than religion.

Parsons gravely prejudiced the claims of his co-religionists to liberty when he re-expressed the teachings of his faith on the subject of heresy, in this case with regard to the ruler. He was considering the question of whether a prince who differed in religion from the true faith should be tolerated. His answer was that there is "but one only religion that can be true among Christians."[2] ". . . Seing that to me ther can be no other fayth or religiō auaylable for my salvation then only that vvich I my selfe do beleeue . . . vnto me and my conscience he vvich . . . beleeueth otherwise than I do, and standeth vvilfully in the same, is an infidel. . . ."[3] Parsons, in other words, considered all men outside his own faith to be spiritual and physical enemies. He continued, "so long as I haue this contrary persuasion of him, I shal do against my conscience and sinne damnably in the sight of God, to prefer him to a charge where he may draw many other to his owne error and perdition. . . ."[4]

It appears strange that Parsons, who here and elsewhere spoke so nobly in the cause of conscience, could not have realized that consciences and wills could be just as inflexible in other faiths than his own; that men in other faiths could be quite as certain of the all-inclusive truth of their convictions. Parsons' theory represents a noble reflection of the thought of an age when universal uniformity of belief was an actuality, when

[1] Parsons, *Conference*, I, 212.   [2] *Ibid.*, I, 214.
[3] *Ibid.*   [4] *Ibid.*; see also I, 216.

States were influenced, if not directed, by spiritual ends. But his logic was as dangerous as high explosives in an age when there was not one faith but many, and not one truth but several. The inexorable rigidity of doctrinal systems had necessarily to relax in order to prevent universal chaos.

The Jesuit disclaimed a principle which had in his own day saved England. He denied that toleration and moderation were possible as policies of State, "for let the bargaines and agreements be vvhat they will, and fayre promises and vayne hopes neuer so great, yet seeing the prince once made and setled, must needes proceede according to the principles of his owne religion . . ." the State will inevitably seek to crush out dissenting groups. In this conviction he over-estimated the importance of religion in sixteenth-century statecraft. He urged that no ruler would keep faith with a religious group not his own. He held that it "is very hard if not impossible for tvvo of different religions to loue sincerely . . ."[1] and that at the best the minority party would be subjected to "so many ielosies, suspitions, accusations, calumnations, and other auersions," that their right freely to worship would be negated.[2]

Even more typical of the Jesuit position on the question of toleration was the view expressed by Father Tichborne in 1598.[3] He held that the early moderation of the Queen had served for nothing else but to make such as "reaped benefit from it to be reputed spies and men of too large a conscience. . . ."[4] Any effective change in the Catholic policy of the Government, he argued, would necessarily come "by some public altering and repealing of laws or some solemn security under the prince's word." He expressed the conviction that a policy of toleration on the part of the Government would mean the ruin of the Catholic cause in England. He urged

[1] Parsons, *Conference*, I, 217. [2] *Ibid.*, I, 218.
[3] Tichborne went over to Rheims in 1583 and joined the Society four years later. In 1597 he was Prefect of the English College at Rome, and was later a Professor in Parsons' Seminary at Seville. He died there in 1606. The letter here considered was sent to Fr. Darbyshire, another prominent Jesuit, and found its way into the hands of the Government. (Cf. also *ante*, 202–209.)
[4] *Henry Tichborne, S.J., to Thomas Darbyshire, S.J.*, February 2, 1598. (*S.P. Dom. Eliz.*, cclxii, 28.)

that toleration was "so dangerous that what rigour of laws could not compass in so many years, this liberty and lenity will effectuate in twenty days, to wit, the disfurnishing of the seminaries, the disanimating of men to come and others to return, the expulsion of the society, a confusion as in Germany, extinction of zeal and fervour, a disanimation of princes from the hot pursuit of the enterprise." Such a policy of toleration, it was urged, would ruin the order and its programmes and would persuade the king of Spain 'our greatest patron' to "stoop to a peace which will be the utter ruin of our edifice, this many years in building."[1]

It is difficult to understand how the Elizabethan Government could possibly have taken any other position than it did toward those who taught these principles. Toleration can scarcely be extended to those who regard it as a danger to their own cause. The Jesuits and the political Catholic group made little contribution to the advancement of religious toleration save as their somewhat unscrupulous tactics convinced men the more that the Christian religion could not be propagated effectively in such wise.

The Roman Catholic pleas for toleration were generally simple in structure and character. Their arguments for spiritual liberty rarely extended beyond the virtues of their own case. They sought liberty of conscience for their own faith on the grounds, whether expressed or implied, that it was the true faith and with no indication that their sufferings had made them ready in the event of their return to power to permit other men to enjoy the freedom for which they now pled.

Parsons in his earlier works pleaded for toleration on the ground that conscience could not be compelled.[2] The great

[1] *Tichborne to Darbyshire.* (*S.P. Dom. Eliz.*, cclxii, 28.) Printed *in extenso* by Law, *Jesuits and Seculars*, 139–143.

[2] Parsons, Robert, *A Brief discourse contayning certayne reasons why Catholiques Refuse to goe to Church* (1580), and *An Epistle of the persecution of Catholickes in England* (1582). We shall reserve the consideration of Parsons' later works, in which his views on the subject of toleration show a considerable progression, for later pages. (*A Treatise Tending to Mitigation towardes Catholicke-Subiectes in England*, 1607 (probably by Parsons), and *A Discussion of the Answere of M. William Barlow*, 1612.) These works belong to a period when Parsons and the Jesuits had begun to despair of

Jesuit was a writer of ability and his argument was close woven and compelling. He held that there were four distinct religions in England, and that the Roman Catholic faith as the oldest of them deserved some favour. He pointed out that it was the source from which the new sects had sprung. It should naturally hope in consequence "to receaue more fauour then the rest, or at least wyse, equall tolleration with other religions disalowed by the State,"[1] On the contrary, other dissenting groups have been tolerated while the Catholic "hath bene soe beaten in, with the terror of lawes, and the rigorous execution of the same, as the verye suspition thereof, hath not escaped unpunished."[2] He held very correctly that the Protestants persecuted with far less cause than the Catholics. For the Catholic faith is ancient and is united, while the Protestants are in no agreement among themselves even in fundamental doctrines such as the number and nature of the Sacraments.[3] He was especially grieved at the confusion appertaining in the religious laws of England between sincere religious worship and treason. He urged that the Catholics are considered *ipso facto* traitors.[4] They are, in fact, "as readye, to spend their goods, landes, liuinges, and lyfe, with al other worldly commodities whasoeuer, in the seruice of your maiestie and their countrie," as any loyal subject is and should be.[5]

The essence of Parsons' argument for liberty of worship for his co-religionists was that conscience may not be compelled. Generally speaking, he held that the persecuted Catholics in England were loyal and peaceful citizens. "The onlie cause of their molestation, is their conscience in religion, whiche beinge setled uppon invincible grounds, as it semethe to them, is not in their power to alter at their pleasure, neither is any persecution in [the world?] able to change the same, but rather confirmeth it more and more, bringinge alwaies an argument withe it, of lack of truthe in the persecutor, whiche seeketh

an immediate return to dominance, and when they had begun to appreciate that a minority party which was suspected and feared must adopt a conciliatory tone.
[1] Parsons, *Certayne Reasons, Dedic.*, iv.
[2] *Ibid.*   [3] Parsons, *Epistle of the Persecution*, 7.
[4] Parsons, *Certayne Reasons, Dedic.* (no pagin.).   [5] *Ibid.*

to supply by externall terror the thynge he is not able to proue by argument."[1] He pleaded ably that the forcing of conscience was a damnable sin. "Al princes also, and potentates of the world, haue abstayned from the beginninge, . . . from enforcinge men to actes against their conscience, especially in religion. . . ."[2]

Persecution cannot possibly secure the desired conformity in religion. If the Government is able to compel a weakling to conform in external matters, he will none the less remain at heart devoted to his previous conviction. In fact, he will be further removed from inward conformity, his soul and conscience having been outraged.[3] The truth of this principle has been recognized even by the greatest enemies of Christianity. Thus the Moslems accord toleration to their Catholic subjects and no man is compelled to embrace their religion.[4] In the Indies and other "farre partes of the worlde, where infinite infidels are vnder the gouernment of Christian princes, it was neuer yet practized, nor euer thought lawful by the Catholicke Church, that such men should be enforced to anye one acte of our religion."[5] Throughout most of Christendom the Jews have been tolerated in their worship. Hence the persecution of Catholics by a Christian prince is all the more lamentable.[6] "I cannot," he declared, "thincke you so fiers and pityles to exercise suche extremitie, uppon poore people for that cause, whereof your own fathers were as guyltie as we are, that is, for our conscience in the auncient religion."[7] Terror cannot destroy truth. Persecution only serves to harden and to propagate the true faith.

English Catholics only ask for the favour which Protestants have secured in other countries.[8] This toleration should proceed "from a mercifull disposition towardes the afflicted," and from a conviction "that mens consciences are not to be constrained."[9]

[1] Parsons, *Epistle of the Persecution*, 8.
[2] Parsons, *Certayne Reasons, Dedic.* (no pagin.).
[3] Parsons, *Epistle of the Persecution*, 9.
[4] *Ibid.*, 36; *Certayne Reasons, Dedic.* (no pagin.).
[5] Parsons, *Certayne Reasons, Dedic.*
[6] Parsons did not make clear that from the Roman Catholic point of view a wholly different principle is involved in the persecution of an unbeliever and of an heretic.   [7] Parsons, *Epistle of the Persecution*, 37.
[8] *Ibid.*, 38.   [9] *Ibid.*

God will hold the Government of England responsible for the judgment of men who are motivated only by the requirements of their consciences, "for . . . suche rigour, to your owne fleshe and bloode, for matter of conscience, which you haue not don to any other most impious, haynous, or detestable malefactor."[1]

In his ninth argument for Roman Catholics absenting themselves from the services of the Established Church, Parsons took a subtle position. All persons who have a sincere regard for their religion desire to worship and commune with believers who hold beliefs identical with their own. "And soe the Anabaptistes at this daye, refuse to goe to the Lutheran church, and the Lutherans to the Trinitaries. In like wise the Puritans of our time in Englād refuse to come to the Protestantes churches."[2] In other countries, the Protestants, alleging conscience, refuse to attend the services of the dominant Catholic Church. Therefore the English Protestants are repudiating their own doctrine "which obiect the same to Catholiques as disobedience, obstinacie, and rebellious dealing, which in other countries they themselues both teach and practise."[3] In this argument he took advantage of the Separatist position that the elect desire to worship together. He pointed out the divisions which marked the Protestantism of his day and enquired how such men could possibly persecute. He did not, it should be noted, abandon the views of his own Church on the subject of heresy; he convicted Protestant intolerance on the evidence of its own teachings and the illogical case it presented for persecution.

He held that the Catholics were willing to render implicit obedience to the Crown in all temporal matters. Any reasonable man, therefore, "Especiallye the Protestant, except he wil mislike with his owne doctrine, which condemneth me of hipocrise, dissimulation, and renouncinge of Christ, and his Gospel, if I present my only bodye, to the Churches of them, whos religion I am not persuaded to be trew,"[4] will be compelled by logic to agree that belief and worship cannot be

[1] Parsons, *Epistle of the Persecution*, 39.
[2] Parsons, *Certayne Reasons*, 53.   [3] *Ibid.*   [4] *Ibid.*, 55.

compelled. No one, he argued, will be so impious as to deny that there is only one religion among Christians which is the true one.[1] "And if euerye man which hath anye religion, and is resolved therein, must needes presuppose this only truth, to be in his own religion: then it followeth necessarily, that he must like wyse perswade him selfe, that all other religions besides his owne, are false and erroneous, and consequently al assemblies, conuenticles, and publike actes of the same" are wicked and dishonourable to God.[2] It is quite as easy to commit treason against God as to be disloyal to the Queen.

Parsons here made use of the generally received notion of absolute truth as an argument for toleration. As we have noted, it was in point of fact one of the principal sources for religious intolerance. Parsons appears to have been unique in his thesis. Every man is convinced of the complete and exclusive truth of his own faith and, correspondingly, of the falsity of other beliefs. To force a man to abandon a faith which has its roots in such conviction would be to force the man into the awful sin of treason against God. The argument was able and it could be used against Catholic intolerance as well as against Protestant bigotry. But the argument was wholly academic as Parsons' own example indicated. The man who is dominated by an absolute conviction of the truth of his belief is so certain of his faith and of the inspiration of God that he inevitably attempts to persecute, in one fashion or another, the error which is quite as clear to him as the truth of his own conviction. Toleration proceeded as the absolute conception of doctrinal truth gave way before the clamourings of a multitude of truths.

Unless Parsons was completely insincere, he came close to enunciating a doctrine of general toleration. Even, he said, if the Protestant religion should be the true faith, "Yet should I be condemned for going amongst them: for that in my sight, iudgment, and conscience (by which onlye I must be iudged), they must needes seemes enemyes to God. . . ."[3] If we interpret him correctly, he came close to asserting that a man is judged, not by the truth of his beliefs, but by the devotion and sincerity with which he adheres to those beliefs. If Parsons meant this,

[1] Parsons, *Certayne Reasons*, 55.   [2] *Ibid.*   [3] *Ibid.*, 58.

he was probably guilty of heresy, but he had advanced a noble heresy.

It is a grievous sin to "compel men by terror, to doe acts of religion against their consciences: as to take othes, receaue sacraments, goe to churches, and the like. . . ."[1] Such oppression results in grave spiritual danger both to the oppressor and to the oppressed. The writer pleaded nobly for a true distinction between civil disobedience and religious Nonconformity. "If by the rackinges, stretchinges, wrestinges, and dreadfull tortures used so often and to so many of our innocent afflicted brethren . . . there hath bene any one thinge wrounge out from them, of treason, conspiracie, or practises against the state, wherewith our aduersaries, without conscience, do use daily to accuse us; let the partis guyltie be punished openly, with infamie also to our cause. Albeit in this later we offer more than reason. But if after all this fierce halinge, and pitifull pullinge of men in pieces, nothinge hath bene founde at all, no one act, no worde, no cogitation of suche matters, but onlye innocencie and zeale of religion in the tormented: then is our case much more hard at home, in our owne countrye, under our owne Soueraigne, than it could be any where els under the extremest aduersaries of our religion in the worlde."[2]

The Government consistently maintained that it made just this distinction. The essential difficulty lay in the definition of "zeale of religion." The Government contended that the zeal of the Jesuit party ceased at a certain point to be spiritual alone and embraced seditious and political designs. The Catholics, basing their arguments upon an older and perhaps a nobler view of the functions of the State, held that the proffered liberty of conscience was an empty bauble if it could not be accompanied with the liberty freely to exercise the rites and

[1] Parsons, *Certayne Reasons*, 58. He explained, however, that under the Roman Catholic doctrine a man, having embraced the faith, and then attempting to rend the robe of Christ by heresy, might be compelled to return to the fold of the Church by the punishment of the civil magistrates. (*Ibid., Dedic.* (no pagin.). Parsons' intolerance lay in the fact that he discerned no inconsistency in advancing an argument with the right hand and recalling it with the left.
[2] Parsons, *Epistle of the Persecution*, 36.

ministrations of the faith and vigorously to prosecute its truths among the erring.

The Catholics held that the Erastian theory and practice of the English Government destroyed the universality of the Church. If, as the English theologians contended, the secular ruler is the head of the Church Universal in his realm, then Christendom has in reality become a collection of wholly independent Churches.[1] If the spiritual authority of the Pope over the Church is denied, then the universal Church becomes non-existent. The doctrine of the royal supremacy will eventually fill the world with as many sects as there are princes.[2] The determination of religion and doctrine is not properly the function of the civil power,[3] as history has well demonstrated. No secular Government will seriously concern itself with questions of faith. To hang on the will of a prince for our religious belief is "the pitifullest hazard."[4] It is absurd to imagine that we must believe in spiritual matters what our secular masters demand, and this is precisely what the English Government required. Thus, the Catholics, "in iustice . . . crave pardon of your honours, for not conforminge our opinions to yours in this matter; We can not doe it without dissimulation and most greeuouse remorse of an accusinge conscience."[5] Parsons and his colleagues held that the presumption that a national Government representing a national Church, could regulate doctrine, prescribe forms of worship, and enforce conformity was a negation of the true nature of religion.[6] The civil governor, they argued, is not infallible and he will seek the lines of least civil resistance rather than the interests and requirements of spiritual truth.

We have met with this argument before from Puritan and from Separatist pens. But neither the Puritan nor the Catholic conception offered anything to the cause of toleration. The one

[1] Strype, *Annals*, I, 2, app. Nos. 6 and 7.
[2] Allen, William, Card., *A True, Sincere, and Modest Defence*, I, 18–19.
[3] Parsons, *Epistle of the Persecution*, 31.
[4] Allen, *An Apologie and Trve Declaration of the Institution and endeauours of the tvvo English Colleges,* . . . 34.
[5] Parsons, *Epistle of the Persecution*, 31.
[6] Allen, J. W., *Political Thought*, 208.

would impose a bigoted and intolerant ministry as the judge of religious concerns and would enforce its decisions by a compliant civil authority; the other would impose a spiritual authority, no less absolute, no less intolerant, which would likewise enforce conformity through a subservient civil power. Both the Puritans and the Catholics sought liberty for their own consciences with the ultimate idea of compelling other men to their beliefs. It is not to be wondered that they hated each other so bitterly. As Professor Allen has brilliantly said, "So far as they were concerned it was merely an accident in the vast process of things, that their efforts to free themselves helped to enlarge human freedom. Had Parsons had his way and England become subject to a Spanish Catholic, had Travers succeeded in getting his 'discipline' established, there would have been far less freedom in England than there was under Elizabeth."[1] The Separatist, on the other hand, denied the right of the magistrate to order religion and to enforce conformity because he regarded the true Church as a miraculous construction of conversion. Conversion cannot be forced by the magistrate and consequently the ruler cannot erect a Church. He posed the sanctity of private judgment against the Erastian dictates of the State-Church. Toleration owes much to the denial of secular interference by the Separatist; little to the position of the Puritan and Catholic. The Separatist desired to establish the judgment of the private man as the supreme arbiter of religious affairs, the Puritan the ministry, the Catholic the papacy.

As we have pointed out, Parsons in the *Conference about the Next Succession* had disclaimed the possibility of the toleration of another faith by the dominant religion. His activity and policy warrant the conviction that he had little sympathy with the concept of religious liberty and that if he and his party had triumphed the moderate character of the English religious settlement would have been quickly blotted out. But he was impelled by the precarious position of the faith for which he laboured so incessantly to pronounce sentiments which are not without importance in the development of religious liberty.

[1] Allen, J. W., *Political Thought*, 209.

393

Parsons' position was not unlike the attitude of the dominant Politico-Religious groups in several European States. He and they were loyal to the ancient doctrine of a uniform faith enforced by rigorous laws against misbelief. But the desperate plight of his party in England compelled Parsons to plead against his will for the cause of conscience and to argue the futility of persecution. So, too, the desperate plight of the social and political order threatened with dissolution in the face of bitter religious struggles compelled the ruling groups to embrace a policy of limited toleration; to avoid the greater evil by the substitution of the lesser.

Parsons pleaded for an equal status of Catholicism with the other minority religious groups in England. He did not demand equality with Anglicanism; only toleration. He protested the loyalty of Catholic subjects and demanded a closer differentiation between treason and the exercise of faith. He urged that the resolute conscience cannot be forced and that any attempt to compel it is brutal, dangerous, and sinful. In his sturdy insistence upon the manifest duty of the Christian to remain true to his religious convictions, whether right or wrong, Parsons made an important contribution to the theory of toleration. A man cannot without grievous sin entrust his conscience to the keeping of the State. The logical application of this doctrine would inevitably lead to toleration. His glance searched the world from India to Germany for examples of different faiths existing side by side in peace under the tolerant mandate of the governor. He argued the inevitable desire of men bound together by the sacred ties of a common belief to commune together and urged that the Protestants could present no valid case for persecution. His argument that even the persecution of a sincere man who holds erroneous convictions is sinful indicates how desperately the Catholic leader was grasping for arguments with which to fortify his case. He disclaimed the authority of the civil Government in affairs of religion. His position, in fine, shows that even the Catholic Church must inevitably modify its teachings and embrace to a limited degree the cause of toleration in those countries in which it finds itself in the unusual rôle of a persecuted minority group.

4. CARDINAL ALLEN

Cardinal Allen in his *A True, Sincere, and Modest Defence of English Catholics that suffer for their faith both at home and abroad* showed a considerable advance beyond the views of Parsons.[1] The treatise was a reply to Burleigh's *Execution of Justice in England*. The purpose of the book was to show that the persecution of English Catholics, whatever the pretended motives might be, was in reality religious. Allen held that the English Catholics sought no more than the author of the *Execution of Justice in England* offered when he said, ". . . he doubteth not but that her majesty would shed no more the blood of her natural subjects, nor use any more bodily punishments at all, if they would desist from their practises abroad, from their writing of railing books, and from wandering in disguised apparel within the realm; and would employ their travail in the works of light and doctrine, according to the usage of their schools: and content themselves with their devotion." Cardinal Allen took Burleigh at his word and sought to outline a possible solution for the English dilemma.

He held that the Catholics stood ready to obey the laws of the realm if they were given toleration; "If they might have had either by licence or connivance, in never so few places of the realm, never so secretly, never so inoffensively, the exercise of that faith and religion which all our fore fathers since our country was converted, lived and died in; and in which themselves were baptized; and from which by no law of God nor man they can be compelled to any sect or rite of religion which they nor their fore fathers ever voluntarily accepted or admitted."[2]

If Burleigh and Allen were both sincere in the outlines of their respective positions, they were not far from an agreement on a policy which might have secured for the Roman Catholics some measure of assured toleration, though more probably by 'connivance' than by 'licence.' But the actions of the Jesuits

[1] First published in 1584. We have used the excellent reprint of 1914 with a preface by Francis, Cardinal Bourne.
[2] Allen, *True . . . and Modest Defence*, II, 143.

belied the conciliatory phrases of Allen. A year before the appearance of his book only the jealousy of France and Spain prevented an invasion of England which the Jesuits had striven so feverishly to launch. In that year Throckmorton's confessions had revealed plots on the Queen's life; plots whose ramifications extended into three countries. In the year of its publication five priests had suffered death at Tyburn, the victims of governmental hysteria.[1] In that year the assassination of William of Orange had shown all too clearly the desperate courage of the political wing of the Catholic party. In the same year the procrastinating Parry was arrested for plotting against the Queen's life. This case was clearly proved and a papal dispensation clinched the Government's case against him. These facts compel us to lend considerably less respect to the words of Allen than to the sentiments of Burleigh.

Allen ignored much of the history of the previous decade when he urged, in the disappointed and despairing tones of a man who was growing old in a cause to which he had given everything, that if only a few churches and colleges had been given to the Catholics the bitterness and persecutions might have been avoided.[2] He held that the Catholics would willingly accept a minority position. If the Catholics could but obtain "Any piece of that liberty which Catholics enjoy in Germany, Switzerland, or other places among Protestants; or half the freedom that the Huguenots have in France and other countries; yea, or but so much courtesy as the Christians find among the very Turks, or very Jews among Christians . . . our adversaries should never have been troubled nor put in jealousy of so many men's malcontentment at home, nor stand in doubt of the departure and absence of so great a number of nobility and principal gentlemen abroad. . . ."[3]

Burleigh had proposed that if the Jesuits and the priests would deal openly and confine their efforts to spiritual ministrations, persecution would cease. Allen held that the persecution must first be terminated and that the Queen must provide

---

[1] February 12, 1584. It has never been proved that they were connected with any plot on the Queen's life.

[2] Allen, *True . . . and Modest Defence*, II, 143.   [3] *Ibid.*, II, 143–144.

some assurance to her Catholic subjects.[1] When this is done by the Government "all priests, religious, and Catholics will appear, and present themselves; and will do all such Christian exercises, duties, and functions, as now by persecution they are forced to do in secret in the face of the whole realm. . . ."[2] The Catholics only desire reasonable security, liberty of conscience, and permission to exercise those ministrations which they consider necessary for their salvation.[3] They desire above all the liberty to exercise publicly those requisites of their worship which persecution forces them to perform secretly. He urged, with truth, that the secrecy with which the Catholics were forced to exercise their religion was the principal cause of misapprehension.[4] If they were granted religious liberty, "those things which now you suspect to be done against the State (for that they be done in covert) may plainly appear unto you nothing else indeed but mere matter of conscience and religion; as in verity they are."[5] If the Government cannot be converted to the Catholic faith, it should at least follow the meritorious example of other Protestant States and accord some measure of toleration to its Catholic subjects.[6] The Government naturally will first try to convert its Catholic subjects. But, that failing, "the next best were in respect of their own security and perpetuity . . . to desist from persecuting their Catholic subjects and bretheren, and to grant some liberty for exercise of their consciences, divine offices, and holy devotions; that so they may pray for her majesty and counsellours as their patrons, whom now they pray for only as their persecutors."[7]

Perhaps two examples of the thought of the lay or spiritual group of English Catholics will suffice to indicate the substantial difference in their position. They argued and petitioned, not quite so well, but we may believe more sincerely than the politico-religious group. They were entirely willing to recognize the inalienable character of their political obligations and sought only liberty to practise the exercise of their faith. This group became increasingly important and numerous as the

[1] Allen, *True . . . and Modest Defence*, II, 145.   [2] *Ibid.*, II, 145–146.
[3] *Ibid.*, II, 148.   [4] *Ibid.*   [5] *Ibid.*   [6] *Ibid.*, II, 150.   [7] *Ibid.*

reign went on, and by its conclusion had half convinced the Crown of its loyalty and had gone far in persuading the Government that some measure of toleration might safely be extended to spiritual Catholicism.[1] We have previously commented upon the development of the party and have noted its important connection with the growing disposition of the Government to accord some religious liberty to its Catholic subjects.[2]

5. THE THOUGHT OF THE NON-POLITICAL CATHOLIC GROUP

As early as 1584 we find a rough outline of *Reasons for and against a Petition to the Queen* which is of a highly interesting character.[3] The paper was probably drawn up by an important Catholic layman, Sir Thomas Tresham.[4] It discussed by the 'objection' and 'solution' method the question of petitioning the Queen for alleviation. In arguing for the petition, it was pointed out that the Queen "is most mercyfull and hathe used great clemencie even now to the priestes, and therefore not to be doubted, in case her Excellencie understood our verie thoughtes and demeanure towardes her Majestie and realme, but that her highnes would extend her mercyfull favour also to us. . . ."[5] The proposed petition to the Queen should not ask for a repeal of the statute of recusancy since that would scarcely be granted and "for that manye be not touched ther with."[6] It is more important that the priests should be permitted to remain in the land in order to maintain the functions of worship.[7] The petition should enumerate the miseries of

---

[1] The terms 'spiritual' and 'politico-religious' seem most accurately to define the tenets and activities of the two Catholic parties.
[2] Cf. *ante*, 202 ff.
[3] *Hist. MSS. Comm., Report on MSS. in Various Collections*, III, 34–37.
[4] Sir Thomas Tresham (1543?–1605) was of a distinguished Northamptonshire family of great landed wealth. He was reared a Protestant, but was converted by Father Parsons in 1580 (*D.N.B.*, lvii, 204), and from that time forward was a leading Catholic layman. He was confined to prison and to his house for a period of seven years for having sheltered Campion. He had no sympathy with the Jesuit party or with foreign interference in English internal affairs. He was released on bail in 1588, but suffered short terms of imprisonment for recusancy at later dates and paid crushing fines. (*Ibid.*, lvii, 205).
[5] *Report on MSS. in Various Collections*, III, 34.   [6] *Ibid.*   [7] *Ibid.*

the Catholics, demonstrate their loyalty, and clear the Catholics "for conversinge with priests who of manye are demed trayters. . . ."[1]

This rough draft, intended only for Catholic eyes, demonstrated the sincerity of the appellants and their desire to attain religious liberty only for the purpose of exercising the spiritual requisites of their faith. It spoke of the clemency of the Queen and appeared to regard the recusancy laws as among the least grievous of their burdens. It was the work of loyal Englishmen who were attempting to assist the State in finding a way out of the admitted impasse of its Catholic policy.

Early in 1585 the *Petition of Loyal Catholic Subjects to the Queen* was drafted, upon the basis of the discussions of the previous year.[2] The document was probably composed by Tresham. The list of the appellants was headed by Shelley, and Lord Vaux. Sir John Arundel and Tresham were among the other signatories. The petitioners stressed their political loyalty in the strongest terms. ". . . yt . . . be our verye bounden duety irrevocablye to beare to your right excellent Majestie all loyaltie, faythe, and Christian obedience, as to our undoubted rightfull, and onlye souergne. . . ."[3] They hoped to clear themselves of any suspicion of plots, and to show the misery which they had undergone in the hope of securing redress and relief.[4] They appealed especially that they might not be subjected to the new and "heavie yokes" which the Parliament of that year was framing in answer to the Jesuit plots.[5] They protested their complete loyalty and obedience to the temporal laws of the realm.

They held that the greatest accusation which might be brought against the Catholics was that of recusancy "whiche hathe devoyded us of all your wonted gracies and speciall favoures. . . ."[6] But that disobedience is grounded not "uppon

[1] *Report on MSS. in Various Collections*, III, 35.
[2] *Ibid.*, III, 37–42. See also reference in Strype, *Annals*, III, 1, 432, and *S.P. Dom. Eliz.*, clxii, 14 (1), for a proposed petition along similar lines, dated August 21, 1583.
[3] *Report on MSS. in Various Collections*, III, 37. [4] *Ibid.*
[5] *Ibid.*, III, 38. [6] *Ibid.*

anye contempte of your Majesties Lawes, or any other wylfull or trayterous intent, but altogether upon meere conscience and feare to offend God."[1] They endeavoured to dissociate their cause from that of the religio-political group. Falsity to the State under pretence of conscience was branded as the most heinous of all crimes, as the Parry case had demonstrated.[2] As a concrete proof of their complete civil loyalty they asserted that "We for our partes utterlye denye that either Pope or Cardynall hath power or authoritie to commaunde or lycence any manne to consent to mortall Synne, or to committe or intend anye other Acte Contra Jus Divinum. Muche lesse can this desloyall, wicked, and unnaturall purpose by any meanes be made lawfull, to wytt, That a native borne subiect may seeke the effusion of the sacred blood of his annoynted Soveraigne."[3] This subscription of loyalty was an important link in the various protestations of loyalty which were finally united in the Jacobean Oath of Allegiance.[4] It was highly important in that it came volitionally from an important group of Catholic laymen and intimated the lines along which the Catholics who were solely interested in religious freedom might be differentiated by the State from their co-religionists whose spiritual ardour was not unmixed with sedition and treason.

They held that they absented themselves from the authorized services only because of conscience.[5] They pointed out that men do not undertake calumny and sufferings unless they are motivated by considerations which are inextricably embedded in conscience.[6] The appellants indicated the essential barrenness of the governmental guarantee of freedom of conscience when they urged that such liberty was without content if the free

---

[1] *Report on MSS. in Various Collections*, III, 38. [2] *Ibid.*, III, 39.
[3] *Ibid.*
[4] We shall have occasion fully to discuss the evolution of the Oath of Allegiance in later pages.
[5] See also *English Protestants' Plea*, 35–36. Their absence from church arises from not "any contempt of your Maiesties Lawes, or any other willful or trayterous intent, but altogether vpon meere conscience, and feare to offende God."
[6] "Yf conscience . . . had not pressed us in this poynte, those of our Religion would never have suffered therfore so manye disgraces and impoverrshmentes." (*Report on MSS. in Various Collections*, III, 39.)

exercise of worship were prohibited. The banishment of their priests would entail the deprivation of Catholics of the sacraments. They promised to expose to the authorities any act of disloyalty on the part of a priest.[1] "Lett not us your Catholique natyve Englishe and obedient Subiects stand in more perill for frequentinge the Blessed Sacramentes and exercysinge the Catholique religion (and that most secretlye) than doe the Catholique subjectes to the Turke publiquelye, then doe the perverse and blasphemous Jewes, hauntinge their Sinagoge under sundrye Christian kinges openlye, and then doe the protestantes enjoyinge their publique Assemblies under divers Catholique kinges and Pryncies quietlye. Lett yt not be Treason for the sickman in bodye (even at the last gaspe) to seeke ghostlye counsell for the salvation of his Soule of a Catholique pryest." The yielding of the Queen to their petition would make her "Tolleration" an event that would be "presented of Recorde from age to age and consecrated to Endlesse glorye and Renoune."[2]

There is among the Hatfield manuscripts a petition to Burleigh from an anonymous refugee at Liege which insisted even more nobly on the sanctity of the rights of conscience.[3] The author urged that every man will be held responsible for his own soul at the day of judgment.[4] Religion, he said, in words that recall the early sentiments of Luther, is a gift of God and cannot be beaten into a man's head with a hammer. The State may force men's bodies, but it cannot compel their minds. When force is employed love is lost and the prince and state endangered.[5] "If a man does a lawful act, yet against his conscience (as thousands in England do to avoid the penalty

---

[1] *Report on MSS. in Various Collections*, III, 41. [2] *Ibid.*, III, 42.
[3] *Unsigned to Burleigh*, August 24, 1597, Liége; *Hatfield MSS.* (*Historical MSS. Comm.*), VII, 363–365. There is every evidence that the document was written by George More. He spoke of dealings with Mary Queen of Scots (VII, 363), for which George More had fled abroad. More was from the North of England, and was perhaps a member of the family of Sir Thomas More. (Strype, *Whitgift*, II, 367.) He was a man of considerable learning and of some political importance. He was cited to appear before the Archbishop of York, but fled abroad to settle at Liége.
[4] *Hatfield MSS.* (*Historical MSS. Comm.*), VII, 364. [5] *Ibid.*

of the law) he damneth his own soul. Therefore men that have a care for their souls, will rather suffer their country to be a spoil to the enemy and themselves brought into bondage, than their souls to be led daily to damnation. . . ."[1] Or, as the author of *The English Protestants' Plea* expressed it, even if the Catholics are wrong in their conscientious conviction, yet "if wee should doe contrarie to that we thinke in conscience to be right" we would be "false dissemblers, hatefull to God and man, and in truth the most dangerous and worst subiectes that may be in a commonwealth. . . ."[2]

The sentiments expressed by Tresham and More must have crystallized the opinions of many thousands of earnest men in England, Catholics and Protestants alike. The appellants sought to establish their identity as loyal Englishmen and to persuade the Government that, despite the conduct of the radical wing of the Catholic party, the mass of Catholics expressed nothing more in their devotions than loyalty to the ancient faith. They recognized that they had broken certain laws of the realm in the exercise of those devotions, but held that their actions rested upon convictions of conscience which no human mandate could rightfully override. They appealed for an extension of liberty of conscience to liberty of worship and suggested a formula by which the Government might test the sincerity of those who professed the Roman faith. We have seen these sentiments uttered repeatedly by men in every minority group and by a substantial section of the dominant group. The view, which has so often been expressed, that no tolerant thought appeared in England during the sixteenth century ignores a large and increasing body of opinion. Catholic thought, the most consistently intolerant of the period, was, in so far as it was English, driven by repression and hardship to the enunciation of views which if properly extended would have resulted in measurable religious liberty. Numerous rivulets of tolerant thought of varying consistency and depth, influenced by different motives and arising in unrelated sources, were converging to form a powerful stream of opinion which

[1] *Hatfield MSS.* (*Historical Comm. MSS.*), VII, 364.
[2] *English Protestants' Plea*, 36.

would eventually sweep away the stupid restrictions on religious worship.

The Jesuits left no stone unturned in their attack on the governmental policy. We are especially struck by their insight in pointing out the dangers which beset the Government in its persecution of Catholics and in its attempt to secure a uniform State religion. They argued the cause of toleration from this basis as manfully as did the *Politiques*, though the former were concerned with the safety of the faith, the latter with the stability of the State. We must admire the Jesuits for their keen prodding of the Achilles' heel of the governmental policy. The Government professed no other motive in the repression of Nonconformist groups than the requirements of a stable Government. The Jesuits sought to point out that its policy of repression was endangering that very end. It was a genuine *Politique* argument cleverly turned to the exigencies of the time.

The case had been powerfully presented in at least three books as early as 1584.[1] Parsons subtly intimated that the Government was dominated by reasons of policy in its religious programme.[2] This being the case, reflection should persuade the Government that "it appearethe no waie to impeache polycie (if respect of conscience were laide aside) to proceede somewhat mylder withe the Catholique parte in Englande."[3] The Government has confused treason with religion. It has interpreted "matters of mere religion and conscience, to cases treasonable as they novv speake; and the dueties done to God, to be vndutifulnes and disobedience to the prince."[4] The English Catholics really suffer for their religion, "for the seruing of God in the maner of al Catholike prouinces, and not for treason, or disobedience to her maties temporal lavves, or the

---

[1] Parsons, *An Epistle of the Persecution of Catholickes in England* . . .; Allen, *An Apologie and True Declaration of the Institution of the two English Colleges* . . .; and in *Leycester's Commonwealth.*
[2] Parsons, *Epistle of the Persecution*, 9. Allen had also noted and lamented the emphasis which was being placed upon the ends of the State in repudiation of the interests of the Church. (Allen, *True . . . Modest Defence*, I, 77–78.)   [3] Parsons, *Epistle of the Persecution*, 9.
[4] Allen, *Apologie . . . for two English Colleges*, 73.

Realmes."[1] Catholicism, rather than being inimical to the State, provides "a Christian commōwealthe, whiche doe not (follow) from the doctrine of our aduersaries."[2]

It is unnecessary, one of the speakers in *Leycester's Commonwealth* was caused to say, that differences in religion should disrupt the peace and harmony of the State.[3] "Wee cannot but mone, to behold contentions advanced so farre foorth as they are: and wee could wish most hartily that for the time to come, these matters might passe with such peace, friendship and tranquility, as they doe in other countries: where difference in religion breaketh not the bond of good fellowship, or fidelity."[4] The author recalled the ill effects of controversy and faction on the State in ancient and modern times.[5] In a section which bears striking resemblance to the arguments of the *Politiques* he suggested that England may be torn to pieces by religious quarrels. Indeed, this fear has made "most English hearts inclined to wish the remedy or prevention thereof, by some reasonable moderation, or reunion among ourselves."[6] The deepening of the existing differences by harsh measures can only result in "rage, fury, and most deadly desperation."[7] The realm requires some measure of toleration for its safety and for the very stability which the Council was striving so desperately to maintain. ". . . If any sweet qualification, or small tolleration among us, were admitted: there is no doubt,

---

[1] Allen, *Apologie . . . for two English Colleges*, 78.
[2] Parsons, *Epistle of the Persecution*, 27.
[3] *Leycester's Commonwealth* was one of the most interesting books of the period. The work was first printed at Antwerp (?) in 1584 under the title *Copie of a leter wryten by a Master of Arts of Cambridge to his friend in London*. A French translation appeared in the following year. A second English edition was published in 1641, and Burgoyne's critical edition, which we have followed, appeared in 1904. The book is a bitter and scurrilous attack on the character of Leicester. In this book he was first charged with the murder of his wife. For many years the authorship was attributed to Parsons (Intro., xi), and it was once held that he wrote it at Burleigh's suggestion. Parsons strongly denied the authorship, and there is no definite proof that the work was from his pen. There are striking similarities to his style and to his quick flow of thought, but the highly tolerant tone of the book was scarcely in keeping with his general notions on the subject. It would be pleasant to think that Parsons was the author, and that under the protection of anonymity these were his personal sentiments.
[4] *Ibid.*, 220.   [5] *Ibid.*, 220–221.   [6] *Ibid.*, 221–222.   [7] *Ibid.*, 222.

but that affaires would passe in our Realme, with more quietnes, safety and publique weale of the same, then it is like to doe long. . . ."[1] As Parsons expressed the idea, even the secret exercise of Roman Catholicism will produce good rather than harm to the State. These facts should induce the Council "to tollerate more, or at least, to shew lesse extremitie against the same, howe muche so euer you thinke us deceaued in not conforminge our selves to the protestantes religion."[2] Only by abandoning religious persecution will men be united in the support of their country.[3]

A gentleman was introduced by the author of *Leycester's Commonwealth* to point out that the practice of toleration in Germany, Poland, Bohemia, and Hungary had made those countries examples of peace and stability which all of Europe might well emulate.[4] The early years of Elizabeth's reign had likewise been a proof of the fine fruits of a policy of toleration and moderation.[5] In that ideal period "the commiserations and lenity that was used towards those of the weaker sort, with a certaine sweet diligence for their gaining, by good meanes, was the cause of much peace, contentation, and other benefit to the whole body."[6] The author pointed out that France was saved from dissolution only by the wisdom of moderate men who insisted upon the adoption of religious toleration.[7] In Flanders, too, the King, though "strait-laced," has been compelled "upon force of reason to abstain from the pursuite and search of men's consciences, not onely in the townes, which upon composition hee receiveth," but throughout his realm.[8]

"Qualification, tollerance, and moderation," it was urged, are the only possible means by which the divisions and factions of England may be healed.[9] By these means alone may England achieve peace and unity. The author's keen insight saw beyond the immediate requirements of his own group. Toleration, he said, will unite all faiths "be they Papists, Puritanes, Famillans,

---

[1] *Leycester's Commonwealth*, 222.
[2] Parsons, *Epistle of the Persecution*, 28.
[3] *Leycester's Commonwealth*, 222.   [4] *Ibid.*
[5] *Ibid.*, 222; 218–219.   [6] *Ibid.*, 222–223.   [7] *Ibid.*, 223.
[8] *Ibid.*, 223–224.   [9] *Ibid.*, 224.

or of whatsoever nice difference or section besides. . . ."[1] He denied, in other words, that religious opinion had any vital connection with political loyalty and urged that a broader basis should be laid for patriotism. He held that toleration was essential to the attainment of this end for it "would be sufficient to retaine all parties, within a temperate obedience to the Magistrate and governement, for conservation of their countrey: which were of no small importance to the contentation of Her Majesty, and weale publike of the whole kingdome."[2]

This view was perhaps the finest and broadest of the Catholic statements in favour of religious toleration during the century. It rested principally upon a *Politique* disavowal of persecution as stupid and as inimical to the interests of the State. But, at the same time, it disclaimed the use of force against religious belief. Cardinal Allen had urged manfully and brilliantly that force could not be a rightful or effective instrument against conscience. If the Government is persuaded of the truth of the English religion, "or at least not with their vvisedome, for that, being thus far gone, the retiring backe might be dangerous to the state: yet for Christes love vve aske it, let their Honours haue some care and consideration of our consciences. . . ."[3] The Catholics are deeply persuaded of the truth of their convictions and force is quite impotent against such persuasion. The State will be made secure if the Catholics may only be granted the right of free worship, for with that precious boon the seminaries and the Jesuit missions will vanish.[4] The Kingdom of God must be sought in the "way to the peace, felicity, and security of al vvorldy vveale. . . ."[5]

We find the *Politique* arguments advanced again after the difficult period which centred about 1588 had passed. Beginning with 1592, the attack was resumed, though less ably than in the earlier period. The literature of the last decade of the reign stressed the necessity of distinguishing between the political and the spiritual groups and was, of course, anti-Jesuit in tone. Thus Constable, the poet, wrote to the Earl of Essex that,

[1] *Leycester's Commonwealth*, 224.　　　　[2] *Ibid.*
[3] Allen, *Apologie . . . for the two English Colleges*, 104.
[4] *Ibid.*　　　　　　　　　　　　　　[5] *Ibid.*

though compelled to live abroad, he was none the less a true Englishman.[1] "I have publicly protested my lawful affections to my country among those with whom I live, and have written to Rome to dissuade the Pope from giving credit to those who would have English Catholics favour the King of Spain's designs against the Queen."[2] He declared that these were the sentiments of most of the exiles in Rome and it had been suggested that they should by oath oppose "themselves against all violent proceedings for religion."[3] He hoped that the Government might be "moved to distinguish between the Catholics who merely desire the peaceable enjoyment of their conscience and such as desire the subversion of the present state."[4] More, in his letter to Burleigh, likewise indicated his loyalty to the Queen and State.[5] He had been utterly ruined by recusancy fines and Star Chamber sentences and had been compelled to abandon his native land. None the less, he had never "entered into any conspiracy against Her Majesty or my country."[6] He had found the seditious faction led by Parsons and Holt so strongly entrenched in Flanders that he had left the Spanish dominions. His only desire was to return "to my country and enjoy liberty of conscience for me and my family."[7] He expressed himself as ready to venture his life in the services of England if "any stranger" should invade the land. But, "without liberty of conscience I will never return. . . ."[8]

Numerous instances could be advanced to show that these sentiments had in the last decade of the reign caught a firm hold among English Catholics, even among the more zealous of those who had been obliged to flee the realm. The gulf between the spiritual group and the politico-religious party was constantly widening and men saw in that distinction a faint chance for the securing of some sort of a guarantee of freedom of worship. Hence they again pointed to the increasing

[1] *Constable to Essex*, Paris, March 10, 1597, *Hatfield MSS.* (*Hist. MSS. Comm.*), VII, 86.
[2] *Ibid.*   [3] *Ibid.*   [4] *Ibid.*
[5] *Unsigned to Burleigh*, Liége, August 24, 1597, *Hatfield MSS.* (*Hist. MSS. Comm.*), VII, 363–365.
[6] *Ibid.*   [7] *Ibid.*   [8] *Ibid.*

danger of faction and urged that the State could achieve stability only through the extension of toleration to religious minorities.

Thus Philopatris denied that the principal danger to England lay in the machinations of the Jesuits and in the existence of a large body of Roman Catholics in the State.[1] He urged that England's greatest weakness lay in the general absence of unity, in "the greate, and irreconcilable differences, and warres in religion, not onely with the Catholiques, but especially betweene the Protestants, and Puritanes them selues, who he[2] saith, are mortall enemyes, and would haue bin long agoe by the eares together, had not the feare of the Catholiques helde them both in awe."[3] Conditions have reached such a state of faction and bitterness is so rife in England that no one is safe "excepte they alwayes cary their pasportes with them in their pocketts, and ride up and downe Ingland, as they would passe thorough Turky."[4] "I know," another Catholic wrote to Burleigh, that England "standeth in most dangerous terms to be a spoil to all the world, and to be brought into perpetual bondage, and . . . I fear, your Lordships and the rest of the Council will see [that] when it is too late."[5]

These Catholic writers earnestly urged that England could find her political salvation only by the establishment of some sort of religious freedom under proper guarantees from the State. Burleigh's correspondent pressed the view that religious toleration would appease the bitterness of men's minds and

---

[1] Philopatris, J. (pseud.), *An advertisement written to a Secretarie of my Lord Treasurer of Ingland, by an Inglishe Intelligencer as he passed through Germanie towardes Italie.* (N. pl., 1592.) The authorship of this extremely rare book has been attributed both to Parsons and to Cresswell. It was poorly executed, the pagination is imperfect, and the final page (67) suggests that it was unfinished. P. 67 in a second copy is in manuscript. The letter to Burleigh is couched in the terms of a friendly report. In reality the book is a fierce assault upon the policy and character of the great minister. The author accused Burleigh, Bacon, Leicester, Walsingham, and Hatton of unduly influencing the Queen in her religious policy and of instigating her to frame harsh laws against her Catholic subjects (11 ff.).

[2] The work was in the form of a letter describing another book, hence the language.

[3] Philopatris, *An Advertisement*, 19.   [4] *Ibid.*, 22.

[5] *Hatfield MSS. (Hist. MSS. Comm.)*, VII, 363-364 (c. 1594-1595).

would enable them to "join all in one for the defence of our country."[1] He pointed, as many writers had before, to the examples of the success of this policy in Europe. The very tiresome reiteration of these examples was important evidence that the policy which divers Continental nations had turned to in desperation was powerfully influencing English opinion. "We see what safety it hath been to France, how peaceable the kingdom of Polonia is where no man's conscience is forced, how the Germans live, being contrary in religion, without giving offence one to another."[2] Why cannot the same results be achieved in England by the substitution of a policy of toleration for repression of conscience? Toleration will make for the quiet state of the Government and of the Church, and it will bring peace to Christendom.[3] From it will spring the unity of religion which is at the present time impeded only by the lack of enquiry and the prevalence of party passions.[4] "And," Constable closed with fine irony, "if this peace deprive you of the present occasion to show your prowess, there will still remain the common foe of all Christendom to display it upon."[5]

Another writer protested strongly against the charge of Catholic disloyalty and argued finely that Catholics were persecuted for conscience rather than for treason.[6] He declared that they had no desire to incense the Queen against other faiths, "being so well acquainted with the smarte of our owne punishmentes, to wishe any Christian to be partaker of our

[1] Hatfield MSS. (Hist. MSS. Comm.), VII, 363–364.
[2] Ibid., VII, 364. See also English Protestants' Plea, 43.
[3] Constable to Essex, Hatfield MSS., VII, 86.   [4] Ibid.   [5] Ibid.
[6] R. Southwell (?), An Hvmble Svpplication to her Maiestie, n. pl., December 1595. The manuscript notes (2–40) are in a hand very like Southwell's. However, since he was executed on February 20, 1594 (5), neither the notes nor the book can be from his hand, if the date of publication is correct. Sidney Lee (D.N.B., liii, 298) believes that the treatise was written in 1591 and first published by Garnet and Blackwell in 1600, the date 1595 being inserted to deceive the authorities. It is difficult to see just what gain deception would have brought, since the author was already dead. Two copies were seized by the Government and survive in the B.M. and at Lambeth. Robert Southwell (1561–1595), the brilliant poet and Jesuit, requires no biographical notice. He was convicted of treason on February 20, 1595, and was hanged the next day.

paines."¹ He only asked that the Catholics should not be so severely and brutally punished for crimes of which they were in no sense guilty.² The Catholics have no desire to convict themselves of treason or to employ force in the propagation of their religion. "Wee come to shed our owne blood, and not to seeke the effusion of others blood. The weapons of our warrefare are spirituall not offensive, and wee carrie our desires, so high lifted aboue sauage and brutish purposes, that we rather hope to make our owne martyrdome, steppes to a glorious eternitie, then [others] deathes, our purchase of eternall dishonour."³

The Remonstrance for Liberty of Conscience in Scotland enlarged the *Politique* argument for toleration.⁴ The authors endeavoured to impress the King with the number and wealth of the Catholics in the two realms.⁵ Further, the Catholics of England and Scotland were declared to be in complete unanimity while the Protestants were completely disunited and hostile to each other. Thus the English service and "heirrithe,"⁶ are as odius to the Scottish ministry as is the Roman Catholic ritual. Neither party can ever be pleased without the granting of liberty of conscience.⁷ James must seek the support, not of one faction in his realm, but of the whole body of his subjects, "for which cause it appears necessary to extend favour upon all, especially in matters of conscience."⁸ The Remonstrants appeared to embrace a principle of general religious toleration in order to secure liberty of worship for their own group.

It was held that the adoption of a policy of toleration would work vast benefit to the State. It would sever the relations of the Catholics with foreign powers and would make them loyal and united in the defence of the realm. James was reminded of the similarity existing between his own case and that of

---

¹ Southwell, *An Hvmble Svpplication*, 48–49.
² *Ibid.*, 49.   ³ *Ibid.*, 59.
⁴ The *Remonstrance* was addressed to James VI and promised Catholic assistance in his pretensions to the throne of England. Though undated, internal evidence would place it some time after the Roman Mission, and shortly prior to the death of the Queen. (*Hatfield MSS. (Hist. MSS. Comm.*), XIV, 335 ff.)   ⁵ *Ibid.*, XIV, 335.   ⁶ Heresy? hierarchy?
⁷ *Hatfield MSS. (Hist. MSS. Comm.)*, XIV, 336.   ⁸ *Ibid.*

Henry IV.[1] In France the positive laws were as much or more against the Protestants as the Acts of Parliament in Scotland are against the Catholics, while the proportional number of Protestants was much less. France found it highly necessary to relieve conscience. "Yea, the French ministers did cry out that there was no Christian liberty where this liberty of conscience was refused."[2] The writers believed that English policy was rapidly shaping itself towards an extension of toleration to Roman Catholic subjects. Some favour has already been shown towards recusants upon the payment of a pecuniary fine, and Elizabeth has permitted some priests to lodge an appeal in Rome against the Archpriest. Even this beginning, they urged, "hath thereby turned the hearts of many stubborn subjects from foreign courses unto loyalty."[3]

A limited group of Catholics had contributed an highly intelligent and reasoned argument for religious toleration on the grounds that only by the effective guarantee of religious liberty could the unity, peace, and stability of the realm be maintained. This reasoning was particularly well attuned to the policy which the Government was obviously attempting to follow, and they may be said to have offered an alternative and superior procedure for the solution of the religious problems of the kingdom. In the period prior to the Armada the Jesuits were chiefly responsible for the development of this point of view; in the subsequent period the spiritual group figured more prominently. The Government, it was declared, professes to be actuated by no other reasons than considerations of state in its Catholic policy. Actually, however, it is persecuting conscience. The dangers of faction and religious discontent were ably presented. The only way in which the State may become closely knit and the dissensions which now beset it quieted is by the adoption of religious toleration. The examples of various European nations were urged. These writers came close to saying that religious opinions had nothing to do with the requirements of political loyalty; a progressive but thoroughly un-Catholic position. In especial, it was urged

---

[1] *Hatfield MSS.* (*Hist. MSS. Comm.*), XIV, 336.
[2] *Ibid.*   [3] *Ibid.*

that force is powerless to achieve a change in the mind and spirit of man and that it only induces obstinacy and foments rebellion. As we would expect, the later group enhanced these arguments by testimonials of their personal loyalty. They urged the Council more carefully to distinguish between sedition and sincere religious conviction that was devoid of political interest. They desired to be considered Englishmen as well as Catholics. This point of view was never so well developed and so carefully urged by any other group in Elizabethan England. It is interesting to speculate on how much it drew from the noble utterances of the *Politiques* in the same period. The points of view of the *Politiques* and of the English Catholics were, of course, precisely opposite, but the arguments of the patriot were easily adopted by the zealot.[1] The position was urged from the point of view of political expediency and the necessity of national unity. They rendered a great service in declaring their willingness and desire to live in a State which guaranteed the right of existence to more than one faith. Suffering had brought the English Catholics far from the dicta of Augustine and Aquinas on the subject of the attitude of the Church towards the question of heresy.

We should notice in concluding our survey of Catholic thought on the question of toleration the relation of the rift between the Jesuits and the seculars to the matter. We have already discussed in some detail the importance of the quarrel from the point of view of the Government and the dominant religion.[2] Fortunately, the violent and extreme views of the Jesuits had little in common with the attitude of the mass of

---

[1] The *Politique* party may be said to have begun after the failure of La Rochelle (1573) and the formation of the Huguenot League. It was obvious from this time forward that heresy in France could never be completely exterminated, and that the continuation of a policy of repression would endanger the very existence of the State. La Noue's *Discours se Politique et Militaire* appeared in 1587; Bodin's *Republic* in 1576, and the *Heptaplomeres* was written in 1588. L'Hôpital's noble efforts to secure toleration had begun as early as 1560. His great speech at Orleans occurred in that year. The *But de la Guerre et de la Paix* was written a decade later. The English adaptation of the *Politique* position may be said to have begun about 1585.   [2] Cf. *ante*, 202 ff.

English Catholics. They remained, for the most part, loyal and English in sentiment throughout the reign. The missionary efforts of the Jesuits had revivified the faith, but their seditious activities had met with little response from the laity and the secular priests. The English Catholics realized that the conduct of the Jesuits had only served to increase the rigour of their lot and they appear to have been considerably more bitter towards the order than towards the Government. By the conclusion of the reign a large section of Anglican Catholicism had been so far offended as to stand prepared to renounce the papal claim to the power of dissolving allegiance in return for some degree of toleration. There was, in fact, considerable danger of a renunciation of papal authority which would have been in its doctrinal consequences not unlike the Henrican Reformation.

Fisher announced in Flanders in 1597 that he was in "greate hope of libertye in conscience in England so that the Jesuitts might be gotten from thence."[1] A letter written by a secular priest two years later, which fell into the widely extended hands of Burleigh, denounced the Jesuits in bitter terms as the source of Roman Catholic misery in England.[2] He said, in speaking of the Archpriest, "We were towards peace with our Prince; why doth he provoke her sword against innocents by bringing into the realm novelties not only against the late parliamental laws, but also the fundamental Catholic laws of our country established three hundred years ago?"[3] He charged that the Jesuits had caused "this kingdom" to be "put to sale three times to three divers nations within sixteen years."[4] They have caused the profession of the Catholic religion to become entangled in a temporal quarrel. They desire that "this kingdom must no more be called Regnum Britannicum but Regnum Jesuiticum, which is the only scope of our archpresbitery." The insolent challenges of the Jesuits to the Government were declared to be the sole "cause of all the hard

---

[1] *Archpriest Controversy*, I, 15.
[2] — to —, 15 June, 1599, *Hatfield MSS.* (*Hist. MSS. Comm.*), IX, 202 ff. (Endorsed by Burleigh, "A Letter brought me by Mr. Wade.")
[3] *Ibid.*   [4] *Ibid.*

laws and edicts made to the undoing and death of so many Catholics. The Archpriest will fly from us into Spain, as Persons did heretofore, and laugh at our miseries. . . ."[1]

By far the most important work of the secular opponents of the Jesuit designs was the *Important Considerations*, in the publication of which William Watson, the leader of the English Catholic party, played an important rôle.[2] Watson hated the Jesuits and blamed their zeal and political machinations for the persecution which the English Catholics had experienced. The author proposed to set forth "a brief relation of the causes moving Her Majesty and the State to make so sharp laws against us all in general for some private men's offences, grown now into a faction of a dangerous sequel: Dangerous (dear Catholics) to our common Mother the weal public, as we are English; Dangerous to our sovereign and the present state, as we are subjects: dangerous to us all, as we are recusants. . . ."[3] The Jesuits have sought to seduce and warp Catholicism to their own ends.[4] They have instigated the Spanish plots against England, and the Spanish are interested, not in the advancement of religion, but in the political conquest of the realm.[5] In a long and bitter argument he assailed Parsons for having been guilty of treason and for having sought to undermine the loyalty of English Catholics by the introduction of the authority of the Archpriest which "doth tend wholly

---

[1] — to —, 15 June, 1599, *Hatfield MSS.* (*Hist. MSS. Comm.*, IX, 203.
[2] *Important Considerations, which ought to move all True and Sound Catholikes, who are not wholly Iesuited, to acknowledge without all equiuocations, ambiguities, or shiftings, that the proceedings of her Majesty, and of the State with them, since the beginning of her Highnesse raigne, haue bene both mild and mercifull . . .* (London, 1601). The book bears little resemblance to Watson's other writings. The important *Epistle* was signed with his initials, and may be fairly certainly ascribed to him, but the authorship of the body of the work is quite uncertain. The book professes to be the work of "sundry of us, the secular priests," and to contain an "historical survey of all the rebellions, plots, and bloody designments set on foot against England by the Pope or other, mainly at the instigation of the Jesuits." It was reprinted without the valuable *Epistle* in various collections, esp. 1675, 1677, and 1689. The *Epistle* was reprinted in 1689. An excellent edition was edited by the Reverend Joseph Mendham. The first edition is rare. The only American copy known to the writer is in the N.Y.P.L.
[3] Watson, *Important Considerations*, 4.   [4] *Ibid.*, 10.   [5] *Ibid.*, 10–12.

to the advancement of the Spanish, and the overthrow of this flourishing commonwealth. . . ."[1]

With these treasonable designs the secular clergy have no sympathy and they utterly disclaim any connection with the Jesuit efforts.[2] He declared the Jesuits and the Archpriest to be "arrant traitors unto their prince and country; whom to death, we will never obey: No, if the Pope's holiness should charge us to obey in this sense, to advance an enemy to the English Crown, we would never yield to it. . . ."[3] The historical method for advancing the Catholic faith has been by the spiritual agencies of the priestly functions, "given ad edificationem non ad destructionem, to teach obedience not rebellions."[4] The secular clergy have sought to maintain and to follow that policy. In their efforts spiritually to advance the cause of the faith they have been hindered by the political designs of the Jesuits "whereby the State hath been most justly irritated and provoked against us."

The writer traced the history of the plots and treasons of the Jesuits, culminating in their share in procuring the Bull of Excommunication against Queen Elizabeth. He correctly regarded this as the critical stage in the development of the governmental policy towards its Catholic subjects. The provocation and danger resulting from the excommunication of the Queen and the absolution of her subjects from their obedience had resulted in a more stringent governmental policy. However, "none of them (i.e. the Catholics) were put to death upon that occasion."[5] Any prince in Christendom would have been compelled to adopt the policy which Elizabeth has pursued.[6] He held that the Bull was a consequence of the activities of the Jesuit order and expressed the view that "many both priests and lay Catholics have greatly wished that it had never been decreed, denounced, published, or heard of."[7] The rigorous legislation of 1571 was likewise not unprovoked, though he regarded it as unnecessarily harsh.[8]

Watson pointed out that the passing and the execution of the penal laws against Roman Catholics closely parallelled the

[1] Watson, *Important Considerations*, 20.   [2] *Ibid.*, 24–25.   [3] *Ibid.*, 25.
[4] *Ibid.*, 36.   [5] *Ibid.*, 43.   [6] *Ibid.*, 44.   [7] *Ibid.*   [8] *Ibid.*

activities and plots of the Jesuits.[1] The Queen cannot be censured for her severity; "What King in the world, being in doubt to be invaded by his enemies, and fearing that some of his own subjects were by indirect means, drawn rather to adhere unto them than to himself; would not make the best trial of them he could for his better satisfaction, whom he might trust to?"[2] When the issue is purely one of political loyalty, a refusal to lend obedience must be condemned and dealt with as treason to the State.[3] The State must maintain its stability, otherwise it is courting complete dissolution.

Naturally the indictment of the Jesuits centred about the events of 1588 and "that most bloody attempt, not only against her majesty and our common enemies, but against ourselves, all Catholics; nay, against this flourishing kingdom and our own native country."[4] Loyal Catholics, if they had been counsellors, could, in the face of such traitorous designs, have done nothing else than consent to the passage of stringent legislation to secure its frustration.[5] The Jesuits have completely subverted their ministry. It is the function of the priesthood to preach and administer in spiritual matters, and not to meddle in affairs of State. The secular clergy lends its full support to this spiritual conception of religion. Its priests "do plainly affirm and resolutely acknowledge it . . . that if the pope himself . . . come or send hither an army under pretence to establish the said Catholic religion, by force, and with the sword, we will ever be most ready, as native born and true subjects of her Highness . . . to withstand and oppose ourselves against him, and to spend the best blood in our bodies in defence of the Queen and our Country."[6]

The Catholic faith, he nobly argued, does not depend for its continuance and stability upon treachery and rebellion. Its sole weapons are spiritual: "The word of the spirit, and not the sword of the flesh, or any arm of man is that, which giveth life and beauty to the Catholic Church."[7] He was persuaded that

---

[1] Watson, *Important Considerations*, 45–52.   [2] *Ibid.*, 53.   [3] *Ibid.*
[4] *Ibid.*, 56–57.   [5] *Ibid.*, 68.   [6] *Ibid.*, 68–69.
[7] *Ibid.*, 70. A direct outcome of this sentiment was the issuance in 1603 (January 13th) of a Protestation of Allegiance to the Crown signed by thirteen

if the Church had not abandoned this policy for one of force and treachery, and if the Pope had dealt moderately and kindly with the Queen, that "there would have been no speeches amongst us of racks and torments, nor any cause to have used them; for none were ever vexed that way simply, for that he was either priest or Catholic, but because they were suspected to have had their hands in some of the said most traitorous designments. . . ."[1]

In the same year, Dr. Humphrey Ely[2] sought to distinguish between the two groups of Catholics and to urge that toleration might safely and wisely be extended to the party which sought only religious freedom.[3] He held that the secular priests and the laity were completely loyal and willing to suffer any persecution for the sake of their faith. They were likewise ready to risk death in the defence of their sovereign and native country "against all whosoeuer shall attempt anything against her royall person or Crowne, be he Spaniard, French, Scott, or whoeuer else."[4] If the Queen appreciated the depths of Catholic loyalty, "she would at the leaste make a distinction betwixt her naturall children and subjects that in all sinceritie doo honor and reuerence her, and those unnaturall bastards th[at] doo attend to nought els but conquests and invasions, by giuing [them] leaue to serue God freely and securely, in easing the yoke of her seuere laws enacted against them for their faith and conscience. . . ."[5]

Thus at the very close of the reign the growing fissure in the Catholic ranks bore rich promise of a development which might lead to the toleration of the spiritual group. The seculars

---

of the leading secular clergy. This was the significant, if belated, answer of the loyal Catholics to the papal Bull of Excommunication, which Watson had so severely criticized.   [1] Watson, *Important Considerations*, 72.
[2] Ely was a brother to the president of St. John's College, Oxford. He was educated at Oxford and Douay. He came to England in disguise in 1580 with a small party of priests. He was captured and was imprisoned for a short time, but was soon released, since he was not in orders. He was ordained shortly after his return to the Continent, and from 1586 to 1604 he was Professor of the Canon and Civil Laws at Pont-à-Mousson. He was in temperament charitable and moderate.
[3] *Ely to Sir Robert Cecil* (?), *Archpriest Controversy*, II, 196 ff.
[4] *Ibid.*, II, 196.   [5] *Ibid.*, II, 196–197.

completely eschewed participation in or sympathy with any political action of Catholicism in achieving its missionary object in England, whether inspired and sanctioned by Jesuits or the papacy. They held that in the event of a political attempt upon England, they were in conscience bound to defend their sovereign.[1] This group aimed at securing some form of toleration for their religion and working out some scheme by which their religion could be woven into the fabric of the State. A point of view was developing which threatened to lead to the creation of a theory of obedience which would deny essential elements of the papal supremacy. Watson endeavoured to show that the English Catholics had suffered solely because of the political character of the Jesuit programme. He and his group were prepared to admit that the Crown had proceeded justly in the stringent repression of these designs. But the time had now come when the cleavage between loyal and disloyal Catholics was clear. The loyal Catholics professed that their weapons were solely spiritual and pleaded for the freedom of employing them in the ministrations of the Church and in the propagation of the faith in the land for which they professed such great love. They recognized that the Government had been moderate in its policy and that its repression had upon occasion been politically necessary. They must have recognized, as well, that its distinction between the secular and spiritual powers had been followed so far as circumstances would permit.[2] But the guarantee of freedom of belief, from the Roman Catholic point of view, was a small balm so long as the exercise of the functions essential to spiritual well-being and the spread of the faith were forbidden by legislation. It has been well said, that the formal right of liberty of conscience is of little use if it exists only in a vacuum of theory. When the principle is honestly and fully extended it means nothing less than toleration. The Roman Catholics, with the sects, urged the rightfulness and the necessity of that extension.

[1] Law, *Jesuits and Seculars*, i.
[2] McIlwain, C. H., *The Political Works of James I*, Intro., xxix.

6. Conclusion

Roman Catholic thought, in summary, made no important contributions to the development of the theory of toleration because it was intimately associated with the general body of Catholic thought which was unprepared, despite the requirements of toleration in numerous soundly orthodox countries, to abandon or to modify the ancient theory of doctrinal uniformity. English Catholic thought was considerably modified by several important forces and, in part, was of doubtful orthodoxy. The thought of the Jesuits must be distinguished from the sentiments of the spiritual group which came rapidly to a sharp differentiation of position as the dubious practices of the Jesuit party came into clearer relief.

In its mistaken zeal and political complexion Jesuit policy had been chiefly responsible for the sufferings of the English Catholics. There is little doubt that if the Jesuits had had their way Catholicism would have been established in England under a persecuting system which would have thrown the country back to the harrowing experiences of Marian times. We must therefore regard with considerable reserve the tolerant sentiments to which the Jesuit party gave periodic expression. Their arguments in this respect simply constituted one of the numerous weapons which they seized without much discrimination for the achievement of their end. But, whether sincerely inspired or no, their utterances in favour of toleration must be regarded as contributing to the creation of a broader and more tolerant sentiment. They denounced the persecution of conscience and held up as examples to be emulated the success of toleration in various countries. Parsons would seem to say that private judgment, right or wrong, should not be violated by the civil power.

The spiritual group of English Catholics based their plea for toleration on their political loyalty and upon a denial of the place of force in the propagation of the faith. Their recusancy, they said, was based upon the deepest sentiments of conscience which may not in justice be violated. They urged that the Government should carefully investigate the loyalty of a suspected

Catholic before bringing punishment to bear upon him. Persecution had brought the lay Catholics of England to a position in theory not unlike that of the Separatists. They had enunciated principles which might eventually lead to the removal of fear from the governmental policy, which was the overshadowing obstacle to Catholic toleration.

A limited group of Catholics had contributed a highly important argument for toleration in insisting that religious liberty must be the basis for a united state. This literature is scattered and small, the theory was only partially developed, but the resemblance to the teachings of the *Politiques* cannot be ignored. They sought to demonstrate to the Government that the very policy to which every interest was so completely subordinated must have, as its central pillar, religious liberty. The dangers of faction and civil war were not neglected. The group came close to the thesis that political loyalty resides in considerations apart from religious belief. The State is impotent before conscience and its attempts to coerce belief only raises the ugly spectre of rebellion. This important tendency of thought was enhanced by the quarrel between the politico-religious and the spiritual groups, which at the conclusion of the reign threatened to stamp English Catholicism as national in character. The spiritual group, by disowning the seditious tactics of the Jesuits and by solemnly averring their loyalty, gave a substantial basis for the argument that a nation may exist in security despite the manifold spiritual loyalties of its subjects. They declared their conviction that the faith of Christ and the cause of the Church might be advanced by the weapons of the spirit alone. These weapons the State had no cause to fear, and by their disavowal of the instruments of force they helped to clear the air of suspicion, to win the sympathy of reasonable men, and to bring the cause of Catholic freedom somewhat closer to attainment.

BIBLIOGRAPHY

ABBREVIATIONS EMPLOYED

Bodl.	Bodleian Library, Oxford.
B.P.L.	Boston Public Library.
B.M.	British Museum.
Camb.	Cambridge University Library.
Gay	Gay Collection in the Harvard University Library.
H.C.L.	Harvard University Library.
Hunt.	The Huntington Library.
Lamb.	Lambeth Palace Library.
McAlpin	The McAlpin Collection in the Union Theological Seminary Library.
M.L.A.	Library of the Mennonite Association, Amsterdam.
P.R.O.	Public Record Office, London.
Sion	Sion College Library, London.
T.T.C.	Library of Trinity College, Cambridge.
Wm.	The Dr. Williams' Library, London.
Y.C.L.	The Yale College Library.
Y.M.	The Library of York Minster.

The figures of a date in black type signify that that edition was used.
The library in black type signifies that the copy in that archive was used.

I. SOURCE MATERIALS

Acontius, Jacobus
De methodo, hoc est, de recta investigandarum tradendarumque scientiarum ratione.
Basle, 1558.
B.M., Berlin (Pub.), Göttingen, Königsberg, Bibl. Natl., Vienna (Pub.).

Satanae Stratagemata libri octo, J. Acontio authore, accessit eruditissima epistola de ratione edendorum librorum, ad Johannem Vuolfium Tigurinum eodem authore.
Basle, 1565.
Berlin, Breslau, Göttingen, Halle, Königsberg, **Paris,** Tübingen, Vienna, Zurich, Brown.

Les Ruzes de Satan, recueillies et comprinses en huit liures.
Basle, 1565.
B.M., Bodl., Bibl. Natl.

421

De Archlisticheden Des Satans, Begrepen in acht Boecken.
Graven-Haghe, 1611.
M.L.A.

Satains Stratagems, or the Devil's Cabinent-Councel Discovered, Whereby he endeavours to hinder the Knowledge of the Truth, through many Delusions . . . and also the testimonies of some Ancient Divines: with an Epistle written by Mr. John Goodwin. And Mr. Duries letter touching the same.
London, 1648.
B.M., McAlpin, Bodl., Library of the late George Brinley, Esq., of Hartford, Conn. (The first English translation of the first four books.)

Darkness Discovered. Or the Devil's Secret Stratagems laid open. Whereby he labors to make havock of the People of God, by his wicked and damnable Designs for destroying the Kingdom of Christ. Wherein is contained an exquisite Method of Disputation about Religion, and putting an end to all controversies in matters of conscience, etc.
London, 1651.
B.P.L., B.M.
(A duplication of the Eng. edition of 1648, with a new title page. This ed. unique in having a fine portrait of the author.)

Acts of the Privy Council of England. (New series.)
Ed. by J. R. Dasent.
London, 1890.

An Admonition to the Parliament.
London, 1571?.
Reprint ed. by W. H. Frere and C. E. Douglas in *Puritan Manifestoes*, etc., London, 1907.

A Seconde Admonition to the Parliament.
London, 1573?.
Reprint ed. by W. H. Frere and C. E. Douglas in *Puritan Manifestoes*, etc., London, 1907.

Ainsworth, Henry
The Confession of Faith of certayne English people living in exile in the low countreys. Together with the preface to the Reader which we wish of all may be read and considered, etc. (Addressed to the Universities of Leyden, St. Andrews, Heidelberg, Geneva, "and other the like famous scholes of learning in the Low-countreyes, . . .")
Preface, ————, 1596; ————, 1598.
B.M., Y.M.

BIBLIOGRAPHY

Alison, Richard
   A Plaine Confutation of Brownisme, published by some of that
   Faction, entituled: A description of the Visible Church, etc.
                London, 1590.
   (An answer to Barrow and Greenwood, A True Description,
   . . . of the Visible Church, 1589.)
   B.M., Hunt.

Allen, P. S.
   Opus Epistolarum Des Erasmi Roterodami; denvo Recognitum
   et auctum per P. S. Allen. 6 vols.
                Oxford, 1906–1928.

Allen, William
   An Apologie and Trve Declaration of the Institution and endeauours of the tvvo English colleges, the one in Rome, and the
   other novv resident in Rhemes: against certaine sinister informa-
   tions giuen vp against the same.
            Mounts (in Henault), 1581.
   B.M.

   A True, Sincere, and Modest Defence of English Catholics that
   suffer for their faith both at home and abroad, against a false,
   Seditious and Slanderous Libel entituled: The Execution of
   Justice in England.
              ————, 1584.
   Reprint of 1914; St. Louis and London. 2 vols. Pref. by Francis,
   Cardinal Bourne.

Aquinas, S. Thomas
   Summa Theologica.
   Ed. by J. P. Migne in *Patrologiae Cursus Completus*.
              Paris, 1841.

The Archpriest Controversy, *see* Law, T. G., ed.

Arminius, Jacob
   Works.
   Transl. by James Nichols. 3 vols.
          London, 1825–1875.

Articles agreed upon by the Archbishops, and Bishops of both
   provinces, and the whole clergy; in the Convocation holden in
   London, in the yeere 1562.
           London, 1628.
   Gay.

Articles for Reformation of the Ministrie.
         London?, 1586.
   Wm.

Articles of the Bishop of Norwich against the Iustices.
London, 1693.

Augustine, Saint
Works.
Transl. in *A Select Library of the Nicene and Post-Nicene Fathers of the Christian Church.*
Ed. by Philip Schaff.
New York, 1892–

B.J.
A bryefe and plaine declaracion of certayne sentēces in this litle boke folowing, to satisfie the consciences of them that haue judged me therby to be a fauoruer of the Anabaptistes, etc.
London, 1547 (no pagin.).
(Attributed to Bradford, J., and Bale, J.)

Bancroft, Richard
Daungerous Positions and Proceedings, published and practised within this Iland of Brytaine, under pretence of Reformation, and for the Presbiteriall Discipline.
London, 1593.
Gay (imperfect pagin.).

Barnes, Robert
That Mens Constitutions, which are not grounded in Scripture, bynde not the conscience of man vnder the payne of deadly synne.
London, 15—.
(Published in the *Works of Tyndal, Frith and Barnes.*)
What the Church is: and Who bee thereof, and whereby men may know her.
London, 15—.
(In *Works of Tyndal, Frith and Barnes.*)

Barrowe, Henry
A Brief of the examination of me, Henry Barrowe, the Nineteenth of Nouember 1586; before the Arch Bishops, Arch Deacon and Doctor Cussins, . . . being at Lambeth, etc.
London, 1586–1587, 1593, 1622.
Reprinted in Harl. Misc., IV, 326 ff.

A Petition directed to her most excellent Maiestie: Wherein is delivered 1. A meane howe to compound the ciuill dissention in the Church of England. 2. A proofe that they who write for Reformation, doe not offend against the stat. of 23 Eliz. c. 2.
Middleburgh?, Dort?, 1590; 1593.
B.M.; 2d ed. is in B.P.L.

A Brief Discourerie of the false Churche. As is the Mother such the daughter is.

> Dort?, Hanse?, **1590**; reprinted with large changes, 1707.

Camb.

A Collection of certaine sclaunderous articles gyven out by the Bisshops against such faithfull Christians as they nowe vniustly deteyne in their prisons together with the answeare of the said prisoners thereunto.

> Dort?, Hanse?, 1590.

B.M.

Mr. Henry Barrowes Platform. Which may serve as a preparative to purge away prelatisme: with some other parts of poperie, etc.

> London, **1593**; 1611.

B.M.

Barrowe, Henry, and Greenwood, John (?)
A True Description, ovt of the Word of God, of the visible Church.

> Dort, **1589** (Anon., no title page. B.M.), Amsterdam, before 1602 (same pagin., but with slight changes in the text. Y.C.L.); ————, 1641 (with title variation).

A Plaine Refutation of M. Giffards Booke, intituled, 'A Short Treatise gainst the Donatistes of England,' etc.

> Middleburgh?, Dort?, Hanse?, 1591.

B.M.

> Amsterdam, 1605 (with additions).

Becon, Thomas
A New Catechisme sette forth Dialogewise in familiare talke betweene the father and the son, etc.
Ed. by the Rev. John Ayre for the Parker Society as *The Catechism of Thomas Becon.*

> Cambridge, 1884.

Beza, Theodore
De haereticis a civili magistratu puniendis libellus, aduersus Martini Belli farraginem, et nouorum Academicorum sectam.

> Geneva?, Paris?, 1554.

B.M.

Iohannis Calvini vita a Theodora Beza descripta.

> Geneva, 1575 (no pagin.).

B.M.

Bilson, Thomas
    The True Difference Betweene Christian Subjection and Vn-
    christian Rebellion: wherein the Princes Lawfvll power to
    commaund for trueth, and indepriuable right to beare the sword
    are defended against the popes censures and the Iesuits sophismes
    vttered in their Apologie and Defence of English Catholikes, etc.
                    Oxford, 1585.
    B.M., H.C.L.

Boccaccio, Giovanni
    The Decameron, or the Ten Days' Entertainment of Boccaccio.
    Revised transl. by W. K. Kelly.
                    London, 1865.
Bodin, Jean
    De Repvblica libri sex. 4th ed.
                    Ursellis, 1601.
    B.M.

Bradshaw, William
    English Puritanisme, Containing the maine opinions of the
    rigidest sort of those called Puritanes in the Realm of England
    (anon.).
                    Amsterdam?, 1605; London, 1640 (Gay); London,
                    1641.
    B.M.

Braght, T. J., van
    Het Bloedig Toonel, . . . martalaers spiegel du doops-gesinde
    of weereloose Christenen, etc.
                    Amsterdam, 1686; Eng. from a Ger. ed., Lancaster
                    (Penn.), 1837.

Bretschneider, C. G., ed., see Corpus Reformatorum

Bridges, John
    The Supremacie of Christian Princes, ouer all persons through-
    out their dominions, in all causes so wel ecclesiastical as temporall,
    both against the Counterblast of Thomas Stapleton . . . and also
    against Nicolas Sanders, etc.
                    London, 1573.
    B.M.

Brinklow, Henry
    Henry Brinklow's Complaynt of Roderyck Mors, sometime a
    gray fryre, vnto the parliament howse of Ingland his natural
    cuntry; for the redress of certen wicked lawes, euel customs,
    and cruel decreys.
                    London, 1542?.
    Ed. by J. M. Cowper for the E.E.T.S.
                    London, 1874.

Browne, Robert

A Booke which Sheweth the life and manners of all true Christians, and howe vnlike they are vnto Turkes and Papistes, and Heathen folke. Also the pointes and partes of all Diuinitie, that is of the reuealed will and worde of God, are declared by their seuerall Definitions, and Diuisions in order as followeth.

Middleburgh, 1582.
Copies in **B.M.**, Y.C.L., Bodl., T.C.C., and Lamb.

A Treatise of Reformation without tarying for anie, and of the wickednesse of those preachers, which will not reforme till the magistrate commande or compell them.

Middleburgh, 1582.
Copies in Y.C.L., Lamb.
Ed. by T. G. Crippen for the Cong. Hist. Soc.

London?, **1903**.

A Treatise vpon the 23 of Matthewe, both for an Order of Studying and handling the Scriptures, and also for auoyding the popishe disorders, and vngodly comunion of all false Christians, and especiallie of wicked preachers and hirelings.

Middleburgh, 1582.
Lamb.

A True and Short Declaration, Both of the gathering and Ioyning Together of Certaine persons: and also of the Lamentable Breach and Division which Fell amongst them.

London?, ————?.
Reprinted London, **1882.**

Letter to Mr. Flower.

————, 1589.
First printed in 1904 as "A New Yeers Guift." Ed. by Champlin Burrage for the Cong. Hist. Soc.

London, 1904.

Bullinger, Heinrich

An holsume antidotus or counterpoysen, agaynst the pestilent heresye and secte of Anabaptistes, newly translated out of Latin into Englysh, by John Veron Senonoys.

London, 1548.
Camb.

A most necessary and frutefull Dialogue betweene ye seditious Libertin or rebel Anabaptist, and the true obedient Chrystiā, wherin, as in a mirrour or glasse ye shal se ye excellencie and worthynesse of a Chrystiā magistrate: and again what obedience is due unto publique rulers of al that professe Christ yea, though

427

ye rulers in externe and outward thinges, to their vtter damp-
natyon, do otherwuse then well. Transl. by John Veron Senonoys.
Worcester, 1551.
B.M.
The Decades of Henry Bullinger.
Ed. for the Parker Society by the Rev. Thomas Harding.
4 vols.
Cambridge, 1849–1852.

Bunny, Edmund
A Treatise Tending to Pacification: By laboring those that are
our adversaries in the cause of religion, to receiue the Gospell,
and to ioyne with vs in the profession thereof.
London, 1585.
Sion.

Burleigh, Lord
The Execution of Justice in England, for Maintenaunce of
publique and Christian Peace, against certeine Stirrers of Sedition, and Adherents to the Traytours and Enemies of the Realme,
without any Persecution of them for Questions of Religion, etc.
London, 1583.
Reprinted in Harl. Misc., II, 122 ff.

Cabot, Sebastian
Ordinances, instructions, and advertisements of and for the
direction of the intended voyage for Cathay, compiled, made,
and delivered by the right Worshipfull M. Sebastian Cabota,
Esquier, . . .
————, 1553.
Printed in Hakluyt, II, 195 ff.

Calendars of State Papers
Letters and Papers Foreign and Domestic of the Reign of
Henry VIII. (Vol. V.)
Ed. by James Gairdner.
London, 1880.

Domestic Series, of the Reigns of Edward VI, Mary, and Elizabeth. (Vol. I, 1547–1580.)
London, 1856.

Domestic Series, of the Reign of Elizabeth. (Vols. II–VII.)
London, 1865–1871.

Domestic Series, of the Reign of James I. (Vols. VIII–XII.)
London, 1857–1872.

Foreign Series, of the Reign of Elizabeth, 1558–1588.
Ed. by Joseph Stevenson, et al.
London, 1863–1927.

Foreign Series, of the Reign of Elizabeth, 1586–1587 (Holland and Flanders).
Ed. by S. C. Lomas and A. B. Hinds.
London, 1927–

Spanish Series, 1558–1603.
Calendar of Letters and State Papers Relating to English Affairs Preserved in, or originally belonging to, the Archives of Simancas.
Ed. by M. A. S. Hume.
4 vols.
London, 1892–1899.

Roman Series, 1558–1576.
Calendar of State Papers Relating to English Affairs, preserved principally at Rome, in the Vatican Archives and Library.
Ed. by J. M. Rigg.
2 vols.
London, 1916–1926.

Venetian Series.
Calendar of State Papers and Manuscripts, relating to English Affairs, Existing in the Archives and Collections of Venice, and in other Libraries of Northern Italy.
London, 1864–1927.

Calvini, Ioannis
Opera quae supersunt omnia.
Ed. by G. Baum, E. Cunitz, and E. Reuss.
59 vols.
Brunswick, 1863–1900.

Camden, William
Annales, or, the History of the Most Renowned and Victorious Princesse Elizabeth, Late Queen of England.
Transl. by Norton.
3rd ed.
London, 1635.

Cardwell, Edward
Documentary annals of the Reformed Church of England; Being a Collection of Injunctions, Declarations, Orders, Acts of Inquiry, . . . from 1546–1716.
2nd ed. 2 vols.
Oxford, 1844.

Cartwright, Thomas
A Replye to an Answere made of M. Doctor Whitgifte, againste the Admonition to the Parliament by T.C., etc.
————, 1573; 1589.
Text in Whitgift's *Defence of the Answer*, Works, vol. I.

The Second Replie of Thomas Cartwright: agaynst Maister Doctor Whitgiftes second answer touching the churche discipline, etc.

Zurich?, 1575.

B.M.

The Rest of the Second Replie of Thomas Cartvuright: agaynst Master Doctor Vuhitgifts second ansvuer, touching the Church Discipline.

London?, Zurich?, 1577.

B.P.L.

A directory of Church-Government; anciently contended for, and as farre as the times would suffer, practised by the first nonconformists in the daies of Queen Elizabeth.

London, 1644.

Gay.

Helpes for the Discovery of the Truth in point of toleration, etc. Attributed to T.C.

London, 1648.

B.M.

Castellion, Sébastien
Traité des Hérétiques. A savoir, si on les doit persécutor, et comment on se doit conduire avec eux, selon l'avis, opinion, et sentence de plusiers auteurs, tant anciens que modernes.
Ed. by A. Olivet.

Genève, 1913.

Contra libellum Calvini in quo ostendere conatur haereticos jure gladii cœrcendos esse.

Amsterdam, 1612.

B.M.

Celsus, Minus
In haereticus coercendis quatemus progedi liceat, Celsi Mini Seninsus disputatio. Ubi nominatim eos ultimo supplicio affici non debere, aperti demonstratur.

—————, **1559**; —————, 1584; Amsterdam, 1662.

B.M.

Cheeke, Sir John
The Trve Subiect to the Rebell. Or, the hurt of Sedition. How grieuovs it is to a Commonwealth.

London, 1549; Oxford, **1641.**

B.M.

BIBLIOGRAPHY

Clapham, Henoch
> Antidoton: or a sovereigne remedie against schisme and heresie, etc.
>> Amsterdam?, 1600.
> Camb.

The Lord Coke his speech and Charge, etc.
>> London, 1607.
> Hunt.; **B.M.**

Collins, E. W., ed.
> Queen Elizabeth's Defence of her Proceedings in Church and State.
>> London, 1899.

A True Confession of the Faith, and Hvmble Acknovvledgment of the Alegeance, vvich vvee hir Maiesties' Subjects, falsely called Brovvnists, doo hould tovvards God, and yeild to hir Majestie and all other that are ouer vs in the Lord. Set dovvn in Articles or positions, for the better and more easie vnderstanding of those that shall read yt: and published for the cleering of our selues from those vnchristian slanders of heresie, schisme, pride, obstinacie, disloyaltie, sedicion, &c vvich by our adversaries are in all places given out against vs.
>> Amsterdam?, 1596.
> B.M.

Another edition: Confessio Fidei Anglorvm Qvorvndam in Belgia Exvlantivm: Vna cum Praefationes ad Lectorem: quam ab omnibus legi et animadverti cupimus.
>> Amsterdam, 1598 (new pref. and slight changes in text).
> Bodl.

Another edition: The Confession of Faith of certayne English people living in exile in the Low Countreys, etc.
>> ————, 1598.
> B.M., Y.M.

Another edition: Dutch translation of 1599 or 1600.

Another edition: The Confession of faith of certayn English people, living in exile in the Low Countreys. Together with a brief note of the special heads of those things wherin we differ frō the Church of England.
>> ————, 1602; 1604; Amsterdam, 1607.
> B.M., Bodl.

Another edition : Dutch translation.
>> Amsterdam, 1614.

Another edition: Dutch translation.
Amsterdam, 1670.

Another edition: Second Latin translation.
Amsterdam?, 1607.
B.M., Y.M.

La Confession de foi des Églises Réformées Walonnes et Flamandes.
Brussels, 1854 (By Soc. Évang. Belge).

An Harmony of the Confessions of the Faith of the Christian and Reformed Chvrches which purelie professe the holy doctrine of the gospell in all the chiefe kingdomes, nations, and prouinces of Europe, the catalogue and order whereof the pages following will declare.
Cambridge, 1586.
Wm.

Cooper, Thomas
An Admonition to the People of England: wherein are ansvvered, not onely the slaunderous vntruethes, reprochfully vttered by Martin the Libeller, but also many other crimes by some of his broode, obiected generally against all Bishops, and the chiefe of the cleargie, purposely to deface and discredite the present state of the Church, etc.
London, 1589; agn. 1589; **1847.**

Coornhert, D. V.
Wercken, waer van eenige noyt voor desen gedruct zyn.
3 vols.
Amsterdam, 1630.

Corpus Reformatorum
Ed. by Bretschneider, C. G., et al.
Halis Saxonum, 1834–

Cranmer, Thomas
The Works of Thomas Cranmer.
Ed. by J. E. Cox for the Parker Society.
2 vols.
Cambridge, 1844–1846.

Dallington, Sir Robert
A Method of Trauell. Shewed by taking the View of France as it stood in the yeare of our Lord 1598.
London, 1598?.
Bodl.

Davies, J.
A Private mans Potion for the health of England, etc.
Anon., B.M. Cat. attribution.
London, 1591.
T.C.C.

A Briefe and plaine Declaration, concerning the desires of all those
faithfull ministers, that haue and do seeke for the Discipline and
Reformation of the Church of England.
London, 1584.
Wm.

A Briefe and Faythfull Declaration of the true fayth of Christ, made
by certeyne men susspected of heresye in these articles following,
etc.
London, 1547.
McAlpin.

D'Ewes, Sir Simonds
The Journals of all the Parliaments during the Reign of Queen
Elizabeth, both of the House of Lords and House of Commons,
etc.
London, 1682.

A Dialogve concerning the strife of our churche: wherein are aun-
swered diuerse of those vniust accusations, wherewith the godly
preachers, and professors of the gospell, are falsely charged.
————, 1584.
Wm., Hunt.

Digges, Sir Dudley
The Compleat Ambassador: or, two treaties of the intended
Marriage of Qu. Elizabeth of glorious memory; comprised in
Letters of negotiation of Sir Francis Walsingham, . . . with the
answers of Lord Burleigh, . . . and others.
London, 1655.
B.M.

The First and Second Booke of Discipline (Scottish).
Leyden?, 1621.
B.M.

Egerton Papers. A Collection of Public and Private Documents,
Chiefly Illustrative of the times of Elizabeth and James I.
Ed. by J. P. Collier for the Camden Society.
London, 1840.

Elizabeth, Queen
> Letters of Queen Elizabeth and King James VI of Scotland.
> Ed. by James Bruce for the Camden Society.
> > London, 1849.

> Queen Elizabeth's Defence of her Proceedings. . . . *See* Collins,
> E. W., Ed.

English Protestants plea, and petition, for English Preists and papists.
> To the present Court of Parliament, and all persecutors of
> them, etc.
> > Douay?, 1621.
> B.M.

Episcopius, Simon
> Opera Theologica.
> Ed. by S. Curcellaeus and P. v. Limboch.
> 2 vols., 4 pts.
> > Amsterdam-Goudae, 1650–1665.
> B.M.

An Exhortation to the Byshops to deale brotherly with theyr
Brethren.
> > London?, 1572, B.M., Mc.
> > London, 1572; 1617.
> Ed. and reprinted by W. H. Frere and C. E. Douglas. London,
> > **1907.**

Fenner, Dudley
> A Defence of the godlie ministers, against the slaunders of D.
> Bridges, contayned in his answere to the Preface before the
> Discourse of Ecclesiasticall Gouernment, with a declaration of
> the Bishops proceeding against them, etc.
> > London, 1587.
> (Anon.: Camb. Cat. ascrpt.; imperfect pagin.)
> B.P.L., Bodl., Lamb., Y.M., Wm.

Fenton, Geoffrey
> A forme of Christian policie drawne out of French by Geffray
> Fenton. A worke very necessary to al sorts of people generally,
> as; wherein is contayned doctrine, both vnoversall, and special
> touching the institution of al Christian profession: and also
> conuenient perticularly for all Magistrates and gouernours of com-
> monweales, for their more happy Regiment according to God.
> > London, 1574.
> B.M., Mc.

434

BIBLIOGRAPHY

Fox, Edward
De Vera Differentia Regiae Potestatis et Ecclesiasticae.
London, 1534.
B.M.
Translated by Lord Stafford as *The True dyfferēs betwen ye regall power and the ecclesiasticall power.*
London, 1548 (rare).
B.M.

Foxe, John
The Acts and Monuments of John Foxe.
4th ed. by the Rev. Josiah Pratt. 8 vols.
London, 1877.

Fulke, William
A briefe Confutation, of a Popish Discourse: Lately set forth, and presumptiously dedicated to the Queenes most excellent Maiestie: by Iohn Howlet, or some other Birde of the night, vnder that name. Contayning certaine reasons, why papistes refuse to come to church, which reasons are here inserted and set downe at large, with their seuerall answeres.
London, 1581.
H.C.L., B.M.

Gardiner, Stephen
De Vera Obediencia. . . .
Eng. transl. by Michal Wood.
Roane, 1553.

Gentilis, Alberico
De Legationibus, libri tres.
London, 1585.
B.M.

De jure belli libri tres.
Hanover, 1598.
B.M.
Hanau, 1612.
Naples, 1770.
London, 1877.

Gifford, George
A briefe discourse of certaine pointes of the religion, which is among the commō sorte of Christians; which may bee termed the countrie divinitie; with a confutation of the same; after the order of a dialogue. (Title missing.)
London, 1581 (?).
Bodl.

A Short Treatise against the Donatists of England, whome we call Brownists, wherein, by the Answeres vnto certayne writings of theyrs, diuers of their heresies are noted, with sundry fantasticall opinions, etc.

London, 1590.

Bodl., B.M.

A Plaine Declaration that our Brownists be full Donatists, by comparing them together from point to point out of the Writings of Augustine. Also a replie to Master Greenwood touching read prayer, etc.

London, 1590.

H.C.L., B.M., Bodl.

Goodman, Christopher
How Superior powers oght to be obeyd of their Subiects: and wherin they may lawfully by Gods worde be disobeyd and resisted. Wherein also is declared the cause of all this present miserie in England and the onely way to remedy the same.

Geneva, 1558.

Grindal, Edmund
The Remains of Edmund Grindal, Successively Bishop of London, and Archbishop of York and Canterbury.
Ed. by William Nicholson for the Parker Society.

Cambridge, 1843.

H.G.
A coppy of a Letter sent from tvvo citizens of London, to theyr friend remayning beyond the Seas for cause of Religion.

————, 1600.

B.M.

Hakluyt, Richard
The Principal Navigations Voyages Traffiques and Discoveries of the English Nation.
12 vols.

Glasgow, 1903–1905.

Hall, Edward
Chronicle: Containing the History of England during the Reign of Henry the Fourth, and the succeeding monarchs, to the end of the Reign of Henry the Eighth, etc.
Ed. by H. Ellis.

London, 1809.

Hanbury, Benjamin
　　Historical Memorials Relating to the Independents, or Congre-
　　gationalists; From their Rise to the Restoration of the Monarchy.
　　3 vols.
　　　　　　　　　London, 1839–1844.

The Harleian Miscellany: or, a collection of scarce, curious, and
　　entertaining Pamphlets and Tracts . . . found in the late Earl
　　of Oxford's Library. . . .
　　8 vols.
　　　　　　　　　London, 1744–1746.

Harrison, Robert
　　A Treatise of the Church and the Kingdome of Christ.
　　　　　　　　　London, 1580–1581.
　　Attributed to Robert Harrison. Printed by Peel, Albert, in *The
　　Brownists in Norwich and Norfolk about 1580.*
　　　　　　　　　Cambridge, 1920.

A letter intercepted from R.H. one of Brownes faction, dis-
covering in part his great disliking of the said Brownes schismatical practises.
Attributed to R.H.
　　　　　　　　　————, 1583.
(In Herbert, 1167; Ath. Cant., II, 178.)

A Little Treatise Vppon the firste verse of the 122 Psalme.
Stirring up vnto carefull desiring and dutifull labouring for true
church gouernment. . . .
　　　　　　　　　Holland?, 1583.
B.M., Bodl., Lamb.

Hastings, Sir Francis
　　A Watchword to all Religious and true hearted English-men.
　　　　　　　　　London, 1598.
　　B.M.

Haynes, Samuel
　　A Collection of State Papers . . . transcribed from the Original
　　Letters and other authentick memorials . . . left by William
　　Cecill Lord Burghley and now remaining at Hatfield House.
　　　　　　　　　London, 1740.
Het Bloedig toonel, etc. Vide Braght, T. J., van.

Historical Manuscripts Commission
Calendar of the Manuscripts of the most Hon. the Marquis of
Salisbury, preserved at Hatfield House, Hertfordshire.
Part IV, London, 1892.
Part VII, London, 1899.
Part IX, London, 1902.
Part XIV, London, 1923.

Report on Manuscripts in Various Collections.
Vol. III, London, 1904.

Hooker, Richard
The Works of that learned and judicious divine, Mr. Richard
Hooker, with an account of his death by Isaac Walton.
Arr. by the Rev. John Keble.
7th ed. 3 vols.
Oxford, 1888.

Hooper, John
Early Writings of John Hooper.
Ed. by Samuel Carr for the Parker Society.
Cambridge, 1843.

Later Writings of Bishop Hooper, together with His Letters
and other Pieces.
Ed. by Chas. Nevinson for the Parker Society.
Cambridge, 1852.

Hutchins, Edward
A Sermon preached in Westchester . . . before the Iudges and
certain Recusantes: wherein the conditions of al heretiques, but
especiallie of stubborn and peruerting Papists, are discouered,
and the duty of al magistrats concerning such persons, applied
and opened.
Oxford, 1586?.
B.M.

Jewel, John
The Works of John Jewel, Bishop of Salisbury.
Ed. by John Ayre for the Parker Society.
4 vols.
Cambridge, 1845–1850.

Johnson, Francis
A Treatise of the Ministery of the Church of England. Wherein
is handled this question, whether it be to be separated from, or
ioyned vnto, which is discussed in two letters, the one written
for it, the other against it. . . .
London, 1595.
Wm., Bodl., Lamb., Y.M., B.P.L.
438

An Answer to Maister H. Iacob, his treatise concerning the Priestes of the Church of England, etc.
>London, 1600.
Wm., B.M., Bodl., Y.M.

An Answer to Maister H. Jacob, his Defence of the Churches and ministery of England by Fr. I., an exile of Jesvs Christ, etc.
>Middleburgh, 1600.
B.M., Bodl., Y.M.

Joye, George
A Present Consolacion for the sufferers of persecucion for ryghtwysenes.
>London, 1544.
B.M.
(Subscribed G.J., i.e. George Joye.)

Knox, John
An Answer to a Great Nomber of blasphemous cauillations written by an Anabaptist, and aduersarie to Gods eternal predestination and confuted by John Knox, etc.
>Geneva?, **1560**, 1591.
Mc.
Reprinted in *Works* (vol. V).
Ed. by David Laing.
6 vols.
>Edinburgh, 1846–1864.

Lactantius
Divinarum Institutionum.
In Migne, *Patrologiae Cursus Completus*, vol. VI.

La Noue, Francois de
Discours politiques et militaires du Seigneur de la Noue. . . .
>Basle, 1587.
Bibl. Natl.

Law, T. G., ed.
Documents Relating to the Dissensions of the Roman Catholic Clergy, 1597–1602. (Referred to as *The Archpriest Controversy*.)
Camden Society.
2 vols.
>London, 1896–1898.

History of Queen Elizabeth, Amy Robsart and the Earl of Leicester.
Being a Reprint of *Leycester's Commonwealth*.
Ed. by Burgoyne, F. J.
>London, 1904.

Published in Antwerp (?) in 1584 under the title, *Copie of a leter Wryten by a Master of Arts of Cambridge to his friend in London*. It was translated and published in French in 1585. A Latin edition appeared in 1585. A 2nd English edition was published in 1641. The edition of 1641 is a reprint of the 2nd English edition, 1904.

L'Hôpital, Michel de
Traité de la Reformation de la Justice.
In Vol. I, 2 de *Oeuvres Completès*.
Ed. par P. J. S. Duféy.
Paris, 1824–1826.

Harangue Prononcée a l'ouverture de la Session des États-Généraux assemblés a Orleans le 13 Decembre, 1560.
In *Oeuvres Complètes*, Vol. I.
Ed. par P. J. S. Duféy.
Paris, 1824–1826.

Proposition et Harangue Faicte . . . sur le Faict de la Religion en la Ville de Poissy.
In *Oeuvres Completès*, Vol. I.
Paris, 1824–1826.

Machyn, Henry
The Diary of Henry Machyn, Citizen and Merchant-Taylor of London, from 1550–1563.
Ed. by J. G. Nichols for the Camden Society.
London, 1848.

Martin Marprelate
Oh Read ouer D. Iohn Bridges, for it is a Worthy Worke, etc.
————, 1588?, 1589, 1843, 1878.
B.M.

McIlwain, C. H., ed.
The Political Works of James I . . . with an Introduction by C. H. McIlwain.
Cambridge, 1918.

More, Sir Thomas
Utopia.
Ed. from the text of the first edition with notes, by Robert Steele.
London, 1908.

A Dialogue of Syr Thomas More Knyghte. . . . Wherin be treatyed diuers maters, as to the veneracion and worship of ymages and relyques, prayng to saintes, and goyng on pylgrimages. With

many other thinges touchyng the pestilent secte of Luther and
Tyndal, etc.
(In *Works*.)
London, 1523?.

The Confutacion of Tyndales Answere made anno 1532 by Syr
Thomas More, knyghte, etc.
(In *Works*.)
London, 1532.

The Answer to the First part of the poysoned booke whych a
nameless heretike hath named the supper of the Lord.
(In *Works*.)
London, 1533.

The Debellacyon of Salem and Bezience made by Syr Thomas
More ... after he had gyven ouer the office of Lorde Chancellour
of Englande.
(In *Works*.)
London, 1533.

The Apology of Syr Thomas More, knight; made by hym ...
after he had gyeuen ouer the office of Lord Chancellour of
Englande.
(In *Works*.)
London, 1533.

The VVorkes of Sir Thomas More.
Ed. by William Rastall.
London, 1557.
H.C.L.

Murdin, William, ed.
A Collection of State Papers relating to affairs in the Reign of
Queen Elizabeth from 1571-1596 ... left by William Cecill
lord Burghley, etc.
2 vols.
London, 1740-1759.

A Necessary doctrine and Erudition for any Chrysten Man, set
furth by the kynges maiestie of England, etc.
London, 1543. (There were ten editions in that
year.)
(This is a review of the *Institutions of a Christen Man*), first
published in 1537, and usually called *The Bishop's Book*. The
Necessary Doctrine was usually known as the *King's Book*. The
Institutions was drawn up by Convocation in 1534, printed three
years later, and was in 1543 enlarged and published in the above
form. The B.M. copy belonged to Herbert.)

Niemeyer, H. A.
> Collectio Confessionum in Ecclesiis Reformaṭis Publicatarum.
> (Appendix, qua continentur Puritanorum libri symbolici.)
> Leipzig, 1840.

Nowell, Alexander
> The Reprovfe of M. Dorman his proufe of certaine Articles in
> Religion, . . . continued by Alexander Nowell. With a defense of
> the chiefe authoritie and gouernment of Christian Princes as
> well in causes ecclesiasticall, as ciuill, within theire owne
> dominions.
> London, 1566.
> B.M.

O.C.
> Elizabethe Queene. Or a short and compendious declaration of
> the peaceable state of England, vnder the gouernment of the
> most mighty and vertuous Princesse Elizabeth. . . .
> (Transl. from the Latin by John Sharrock.)
> Perhaps by C. Ockland.
> London, 1585 (no pagin.).
> B.M.

Ochino, Bernardino
> Dialogi xxx in duos libros divisi, quorum primus est de Messia
> continetque dialogos xviii. Secundus est cum de rebus variis,
> tum potissimum de Trinitate. Quorum argumenta in secunda
> utrivsque pagina invenies.
> 2 vols.
> Basle, 1563.
> B.M.

Parker, Matthew
> Correspondence of Matthew Parker, Archbishop of Canterbury.
> Comprising Letters Written by and to him, from 1535–1575.
> Ed. for the Parker Society by John Bruce and the Rev. T. T.
> Perowne.
> Cambridge, 1853.

Parsons, Robert
> A brief discours contayning certayne Reasons why Catholiques
> Refuse to goe to Church. Written by a learned and vertuous man,
> to a friend of his in England, and dedicated by I.H. to the Queenes
> most excellent Maiestie.
> Douay, 1580, 1599, 1601, 1621.
> B.M.

442

An epistle of the Persecution of Catholickes in England. Translated ovvt of frenche into Englishe and conferred vvith the Latyne copie by G.T. To whiche is added an epistle of the translator to the right honorable Lordes of her Maiesties preeuie councell touchynge the same matter.

Douay, 1582.

H.C.L., B.M.

A Conference abovt the Next Succession to the Crowne of Ingland, etc.

————, 1594.

H.C.L., B.M.

Peck, Francis
Desiderata Curiosa . . . memoirs, letters, wills and epitaphs, . . . all now published from original MSS.
2 vols.

London, 1732–1735.

Peel, Albert, Ed.
Second Parte of a Register. Vide *Register*.

Penry, John
An Exhortation vnto the gouernours, and people of hir maiesties countrie of Wales, to labour earnestly to haue the preaching of the Gospell planted among them, etc.

————, 1587?, **1588.**

B.M.

A Defence of that which hath bin written in the questions of the ignorant ministrie, and the communicating with them.

London?, 1588?.

Wm., Bodl., Lamb.

Th' Appelation of Iohn Penrie, vnto the Highe Court of Parliament, from the bad and injurious dealing of th' Arch. of Canterb. and other his colleagues of the High Commission: Wherin the complainant, humbly submitting himselfe and his cause vnto the determination of this honorable assembly, craueth nothing els, but either release from trouble and persecution, or iust tryall, etc.

London, 1589.

H.C.L., B.M., Bodl., Lamb.

An hvmble motion with svbmission vnto the right honorable LL. of Hir Maiesties Priuie covnsell. Wherein is Laid open to be considered, how necessarie it were for the good of this Lande, and the Queenes maiesties safetie, that Ecclesiasticall discipline

443

were reformed after the worde of God: and how easily there might be provision for a learned ministery.

————, 1590.

B.M., Bodl., Lamb., T.C.C., Y.M.

London, 1599?, 1641.

A Treatise wherein is manifestlie proved, that Reformation and those that sincerely fauor the same, are unjustly charged to be enemies, vnto hir maiestie, and the State, etc.

Edinburgh?, 1590 (no pagin.).

B.M., Y.M., Bodl., Lamb.

Confession of Faith and Apology.

————, 1593.

Printed in Burrage, C., *The Early English Dissenters*, II, 87 ff.

. . . The Historie of Corah, Dathan, and Abiram, . . . Applied to the prelacy ministerie and Church-assemblies of England. (Unfinished.)

London, 1609.

Bodl., B.M.

The Humble Petition of the Imprisoned Barrowists to the . . . Magistrates of our most Mercifull Soueraign Lady Queene Elizabeth in their seuerall places.

London, 1593.

Printed in Burrage, C., *The Early English Dissenters*.

The Petition of six Norwich Ministers to (Burleigh).

————, c. 1576.

In *Seconde Parte of a Register, Morrice MSS.*

Wm.

Catholic Petition to Queen Elizabeth.

————, 1585.

Printed in *English Protestants' Plea*, etc. (1621).

B.M.

Philopatris, J.

An Advertisement written to a Secretarie of my L. Treasurers of Ingland by an Inglishe Intelligencer as he passed through Germanie towardes Italie. . . .

London?, 1592.

B.M.

(Very rare. The pagin. is imperfect.)

(Attributed to Parsons, R., and Cresswell, J.)

Pilkington, James

The Works of James Pilkington, Lord Bishop of Durham.
Edited by James Scholefield for the Parker Society.
2 vols.

Cambridge, 1842.

A Shorte Treatse of Politike Povver, and the true Obedience which
subiectes owe to kynges and other ciuile Gouernours, with an
Exhortacion to all true naturall Englishmen.
(No pagin.)
————, 1556.
B.M.

Prothero, G. W., Ed.
Select Statutes and Other Constitutional Documents Illustrative
of the Reigns of Elizabeth and James I.
Oxford, 1894.

Pulci, Luigi
Il Morgante Maggiore.
Con note di Eugenio Camerini, del Sermolli ed altri.
Milan, 1875.

The Reformation of Religion of Iosiah a commendable example for
all Princes professing the Gospel to follovve, with a warninge
to all faithfull and true-hearted Subiectes, to encourage their
princes in so happie a course, etc.
————, 1590.
Wm. (cropped; no pagin.)

A Parte of a Register, contayninge sundrie memorable matters,
written of diuers godly and learned in our own time, which
stande for, and desire the reformation of our church, in Discipline and ceremonies, accordinge to the pure worde of God,
and the Law of our Lande, etc.
Middleburgh?, 1593.
Wm.

The Seconde Parte of a Register: being a Calendar of Manuscripts
under that title intended for publication by the Puritans about
1593, and now in the Dr. Williams' Library, London.
Ed. by Albert Peel.
2 vols.
Cambridge, 1915.

Rymer, Thomas.
Foedera, conventiones, literae, et cujuscunque generis Acta
publica, inter Reges Anglia, et alios quosvis Imperatores, Reges
Pontifices, Principes, vel Communitates, . . . ab anno 1101, ad
nostra usque tempora, etc.
20 vols.
London, 1704–1732.

445

S.C.

A Briefe Resolution of a Right Religion. Tovching the controversies, that are nowe in England.

London, 1590.

Wm.

Saint Germain, Christopher

Dyaloge Betwyxt a Doctoure of Dyuynyte and a Student in the Laues of Englande: of the groundes of the sayd Laues and of consycence.

London, 1530.

B.M.

A Treatise concernynge the diuision betwene the spirytualtie and temporaltie.

London, 1530?, **1532.**

Salem and Bizance. A Dialogue Betwixte two Englyshe men. Whereof one was called Salem, and the other Bizance.

London, **1533**, 1537.

Sandys, Edwin, Abp.

A Proposal of union amongst Protestants, from the last-will of the most Reverend Dr. Sands, sometime Archbishop of York.

London, 1590.

(Lincoln's Inn.)

The Sermons of Edwin Sandys, . . . to which are added some miscellaneous pieces, etc.

Ed. by John Ayres for the Parker Society.

Cambridge, 1842.

Sandys, Sir Edwin

Europae Speculum, or, a View or Survey of the State of Religion in the Westerne parts of the World. Wherein the Romane Religion, and the pregnant policies of the Church of Rome to support the same, are notably displayed, etc.

London, 1605? (anon.).

B.M., Hunt.

London, 1605.

Harms.

London, 1605?.

Hunt., Camb., Mc.

London, 1629.

Mc.

London, **1637.** (7th ed.?)

H.C.L., Mc.

446

Savage, Francis
A conference Betwixt a Mother a Devovt Recusant, and her
Sonne a zealous protestant, seeking by humble and dutifull
satisfaction to winne her vnto the trueth, and publike worship
of God established nowe in England, etc.
Cambridge, 1600.
B.M.

Schwenckfeld, Caspar
Corpus Schwenckfeldianorum.
Pub. under the auspices of the Schwenckfelder Church and the
Hartford Theological Seminary.
Ed. by C. D. Hartranft, et al.
Leipzig, etc., 1907–

Some, Robert
A Godly Treatise containing and deciding certaine questions,
mooued of late in London and other places, touching the minis-
terie, Sacraments, and church.
London, 1588.
Wm.

A Defence of Svch points in R. Somes last Treatise as M. Penry
hath dealt against, etc.
London, 1588.
Wm.

A Godly Treatise wherein are examined and confuted many
execrable fancies, given out and holden, partly by Henry Barrow
and John Greenwood; partly, by other of the Anabaptisticall
order, etc.
London, 1589.
H.C.L. (photostat), Bodl.

Some, Robert, and Pilkington, J.
A godlie Treatise, against the foule and grosse sinne of oppres-
sion.
London?, 1585.
B.M., Wm.

Somers, J.
A Collection of Scarce and Valuable Tracts, etc.
2nd ed., edited by Walter Scott.
13 vols.
London, 1809–1815.

Southwell, Robert
An Hvmble Svpplication to her Maiestie.
(Attributed to R.S.)
————, 1595.
B.M.

Starkey, Thomas
A Dialogue Between Cardinal Pole and Thomas Lupset, Lecturer in Rhetoric at Oxford.
Ed. by J. M. Cowper for the E.E.T.S.
London, 1878.

A Complete Collection of State Trials.
Ed. by J. B. Howell and contd. by T. J. Howell.
33 vols.
London, 1816–1826.

Stow, John
The Annales of England, etc.
London, 1605.

Strype, John
Annals of the Reformation and Establishment of Religion, and various occurrences in the Church of England, during Queen Elizabeth's Happy Reign.
4 vols. in 7 parts. 4th ed.
Oxford, 1824.

Memorials of the Most Reverend Father in God Thomas Cranmer, etc.
2 vols.
Oxford, 1812.

History of the Life and Acts of . . . Edmund Grindal, etc.
Oxford, 1821.

Historical Collections of the Life and Acts of John Aylmer, etc.
Oxford, 1821.

The Life and Acts of Matthew Parker, etc.
3 vols.
Oxford, 1821.

Ecclesiastical memorials relating chiefly to religion, and the reformation of it, and the emergencies of the Church of England under King Henry VIII, King Edward VI, and Queen Mary the First.
3 vols.
Oxford, 1822.

History of the Life and Acts of John Whitgift.
3 vols.
>Oxford, 1822.

Sulpicius, Severus
Chronicorum quae vulgo inscribuntur Historia Sacra, libri duo.
In Migne, *Patrologiae Cursus Completus*, XX.

T.T.
A Myrrour for Martinists, and all other Schismatiques, which
in these dangerous daies doe breake the godlie vnitie, and dis-
turbe the Christian peace of the Church, etc.
(Attributed to T. Turswell.)
>London, 1590.
Lamb.

Tanner, J. R., Ed.
Tudor Constitutional Documents, 1485–1603, with an historical
commentary.
>Cambridge, 1922.

Tertullian
Adversus Gnosticos Scorpiace.
In Migne, *Patrologiae Cursus Completus*, I.
Apologeticus Adversus Gentes pro Christianis.
In Migne, *Patrologiae Cursus Completus*, I.
Liber ad Scapulam.
In Migne, *Patrologiae Cursus Completus*, I.

Townshend, Heywood
Historical Collections; or, An Exact Account of the Proceedings
of the four Last Parliaments of Q. Elizabeth of famous Memory.
Wherein is contained the compleate journals both of the Lords
and Commons, taken from the Original Records of their Houses.
>London, 1680.

Travers, Walter
A full and plaine declaration of Ecclesiasticall Discipline owt off
the Word of God, and off the Declininge off the Churche of
England from the same.
(Anon., transl. by Thomas Cartwright. This is an English ver-
sion of Traver's *Explicio*.)
>————, 1574.
B.P.L., Mc.

An Answere to a Svpplicatorie Epistle, of G.T. for the pretended
Catholiques: written to the Right honorable lords of her Maiesties
priuy Councell.
>London, 1583?.
B.M., Mc.

A Defence of the Ecclesiastical Discipline ordayned of God to be used in his Church. Against a Replie of Maister Bridges, to a briefe and plain Declaration of it. . . . Which replie he termeth, A Defence of the gouernment established in the Church of Englande, for Ecclesiasticall matters.
(Attributed to W.T.)

London, 1588.

B.M., Bodl.

A Triall of Subscription, by way of a Preface vnto certaine svbscribers; and reasons for lesse rigour against non-subscribers.
(Anon.)

Middleburgh, 1599.

Wm., Bodl.

Turner, William

A   Neue Dialogue, VVherin is conteyned the examinatiō of the Messe and of that kind of priesthode, whiche is ordeyned to saye messe: and to offer vp for remission of synne, the body and bloud of Christe againe.

London, 1548?, 1549?, 1550?.

B.M.

A Preseruatiue, or triacle, agaynst the poyson of Pelagius, lately revived, and styrred vp agayn, by the furious secte of Anabaptistes: deuysed by Wyllyam Turner, etc.
(No pagin.)

London, 1551.

B.M.

A nevv booke of spirituall Physik for dyuerse diseases of the nobilitie and gentlemen of Englande, etc.

Rome (Basle?), 1555.

Udall, John

A Demonstration of the trueth of that Discipline which Christe hath prescribed in his Worde for the gouernement of his Church, in all times and places, vntill the ende of the worlde, etc.

————, 1588.

(Anon.: Camb. Cat. and P. & R. ascription.)

B.M., Bodl.

The State of the Church of Englande, laide open in a conference betweene Diotrephes a Byshop, Tertullus a Papist, Demetrivs an vsurer, Pandocheus an Inne Keeper, and Paule a preacher of the Worde of God.

London?, 1588?.

B.M.

The Vnlawful Practises of prelates against godly ministers.
London, 1584?.
B.M.

Walsingham, Sir Francis
Walsingham to M. Cretoy, . . . in defence of the Queens Majesty, in her proceedings in causes ecclesiastical against Catholics. (MS. at Helmingham Hall, Suffolk; copy in Sloan MSS. in B.M.; printed in Burnet, III, 419 ff.; Neal, Bk. I, c. viii; and in Spedding, I, 42 ff.)

Watson, William
Important Considerations, which ought to move all True and sound Catholikes, who are not wholly Iesiuted, to acknowledge without all equiuocations, ambiguities, or shiftings, that the proceedings of her majesty, and of the State with them, since the beginning of her Highnesse raigne, haue bene both mild and mercifull. Published by Sundry of vs Secular Priests, in dislike of many treatises, letters, and reports, which have been written and made in diverse places to the contrarie: together with our opinions of a better course hereafter, for the premoting of the Catholike faith in England.
London, 1601
Ed. by the Rev. Joseph Mendham, London, 1831.
B.M., N.Y.P.L.

Whitgift, John
Works.
Ed. by John Ayre for the Parker Society.
3 vols.
Cambridge, 1851–1853.

An answere to a certen Libel intituled, An Admonition to the Parliament.
London, 1572.
(v. I. of *Works*.)

The Defense of the Aunswere to the admonition, against the Replie of T.C.
London, 1574.
(v. I of *Works*.)

A godlie Sermon preched Before the Queenes maiestie at Greenevviche the 26 of March last past.
(v. III of *Works*.)
London, 1574.

Contents of the Archbishops Sermon preached at the Cathedral of St. Paul's, London, November 17, 1583. Being the Anniversary Day of Q. Elizabeth's coming to the crown.
(v. III of *Works*.)

Wilkins, David
Concilia Magnae Britanniæ et Hiberniae, a Synodo Verolamiensi, a.d. CCCCXLVI ad Londinensen a.d. MDCCXVII. Accedunt constitutiones et alia ad historian Ecclesiae Anglicanae spectantia.
London, 1737.
4 vols.

Wood, Anthony A.
Athenae Oxonienses . . . to which are added the Fasti or Annals of the said university, etc.
3rd ed. contd. by P. Bliss.
3 vols.
London, 1813–1820.

The Whole Workes of W. Tyndall, Iohn Frith, and Doct. Barnes, three worthey martyrs, and principall teachers of this Churche of England, Collected and compiled in one tome together.
London, 1573.

Wriothesley, Charles
A chronicle of England during the Reigns of the Tudors, etc.
Ed. by W. D. Hamilton for the Camden Society.
2 vols.
London, 1875–1877.

The Zurich Letters Comprising the Correspondence of Several English Bishops and Others, with some of the Helvetian Reformers, etc.
(First Series.)
Ed. by H. Robinson for the Parker Society.
Cambridge, 1842.

The Zurich Letters . . . Second Series.
Ed. by H. Robinson for the Parker Society.
Cambridge, 1845.

Zwingli, Ulrich
Sämtliche Werke.
Ed. von Emil Egli, Georg Finsler, *et al* in the *Corpus Reformatorum*, lxxxviii, ff.
Berlin, Leipzig, 1905.

Articuli sive conclusiones lxvii (1523).
In *Sämtliche Werke*, I; Niemeyer, *Collectio*, 1–13.

Christianae Fidei ab. H. Zwinglio Praedecatae et clara espositio (1531).
In Niemeyer, *Collectio*, 36 ff.

Theses Bernenses.
In Niemeyer, *Collectio*, 14–15.

II. SECONDARY MATERIALS

Acton, J. E. E.
  The History of Freedom, and other essays, etc.
  Ed. with an Introduction by J. N. Figgis and R. V. Lawrence.
      London, 1909.

Allen, J. W.
  A History of Political Thought in the Sixteenth Century.
      London, 1928.

Arber, J. W.
  An Introductory Sketch to the Martin Marprelate Controversy, 1588–1590.
      London, 1880.

Arnold, Gottfried
  Unparteyische Kirchen-und Ketzer-historie, vom anfang des Neuen Testaments biss auff das jahr Christi, 1688.
  4 Thle.
      Frankfort-a.-M., 1700–1715.

Bayle, Pierre
  Commentaire Philosophique sur ces paroles de Jésus-Christ, "contrain les d'entrer," ou Traité de la Tolérance Universelle.
  2 vols.
      Rotterdam, 1713.

  Dictionaire Historique et Critique, etc.
  5th ed., 4 vols.
      Amsterdam, 1740.

Beard, Charles
  The Reformation of the Sixteenth Century in its Relation to Modern Thought and Knowledge.
      London, 1883.

Belasco, P.S.
  Authority in Church and State, etc.
      London, 1928.

453

Benôit, A. V.
De liberté religieuse.
Paris, 1819.

Benrath, Karl
Bernardino Ochino von Siena. Ein Beitrag zur Geschichte der Reformation.
Leipzig, 1875.

Blunt, J. H.
The Reformation of the Church of England. Its History, Principles, and Results.
2 vols.
London, 1882.

Bluntschli, J. C.
Geschichte des Rechts der religiösen Bekenntnissfreiheit. Ein öffentlichen Vortrag.
Elberfeld, 1867.

Bonet-Maury, Gaston
Des Origines de Christianisme Unitaire chez les Anglais.
Paris, 1881.

Brandt, Gerrit
The History of the Reformation and other Ecclesiastical Transactions in and about the Low Countries, etc.
4 vols.
London, 1720–1722.

Brook, Benjamin
The Lives of the Puritans: containing a biographical account of those divines who distinguished themselves in the cause of religious liberty from the Reformation under Queen Elizabeth, to the Act of Uniformity in 1662.
3 vols.
London, 1813.

The History of Religious Liberty from the first Propagation of Christianity in Britain, to the Death of George III.
2 vols.
London, 1820.

Brooks, Phillips
Tolerance.
New York, 1887.

454

Buckle, H. T.
History of Civilization in England.
3 vols.
Toronto, 1878.

Buisson, Ferdinand
Sébastien Castellion: Sa vie et son oeuvre (1515-1563). Étude
sur les origines du protestantisme libéral français.
2 vols.
Paris, 1892.

Burckhardt, Jacob
The Civilization of the Period of the Renaissance in Italy.
Transl. by S. G. C. Middlemore (with additions by L. Geiger).
2 vols.
London, 1878.

Burnet, Gilbert
The History of the Reformation of the Church of England.
Revised ed. by Nicholas Pocock.
7 vols.
Oxford, 1865.

Burrage, Champlin
The Church Covenant Idea: Its Origin and its Development.
Philadelphia, 1904.

The True Story of Robert Browne, Father of Congregationalism,
including various points hitherto unknown or misunderstood,
with some account of the development of his religious views, and
an extended and improved list of his writings.
Oxford, 1906.

The Early English Dissenters in the Light of Recent Research
(1550-1641).
2 vols.
Cambridge, 1912.

Bury, J. B.
A History of Freedom of Thought.
2nd ed.
London, 1920.

Calder, Frederick
Memoirs of Simon Episcopius . . . To which is added a brief
account of the Synod of Dort.
London, 1835.

455

Calthorp, M. M. C.
    The Ecclesiastical History of Dorset.
    (In the Victoria County History, *Dorset*, v. II.)
        London, 1908.

Campbell, Douglas
    The Puritan in Holland, England, and America, etc.
    2 vols. in 1.
        New York, 1892.

Carlile, J. C.
    The Story of the English Baptists.
        London, 1905.

The Catholic Encyclopedia.
    Ed. by C. G. Herbermann, *et al.*
    16 vols.
        New York, 1907–1914.

Chambers, R. W.
    The Saga and the Myth of Sir Thomas More.
    (From the Proceedings of the British Academy.)
        London, 1927.

Charbonnel, J. R.
    La Pensée Italienne au xvi siècle et le courant libertin.
        Paris, 1919.

Clark, H. W.
    History of English Nonconformity from Wiclif to the close of
    the nineteenth century.
    2 vols.
        London, 1911.

Cobbett, William
    The Parliamentary History of England from the earliest Period
    to 1803, etc.
    36 vols.
        London, 1806–1820.

Collier, Jeremy
    An Ecclesiastical History of Great Britain, chiefly of England,
    from the first planting of Christianity, to the end of the Reign
    of King Charles the Second. . . .
    Ed. by Thomas Lathbury, with a life of the author.
    9 vols.
        London, 1852.

BIBLIOGRAPHY

Constant, G.
    La Réforme en Angleterre.
        Paris, 1930.

Cooper, C. H. and T.
    Athenae Cantabrigienses.
    Cont. and corrected by Henry Bradshaw, *et al.*
    3 vols.
        Cambridge, 1858, 1861, 1913.

Coulton, G. G.
    A Protestant View of Toleration.
    Contemporary Review, 777, September 1930.

Creighton, Mandell
    Persecution and Tolerance. Being the Hulsean Lectures preached
    before the University of Cambridge in 1893–1894.
    New ed.
        London, 1906.

Crenius, Thomas (i.e. Crusius, Thomas Theodorus)
    Animadversiones philogicae et historicae, novas librorum edi-
    tiones, praefationes, indices, nonnullasque summorum aliquot
    virorum labeculas notatas, excutientes.
    3 vols., 19 pts.
        Rotterdam, 1695–1720.

Deslandes, M.
    Histoire Critique de la Philosophie.
    4 vols.
        Amsterdam, 1756.

Destombes, C. J. B.
    La persécution religeuse en Angleterre sous le Règne d'Elizabeth.
        Paris, 1863.

Dexter, H. M.
    The Congregationalism of the Last Three Hundred Years, as
    Seen in Its Literature, etc.
        New York, 1880.

The Dictionary of National Biography
    Ed. by Sir Leslie Stephen.
    63 vols.
        London, 1885–1900.

Dixon, R. W.
    History of the Church of England, 1529–1570.
    6 vols.
        London, 1878–1902.

Dodd, Charles
Church History of England from the Commencement of the Sixteenth Century to the Revolution in 1688. With notes, additions, and a continuation by M. A. Tierney.
(Pseud.: C.D., i.e. Hugh Tootell.) Referred to as Tierney.
5 vols.
London, 1839–1843.

Dudley, A. A.
The Attitude to the State in Anglican Literature, 1525–1550.
In *Economica*, 9 (25), April 1929.

Echard, Laurence
The History of England from the First Entrance of Julius Cæsar . . . to the Conclusion of the Reign of James the Second, etc.
3rd ed.
London, 1720.

Evans, B.
The Early English Baptists.
2 vols.
London, 1862–1864.

Fairbairn, A. M.
Calvin and the Reformed Church-Tendencies of European Thought in the Age of the Reformation.
In the *Camb. Mod. History*, II, c. xix.
Cambridge, 1903.

Studies in Religion and Theology. The Church: in Idea and in History.
London, 1910.

Fawker, A.
Art. *Persecution*. In Encyclopedia of Religion and Ethics.
Ed. by James Hastings, *et al.*
New York, 1922.

Figgis, J. N.
Political Thought in the Sixteenth Century.
In *Camb. Mod. History*, III, c. xxii.
Cambridge, 1904.

Studies of Political Thought from Gerson to Grotius, 1414–1625, etc.
Cambridge, 1907.

Frere, W. H.
The English Church in the Reigns of Elizabeth and James I, 1558–1625.
London, 1904.

BIBLIOGRAPHY

Freund, Michael
Die Idee der Toleranz im England Der Grossen Revolution.
Halle-Salle, 1927.

Froude, J. A.
History of England from the Fall of Wolsey to the Defeat of the
Spanish Armada.
12 vols.
London, 1870.

Fuller, Thomas
The Church History of Britain; from the Birth of Jesus Christ
Until the Year MDCXLVIII.
New ed. by J. S. Brewer.
6 vols.
Oxford, 1845.

Gardiner, S. R.
History of England from the Accession of James the First to the
Outbreak of the Great Civil War, 1603–1642.
10 vols.
London, 1883–1884.

Gee, Henry
The Elizabethan Clergy and the Settlement of Religion, 1558–
1564, etc.
Oxford, 1898.

Giran, Étienne
Sébastien Castellion et la Réforme Calviniste. Les deux
Réformes.
Paris, 1914.

Gordon, Alexander
The Sozzini and Their School.
In *The Theological Review*, 1879.

Gow, Henry
The Unitarians.
London, 1928.

Green, J. R.
History of the English People.
6 vols.
New York, n.d., published by Sully and Kleinteich.

Greville, Sir Fulke
Of the Life of the Renowned Sr. Philip Sidney, With the true
interest of England, as it then stood in relation to all forrain

princes: and particularly for suppressing the power of Spain. . . .
Together with a short account of the maxims and policies used
by Queen Elizabeth in her government.
London, 1652.

Hallam, Henry
Introduction to the Literature of Europe in the Fifteenth, Sixteenth, and Seventeenth Centuries.
2nd ed., 3 vols.
London, 1843.

The Constitutional History of England.
7th ed., 3 vols.
London, 1854.

Hardwick, Charles
A History of the Articles of Religion.
2nd ed.
Cambridge, 1859.

Harnack, Adolph
History of Dogma.
Transl. by Neil Buchanan from the 3rd German ed.
7 vols.
London, 1894–1899.

Haynes, E. S. P.
Religious Persecution: A Study in Political Psychology.
London, 1904.

Hessels, J. H., ed.
Ecclesiae Londino-Batavae Archivum.
London, 1889–1897.

Hollis, Christopher
The Monstrous Regiment. (A study of Queen Elizabeth's Religious
Policy.)
London, 1929.

Hume, Mary B.
The History of the oath *ex officio* in England.
(Ph.D. Thesis (MS.), Radcliffe College, 1923.)

Hunt, John
Religious Thought in England from the Reformation to the End
of the Last Century.
3 vols.
London, 1870–1873.

Innes, A. D.
England Under the Tudors.
London, 1905.

Janet, Paul
Histoire de la Science Politique dans ses rapports avec la morale.
3 vols.
Paris, 1872.

Jones, R. M.
Spiritual Reformers in the Sixteenth and Seventeenth Centuries.
London, 1914.

The Church's Debt to Heretics.
London, 1924.

Kitchin, G. W.
A History of France.
3rd ed., 3 vols.
Oxford, 1892.

Klein, A. J.
Intolerance in the Reign of Elizabeth, Queen of England.
Boston and New York, 1917.

Krasinski, Count Valerian
Historical Sketch of the Rise, Progress, and Decline of the
Reformation in Poland.
2 vols.
London, 1838–1840.

Law, T. G.
A Historical sketch of the Conflicts between Jesuits and Seculars
in the Reign of Queen Elizabeth: with a Reprint of Christopher
Bagshaw's *True Relation of the Faction Begun at Wisbich*, and
illustrative documents.
London, 1889.

Lea, H. C.
A History of the Inquisition of the Middle Ages.
3 vols.
New York, 1888.

Lecky, W. E. H.
History of the Rise and Influences of the Spirit of Rationalism
in Europe.
2 vols.
New York, 1866.

461

Le Neve, John
    Fasti Ecclesiae Anglicanae, etc.
    Corrected and contd. . . . by T. D. Hardy.
    3 vols.
                Oxford, 1854.

Lingard, John
    A History of England from the First Invasion by the Romans (to
    the Revolt in 1688).
    10 vols.
                Dublin, 1888.

Matagrin, Amedée
    Histoire de la tolérance religieuse, Évolution d'un principe social.
                Paris, 1905.

Matthews, W. R.
    Dogma in History and Thought.
                London, 1929.

Maurice, J. F. D.
    Modern Philosophy; or, a Treatise of Moral and Metaphysical
    Philosophy from the Fourteenth Century to the French Revolu-
    tion, etc.
                London, 1862.

Meyer, A. O.
    England and the Catholic Church under Queen Elizabeth.
    Transl. by the Rev. J. R. McKee.
                London, 1916.

Moreton, H. A.
    La Réforme Anglicane au xviie Siècle.
                Paris, 1930.

Murray, R. H.
    Utopian Toleration.
    In the Edinburgh Review, 447, January 1914.

    The Political Consequences of the Reformation. Studies in
    Sixteenth Century Political Thought.
                Boston, 1926.

Naunton, Sir Robert
    Fragmenta Regalia: (or, Observations of the late Queen Elizabeth,
    her times and favourites).
                London, 1653.

BIBLIOGRAPHY

Neal, Daniel
  The History of the Puritans; Or, the Protestant Nonconformists;
  from the Reformation in 1517, to the Revolution in 1688; com-
  prising an account of their Principles; their attempts for a farther
  Reformation of the Church; their Sufferings, and the Lives and
  Characters of their Most Considerable Divines.
  (From the Toumlin text, with revisions.)
  3 vols.
                    London, 1837.

Nezard, Henry
  Albericus Gentilis.
  In *Les Fondateurs du Droit International*, etc.
                    Paris, 1904.

Nouvelle Biographie Générale.
  46 vols.
                    Paris, 1855.

Oldmixon, John
  The History of England, During the Reigns of Henry VIII,
  Edward VI, Queen Mary, Queen Elizabeth including the
  History of the Reformation of the Churches of England and
  Scotland, etc.
                    London, 1739.

Osborne, C. E.
  Christian Ideas in Political History.
  (Holland Memorial Lectures, 1925.)
                    London, 1929.

Owen, John
  The Skeptics of the Italian Renaissance.
                    London, 1893.

Paulus, Nikolaus
  Protestantismus und Toleranz im 16-Jahrhundert.
                    Freiburg, 1911.

Pearson, A. F. S.
  Thomas Cartwright and Elizabethan Puritanism, 1535–1603.
                    Cambridge, 1925.

  Church and State: Political Aspects of Sixteenth-Century
  Puritanism.
                    Cambridge, 1928.

Phillipson, Coleman
    The Great Jurists of the World, Albericus Gentilis.
    Reprinted from the Journal of the *Society of Comparative Legislation*, August 1911.

Pollard, A. F.
    Thomas Cranmer and the English Reformation, 1489–1556.
        New York and London, 1904.

    The History of England from the Accession of Edward VI to the death of Elizabeth, 1547–1603.
        London, 1911.

Pollen, J. H.
    The English Catholics in the Reign of Queen Elizabeth. A Study of their politics, civil life, and government.
        London, 1920.

Pollock, Sir Frederick
    Essays in Jurisprudence and Ethics.
        London, 1882.

Poynter, J. W.
    The Reformation, Catholicism, and Freedom, etc.
        London, 1930.

Ranke, Leopold v.
    A History of England Principally in the Seventeenth Century.
    6 vols.
        Oxford, 1875.

Read, Conyers
    Walsingham and Burghley in Queen Elizabeth's Privy Council.
    In the *English Historical Review* (January 1913), 28, 34.

    Mr. Secretary Walsingham and the Policy of Queen Elizabeth.
    3 vols.
        Cambridge and Oxford, 1925.

Renan, J. E.
    Averroes et l'Averroïsme: Essai Historique.
    2nd ed.
        Paris, 1861.

Robertson, J. M.
    A Short History of Free Thought, etc.
    3rd ed., revised and expanded.
    2 vols.
        London, 1915.

BIBLIOGRAPHY

Roper, William
 The Life of Sir Thomas More.
 New ed. revised and corrected by S. W. Singer.
  London, 1822.

Ruffini, Francesco
 Religious Liberty.
 Transl. by J. P. Heyes . . . with a preface by J. B. Bury.
  New York, 1912.

St. John, Wallace
 The Contest for Liberty of Conscience in England.
  Chicago, 1900.

Sanders, Nicolas
 Rise and Growth of the Anglican Schism, etc.
 Contd. by the Rev. Edward Rishton, and edited by David Lewis.
  London, 1877.

Schaff, Philip
 The Creeds of Christendom, with a History and Critical Notes.
 2nd ed., 3 vols.
  New York, 1878.

Seaton, A. A.
 The Theory of Toleration Under the Later Stuarts.
  Cambridge, 1911.

Seeberg, Erich
 Gottfried Arnold. Die Wissenschaft und die Mystik seiner
 Zeit, etc.
  Meerane i. Sa., 1923.

Seeberg, Reinhold
 Lehrbuch der Dogmengeschichte.
 Bd. IV, 2 hälfte.
 Die Fortbildung der Reformatorischen Lehre und die gegenre-
 formatorische Lehre.
  Leipzig, 1920.

Selbie, W. B.
 Congregationalism.
  London, 1927.

Simpson, Richard
 Edmund Campion.
  London, 1867.

Smith, Preserved
The Age of the Reformation.
New York, 1921.

Spedding, James
An Account of the Life and Times of Francis Bacon.
2 vols.
Boston, 1880.

Stratford, Esme C. Wingfield-
The History of British Civilization.
2 vols.
London, 1928.

Symonds, J. A.
The Renaissance in Italy.
New ed., 7 vols.
London, 1898.

Tawney, R. H.
Religion and the Rise of Capitalism. A Historical Study.
New York, 1926.

Teulet, Alexandre
Relations Politique de la France et l'Espagne avec l'Écosse au
xvi Siècle, etc.
5 vols.
Paris, 1862.

Trechsel, Friedriech
Die Protestantischen Antitrinitarier vor Faustus Socin nach
Quellen und Urkunden Geschichtlich dargestellt, etc.
2 vols.
Heidelberg, 1839–1844.

Troeltsch, Ernst
Protestantism and Progress: a Historical Study of the Relation
of Protestantism to the Modern World.
Transl. by W. Montgomery.
London, 1912.

Die Soziallehren der Christlichen Kirchen und Gruppen.
Tübingen, 1923.

Tulloch, John
Rational Theology and Christian Philosophy in England in the
Seventeenth Century, etc.
2 vols.
London and Edinburgh, 1872.

BIBLIOGRAPHY

Twiss, Horace
    The Public and Private Life of Lord Chancellor Eldon with Selections from his Correspondence.
    3 vols.
                London, 1844.

Usher, R. G.
    The Reconstruction of the English Church.
    2 vols.
            New York and London, 1910.

Voetius, Gisberti
    Selectarum Disputationum Theologicarum pars prima (—quinta. Accedunt Dissertatio epistolica de termino vitae. Exercitatio de prognosticis cometarum, . . .)
            Ultrajecti, 1648–1649.

Walker, Williston
    The Creeds and Platforms of Congregationalism.
            New York, 1893.

Walton, Izaak
    The Lives of Dr. John Donne, Sir Henry Wotton, Mr. Richard Hooker, Mr. George Herbert, and Dr. Robert Sanderson, etc.
    4th ed.
            London, 1825.

Wand, J. W. C.
    A History of the Modern Church, from 1500 to the Present Day.
            London, 1930.

Weber, Max
    The Protestant Ethic and the Spirit of Capitalism.
    Transl. by Talcott Parsons.
            London, 1930.

Weis, F. L.
    The Life, Teachings, and Works of Johannes Denck, 1495–1527.
            Strassburg, 1924.

Willis-Bund, J. W.
    Ecclesiastical History of Worcestershire.
    In V.C.H., *History of Worcestershire*, Vol. II.
            London, 1907.

Wilson, James
    Ecclesiastical History of Cumberland.
    In V.C.H., *History of Cumberland*, Vol. II.
            London, 1905.

Wright, Thomas, ed.
> Queen Elizabeth and Her Times, a series of Original Letters, Selected from the unedited Private Correspondence of the Lord Treasurer Burleigh, the Earl of Leicester, the Secretaries Walsingham and Smith, Sir Christopher Hatton, and Most of the Distinguished Persons of the Period.
> 2 vols.
>> London, 1838.

Wulf, Maurice de
> History of Medieval Philosophy.
> Transl. by P. Coffey.
> 3rd ed.
>> New York, 1909.

III. BIBLIOGRAPHICAL WORKS

This list is in no sense complete. A few of the bibliographical works which were of especial assistance are listed.

Arber, Edward
> Transcripts of the Registers of the Company of Stationers of London, 1554–1640.
> 5 vols.
>> London, 1875–1894.

Bloom, J. H.
> English Tracts and Printed Sheets, 1473–1640.
> Vols. I and II.
>> London, 1922–1923.

British Museum Catalogue of Printed Books
>> London, 1885.

Cambridge University Catalogue
> Early English Printed Books in the University Library, Cambridge (1475–1640).
> 4 vols.
>> Cambridge, 1900–1907.

Dexter, H. M.
> The Congregationalism of the Last Three Hundred Years, as Seen in Its Literature, etc.
>> New York, 1880.

Halkett, S., and Laing, J.
A Dictionary of the Anonymous and Pseudonymous Literature
of Great Britain.
4 vols.
Edinburgh, 1882–1888.

Huntington Library
Check List or Brief Catalogue of the Library of Henry E.
Huntington. (English Literature to 1640.)
New York, 1919.

McAlpin Collection.
Catalogue of the McAlpin Collection of British History and
Theology in the Union Theological Seminary Library.
Compiled and edited by C. R. Gillett.
4 vols.
New York, 1927–1929.

Pollard, A. W., and Redgrave, G. R., and Others.
A Short Title Catalogue of Books Printed in England, Scotland,
and Ireland, and of English Books Printed Abroad, 1475–1640.
London, 1926.

Usher, R. G.
The Reconstruction of the English Church. (Vol. II, app. of.)
2 vols.
New York, 1910.

Whitley, W. T.
A Baptist Bibliography.
2 vols.
London, 1916.

The Williams' Library
Catalogue of the Library . . . founded pursuant to the Will of
the Reverend Daniel Williams.
2 vols. and a suppl.
London, 1841, 1870.

IV. SUPPLEMENTARY BIBLIOGRAPHY

(Works used with some profit, but not quoted.)

A. Source Materials

Asinus Onustus: The Asse Overladed. To his Loving, and Deare
Mistresse, Elizabeth, the Blessed Queene of England.
London, 1589, **1642**, 1689.
B.M.

Barnes, Richard
> The Injunctions and other Ecclesiastical Proceedings of Bishop
> Barnes of Durham, 1575–1587.
> Edited by James Kaine for the Surtees Society (vol. xxii).
>> Durham, etc., 1850.

Barthlet, John
> The Pedegrewe of Heretiques: Wherein is truely and plainly set
> out, the first roote of Heretiques begon in the Church, since the
> time and passage of the gospell, together with an example of the
> Spring of the Same.
>> London, 1565(6).
> **H.C.L., B.M.**

Bilson, Thomas
> The Perpetual Government of Christ, His Church, etc.
>> London, **1593**, 1610, 1842.
> H.C.L.

Bullinger, Henry
> A Treatise or Sermon of Henry Bullynger . . . Concernynge
> Magistrates and obedience of Subiectes. Also concernyng the
> affayres of warre, and what Scryptures make mension thereof.
> Transl. from the Latin text by G. Lynne.
>> London, 1549.
> B.M.
>
> A Collection of Letters from the Bishops to the Privy Council
> (1564).
> (Vol. ix of the *Camden Miscellany*.)
>> London, 1893

Calvin, John
> Declaration pour maintenit la vraye foy que tiennent tous Chres-
> tiens de la Trinité des personnes en un seul Dieu, par Jean
> Calvin, etc.
>> Geneva, 1544.

Churchson, John
> A brefe Treatyse declaryng what and where the Churche is, that
> it is knowen, and whereby it is tryed and knowen.
>> London, 1556.
> B.M.

Clerke, William
> The Triall of Bastardie: That part of the second part of policie,
> or maner of gouernment of the realme of England: so termed,
> spirituall, or ecclesiasticall, etc.
>> London, 1594.
> **Mc., B.M.**

BIBLIOGRAPHY

Cosin, John
   The Correspondence of John Cosin, Bishop of Durham, together
   with other papers illustrative of his Life and Times.
   Ed. by George Ornsby for the Surtees Society (vols. lii and lv).
   2 vols.
                    Durham, etc., 1869–1872.

Cosin, Richard
   An Apologie for sundrie proceedings by Iurisdiction ecclesiasticall, of late times by some chalenged, and also diuersly by them
   impugned . . . whereunto . . . I have presumed to adione . . .
   concerning oaths . . . by M. Lancelot Andrewes, etc.
                    London, 1593.
   H.C.L.

   A *Defence* of the Ecclesiastical Discipline Ordayned of God to
   be vsed in His Church. Against a Replie of M. Maister Bridges
   to a Briefe and Plaine Declaration of it, etc.
                    London, 1588.
   H.C.L.

Digges, Thomas
   Humble motives for association to maintaine Religion Established. Published as an antidote against the pestilent treatises
   of secular priests.
                    London, 1601.
   B.M.

Floyd, Thomas
   The Picture of a perfit Commonwealth, describing as well the
   offices of Princes and inferiour Magistrates ouer their subiects,
   as also the duties of subiects towards their gouernours, etc.
                    London, 1600.
   B.M.

Frere, W. H., and Douglas, C. E. (Editors)
   Certaine Articles, collected and Taken (as it is thought) by the
   Byshops out of a litle Boke entituled an Admonition to the
   Parliament, with an answere to the same.
   Reprinted in *Puritan Manifestoes*.
   London, 1907.

Gifford, George
   A Dialogue betweene a Papist and a Protestant, applied to the
   capacitie of the Vnlearned.
                    London, 1582.
   B.M.

Hide, Thomas
A Consolatorie Epistle to the afflicted Catholikes: set foorth by
T. Hide Priest.
Louvain, 1580.
B.M.

Horne, Robert
An Ansvveare made by Rob. Bishoppe of VVynchester, to a
booke entituled, the Declaration of Suche Scruples, and staies
of Conscience, touchinge the Othe of the Supremacy, as M. John
Fekenham, by vvrytinge did deliver vnto the L. Bishop of
VVinchester, vvith his Resolutions made thereunto.
London, 1566.
B.M.

Latimer, Hugh
Works.
Ed. for the Parker Society by G. E. Corrie.
2 vols.
Cambridge, 1844–1845.

Law, T. G.
Catholik Tractates of the Sixteenth Century, 1573–1600.
Selections, with an Intro. and Glossary.
Edited for the Scottish Text. Society.
Edinburgh, 1901.

Merbury, Charles
A Briefe Discourse of Royall Monarchie, as of the best common-
weale, etc.
London, 1581.
H.C.L., B.M.

Smith, Richard
A brief treatyse settynge forth diuers truthes necessary both to
be beleued of chrysten people, and kepte also, whiche are not
expressed in the Scripture, but left to ye Church by the Apostles
traditiō.
London, 1547.
B.M.

Smith, Sir Thomas
De Repvblica Anglorvm. The Maner of governement or policie
of the Realme of England, etc.
London, 1584.
B.M.

BIBLIOGRAPHY

Stapleton, Thomas
  A counterblast to M. Hornes Vayne Blaste against M. Fekenham, etc.
        Louvain, 1567.
  McAlpin, H.C.L.

Starkey, Thomas
  An Exhortation to the people Instructynge thym to Unitie and Obedience.
        London, 1540?.
  B.M.

Sutcliffe, Mathew
  An Ansvver to a certaine libel svpplicatorie, or rather Deffamatory, and also to certaine calumnious Articles and Interrogatories, both printed and scattered in secret corners, to the slaunder of the Ecclesiastical State, and put forth vnder the name and title of a Petition directed to her maiestie
        London, 1592.
  B.M.

T. J.
  An Apologie or defence agaynst the calumnacion of certayne men, which . . . do sclaunder those men, which for the better seruinge of God with a more pure conscience, according to his holy Word, haue abandoned theyr liuinges and vocacion, abydinge as exyles in poore estate oute of theyr natyue countrye.
        n. pl., 1555.
  B.M.

Tyndale, William
  The obedience of a Christen man, and how Christen rulers ought to gouerne, wherein also yf thow marke diligently thow shalt fynde eyes to perceaue the crafty conueyance of all Iugglers. Newly printed and diligently corrected.
        Marlborough, Hesse (London?), 1535.
  Mc.
  Answer to Sir Thomas More's Dialogue, the Supper of the Lord, after the True Meaning of John vi and Cor. xi and William Tracy's Testament expounded.
  Ed. by Henry Walter for the Parker Society.
        Cambridge, 1850.

Veron, John
  Certayne Litel Treaties set forth by John Veron Senonoys, for the erudition and learnyng of the symple and ingnorant (sic) peopell.
        London?, 1548.
  B.M.

Wentworth, Peter
A Pithie Exhortation to Her Maiestie for Establishing her Svccessor to the Crowne. Whereunto is added a discourse containing the Authors opinion of the true and lawfull successor to her Majestie.
London, 1598.
B.M.

Whetstone, George
The Censure of a loyall subiect: vpon certaine noted Speach and behauiours, of those . . . notable Traitors at the place of their executions, the xx and xxi of September last past.
London, 1585.
B.M.

B. SECONDARY MATERIALS

Bax, E. B.
Rise and Fall of the Anabaptists.
London, 1903.

Brook, Benjamin
Memoir of the Life and Writings of Thomas Cartwright, B.D., the Distinguished Puritan Reformer; including the principal ecclesiastical movements in the reign of Queen Elizabeth.
London, 1845.

Brown, John
The English Puritans.
Cambridge, 1912.

Delahaye, A.
De la liberté des cultes.
Paris, 1854.

Ellys, Anthony
Tracts on the Liberty, Spiritual and Temporal, of Protestants (and) of subjects in England.
2 vols.
London, 1763.

Flynn, J. S.
Influence of Puritanism on Religious and Political Thought in England.
New York, 1920.

BIBLIOGRAPHY

Gregory, J.
Puritanism in the Old World and in the New from its Inception in the Reign of Elizabeth to the Establishment of the Puritan Theocracy in New England.
New York, 1896.

Herford, C. H.
Studies in the Literary Relations of England and Germany in the Sixteenth Century.
Cambridge, 1886.

Heylyn, Peter
Ecclesia Restaurata; or, the History of the Reformation of the Church of England, etc.
Edited by J. C. Robertson.
2 vols.
Cambridge, 1849.

Höffding, Harald
A History of Modern Philosophy. A Sketch of the History of Philosophy from the close of the Renaissance to our own day.
Transl. from the German ed. by B. E. Meyer.
2 vols.
London, 1900.

Hopkins, S.
The Puritans: Or, the Church, Court, and Parliament of England during the Reigns of Edward VI and Queen Elizabeth.
3 vols.
Boston, 1860–1861.

Hulbert, E. B.
The English Reformation and the Puritans.
Chicago, 1908.

Hume, M. A. S.
The Great Lord Burghley: a Study in Elizabethan Statecraft.
London, 1898.

Hyland, St. George K.
A Century of Persecution, under Tudor and Stuart Sovereigns, from Contemporary Records, etc.
London, 1920.

Jenkins, John
The Laws Relating to Religious Liberty and Public Worship.
London, 1880.

Kuhn, Johannes
Toleranz und Offenbaraung. Eine Untersuchung der motive und Motivformen der Toleranz im offenbarungsglaubigen Protestantismus.
Leipzig, 1923.

Lloyd, Walter
The Story of Protestant Dissent and English Unitarianism.
London, 1899.

Lupton, J. H.
The Life of John Colet . . . with an appendix of some of his English Writings.
London, 1887.

Mackinnon, James
History of Modern Liberty.
3 vols.
London, 1906–1908.

Makower, Felix
The Constitutional History and Constitution of the Church of England.
London, 1895.

Murray, R. H.
Erasmus and Luther: Their Attitude towards Toleration.
London, 1920.

Parry, C. H.
The Parliaments and Councils of England, Chronologically arranged from the Reign of William I to the Revolution in 1688.
London, 1839.

Patterson, M. W.
A History of the Church of England.
London, 1909.

Pierce, William
An Historical Introduction to the Marprelate Tracts; a chapter in the evolution of religious and civil liberty in England.
London, 1908.

Powicke, F. J.
Robert Browne, Pioneer of Modern Congregationalism.
London, 1910.

Schaff, Philip
    History of the Christian Church.
    2nd revised ed. 8 vols.
          New York, 1886–1910.

Smith, Preserved
    A History of Modern Culture, 1543–1687.
          New York, 1930–

Tarrant, W. G.
    Unitarianism.
          London, 1912.

Taylor, H. O.
    Thought and Expression in the Sixteenth Century.
    2 vols.
          New York, 1920.

Thornton, L. S.
    Richard Hooker: A Study in his Theology.
          London, 1924.

Troeltsch, Ernst
    Christian Thought; its History and Application. Lectures . . .
    translated . . . by various hands, and edited with an introduction
    . . . by Baron F. v. Hügel.
          London, 1923.

Wallace, Robert
    Antitrinitarian Biography.
    3 vols.
          London, 1850.

Whitney, J. P.
    Reformation Literature in England.
    In Vol. III of the *Camb. Hist. of English Literature.*

INDEX

INDEX

Liberty of conscience—
Aglionby on, 130–131.
Allen on, 395–398.
Beale on, 193.
Confession in Order of Exercises on, 254–255.
Dering on, 255.
distinguished from toleration, 18–19.
Exhortation to the Bishops on, 254.
Humphrey on, 252–253, 255–256.
plea of Watson for, 415–417.
pleas in Parliament for, 130–131.
Puritan insistence on, 251–258, 260–261.
Sampson on, 252–253.
Separatist pleas for, 288–291.
Triall of Subscription on, 257–259.
Turner on, 74.
see also Toleration.
Locke, John, 363.
London, 263, 295, 297.
Luther, Martin, 31, 45, 145, 194, 332, 401.

Magistrate, power of, in the Church, 49–57, 80, 91–95, 101–102, 139–142, 152–153, 156, 243–248.
Admonition on, 244.
Barnes on, 65.
Barrowe on, 277–278.
Becon on, 53.
Beza on, 51, n.
Bilson on, 186.
Browne on, 264–265.
Bullinger on, 51, n.
Cartwright on, 139–140.
Cranmer on, 51–52.
Fenner on, 246.
Fenton on, 156.
Gifford on, 221.
Hooker on, 223–224.
Hutchins on, 187–188.
Jewel, on, 101–102.
Nowell on, 156.
Parsons on, 383–384.
Penry on, 284–285.
Pilkington on, 152.
Reformation of Religion of Iosiah on, 247.

Magistrate—*continued.*
Sandys on, 152-153.
Second Admonition on, 244–245.
Travers on, 245, 247, 248.
Udall on, 247.
Magna Carta, 216.
Manichaeism, 377.
Martin Marprelate controversy, 23, 188, 212, 250.
Martius, Galeottus, rationalism of, 326.
Mary Stuart, Queen of Scots, 112, 117, 120, 128.
Mary Tudor, Queen of England, 81, 89, 90, 126, 172, 174, 181.
policy of, stimulates radical theories, 54 ff.
Matagrin, A., 27, 29.
Melanchthon, Philipp, 71.
Mildmay, Sir Walter, 168.
Mofa, Matteo Gribaldi, 308.
Montagu, Lord—
biog. n. on, 103, n.
condemns persecution, 103–104.
Moore, Sir George, orthodox views of, 216.
More, Sir Thomas, 30, 41–49, 80.
early tolerance of, 41–44.
effect of spiritual anarchy on, 44 ff.
controversy with St. Germain, 59–60.
Morton, Nicholas, 117.
Mush, John, 204.

Nantes, Edict of, 38.
Netherlands, The, 38, 192, 302.
Nevill, Sir John, proposes toleration of Catholics, 128–129.
Nowell, Alexander—
on heresy, 156.
on the magistrate in the Church, 156.
on the Roman Catholics, 99.
Nonconformity, 68, 109, 151, 161, 174.
Anglican attitude towards, 132–159.
Government's handling of, 1558–1568, 99 ff.
vigorous repression of, 182 ff.

485

GEORGE ALLEN & UNWIN LTD
LONDON: 40 MUSEUM STREET, W.C.1
CAPE TOWN: 73 ST. GEORGE'S STREET
SYDNEY, N.S.W.: WYNYARD SQUARE
AUCKLAND, N.Z.: 41 ALBERT STREET
TORONTO: 91 WELLINGTON STREET, WEST

The Social Teaching of the Christian Churches

by ERNST TROELTSCH

TRANSLATED BY OLIVE WYON

Sm. Royal 8vo.   *Two Vols.*   42s. *the set*

Dean Inge, in the *Church of England Newspaper*, writes: "It is the standard work on the subject, immensely learned, judicially impartial, and full of interest to all who are occupied with modern social problems."

Alexandrine Teaching on the Universe

by R. B. TOLLINTON, D.D., D.Litt.

Cr. 8vo.   5s.

Lectures delivered in Cambridge in 1931 which describe the views of the Universe held by the greatest teachers of ancient Alexandria. Philo, Clement, Origen, Plotinus and the Gnostics are considered and their outlook compared and contrasted with certain phases of modern scientific opinion.

Personal Problems of Conduct and Religion

by J. G. McKENZIE, B.D.

Cr. 8vo.   5s.

"His counsel is marked by a simple common sense, all the more valuable because it is reinforced by the fruits of his knowledge as an expert psychologist."—*Times Literary Supplement*

By the same Author

SOULS IN THE MAKING. 7s. 6d.

The Holy and the Living God

by M. D. R. WILLINK

Demy 8vo.   10s.

"Profoundly able and heart-searching . . . very much in the line of Rudolf Otto's great work on *The Idea of the Holy*, and well worthy to stand in that noble succession."—*Expository Times*

Religion, Morals and the Intellect

by F. E. POLLARD

Cr. 8vo.   5s.

This book examines the part played by the intellect in the grasping of religious truth and in the moral life. Does reason lead us to reality? Is the unintelligible an essential element? Are the Churches attending to the results of modern criticism? Are rites and symbols a real help? A rational morality alone can cope with the needs of to-day. There are indisputable facts of inward experience which it is for reason to see and interpret.

All prices are net

LONDON: GEORGE ALLEN & UNWIN LTD

283.42
J82
c.2

3 4711 00161 2060